A FANTASTIC JOURNEY
THE LIFE AND LITERATURE OF LAFCADIO HEARN

Lafcadio Hearn aged 35, photographed in New Orleans
by W. W. Washburn; dated 11 July 1885

A FANTASTIC JOURNEY

THE LIFE AND LITERATURE OF
LAFCADIO HEARN

PAUL MURRAY

空想的な旅行 ラフカーディオ・ハーンの生涯と文学

ANN ARBOR

THE UNIVERSITY OF MICHIGAN PRESS

First published in the United States of America in 1997
by the University of Michigan Press
Manufactured in the United States of America
⊗ Printed on acid-free paper

2000   1999   1998   1997   4   3   2   1

First published in Great Britain in 1993
by Japan Library,
Knoll House, 35 The Crescent, Sandgate
Folkestone, Kent CT20 3EE

A British catalog record for this book is available
from the British Library.

Library of Congress Cataloging-in-Publication Data

Murray, Paul, 1949–
    A fantastic journey : the life and literature of Lafcadio Hearn /
Paul Murray.
        p.   cm.
    Includes bibliographical references (p.   ) and index.
    ISBN 0-472-10834-4 (cloth)
    1. Hearn, Lafcadio, 1850–1904.   2. Authors, American—19th
century—Biography.   3. Americans—Japan—History—19th Century.
4. Journalists—United States—Biography.   5. Japan—In literature.
I. Title.
PS1918.M87   1997
813'.4—dc21   97-12758
    [B]   CIP

For Elizabeth, Daniel and Stephen

CONTENTS

LIST OF ILLUSTRATIONS

Headstone of Lafcadio Hearn in the Yoshigaya Cemetery, Tokyo

FOREWORD

by
R. F. FOSTER
Carroll Professor of Irish History,
University of Oxford

IT IS FITTING that this study of a unique interpreter of Japan is by an Irishman who has himself lived there and knows its language and culture well. For it might be claimed that Lafcadio Hearn presents us with a distinctively Irish imagination. This may seem an odd assertion, given the patchy and obscure nature of his Irish background; but this book is the first to clarify it, and in the process builds up a picture which sets off resonances with other nineteenth-century Irish literary achievements.

Even more than the work of Edgar Allan Poe (sometimes seen as his inspiration), Hearn's cast of mind can be seen as stemming from the tradition of Irish-Victorian Gothic. Moreover, this biography clarifies the aspects of his life which put him squarely in this succession. A fractured and uncertain background, oscillating between present economic insecurity and the memories of past power and affluence; the tension between declining Protestantism and newly-Establishment Catholicism (vividly manifested in Hearn's own Protestant-Catholic family); the sense of being *déclassé*; eventually, like so many Irish writers in later generations, the conscious embrace of an expatriate life. For all Hearn's cult of Herbert Spencer, another Irish element is represented by his governing preoccupation with religion as an essential part of sociological formation. And finally, his obsession with the occult is inseparable from a belief characteristic of the contemporary Irish literary renaissance: the significance of folk-tales as emblems of ancient civilization, and repositories which give access to eternal truths lost to the degraded materialism of modern society.

As this indicates, Hearn was a child of his time. Behind him lies not only the cult of Poe but the West's discovery of oriental religion in the 1880s and the fashion for the *Golden Bough*'s version of comparative anthropology. He was always drawn, as Murray shows, to 'hosts of fantastic heterodoxies'. But there was a specifically Irish dimension too. The years when his art matured were also those of the Celtic Revival. It seems impossible that he did not read W.B. Yeats's *The Celtic Twilight* (1893), given his own subsequent use of folk-tales and ghost stories to define cultural identity; he certainly analysed Yeats's style closely, and followed the master in moving from a highly decorated fin-de-siècle manner to a deliberately unadorned style – with maximum effect. Indeed, he identified with Yeats's work strongly enough to send him a characteristically emphatic letter in 1901, abusing him roundly for altering 'The Hosts of the Air' in its latest publication. From Yeats's surprisingly meek reply, it is unclear whether he knew Hearn's writing at this stage; but he certainly was familiar enough within a few years to refer to it casually. Yeats's own preoccupation with Japan developed later still, under the influence of Ezra Pound, who introduced him to Fenellosa's writings in 1913. But it is at least interesting to note that the name 'Hearn', or versions of it, turns up repeatedly in Yeats's early fiction, often attached to figures with occult and Eastern interests. For instance, his autobiographical hero Michael in the unfinished novel *The Speckled Bird* is named 'De Burgh' or 'Leroy' in early versions; but in the final draft of 1902–1903 this seeker after occult wisdom becomes 'Hearne'.

Less speculatively, Yeats and the real Hearn held much in common: notions of universal religion, a longing to repudiate industrialised life, an interest in symbolism and 'decadents' (including, in both cases, Villiers de L'Isle Adam). Murray shows us a Hearn who, if he had stayed in Ireland, would have become a Celtic Revivalist; and who, after his death, was claimed by some of his contemporaries as a dissolute representative of Yeats's 'Tragic Generation'. Both Hearn and Yeats came to believe that in matters of self-presentation 'The Mask' was a necessary part of civilization; formalizing such a process was, in fact, an index of civilized life.

There are further parallels too. Like Yeats, Hearn had

memories of an insecure childhood, dominated by grandparents and great-aunts who disapproved of his parents' fecklessness; like Yeats, Hearn kept these memories alive and in late autobiographical writings re-lived their potency and pain. Both men, from their marginalised Irish backgrounds, held to a view of social relations which emphasised the supposed links between aristocrat and peasant (Yeats's 'dream of the noble and the beggarman'), rather than the middle-classes who actually bought their books. Yeats's reinvention of relationships in a supposed Italian Renaissance or Irish eighteenth-century parallel what Hearn discovered in Japan as 'the religion of loyalty'. With both men, this idealised relationship harked back to storytelling in their childhood. Yeats remembered the tales of servants in Sligo and fishermen's wives in Howth as the only thing that apparently roused his shadowy mother's enthusiasm and held her attention; Hearn's similar taste for re-living his childhood by listening to folktales in the kitchen led to his precipitate and disastrous first marriage to Mattie Foley. More happily, he would eventually tell his Japanese wife, 'I owe you everything; I have written all these books listening to your stories.'

Hearn's associated interest in the inheritance of ancestral memories (mediated through dreams), the theme of ancestor-worship, and the transmigration of souls, raises Yeatsian echoes too. And in his last and most influential book, *Japan: an attempt at interpretation*, Hearn discussed the Japanese belief that the dead take a continuing part in the lives of the living. This was also the basic article of Yeats's faith, derived from Swedenborg's spiritual theories and Irish folk belief. 'What made the aspirational in life?' Hearn asked rhetorically in a letter of 1893. 'Ghosts. Some were called gods, some demons, some angels; they changed the world for man – they gave him courage and purpose and the awe of nature that slowly changed into love, they filled all things with a sense and motion of invisible life; they made both terror and beauty.'

By his later stories, Hearn had discovered in supernatural Japanese folktales a resonant economy of effect; this made concrete his belief that 'there is something ghostly in all great art'. Yeats noted this judgement, repeated it, and specifically approved of it. This, too, connects with a distinctly Irish-Victorian provenance, following a tradition that takes in Maturin and LeFanu (related by marriage to Hearn), as well as Stoker and Yeats: supernaturalist writers who were members of a declining elite. Marginalization, insecurity, resentment at the evaporation of social authority, and a mingled repulsion from and attraction towards the certainties of triumphant Catholicism – for all these writers, such identifications lay behind a deep attachment to a violent past where ancestral pride mingled with bad conscience, and an obsession with the hauntings of history. In this absorbing sub-culture, Lafcadio Hearn may take his place. Like them, he was a displaced person, at odds with the conventional expectations of society; his life is a search for location.

The structure of Paul Murray's biography first situates Hearn at the edge of the Orient, then casts him back to his disorganised, somewhat desperate, psychologically unstable American years; this forms the background to his self-definition in Japan. But at that point we are skilfully returned, 'by a commodious viscus of recirculation', to Hearn's Irish origins. In the process a unique Irish writer is redefined and, in a sense, reclaimed; and that is not the least important achievement of this book.

R.F.FOSTER
Oxford, September 1993

ACKNOWLEDGEMENTS

I SHOULD LIKE to acknowledge my debt to the following people and institutions for assisting me in a variety of ways:

My wife, Elizabeth Fitz-Simon, whose practical help included transcribing large amounts of Hearn material in various New York institutions; Professor Sukehiro Hirakawa Professor Emeritus, Tokyo University, for providing so stimulating an introduction; Professor Roy Foster, Carroll Professor of Irish History at Oxford, for his preface, practical help (including first bringing the Yeats-Hearn connection to my attention), and enthusiastic encouragement; Dr John Kelly, St John's College, Oxford, for providing me with material on the relationship between Hearn and W.B. Yeats; Frank Delaney; my publisher, Paul Norbury, for his constructive guidance; Dr Michael Sharratt, for his invaluable assistance in making Hearn's school records available to me, as well as bringing St Cuthbert's marvellous collection of 1860s photographs to my attention, and his successor as Librarian at Ushaw, Dr J.T. Rhodes; Bon Koizumi, Hearn's great-grandson, and curator of the Lafcadio Hearn Memorial Museum in Matsue; David Woodworth, the GPA-Bolton Library, Cashel, for supplying information on Archdeacon Daniel Hearn; Kenneth McConkey, Head of the Department of Historical and Critical Studies at Newcastle upon Tyne Polytechnic, for his assistance in tracing the career of Richard Hearn, Lafcadio's artist uncle; Dr Ruth Dudley Edwards; my brother-in-law, Stephen Fitz-Simon, and his wife, Barbara Hulanicki; Sean G. Ronan, retired Irish Ambassador and Hearn scholar; and, His Excellency, Joseph Small, my Ambassador in London.

I am grateful to the Librarian and staff at all the institutions which are listed as sources of material in the bibliography. However, I should like to express a particular debt of gratitude to the following:

William A. Moffett, Librarian, and Carolyn Powell, The Huntington Library; Charles E. Pearce, Jr., Director, and Christine Nelson Assistant Curator of Autograph Manuscripts, The Pierpont Morgan Library, New York; Dr Wilbur E. Meneray, Head, Rare Books and Manuscripts, and Sylvia V. Metzinger, Rare Books Librarian, Howard-Tilton Memorial Library, Tulane University; Michael Plunkett, Curator of Manuscripts, University Archivist, and Gregory A. Johnson, Senior Public Services Assistant, Special Collections Department/Alderman Library, University of Virginia Library; Leslie A. Morris, Curator of Manuscripts, The Houghton Library, Harvard University; Margaret Cook, Curator, Manuscripts and Rare Books, The Earl Gregg Swem Library, The College of William and Mary; Bernard R. Crystal, Rare Books and Manuscript Library, the Butler Library, Columbia University; Cathy Henderson, Research Librarian, Harry Ransom Humanities Research Centre, The University of Texas at Austin; Bob Buckeye, Abernethy Curator, Abernethy Library/Starr Library, Special Collections Middlebury College; Wayne Furman, Office of Special Collections, The Research Libraries, New York Public Library; Saundra Taylor, Curator of Manuscripts, The Lilly Library, Indiana University; Professor F. Rhodes, President, Cornell University; James H. Hutson, Chief, Manuscripts Division, and Jim Cole, Copyright Office, Library of Congress, Washington DC; Frank Waller, Fales Librarian, New York University

I am particularly grateful to Toki Koizumi, grandson of Lafcadio Hearn, for permission to quote from unpublished Hearn material, and to the following institutions for providing access to and/or permission to quote from their collections of mostly unpublished Hearn material:

The Pierpont Morgan Library (Harper and Hearn-Freeman-Watkin Collections MA 1950, MA 2532, MA 2533, MA 2534–35), New York; Fales Library, New York University, New York; The Research Libraries, (Henry W. and Albert A. Berg Collection, The New York Public Library, Astor Lenox and Tilden Foundations, and Lafcadio Hearn. Personal Miscellaneous Papers, Rare Books and Manuscripts Division, The New York Public Library, Astor, Lenox and Tilden Foundations) The New

York Public Libraries, New York; The Huntingdon Library, San Marino, California; Special Collections Department/Alderman Library, University of Virginia Library, Charlottesville, Virginia; Manuscript Division, Library of Congress, Washington, DC; Harry Ransom Humanities Research Centre, The University of Texas at Austin, Austin, Texas; The University Libraries, Indiana University, Bloomington, Indiana; Tucker-Coleman Papers, Swem Library, College of William and Mary, Williamsburg, Virginia; Abernethy Library, Starr Library, Middlebury College, Middlebury, Vermont; Harper Brothers Records, Edmund C. Stedman Papers, Lafcadio Hearn Papers, Rare Books and Manuscript Library, Butler Library, Columbia University, New York; by permission of the Houghton Library, Harvard University, Cambridge, Massachusetts.

The views expressed in this book are entirely my own. The only connection between it and my profession as an Irish diplomat is that my postings, purely by chance, enabled me to follow in Hearn's footsteps, except in the West Indies (where Ireland does not have any embassies).

While I have, in general, followed the English spelling system, I have not altered the spelling in documents from which I quote. Thus, when quoting from original Hearn documents, or his books, I have retained his American spelling. When quoting from Bisland's *Life and Letters* and *Japanese Letters*, I have allowed alterations to English spelling to stand.

The family name comes first in Japanese. However, I have usually followed the Western convention of putting the given name first and the family name second for all names, irrespective of nationality, to avoid confusion for readers unfamiliar with Japanese.

PAUL MURRAY
London, September 1993

Caricature of Lafcadio Hearn by John H. Garney, 1897

INTRODUCTION

LAFCADIO HEARN: TOWARDS
AN IRISH INTERPRETATION

by
SUKEHIRO HIRAKAWA
Professor Emeritus, Tokyo University
Honorary Member, MLA

TO RE-EXAMINE LAFCADIO HEARN by perusing not only
his published writings but also his scattered letters and
manuscripts is a most timely endeavour and will surely prove
to be most rewarding, now that Hearn's significance as Japan's
great interpreter is being seriously reconsidered both in the West
and in Japan. Indeed, Hearn was that *rara avis*, a Western observer
of Japan who, coming to the Far East in the 1890s, did not take
as an article of faith the superiority of the industrial civilisation of
the West. For example, far from adhering to the opinions of the
mainstream of Western orientalists, Hearn was adamant in his
conviction that for ordinary citizens of the lower strata of society,
that fundamental human rights, freedom from horror, was
safeguarded better in Japanese slums than in European capitals or
America's great cities.

Hearn was mercifully free also from many commonly-shared
prejudices of certain over-zealous Christian missionaries and
Europe-centred professors of the nineteenth century and he was
at that time apparently the only Westerner who recognised the
importance of Shinto, the indigenous animistic religion of the
Japanese. How was it possible for Hearn to make the very
perspicacious sociological and religious observations which he so

1

modestly called 'glimpses'? And how was it possible for him to intuit so well the subtleties of *kokoro* or the psyche of the Japanese? There is a great variety of possible answers to all these intriguing questions about Lafcadio Hearn, a man of undeniably many parts, and Mr Paul Murray tries to answer them by opening a new biographical and interpretative perspective which might be called Irish, and this Hibernian perspective, which hitherto has not been adequately explored, is, in my opinion, very important and suggestive.

It has long been believed that Patrick Lafcadio Hearn, on his arrival in the United States dropped his first name Patrick: he did not like his dead Anglo-Irish father who had been the cause of so many of his miseries: in Dublin 'the child' was separated from his Greek mother at the tender age of four, when the father obliged her to go back to an Ionian island. Penniless, at the age of nineteen, he left England for America. It is psychologically understandable that Hearn wished to obliterate his paternal background and that he harboured a strong antipathy against what his father, officer surgeon of Queen Victoria's regiment, stood for. However, as is documented by Mr Paul Murray in such detail, Lafcadio Hearn's Irish connection was too deeply embedded in his psyche to be wiped away so quickly. This study clearly shows that, contrary to what Hearn himself wrote later, he remained Paddy Hearn in his early Cincinnati days. Then he transmogrified himself completely into the Greek romantic figure of Lafcadio Hearn in New Orleans.

However, what did 'Greece' mean to Hearn whose linguistic knowledge of Greek was so poor as to be later mocked by the philosophy professor von Koeber, a colleague of his at Tokyo University? Where did this need to re-invent himself come from? And why was he so successful as a Japan interpreter? Was there any connection between his insecure childhood and his sympathetic understanding of ghostly Japan? Or was his success bogus, as the aged dean of Western Japanologists, Basil Hall Chamberlain, intimated in the article 'Lafcadio Hearn' which appeared in the 1939 edition of *Things Japanese*? These are the questions concerning Lafcadio Hearn mainly in the West, while in his country of adoption Hearn has become more popular under his Japanese name of Koizumi Yakumo, and there is a considerable difference in appreciation between literary historians of the West and Japanese Hearn admirers. Does the contrasting difference in appreciation derive from infatuation, narcissism or nostalgia for their romantically idealised pre-industrial past by the Japanese? Or does the difference in deprecation derive from the incredible act, in the respectable reign of Queen Victoria, of a British subject's going native and becoming a naturalised Japanese citizen?

Before answering all these questions, let me clarify first Hearn's posthumous literary fame and his gradual acceptance in Japan, as information in this area is not always easily accessible to Western Hearn specialists; and by showing an example of Japanese understanding of Lafcadio Hearn, I'll try to explain the need for us all to know more about his Irish background.

Hearn is today remembered in Japan mainly by his *kwaidan* or ghost stories. One of the first folk-tales retold by Hearn is included in an essay 'By the Japanese Sea' in *Glimpses of Unfamiliar Japan* (1894).

> Once there lived in the Izumo village called Mochida-no-ura a peasant who was so poor that he was afraid to have children, and each time that his wife bore him a child he cast it into the river, and pretended that it had been born dead. Sometimes it was a son, sometimes a daughter; but always the infant was thrown into the river at night. Six were murdered thus.
>
> But, as the years passed, the peasant found himself more prosperous. He had been able to purchase land and to lay by money. And at last his wife bore him a seventh child, – a boy.
>
> Then the man said: 'Now we can support a child, and we shall need a son to aid us when we are old. And this boy is beautiful, so we will bring him up.
>
> And the infant thrived; and each day the hard peasant wondered more at his own heart, – for each day he knew that he loved his son more.
>
> One summer's night he walked out into his garden, carrying his child in his arms. The little one was five years old.
>
> And the night was so beautiful, with its great moon, that the peasant cried out, –
>
> '*Aa! kon ya medzurashii e yo ka!*' (Ah! tonight truly a wondrously beautiful night it is!)
>
> Then the infant, looking up into his face and speaking the speech of a man, said –
>
> 'Why, father! *the LAST time you threw me away* the night

was just like this, and the moon looked just the same, did it not?'

And thereafter, the child remained as other children of the same age, and spoke no word.

The peasant became a monk.

I am of the opinion that the Japanese ethnological studies undertaken by Yanagita Kunio at the beginning of the twentieth century got a strong impetus from Hearn's writing of this kind. Stimulated by Hearn's example, Japanese pioneer folklorists belatedly began to collect and write down oral legends, though this legend of Mochida-no-ura itself was never recorded in Japanese except the Izumo dialect of the father's cry used in the test and the boy's speech footnoted by Hearn. The curiosity of Japanese comparative literary historians, too, was aroused by this kind of retold story. While analysing the intrinsic value of the retold tale itself, we are inevitably reminded of the writer's own childhood. Was not Lafcadio psychologically an abandoned child himself?

We have also remarked that the empathy with which Hearn retells Japanese stories has in many cases two kinds of root: one has something to do with his own personal experience. Longing for his early separated mother is apparently transplanted in stories such as Urashima ('The Dream of a Summer Day') or the rebirth of a betrothed girl ('The Story of O-Tei'). The other derives from his bookish knowledge or literary experience gained in his formative years. While retelling Japanese stores, Hearn might have mingled or used consciously or unconsciously some such Western elements. Let us compare the Mochida-no-ura legend with a Scottish ballad Hearn later taught to Tokyo university students:

> She leaned her head against a thorn,
> *(The sun shines fair on Carlisle wall!)*
> And there she has her young babe born.
> *(And the lion shall be lord of all!)*
>
> 'Smile not so sweet, my bonny babe,
> *(The sun shines fair on Carlisle wall!)*
> An ye smile so sweet, ye'll smile me dead.'
> *(And the lion shall be lord of all!)*
>
> She's howket a grave by the light of the moon,
> *(The sun shines fair on Carlisle wall!)*

4

And there she's buried her sweet babe in.
(And the lion shall be lord of all!)

As she was going to the church,
(The sun shines fair on Carlisle wall!)
She saw a sweet babe in the porch.
(And the lion shall be lord of all!)

O bonny babe, an ye were mine,
(The sun shines fair on Carlisle wall!)
I'd clad ye in silk and sabelline,
(And the lion shall be lord of all!)

O mother mind, when I was thine,
(The sun shines fair on Carlisle wall!)
To me ye were not half so kind.
(And the lion shall be lord of all!)

But now I'm in the heavens hie,
(The sun shines fair on Carlisle wall!)
And ye have the pains of hell to dree.
(And the lion shall be lord of all!)

Hearn adds the following comment:

Here we have a story told in a few lines, but with
extraordinary power, for once read, this ballad never can be
forgotten. A young girl, to hide her shame, determines to
kill her illegitimate child, but at the moment of the act, the
child smiles in her face, and this almost prevents the crime.
Nevertheless it is accomplished, the child is secretly buried;
no one knows of the act: and the mother returns to her life
in society as if nothing had happened. But one day as she is
about to enter a church, she sees a child of such remarkable
beauty that her natural affection is aroused, and she cannot
help saying to the little creature, 'Oh, how beautifully I
should dress you if you were my boy.' The child's answer
immediately reveals to her that she is speaking to the ghost
of the child she has murdered. - 'O mother, when I was
your boy, you were not so kind!' The great art of this poem
– probably the composition of some peasant – is all in the
second verse. This is intensely human, and terribly
touching.

The subject of the ballad is very similar to the Japanese legend.
The difference is that in the Scottish ballad it is not the father but
the mother of the child that killed it. In the ballad the child was
killed only once while in the Japanese legend six children were
killed, as the Buddhistic transmigration is often associated with

the number seven. However, the most impressive point is that the ghost of the murdered child speaks to the parent through the mouth of another new-born baby. This point is the same in the two pieces: the child's voice reminds the parent of the past crime. According to Hearn's paraphrase, the child that the mother sees at the entrance of a church is a boy. I am wondering if the child is really a boy. Is there not a possibility that 'my bonny babe' is a girl? In the fifth stanza the mother says: 'I'd like to clad ye in silk and sabelline'. The expression 'Oh, how beautifully I should dress you' seems to me to fit better 'if you were my *girl*'. However, for the once abandoned Lafcadio the bonny babe should be, like himself, a boy.

The question now is whether Hearn was conscious of this ballad when he retold in English the legend of Mochida-no-ura. As the original Japanese oral story is not recorded in a written form, we cannot give any satisfactory answer. However, it is very probable that Hearn was reminded of this ballad while rewriting the Japanese tale. His childhood experience, too, must have played a certain part in this recreation of many of his Japanese stories and observations. In fact, towards the end of 'By the Japanese Sea', in which the supernatural tale of the abandoned child is told, Hearn all of a sudden refers to a Celtic lullaby sung in a dream by a woman with black hair and to an Irish folk-saying that any dream may be remembered if the dreamer, after awakening, forbear to scratch his head in the effort to recall it, as is remarked by Mr Murray in this book. There is, therefore, a conscious or unconscious association between them.

If even a retold Japanese story can be profitably re-examined in a Celtic perspective, then how about Hearn's interpretations of Japanese goblins, ghosts and souls? Would it not be possible for us to reconsider them under an Irish angle? In his opening chapter, 'Discovering Hearn', Mr Murray says:

> It has been accepted in Hearn biography that his experience in Japan was a curve, veering from early infatuation to disillusioned realism. A close examination of the evidence, however, reveals that he formed his views on Japan in his first few months there and never fundamentally altered them up to the time of this death, fourteen years later.

I am also of this opinion. It is true that Hearn's attitude toward Japan and the Japanese was ambivalent and that there were inevitable fluctuations in his love-hate relationship with Japan, as is sensitively explained by Makino Yôko in her concise analysis *Rafukadio Haan* (Chûkô-shinsho, 1992). However, there was not much change in his interpretations of Shintô. This means either that Hearn formed his views on Japanese religions in his first few months or that he had come to Japan with an almost preestablished idea concerning the relationships between underlying indigenous religion and a superimposed imported religion. In this context Hearn's prior experience in the French West Indies as well as his childhood experience become very significant, as some of his keen observations and sharp interpretations of the religious state of mind of the Japanese were made against those earlier backgrounds.

Lafcadio Hearn was already cynical towards missionaries and their evangelical work in his Martinique days. He saw clearly and rightly that what Creole populations there worshipped in distorted figures of Mary, Christ or Catholic saints was in reality something considerably different from orthodox Christianity. Martinique was indeed full of ghosts and ghost stories related with religions of African origin; it was there that Hearn first successfully collected ghost stories, and thanks to his recording of them those Creole stories are still read and enjoyed by the local population a century later, and Hearn's name is as well remembered in the French West Indies as it is popular in Japan today. 'Un Revenant' is a superb piece, and I quite agree with the view that there was much in *Two Years in the French West Indies* which anticipated important elements of Hearn's Japanese work.

On his arrival in Japan, I believe that Hearn was already sure that Buddhism in this island country must have been very much Japanised, and he was right; Buddhism in Japan is as different from other national Buddhisms as Japanese temples are different in colour and in form from Buddhist temples in China, Korea or Ceylon. The problem with Japanese Buddhists, however, is that they insist that Buddhism in its Japanese form is the true one. It is curious but the Japanisation of Buddhism under the influence of Shinto has not always been objectively studied by native Buddhist monks and believers, as the present form suits their interests and tastes best. Hearn's observations concerning Japanese religious matters had from the beginning the advantage

7

of perspective and points of comparison with other countries.

In his New Orleans days Hearn translated some passages from Loti, and he admired the dance of the festival of the dead in Senegal beautifully described by the French author. 'At the Market of the Dead' and 'Bon-Odori' in *Glimpses of Unfamiliar Japan* are what Hearn actually observed in the first months of his stay in Japan; however, he had already learnt how to observe a phantasmal dance from the final chapters of Loti's *le Roman d'un Spahi*. Still, we would like to know why it was possible for Hearn to convey so expertly the feelings of the foreigner who was making his first acquaintance with the *bon-odori*, the dance of the festival of the dead. Moreover, why was it so easy for him to understand that the traditional festival of the dead, *o-bon*, had originally little to do with Buddhism? Was it because Halloween in the West has roots going far back into pre-Christian times? Was Hearn's approach to Japan essentially analogical? And why did he understand so early the *bon* festival's ancestral character, while coming to Matsue, the chief city of the province of gods? Why could he enter into that gathering of Japanese ghosts?

Here we are ineluctably reminded of Yeats' connection with Japan. William Butler Yeats intuited remarkably well the world of Nô plays, which is no other than a world of ghosts, probably because he was already familiar with Irish faery tales and ghost stories. If Yeats, who had never been to Japan, was able to empathise with the ghostly world of the Japanese through his reading of the Fenollosa-Pound translations of Nô plays, why would it not be possible for Lafcadio Hearn, a child of similar Irish background, to sympathise with Japanese ghostly folklore and customs? Both Yeats and Hearn were agnostics of a kind; but this does not mean that both poets were not gifted with religious sensitivity. On the contrary, Yeats and Hearn were religious in the sense that in the vacuum caused by their loss of faith in a monotheistic religion there entered furtively a legion of pagan gods, ghosts and goblins. To their mind's eye began to appear many faeries and spirits. The Japanese world of the dead began to be familiar to Lafcadio's mind's eye. Here is a first example of his penetration into the religious world of the Japanese, which I quote from the same travel essay 'By the Japanese Sea'. The Mochida-no-ura legend of the transmigration of the soul of a murdered child, although Buddhistic in form, is indirectly related to the following belief in returning ghosts:

> Though during a week the sky has remained unclouded,
> the sea has for several days been growing angrier; and now
> the muttering of its surf sounds far into the land. They say
> that it always roughens thus during the period of the
> Festival of the Dead, – the three days of the Bon, which are
> the thirteenth, fourteenth and fifteenth of the seventh
> month by the ancient calendar. And on the sixteenth day,
> after the shôryôbune, which are the Ships of Souls, have
> been launched, no one dares to enter it: no boats can then
> be hired; all the fishermen remain at home. For on that day
> the sea is the highway of the dead, who must pass back over
> its waters to their mysterious home; and therefore upon that
> day is it called Hotoke-umi, – the Buddha-Flood, – the
> Tide of the Returning Ghosts. And even upon the night of
> that sixteenth day, – whether the sea be calm or
> tumultuous, – all its surfaces shimmers with faint lights
> gliding out to the open,– the dim fires of the dead; and
> there is heard a murmuring of voices, like the murmur of a
> city far-off, – the indistinguishable speech of souls.

And Hearn tells us his visit to the village hakaba or graveyard:

> After the supper and the bath, feeling too warm to sleep, I
> wander out alone to visit the village hakaba, a long
> cemetery upon a sandhill, or rather a prodigious dune,
> thinly covered at its summit with soil, but revealing through
> its crumbling flanks the story of its creation by ancient tides,
> mightier than tides of today.
>
> I wade to my knees in sand to reach the cemetery. It is a
> warm moonlight night, with a great breeze. There are
> many bon-lanterns (bondôrô), but the seawind has blown
> out most of them; only a few here and there still shed a soft
> white glow, – pretty shrine-shaped cases of wood, with
> apertures of symbolic outline, covered with white paper.
> Visitors beside myself there are none, for it is late. But much
> gentle work has been done here today, for all the bamboo
> vases have been furnished with fresh flowers or sprays, and
> the water basins filled with fresh water, and the monuments
> cleansed and beautified. And in the farthest nook of the
> cemetery I find, before one very humble tomb, a pretty zen
> or lacquered dining tray, covered with dishes and bowls
> containing a perfect dainty little Japanese repast. There is
> also a pair of new chopsticks, and a little cup of tea, and
> some of the dishes are still warm.

Festivals of the dead took place in many parts of the world.

Now let us have a look at the following description:

> The second of November is the festival of All the Souls of the Faithful Departed, and, in accordance with ancient church practice, prayers for the repose of the souls of the dead were recited on this day.
>
> A widespread belief was that dead members of the family returned to visit their old home on this night, and that care should be taken to show that their visit was welcome.
>
> All Souls Eve is sacred to the memory of the departed. After the floor has been swept and good fire put down on the hearth, the family retires early, leaving the door unlatched and a bowl of spring water on the table, so that any relative who had died may find a place prepared for him at his own fireside. On that one night in the year the souls of the dead are loosed and have liberty to visit their former homes.
>
> Many people lit one candle for each dead member of the family when evening prayers were being said. In some cases the candles were quenched when the prayers were ended, in others they were left to burn out. Many people made visits to the graveyard where their relatives were buried, to pray for their souls and clean and tidy the graves; some placed lighted candles on the graves while praying.
>
> The belief that the souls of dead kinsfolk could come to the aid of the living at this time was current. The present writer, as a child, asked an old storyteller in County Limerick 'if he wasn't afraid to go into the haunted house?' and got the reply 'In dread, is it? What would I be in dread of, and the souls of my own dead as thick as bees around me?'
>
> It is said that on this one day in the year the souls of the dead are allowed to re-visit their native districts: and if only human eye had the power to see them, they would be observed about one on every side ' as plenty as thraneens in an uncut meadow'.

The quotation is from Kevin Danaher: *The Year in Ireland* (The Mercier Press, Cork, 1972). We know that the dead take a continuing part in the lives of the living not only in Japan of Shinto traditions but also in many areas of rural Ireland. So long as we humans feel a need to believe it, communications between out ancestors and us continue and this belief in East Asia is generally known by the name of 'ancestor-worship'.

Finally, let me dwell a bit on the relationship between Hearn's Greece and Ireland. In many of his writings Lafcadio Hearn fondly compared Japan with Greece. In the case of his *Japan: an Attempt at Interpretation* Hearn's repetitive references to Greek antecedents are quite understandable, as the book was modelled after Fustel de Coulanges' *la Cité Antique*. The tables of contents of both books contain the same chapter titles such as 'antiques croyances', 'le culte des morts', 'le feu sacré', 'la religion domestique', 'la famille' for Fustel de Coulanges' book and 'the ancient cult', 'the religion of the home', 'the Japanese family', 'the communal cult', 'developments of Shintô' for Hearn's book. Hearn's approach was so remarkably similar that Marc Logé, the French translator of *Japan: an Attempt at Interpretation*, called it in the preface *la Cité Extrême-Orientale*. Incidentally, *la Cité Antique* was extremely popular among the leading jurists of Meiji Japan, who, like Hearn, believed they had found in the French historian's description of ancient Greek society, a society very similar to that of nineteenth-century Japan.

As Hearn was a firm believer in the linear evolution of mankind, he imagined that he himself was living in Japan at the same stage lived by his ancestors several thousand years before. However, what is interesting about the use of the adjective 'Greek' by Hearn, and to a certain extent by Fustel de Coulanges himself, is that it often means 'pre-Christian'. The French historian depicts European society before it was christianised or before ancient cults were eradicated and their gods expelled. In spite of his rather weak knowledge of things Greek, Hearn was easily able to empathise with the 'Greek' world as it was described by Fustel de Coulanges, because it was a world full of ghosts, and that world haunted by the spirits of the dead was in many ways similar to the Celtic world.

Yes, it may be claimed that Lafcadio Hearn presents us with a distinctively Irish imagination. Brought up in Dublin, listening to so many Irish folk-tales told by unspoiled peasant maids and servant-boys coming from the countryside, Hearn was obsessed with the world of the occult. He was probably conscious of this Irish background which enabled him to enter into and feel the ghostly Japan so well. However, for the reason already mentioned, Lafcadio did not wish to mention his indebtedness towards his paternal country. When he began to write autobiographical fragments, vaguely recognising his own background, Hearn suddenly passed away at the age of fifty-four. Do

I insist too much on the Irish in him, if I sometimes change 'Greek' to 'Celtic', while reading Hearn's writings? At any rate how satisfying it is to see in the same perspective Yeats and Hearn together! It is almost certain that Hearn is going to be redefined and revived with an Irish dimension.

CHAPTER ONE

DISCOVERING HEARN

> I refer to the civilized nomad, whose wanderings are not
> prompted by the hope of gain, nor determined by pleasure,
> but simply controlled by certain necessities of his being,-
> the man whose inner secret nature is totally at variance with
> the stable conditions of a society to which he belongs only
> by accident.[1]

IN APRIL 1890, a small, unprepossessing figure stepped ashore
in brilliant spring sunshine onto the quay at Yokohama. Patrick
Lafcadio Hearn was approaching his fortieth birthday and did not
seem to have too much to show for a fairly frenetic life. Contrary
to what many have thought, he had achieved a good deal. He
had been a successful, well-paid, journalist and *littérateur* in two
American cities; two years in the West Indies had yielded a
highly-regarded book. But somehow the achievement had never
lasted. He always kicked over the traces, and walked away from
success he had worked hard to achieve.

Part of the phenomenon was a need to constantly re-invent
himself, firstly as Paddy Hearn, the muckraking journalist from
Ireland whose sensationalism rocked Cincinnati in the 1870s.
Then, in New Orleans, he transmogrified himself into the Greek
romantic figure of Lafcadio Hearn. In the West Indies, in the
later 1880s, he was the superior Northern observer reporting on
a fascinating, but inferior, culture. In Japan, he would reverse this
stance and hold up the mirror of Japanese moral superiority to his
Western audience. Most surprisingly, the man whose obsession

with the Roman Catholic Church, the Jesuits in particular, seemed to reach levels of acute paranoia, would use religion as the major component of his interpretation of Japan.

It is easy to ridicule the seeming contradictions of Patrick Lafcadio Hearn. He made many enemies in his lifetime and, after his death, some of them emerged to assail his reputation in a manner from which it has never recovered. I began researching this book in the early 1980s because I could not reconcile the intelligence, and astonishing modernity, of Hearn with the caricature of much of what has passed for biography. The tone of so much of it seemed to range from hostility to condescension. This was made possible by ignoring, or glossing over, most of Hearn's achievement.

During his life, and often since then, Hearn was treated as a poetically-inspired writer, but a practical idiot otherwise. Few bothered to look at the prescient intelligence evident in his journalism. Even though it is for his Japanese work that Hearn is now remembered, no previous biographer has lived in Japan and none made the effort to interpret his crowning achievement. The anthologies of his writings on Japan seemed to plod along in the same tracks, concentrating, significantly, on the descriptive rather than the analytical.

This book starts from the proposition, therefore, that Hearn's work on Japan is among the best ever written on that country, and is of continuing relevance. In human terms, it sees Hearn as capable of being difficult, devious, dishonest and irrational certainly, but also as a man of conscious artistic mission who was not invariably in the wrong in his dealings with other people. The quality of his friendship was not always reciprocated by 'friends' with their own axes to grind.

The first duty of the biographer is to look at the facts and try to make sense of them. For this biography, all of Hearn's work has been closely examined, both from a biographical angle and in terms of its inherent literary worth. Many new sources have been discovered and many old ones looked at afresh for the first time in decades. The task facing a biographer of Hearn should not be underestimated: the sheer volume of primary, let alone secondary, material is vast. He produced a huge corpus of published work, in the form of books, articles, lectures and translations, as well as leaving behind an enormous volume of correspondence and other personal writings. While freely acknowledging the debt which all those interested in the subject owe to the great line of previous Hearn biographers – Bisland, Kennard, McWilliams, Frost, and Stevenson, among others – I nevertheless felt that the time had come to look afresh at the whole canon of Hearn sources, using an historian's methodology, while trying to give due emphasis to the literary side.

The original plan of the book followed a straight chronology. This seemed less than satisfactory because a close examination of the formative years of Hearn's youth does not work best in a vacuum. Much of the subjective material derived from Hearn himself when, in later life, he was trying to make sense of his own childhood. It therefore unfolds to best effect later in the story. However, it is probably useful to give the reader an outline of Hearn's life at the outset.

He was born on a Greek island in June 1850 to an Irish officer/surgeon in the British Army and a local Greek woman. He was one of three children which resulted from a passionate liaison: the first was born illegitimate and the second, Patrick Lafcadio, was in gestation when the couple married. Within months of his birth, his father was transferred to the West Indies which essentially marked the end of the couple's real relationship.

His good-looking, passionate and illiterate mother took him to Dublin when he was two, to stay with her Hearn in-laws. It was not a success and she returned to Greece two years later, leaving the young Patrick Lafcadio in the care of a widowed elderly great-aunt, Mrs Brenane. He was never to see his mother again.

The Hearns were middle-ranking Protestants with a stern tradition of service to the British Army and the Church of Ireland, part of the elite which ruled the mostly Roman Catholic island of Ireland at a time when all of it belonged to the United Kingdom of Britain and Ireland. Patrick Lafcadio's father was Protestant and his mother Greek Orthodox; Mrs Brenane, who had converted from the Church of Ireland to marry a wealthy Roman Catholic, brought him up in her adopted faith.

From the earliest Hearn biography to the present day, Mrs Brenane has been cast as a bigot with the vengeful zeal of the convert, imposing rigid Roman Catholicism on her unwilling charge.[2] Closely examined, the evidence suggests the opposite: in her care, young Patrick enjoyed a life of cultured leisure with, critically, untrammelled access to books of all sorts.

The idyll came to an end, however, when Patrick Lafcadio was in his early teens and Mrs Brenane fell under the spell of a young English Roman Catholic couple on the make. He was then packed off to an English boarding school run by Roman Catholic priests on rigidly religious lines. Here young Paddy Hearn, as he was then called, was subjected to a religious regime for which his *laissez-faire* upbringing had ill-prepared him. The school buildings were masterpieces of Victorian Gothic and were to have an abiding influence on a mind which would always be tormented by Gothic horror.

He also seems to have been effectively abandoned by Mrs Brenane at this stage, no longer wanted in a home dominated by strangers and condemned to spend his holidays at the school. Further misfortunes rained down on him: he lost an eye in a accident during a game at the school, leaving a disfigurement which, added to his small stature and acute shyness, induced social misery for the rest of his life. The denouement of this catalogue of misfortune was his great-aunt's financial ruin which saw him cast down in his later teens from privilege to living with a former maid of Mrs Brenane's and her husband in a squalid quarter of London.

In 1869, at the age of nineteen, he was dispatched to America and went to Cincinnati where he was taken on by a middle-aged English printer, Henry Watkin. He progressed to journalism, making a name for himself by writing luridly horrific accounts of the low life of the burgeoning industrial city. At this stage, he was still Paddy Hearn, conscious of his position as an Irish immigrant. He was well-paid and could have settled into a comfortable local niche, even if his career was interrupted by a short-lived marriage to a negress who had been born into slavery.

But Hearn was in the grip of an artistic imperative. Lacking, he felt, the ability to be a wholly original writer, he began translating his French Romantic literary idols into English, firstly through the medium of short pieces published in the newspapers, and then in longer works intended to appear as books. Victorian American, however, was not interested: publishers had to be wary of the then scandalous sexual licence which underlay

French Romanticism, and in which Hearn frankly gloated. His uninhibited attitude to sex, which shocked his contemporaries and many since, is unremarkable today. Later, under the influence of Japanese restraint, he would condemn the latent, but universal, sexuality which he came to see as permeating all Western civilisation.

His flouting of the mores of conventional society, both in his work and his life, emphasised the marginal nature of Hearn's relationship to it. In Ireland he was the half-Greek, Roman Catholic scion of the Protestant Hearns. He was marginalised in Mrs Brenane's household by the adventurer, Molyneux, who ruined her. In London he lived among the dregs of society.

In Cincinnati, he marginalised himself. His mainstream journalism probed the rotten underbelly of society – grotesque murders, hangings, slaughter houses, dissection rooms, city dumps, the poor black quarter, and, more dangerously, municipal corruption. In his personal work, he translated unacceptably salacious French Romanticism. In his private life he flouted the law which forbad racial inter-marriage. Yet society rewarded as well as punished him. He was a well-paid and highly-regarded journalist. If news of his marriage precipitated his dismissal from one newspaper, he was taken on by another. Notwithstanding his self-proclaimed demophobia, he enjoyed the friendship of serious people. Prostitutes may have been his main sexual outlet but he also attracted a woman of social rank.

Cincinnati, in other words, treated him well but after a few years he had outgrown it. In his late twenties he moved south to New Orleans where he finally discarded 'Paddy' and became Lafcadio Hearn, Latin *litterateur*, even if journalism still provided a living. He marginalised himself once again in New Orleans, self-consciously rejecting the mainstream American city in favour of the archaic Creole quarter, damning the technological advances of the nineteenth century from a romantic distance. Hearn had discovered ancient Greek culture in his teens and now, in New Orleans, he claimed it as his inheritance from his Greek mother. He identified himself with the warm, pre-industrial South and determined to reject the inheritance of his father's cold North. Even then, he knew it was not quite so simple, but that was the direction he wanted to follow.

He still had to practise the despised trade of journalism but he no longer trod the streets in search of stories. He was a commentator and editorialist and, increasingly, a translator. His search for ever more exotic material, and his French literary idols, brought him into contact with the Orient. This, together with his discovery of the 'synthetic philosophy' of Herbert Spencer, began the process which ultimately brought him to Japan.

Even more than Cincinnati, New Orleans treated him well. He was the star name of his newspaper and enjoyed easy intimacy with the editor and his family. He was allowed to publish what he wanted, including his first attempts at original creative writing. He was accepted by the Creoles and New Orleans cultured society in general. He was lionised at literary soirees and wheeled out for visiting cultural dignitaries. His books began to be published, particularly *Stray Leaves from Stray Literature* and *Some Chinese Ghosts*, both translations of Eastern tales. Here, one would have thought, he had found his niche. He had not. He wanted to go further south, craving new adventures and new sensations. He found them initially in Grande Isle, at the mouth of the Mississippi; vacations there provided the inspiration for *Chita*, his first piece of extended fiction. It was well received, both by the critics and the public, and he was now a coming man in the field of popular literature.

Armed with a commission of sorts from a major publisher, Harper, he set off for the West Indies, to encounter what was probably the greatest disappointment of his career. He might fantasise about being a simple man of the South but was, in reality, a Northern intellectual who could not adjust to the climate and found the local culture vapid. The *enfant terrible* of Cincinnati had been in the process of becoming steadily more conservative in his years in New Orleans and his perspective now was that of the superior Northerner, viewing a charming but childish society with sympathy and firm detachment. The experience did yield *Two Years in the French West Indies*, the prototype for the format of his Japanese books, and *Youma*, another piece of extended popular fiction.

Hearn's first attempt to live solely by his pen, without the underpinning of a journalistic income, proved to be a failure and led to strains with his publisher which would explode early on in his stay in Japan. Some desperate months spent back in the United States in 1889 began initially with a doctor in

Philadelphia, George Gould, who had befriended him through correspondence. The bizarre, and highly ambiguous, relationship between the two men broke down; it would lead to a spectacular literary controversy after Lafcadio's death. He then returned to New York and undertook hack literary work to keep himself afloat. Most people in his position at this stage would have churned out popular fiction, building on the success of *Chita* and *Youma*. He was urged to do this by his closest friends throughout his career but it was a course he resolutely refused to countenance. He was more discerning than his readers and knew that his artistic vocation did not lie in that direction.

Instead, at the age of almost forty, when most people have already shaped their lives, he set off for Japan with only the most tenuous of undertakings from his publisher. The relationship failed after a few weeks in Japan and Hearn was on his own in a strange society with no means of support. For a man whose early experiences had imprinted vividly on his psyche the horror of being destitute, and the value of money, Lafcadio's repeated willingness to abjure comfortable circumstances and face alien societies alone was a measure of his inner steel. He may have known that he would not be a major literary figure of a conventional sort but he knew he had an artistic purpose to fulfil and he would let nothing stand in the way of achieving it, even if for the time being he was not quite sure what is was.

Japan was to provide Hearn with the means of artistic fulfilment for which, in retrospect, he had spent his life up to this point preparing; henceforth he would be preoccupied with articulating his vision of a country whose language he never learned to speak but with whose culture he developed an extraordinary empathy. It was, in fact, a double vision: he was concerned not just with explaining Japan to his Western audience; he used Japan as a mirror to show to the West its moral inadequacy. This had long been a theme of his, but never so powerfully or coherently expressed.

In London, as a teenager, he had recoiled in horror at his first encounter with an industrial society. In Cincinnati, he had thrown the foulest abasement in his readers faces, reminding them of what lay beneath society's veneer of respectability. In New Orleans, he had used ancient Greek civilisation as a yardstick to measure the shortcomings of the nineteenth century.

He also used the 'common' people as an instrument to articulate his dissatisfaction with industrial society. He had always been interested in folklore, contrasting the superiority of the unsophisticated to contemporary bourgeois culture. The roots of this attitude went back to his childhood in Ireland where the reclamation of the old Gaelic folk culture was laying the foundations for the literary revival pioneered by Lafcadio's great Irish contemporaries, Yeats in particular.

In Cincinnati, his work on the popular culture of the negro levee quarter is now recognised as trailblazing. In New Orleans, he immersed himself in the romantic, doomed, *ante bellum* world of the Creoles. In the West Indies, the common man was again his theme, even if his views on the race question, formed by his identification with the *ancien regime* in New Orleans, led him to adopt patronising attitudes. But he was never patronising towards the Japanese. He knew from the start that he was in the presence of a major culture and his modern, anti-imperialist, attitudes marked him out from even his greatest Western contemporaries, such as Basil Hall Chamberlain. He would be ambiguous, alternatively loving and hating the country, but in that he was no different from many long-term foreign residents in Japan over the years. In any case, a Joycean ambiguity about the country in which he had been formed, Ireland, and the countries in which he lived afterwards – England, the United States, the West Indies, and Japan – was an ingrained characteristic of Patrick Lafcadio Hearn.

It has been accepted in Hearn biography that his experience in Japan was a curve, veering from early infatuation to disillusioned realism. A close examination of the evidence, however, reveals that he formed his views on Japan in his first few months there and never fundamentally altered them up to the time of his death, fourteen years later. In that time he wrote a dozen books on Japan, containing an immortal corpus of interpretation. While much has been written about Lafcadio Hearn *in* Japan, not too much attention has been paid to what he wrote *about* Japan. In New Orleans he had become interested in Buddhism and began a life-long attempt to reconcile it with Herbert Spencer's evolutionary philosophy. When he reached Japan, he was initially fascinated to find himself surrounded by a real, living, Buddhism; soon, however, he came to the conclusion that

Buddhism was a foreign superstructure grafted onto the ancient substructure of Japanese society, the core of which was Shinto, the indigenous form of ancestor-worship. At this stage he gathered the analytical tools – Shinto, ancient Greek civilisation and Spencer's evolutionary philosophy – which he would use to penetrate the increasingly Westernised exterior of a Japan then in the throes of Meiji modernisation through to the old, eternal, essence of the real Japan which, he believed, lived on in the common people. Not that Hearn's vision of Japan was a folksy one; on the contrary, essays such as 'Jiujutsu' are marvellous analyses of the *realpolitik* underlying Japanese policy, particularly towards the outside world.

Spencer was perhaps the most contentious influence and caused Hearn sometimes to advance propositions directly at odds with the fruits of his experience. His philosophy did, however, provide a structure with which a writer woefully lacking in architectonic ability could give some backbone to his approach, particularly in *Japan: an Attempt at Interpretation*, his late attempt to summarise his outlook on Japan in a single work. From an analytical standpoint, the best material is in the early books, *Glimpses of Unfamiliar Japan*, *Out of the East*, and *Kokoro*, published during his first six years in Japan. These books were the products of his time at Yokohama, Matsue, Kumamoto, and Kobe. He went to Matsue, a relatively remote city on Japan's west coast in September 1890, where he had been offered a job as a schoolteacher. Lafcadio was an instant success as a teacher and he spent a happy year in Matsue, where he married a Japanese before the harshness of the winter drove him to another teaching post in Kumamoto, on the southern island of Kyushu. The three years he spent here, however, were unhappy, yet productive.

In October 1894, the Hearns moved to the 'open port' of Kobe where Lafcadio went into journalism again – for the last time. Sadly, after a few months, his eyesight failed and he was out of work for two years, until his appointment to Tokyo University in 1896. He was given this lectureship (in English language and literature) at a time when the Japanese were anxious to avail themselves of foreign expertise. Hearn held the post for seven years, unaware that, towards the end, the great Japanese novelist, Soseki, was being groomed to replace him. His lectures at Tokyo University have survived and contain a body of clear and simple literary criticism, as well as a good deal of autobiographical revelation. He continued to produce books on Japan in which he pursued, progressively, his own enthusiasms.

The birth of his first son, Kazuo, stirred an emotional earthquake in Hearn and he began to explore his own childhood, to peel back the romantic layers he had been superimposing on it for most of his life. It is for this reason that the childhood section of the biography has been placed at this point in the book. It makes more sense to accompany Hearn on his voyage of self-discovery than to go through the process of disentanglement at the beginning of the book, when the reader would have far less sense of its relevance.

Hearn was relentlessly autobiographical in every medium in which he wrote. An attempt is made in this book to gather together and analyse the full wealth and complexity of these sources. Critically examined, they show that interpreting what others have accepted as straightforward needs a much more subtle approach. Legal documents have been unearthed from Irish State archives which cast a radically different light on the background of the Hearn family, particularly the relationship of Mrs Brenane with Lafcadio' father.

Hearn's later years in Tokyo were lonely and sad. With the onset of the heart disease which would eventually kill him, he lost much of the vigour which had sustained so many friendships over the years, even if his intellectual powers were undimmed. The loss of his Tokyo University post was a hammer-blow, even if he did quickly find another prestigious lectureship. He died peacefully at his home in September 1904.

There was intense interest in Hearn in the years immediately following his death but this had turned into the most amazing controversy within a few years. Posthumous stories about his private life led to abusive media attacks on his reputation. The publication of his letters in a loose attempt at biography by his old friend, Elizabeth Bisland, caused George Gould to write one of the most bitter denunciations in the history of literature in his book, *Concerning Lafcadio Hearn*. The ensuing uproar divided opinion in America in the first decade of the century.

An Irishwoman, and friend of the Hearn family, Nina Kennard went to Japan with Lafcadio's half-sister in 1909 in a vain attempt to see if Hearn's wishes about educating his eldest son abroad could be put into effect. She wrote a biography, now a valuable primary source, many of whose insights, such as Hearn's transmogrification of his early experiences from one country to another, have been politely ignored by many writers on Hearn since then.

Interest in Hearn was maintained up to the Second World War, when he became a political football, with some scholars arguing that the United States might have understood Japan better before Pearl Harbor had more heed been paid to his writings. After the War his reputation in the West went into eclipse, possibly because Shinto was identified with the militarism which had led Japan to catastrophe. This cloud is now beginning to clear and it is surely time to see an authentic original for what he really was rather than through the prism of personal, historical or national prejudice.

CHAPTER TWO

GHOUL

HEARN CREATED a romantic fog around his early years in America so that it is impossible to be sure what exactly happened on his arrival in the USA. He claimed later that he had been sent without any money to make his own way and had spent two years 'roughing it' before he was taken up in Cincinnati by Henry Watkin, an English printer who cared for him until he got 'fledged'.[1] The years – or months, depending on the version used – in New York were spent 'as a restaurant waiter, dishwasher, itinerant vendor, odd-job man, anything by which I could turn an honest dollar', while he 'trod the borderland of despair', with only 'hereditary desires' keeping him from 'relinquishment', presumably meaning suicide. He was then supposed to have received advice from home suggesting that he contact a family connection in Cincinnati and he went, on the basis that any change could be an improvement.[2]

Hearn did labour through various autobiographical drafts years later in Japan when he was trying to disentangle his early memories, which portrayed in detail sleeping in a stable and being fed surreptitiously by some kindly hand.[3] He wrote of being nineteen years old 'in the great strange world of America and grievously tormented by grim realities', to escape which he wandered the streets and nourished his dreams in the public library.[4] Hearn's first biographer and virtual disciple, Elizabeth Bisland, accepted that he had spent 1869 and 1870 in New York in great poverty where 'a friendly Irish workman' allowed him to sleep on the shavings in his carpenter's shop in return for book-keeping and running errands. Bisland, however, attributes an autobiographical fragment, 'Intuition' to this period while it clearly belongs to Cincinnati.[5] The character described in it is Henry Watkin though neither he nor the city is identified. In this fragment, Hearn gives his own age as nineteen. If this is accepted, there could have been no New York interlude of any duration.

That the real facts of the case were somewhat more mundane than some of Hearn's more dramatic statements is also suggested by the story he told his half-sister, Minnie Atkinson. She would have been more likely than his other correspondents to have known what actually happened from family sources. The ruin of his great-aunt, Mrs Brenane, who had brought him up, had been brought about by Henry Molyneux, an English financial bungler. Molyneux's sister, Frances Anne, was married to an Irishman, Thomas Cullinan in Cincinnati, Ohio. The likelihood is that young Patrick Lafcadio was sent to Cullinan's care and that he introduced him to Henry Watkin, who gave him his first job. Lafcadio told Minnie Atkinson that he was sent to some of Henry Molyneux's friends in America who gave him five dollars a week for a few months: 'Then I was told to go to the devil and take care of myself. I did both'.[6] Thomas Cullinan's version was that Lafcadio had been sent to him by his brother-in-law and Mrs Brenane had sent him money to give to her great-nephew to pay his bills. Hearn had come to his house three times. After that, he found work and never came to see him again, not surprising as his attitude towards Patrick Lafcadio had been one of frank dislike.[7]

An 1892 article on Hearn claimed that he had first worked in Cincinnati as a waiter in 'Hunt's' restaurant. This might suggest that he went to Cincinnati more-or-less directly in 1869 but worked at menial jobs initially and perhaps lived in rough circumstances until he was taken in by Henry Watkin.[8] However, Watkin's later account, that Hearn had come to see him a few days after his arrival in Cincinnati, would rule this out though Watkin's palpably absurd claim that Hearn was still wearing the clerical garb of his French monastery is a sign perhaps that his memory had failed somewhat by the time he gave this account. Lafcadio was introduced to him by a Mr McDermott, probably a friend of Cullinan, who, anxious to be rid of this embarrassing burden, arranged the introduction to

Watkin. Hearn made clear his literary ambition from the outset;
Watkin asked:

> 'Well, young man, what ambition do you nourish?'
> 'To write, sir'.
> 'Mercy on us. Learn something that will put bread in your
> mouth first, try your hand at writing later on'.[9]

The older man, struck by Lafcadio's 'intangible air of
breeding', offered to teach him the printing trade.[10] For two
years Hearn slept on a bed of paper-shavings in the office, ran
errands and kept the place tidy, was fed but not paid. Watkin
found young Lafcadio an indifferent worker and could do little
with him initially. Still, the two liked to read aloud to each other
in the evenings and had in common a fascination with 'weird
places and strange peoples'. Meanwhile, the ragbag of radicals
who hung around the printing shop provided the young
Irishman with a strange education in contemporary alternative
philosophy. Watkin himself was 'something of a Fourierist', and
he introduced his young charge to 'hosts of fantastic
heterodoxies', including anarchists who 'spoke very eloquently
about the religion of humanity and the atrocities of modern
civilisation'. He sympathised and entered into the spirit of
Watkin's office with zest; retrospectively he saw himself as an ass
who thought he could overturn the universe: 'I was a new
Archimedes: the lever was enthusiasm! all radicals were my
brothers, and had I been in Russia I might have tried to blow up
the Czar'. Watkin regarded these boyish enthusiasms with
amused sympathy.[11]

That he was able to hold his own with the habitués of
Watkin's shop from the beginning is indicated by the articles
which young Patrick Hearn wrote for the Boston *Investigator*, a
freethought weekly, under the pseudonym 'Fiat Lux' in 1870
and 1871. These articles show their author ruminating on the
philosophical questions which were to occupy Hearn all his life:
religion, Eastern philosophy and the nature of matter.[12] If he
really was radical at this stage, it was a very temporary
phenomenon, as Hearn progressed from youthful, wry,
cynicism to increasing conservatism even while he was still a
young man.

Hearn may have done some part-time work for a librarian,
Thomas Vickers, and been a proof-reader with the Robert

Clarke printing firm in these years.[13] He was, for a short time, the Assistant Editor of the *Trade List*, a small business paper. Then, in October 1872, John A. Cockerill, editor of the Cincinnati *Enquirer* was surprised when 'a quaint dark-skinned little fellow strangely diffident' came into his office and asked if he paid for outside contributions. When Cockerill replied that money was tight but he would consider what was offered, Hearn laid a manuscript on the table and stole away. Cockerill was 'astonished to find it charmingly written and full of ideas that were bright and forceful'.[14] Paddy Hearn, as he then still was, was prolific from the start: his first piece appeared on 4 November 1872 and he had a further 14 pieces published before the end of the year. The figure for 1873 jumped to 79; in 1874, when he certainly was full-time with the paper, it was 206.[15] The subject-matter of these very early stories – the processing of the carcasses of dead, diseased animals, the lot of tramps forced to sleep on bricks, an attack on the YMCA, suicide and the origins of words – set the tone for his Cincinnati journalism.

By 1874, Hearn was already revelling in the considerable latitude he was being given by the *Enquirer* to indulge in his own particular interests. In 'Among the Spirits', it was the public exploration of autobiographical experience, something he continued to do in print for the rest of his life. Here it concerned his father whose ghost was supposedly conjured up by a medium. He was seemingly convinced by the detail which the spirit communicated about 'a rather curious bit of private family history.'[16] He could offer no explanation for what had occurred. Others have tried: one rationale is that the medium, who had been exposed before by Hearn, was determined on revenge and got the information on his family background from Mr Cullinan.[17]

He probed his background again in March 1874 in a humorous account of a visit to a barber who guesses his nationality:

> 'I think you are an Irishman', softly murmured the Babbling Brook, with a triumphant smile.
> 'It's none of your infernal business', cried the miserable reporter, 'what country I belong to. . .'[18]

This piece revealed the insecurity of the immigrant, something which had been evident two months previously when he wrote of himself as a 'foreigner' who had been 'but a few years' in the United States.[19]

The foreigner was not popular with his colleagues: they did not regard him as a good journalist in the pure sense, feeling that he had little instinct for real news, relying instead on his ghoulish imagination for impact. They did not respect the way he seemed to live in a dreamland, his idea of fun being to haunt the second-hand bookshops.[20] He was shy and never 'one of the boys', and his appearance made him the butt of their rough jokes.[21] He naturally disliked being 'guyed' by them and found he could not converse easily with them. An element of professional jealousy may of course have been at work here. His abilities were put in perspective by Edwin Henderson, later his city editor on the Cincinnati *Commercial*, who saw that, notwithstanding his lack of size, he had the courage of a lion, 'and there was no assignment of peril that he would not bid for avidly'; because of his myopia, he could not, Henderson believed, see what he described and his descriptive powers must have been the product of his imagination; he might not have had a good instinct for news in the conventional sense but he could write a story 'as polished and as full of colour as if it had come from the pen of Gautier himself.'[22] His editor on the *Enquirer*, Cockerill, was also pleased with the young reporter. He admired the poetic nature that could quarry charming stories from the darkest side of life and a prose style which he felt added tone to the *Enquirer* as a whole.[23]

Cockerill did not exaggerate Lafcadio's ability to quarry stories from the dark side of life but charming would hardly apply to his most distinctive work on the *Enquirer*. It was a particularly gruesome story that really established him as a journalist. In November 1874, 'a murder so atrocious and so horrible that the soul sickens at its revolting details' was committed in Cincinnati; the staff who would have covered it were not at the newspaper when the story broke and Hearn was assigned to it. The following day, under the title, 'Violent Cremation', the *Enquirer* splashed over its front page Hearn's sensationally graphic treatment of a sensational crime – the 'Tan-yard Murder'.[24] In a terrible act of revenge for the death of his pregnant fifteen-year-old daughter, her father, brother and another man had attacked the presumed culprit and, after a bloody struggle, thrust him, apparently still alive, into a furnace.

As a newspaperman, Hearn was never content merely to report the facts and it is his imagination, his vivid re-enactment of the terrible crime, which gives his coverage of the 'Tan-yard Murder' its lasting value. His explicit treatment of the sexual licence which formed the background in the opening paragraphs must have startled his Victorian audience almost as much as his account of the murder. The accused murderer, Egner, had had a daughter,

> . . .about fifteen years of age, whose morals, from common report, were none of the best, and she and the deceased, Schilling, became very intimate. In fact, so intimate did they become that Schilling was found by the father, late one night, in her bedroom, under circumstances that proved that they were criminally so, and Schilling only escaped the father's vengeance at the time by jumping through the window to the ground and temporary safety. Egner claimed that Schilling had seduced his daughter, which charge was denied by the accused, who, while admitting his criminal connection with the girl, alleged that he was not the first or only one so favoured. At all events, the girl became pregnant and died at the Hospital on the 6th of August last from cancer of the vulva, being seven months advanced in pregnancy at the time.

After sketching the circumstances surrounding the murder, Hearn focused on the autopsy the following day. The grim humour and juxtaposition of the innocuous and the horrible which were to become his trademarks were already in evidence. The body of the murdered man smelt of 'burnt beef, yet heavier and fouler . . . The liver was simply roasted and the kidneys fairly fried'. The unflinching description of the remains must have astounded the *Enquirer*'s readers:

> . . .masses of crumbling human bones, strung together by half-burnt sinews, or glued one upon another by a hideous adhesion of half-molten flesh, boiled brains and jellied blood mingled with coal. The skull had burst like a shell in the fierce furnace-heat; and the whole upper portion seemed as though it had been blown out by the steam from the boiling and bubbling brains. The brain had all boiled away, save a small wasted lump at the base of the skull about the size of a lemon. It was crisped and still warm to the touch. On pushing the finger through, the crisp interior felt

about the consistency of banana fruit, and the yellow fibres seemed to writhe like worms in the Coroner's hands.

His readers could hardly have failed to notice that the intrepid reporter had not flinched from the most gruesome examination of the corpse. However, it is Hearn's entirely speculative reconstruction of the scene of the crime (there were no eye-witnesses) which has the most powerful effect:

> Fancy the shrieks for mercy, the mad expostulation, the frightful fight for life, the superhuman struggles for existence – a century of agony crowded into a moment - the shrieks growing feebler – the desperate struggles dying into feeble writhings. And through all the grim murderers, demonically pitiless, devilishly desperate, gasping with their exertions to destroy a poor human life, looking on in silent triumph!

'Violent Cremation' was a scoop which was picked up by other newspapers across America. His enhanced value to the *Enquirer* was reflected in a pay rise. He became a well-known local figure, if not exactly a celebrity. By November 1874, he could well describe himself as 'the *Enquirer's* Dismal Man, whose rueful countenance was flushed with the hope of hearing or seeing something more than the usually horrible.'[25] In what might be seen in retrospect as a series of trial pieces, Hearn had been exploring similar subject-matter at length since the beginning of the year, trawling extraordinarily necrophilic depths for a daily newspaper. 'Shall We Burn or Bury?', which appeared in the *Enquirer* in March 1874, gave him an excuse the describe in detail the decay of a corpse, firstly in the immediate aftermath of death, and then some time later:

> Dissolution has been steadily going on, the gases generated by corruption have twisted the inanimate body, rent the integuments and torn the limbs, as with piteous sounds they have freed themselves from confines now too narrow for their expansive power. All trace of life has vanished; comeliness in form has fled; there remains but the polluted cerements, handfuls of hair, teeth and bones, a mass of putrid matter, foul liquids and effluvia which is death to the living and food for the grovelling worms that gather from the dark recesses of the earth to feed and revel upon it.[26]

'The Dance of Death' followed a similar interest, this time from the perspective of the dissecting-room. There was a studied casualness in the description of how the medical students drew lots for different parts of the newly-arrived corpse. There was Joe, his guide, 'exultingly' showing him around, pointing out the remains of the girl reduced to a 'ghastly, headless thing'. What had once been a tall, graceful, supple-limbed Germanic girl, who had loved and been loved, was now a 'frightful mass of bleeding flesh and blackened bone', which had been 'mangled and torn . . .limb from limb with jests and laughter' by the students. Even the self-confessed 'ghoul' had had enough by the time he had been shown yet another corpse being slashed and poked with knives by a row of medical students and declined the offer of seeing the boiling of flesh off the bones in a caldron in the next room.[27]

Almost as if he were searching for the foulest debasement with which to affront his readers, Hearn went to the city dumps in search of material. There he found fresh hideousness - 'abominations unutterable' – and the human scavengers who eked out a living by picking though the rubbish. There were old men, begrimed and feeble from disease, children who had never had a childhood and, best of all, a woman whom he approached from behind. He touched her on the arm and she turned to reveal a face which would not have been out of place in his later stories of Japanese spectres:

> It was a goblin-like face, horrible to grotesqueness. A huge vulture nose, great black eyes, deep-set, and glowing with a brilliancy that seemed phosphorescent, a high, bold, frowning forehead, crowned with a filthy turban, long, thin, bloodless lips, and a long, massive chin, all begrimed to deep blackness by the filth of the dumps.[28]

In the back streets of America Hearn had found the perfect material to feed his ghoulish tastes and fantasies. Edgar Allan Poe has, in the past, been credited with being a decisive literary influence on the gruesome young journalist. Hearn was certainly interested in Poe and the biographical parallels with himself are obvious in his view of the great horror writer: Poe was, he wrote, descended from an ancient Irish family which included poets and soldiers and was 'improvident, adventurous and recklessly brave'. He had been orphaned and adopted by a wealthy man who intended to make him his heir and sent him to school in England. Like Hearn he was industrious, a 'gentleman', of less than average height, and proud of his athletic prowess but destined to blunder through life and doomed to remain without intellectual sympathy 'in the dreariness of American city life.' However, Hearn's comments on the poet's literary ability were judiciously critical whereas his enthusiasm for literary or philosophical figures he revered tended to be unrestrained, and his nickname, 'The Raven', was not a product of self-identification with Poe but was dubbed on him by Watkin because his morbidity and love of the weird reminded the printer of Poe.[29]

Hearn shared these predilections with a number of other Irish nineteenth-century writers. Professor Roy Foster, the outstanding modern Irish historian, sees horror firmly rooted in the Anglo-Irish tradition:

> . . .the line of Irish Protestant supernatural fiction is an obvious one, though it has not been analysed as such. It leads from Maturin and Le Fanu to Bram Stoker and Elizabeth Bowen and W.B. Yeats − marginalised Irish Protestants all, often living in England but regretting Ireland, stemming from families with strong clerical and professional colorations, whose occult preoccupations surely mirror a sense of displacement, a loss of social and psychological integration, and an escapism motivated by the threat of a take-over by the Catholic middle classes. . .

This surely applies to the Hearns, with their solid background of the Church of Ireland, the British Army and the professions, living precariously on the margin until the financial irresponsibility of Lafcadio's father, together with that of Molyneux, pushed them over the brink. Foster goes on to link occult investigations, which was to become a major preoccupation of Hearn's, with an interest in folklore: 'Yeats was a committed gatherer of folklore, and an equally committed enemy of rationalising folklore scholarship. Folktales embodied a secret truth. . .' This could be applied equally to Hearn.[30]

The American scholar, Albert Mordell, believed that Lafcadio's ideas had been formed to some extent before he went to the USA.[31] We do know that the milieu in which he grew up in Dublin allowed him great scope in his reading and access to a wide range of literature and philosophy. The Anglo-Irish elite had, from the late eighteenth century onwards, shared with similar classes elsewhere in Europe an enthusiasm for the folk culture of the ordinary people. This, in turn, formed a link between Ireland and French Romanticism, from the vogue for the ancient hero, Ossian or Oisin, through the inspiration provided by Thomas Moore to such as Berlioz and Augustine Thierry and the influence exercised by Charles Maturin on Baudelaire and Balzac. French as well as Irish romanticism had its roots nurtured by the antiquarianism which was so notable a feature of Irish intellectual life when Patrick Lafcadio was growing up in Dublin.[32]

Hearn's taste was always passionately romantic and he was a master of horror like Sheridan Le Fanu and Bram Stoker, contemporaneous Dubliners educated at Trinity College, *alma mater* of so many members of the Hearn family. Lafcadio defined romanticism in literature as 'seeking for beauty in the past rather than the present'.[33] Conditions in Ireland in his youth were conducive to such backward vision. The loss in 1800 of the political autonomy represented by the Irish Parliament was followed by the decline of Dublin from the second city of the British Empire to a provincial backwater. The industrial revolution in Britain, that generator of Victorian confidence, passed most of Ireland by. The appalling famine of the mid-nineteenth century, the terrible aftermath of which would have dominated life in Ireland in Lafcadio's formative years, devastated an already demoralised people. In the circumstances, the past clearly had its attractions.

There was, at the same time, a new interest in, and value placed on, the peasant and his folklore. Hearn believed that study of the peasantry was essential to understanding a country. He connected romanticism, folklore and horror; the Celtic belief in fairies had created an imagination that was 'romantic, poetic and also terrible'. He believed that it had produced one 'representative' poet, W.B.Yeats, 'who himself collected a great number of stories and legends about fairies from the peasantry of Southern Ireland'. Yeats' poem, *The Host of the Air*, he regarded as the outstanding contemporary fairy poem which, of its type, could not, he believed, be surpassed. It had an extraordinary ability to communicate 'the pleasure of fear', an art Hearn greatly admired. Not only did he appreciate the 'rare excellence' of the early Yeats – the poet was thirty-nine when Lafcadio died in 1904 – he also understood that ancient Celtic literature had inspired much of his poetry.[35] Indeed, so passionate did he feel about this excellence that he wrote a letter of violent protest to Yeats in 1901 when *The Host of the Air* appeared in *The Wind Among the Reeds* revised from its earlier form. Hearn alleged that 'this wonderful thing which must have been blown into you and through you as by the wind of the Holy Ghost' had been 'destroyed totally'; the crime, as Hearn saw it, had been the attempt to change a plain ballad into a mystical poem.[35a] He would, on the other hand, have been delighted to know that Yeats considered his explanation of poetry – 'there is something ghostly in all great art' – as possibly the best definition there was.[35b]

Hearn was also appreciative of the 'extraordinary power in arousing the sensation of the weird' in the 'excellent poetry' of Sir Samuel Ferguson, the first Irish poet to use the early saga material being made available by scholars in the mid-nineteenth century.[36] He was perhaps excessive in describing a poem of William Allingham, who also influenced Yeats and the Celtic revival, as great poetry.[37] Explaining why he devoted a lot of time to what he termed 'superstition' – Irish peasant beliefs about the power of fairies, etc. – in his Tokyo University lectures, Hearn told his students that if they could appreciate the value of such ideas to European poetry and romance, they would be better able to understand the literary value of Oriental folk material, then dying out: 'To an unimaginative and dryly practical man such things are simply superstition, absurd rubbish. But to the true poet or dramatist or story-teller they are all, or nearly all, of priceless value.'[38]

That Lafcadio's knowledge of these matters was not acquired in later life is demonstrated by an hilarious satire of Irish mythology which he wrote as a young journalist in Cincinnati: '. . . the picture spoken of is an elegant green and yellow chromo of the great Irish hero, Finn Maccuhail, founder of the Benevolent Society of Fenians, and father of Ossian, who supported himself (he had no father) by eating delicate sea shells. . .'[39] This satire was essentially non-malicious and Hearn, in fact, believed that the peasant, with little formal education, could effortlessly equal the greatest modern poets; education, however, took the poetry out of his soul. His vision of peasant life was remarkably similar to his later view of Shinto in Japan:

Anciently woods and streams were peopled for him with
invisible beings; angels and demons walked at his side; the
woods had their fairies, the mountains their goblins, the
marches their flitting spirits, and the dead came back to him
at times to bear a message or to rebuke a fault. Also the
ground that he trod upon, the plants growing in the field,
the cloud above him, the lights of heaven all were full of
mystery and ghostliness.[40]

As a young man in New Orleans, correspondence with a
American friend on the subject of the Irish keening wail (part of
the 'wake' for the dead) produced a remarkable anticipation of
Joyce: 'Your last letter strengthened a strange fancy that has come
over me at intervals since my familiarity with the Chinese
physiognomy – namely that there are such strong similarities
between the Mongolian and certain types of the Irish face that
one is inclined to suspect a far-distant origin of the Celts in the
East.'[41] Contrast this with an almost identical observation by
James Joyce in Stephen Hero: '. . .it was in the constant
observance of the peasantry that Stephen delighted. Physically,
they were almost Mongolian types, tall, angular and oblique-
eyed.'[42] Psychologically, for Hearn, the notion of an Oriental
origin for the Irish could have the happy effect of reconciling the
divergent streams of his Irish and Greek – he regarded Greece as
part of the Orient – parents.

It is likely that household servants, some of whom at least
would probably have been of peasant background, played an
important role in his development as a child in Ireland. Indeed,
there is some confirmation of this in his correspondence with
W.B. Yeats: replying to a letter from the poet, in September
1901, he was concerned that Yeats should not misinterpret his
passionate desire that *The Folk of the Air* be left unchanged: 'But I
hope you will not think me unsympathetic in regard to Irish
matters: I mean only this,– that you *can* speak, if you will, to a
hundred million hearts at once,– why not some time again do it?
(One little song,– one twitter of the white Soul-bird! what may it
not do?) But forty-five years ago, I was a horrid little boy "with
never a crack in his heart", who lived in Upper Leeson Street,
Dublin; and I had a Connaught nurse who told me fairy-tales and
ghost-stories. So I *ought* to love Irish Things, and do.' Even in
this letter, however, there was a hint of the nightmare which
followed these tales, when he referred to 'the *suspicion* that comes

before the fear of dreams'.[42a] At the same time, his respect for the songs of Thomas Moore, some of which he considered to be 'very beautiful from a literary point of view',[43] was probably a result of exposure, in the same house, to middle class Victorian drawing-room culture, as was his appreciation of such standards of that world as *The Bells of Shandon*.[44]

However, it was not the welcoming drawing-rooms of Victorian Cincinnati that won Hearn's affections but the levee, the city's riverside dockland. Here was both folklore and marginalisation. He displayed little interest in anything other than the sensational aspects of mainstream Northern life but found in the levee an exotic, colourful, Southern – which to him was synonymous with 'Oriental' – and endlessly fascinating world with an indigenous music and folklore. Here was a community within – but virtually unconnected with – the wider community of settled society – in much the same way he would find a Creole culture in New Orleans encircled by, but cut off from, the Americanised city and, in Japan, reject the foreign communities in favour of ordinary Japanese.

Had he stayed in Ireland, he would, in all likelihood, have earnestly immersed himself in the culture and folklore of the Irish peasant, like Yeats, Lady Gregory, Synge and the other figure of the Irish literary revival. As it was, he found himself in Cincinnati and it was the levee, with its Southern negro hue, which claimed his attention. The levee was, in Hearn's view, primitive and savagely simple, with an emotional range little beyond the animal. Here we see the superior Northern observer, recording 'the peculiarities of this grotesquely-picturesque roustabout life' and finding it all 'pitiful'.[45]

It was, however, to be the beginning of a long-term fascination with negro music and folklore. In New Orleans, his black 'nurse', Louise Roche, would sing voodoo songs for him and he would collaborate with his friend, Krehbiel, in gathering material for a study of Creole music, even though his suggestion that they jointly produce a book on negro music came to nothing. He would search the Creole songs of Louisiana for relics of African survivals. Krehbiel paid posthumous tribute to Lafcadio's ability to detect the imposition of French and Spanish melody on African rhythm later still, in the West Indies.[45a]

Hearn was able to fit in unobtrusively into this strange life of the city's dockland underbelly. In spite of his sympathy with the underdog, he displayed an easy intimacy with the police, who were of course important sources of information on the life of the levee. They emerge as low-key, decent figures, kindly though firm, displaying a wry understanding of the psychology of the cast of curious characters who peopled their beat.[46] If policemen are the understated heroes, the other whites in the levee were the villains; though most coloured people on the levee carried knives, they seldom quarrelled; the fights, according to Hearn, were the work of white roughs whose only interest in the area was crime. His comparison of the two races was generally unflattering to the race of his readership.[47]

His physical absorption in the levee was paralleled mentally by immersion in the Latin and Oriental exoticism of the literature which he now began to translate with lonely passion. Journalism he regarded only as a means to the end of becoming a writer; translation was the second step on that road. He began in earnest with the works of his idol, Gautier. *One of Cleopatra's Nights*, was translated in this period but had to wait until 1882 before it was published. His friend, Joseph Tunison – who attested to the positive response of many contemporary scholars to the translation – recalled that he was determined to publish it at his own expense in Cincinnati but it never got beyond a few pages of printed proofs.[48]

Another friend, Elizabeth Bisland, believed that he began the translation of *The Temptation of St Anthony* by Flaubert in Cincinnati in 1875/6. It was not published until well after his death. According to her, the manuscript could not even get a reading because artists had so erotically dramatised the subject. Bisland felt that Hearn had failed to see the comic side of the publishers' timidity; a few years later, in New Orleans, she ardently applauded his tirades against 'the stultifying influence of blind puritanism upon American literature'.[49] Considering what the effort the translation must have been – it came to over 260 pages in printed form – it is perhaps not surprising that he was not amused. What he could not have known was that with his three major preoccupations of that era – folklore, the classical world and the Orient – he was sharpening the tools he would later use to fashion his finest Japanese work.

Hearn would, however, explore some dead ends before finding the style and the material which would form his mature work. One of these was *Ye Giglampz*, a weekly illustrated journal which he founded in 1874 in collaboration with the artist, H.F.Farny. Bravely dedicated to 'Art, Literature and Satire', it lasted less than two months, late June to mid-August 1874, and nine issues. Each issue had eight pages, three of which were illustrated by Farny. Hearn's contribution to the editorial content of the publication dwindled from two-thirds of the first issue to almost nothing at the end. This reflected the wrangling between the co-founders, with Farny 'compelling' his partner, in his own words, 'to moderate the boldness of sentences which would by their sensualism and licence shock their Cincinnati readers'.[50]

The *Giglampz* was started speculatively without adequate funds, subscribers, advertisers or staff. Farny, a 'brilliantly-facetious, dashingly-unconventional and abnormally-intellectual Bohemian paragon', believed that the brilliance of its two founders would compel success on their own terms. There had been, however, no definition of policy on content and tone prior to publication of the first issue. Farny had taken on as his partner a journalist whose track record on the *Enquirer* had fully lived up to his self-image as having tastes 'whimsically grotesque and arabesque', who indulged in 'the Revoltingly Horrible or the Excruciatingly Beautiful'. He had 'worshipped the French school of sensation' and delighted in nauseating his readers at breakfast time. But this was not what Farny wanted. He might have hoped that Hearn would be able to rein in his more extreme ghoulish tendencies and produce purely comic material. Before the first issue, Farny told him to seek inspiration in an old issue of *Punch*; Hearn decided to rely on his imagination.[51]

He contributed most of the copy for the first issue, attacking the local police, organised religion and Spaniards, whose destiny it was, he wrote, to cut each others' throats; the sooner the better. This racism seems to have been prompted by opposition to Spanish colonial exploitation. Britain was accused of relieving starvation in its colonies while ignoring it at home where it was hidden away '. . .in the filthy alleys, the noisome tenement-houses, the foul and dismal garrets of the great metropolis. . .'[52] The scars of London were still fresh and may explain his aversion to *Punch*'s brand of humour.

One of his features in the first issue was on Tahiti as the 'Paradise of the Pacific' which was similar in tone to his later reaction to the West Indies and Japan. He was already rejecting mainstream Western society in favour of survivals of the pre-industrial era. Tahiti before the white man came was portrayed as a paradise where the people lived in a state of primitive contentment, in the pursuit of every sensuous enjoyment, with little or no labour, marriage, wars or crime. All this was inverted by the first settlers and missionaries. Disease and vice came with forcible conversion. The wealth and produce of an enslaved people were shipped to Europe and '. . .harnessed like brutes to carriages, they drew the saintly wives of those pious evangelists from place to place. . .'[53]

The people of Cincinnati were unimpressed. The first issue was a disaster, selling only a fraction of the copies necessary to cover its production costs. Farny thought it had been too heavy and insufficiently funny. Hearn decided that sensation, 'embodying the extremes of horror and the agony of aesthetics' was the answer: 'So the Ghoul produced a series of translations from *Charivari* and a succession of elaborately florid fantasies, and hopefully awaited the result'. Farny's reaction was that Hearn was 'pandering to depraved tastes'; he refused to accept some copy and insisted that the rest be toned down.[54]

The third week, Farny denounced 'Fantasies for Summer Seasons, or a Ravishing Picture of Free Love in the Sandwich Islands' as the work of 'the brain of a Satyr'. Hearn's most salacious piece, however, was 'The Tale a Picture Tells', with the subheading, 'Butchered to make a Roman Holiday'. The reproduction of a picture in a magazine prompted a sensuously, romantically violent reconstruction by Hearn of the destruction of a young girl in the Roman amphitheatre. There was prurient sensuality as well as horror with more than a hint of sadism in the work.[55] It was not, however, Hearn's cruel sensualism but Farny's lack of judgement which finally killed the *Giglampz*. He thought that his own illustrations for the eighth issue of a steamer disaster were a coup; the public assumed that they were heartless caricatures of a tragedy which had touched them deeply and the journal collapsed.

The title of the *Giglampz* had a pun on Lafcadio's huge spectacles, an early example of his self-deprecating humour. He was seen by his Cincinnati contemporaries in unflattering terms, a fellow journalist recalling him as small in stature, stoop-shouldered, his one good eye so nearsighted that even with spectacles he was forced to put his face right down to the print to be able to read it.[56] Another Cincinnati journalist remembered him as unattractive and shabbily dressed though not unclean.[57] Watkin, not unnaturally perhaps, was more positive; conceding that he was less than average in height, he nevertheless recalled his friend as having been 'perfectly moulded, and without scar or blemish', except for his eye which, unfortunately, marred what would otherwise have been a refined, intellectual face.[58] Hearn had been blinded in one eye as a result of an accident in a schoolboys' game at the age of sixteen and he was hyper-sensitive about the resulting disfigurement. This came across in an early piece in the *Enquirer*:

> The reporter chosen for the expedition unfortunately happens to be the ugliest local in the office. . .and his spectacled visage, which bears a grotesque resemblance to the countenance of an owl, called forth a number of very uncomplimentary remarks from Ethiopian maidens during his progress through the negro quarter. As he toiled up the hill beyond, the solemn helplessness of his demeanour encouraged nasty little boys to pelt him with snow-balls from a safe distance, and a horrid little dog assaulted him vigorously, until demoralised by a frantic kick in the region of his canine epigastrium.[59]

This awareness of his physical defects was Watkin's explanation of the disastrous marriage which Hearn contracted at this time.[60] It says a great deal about Hearn that he always blamed himself for the catastrophic consequences – personal, professional and social – of this tragic marriage when he might well have seen himself as the ill-used victim.[61] In 1906, Alethea ('Mattie') Foley, wishing to lay claim to the vast fortune she believed he had left, gave her account of her marriage to Hearn to the Cincinnati *Enquirer*, ironically the paper which fired him for this very act. She had been born into slavery in Kentucky, the daughter of a slave and her white owner. He gave her as a wedding present to his legitimate daughter. By the time she came into contact with Hearn, she had had a son who bore his father's name, Anderson.

Mattie worked in a boarding house at which Hearn was

staying in Cincinnati. He used to spend time in the kitchen talking to her. Although illiterate, she was an outstanding story-teller. He proposed marriage and the ceremony took place on 14 June 1874. Hearn described Mattie in an article in the Cincinnati *Commercial* in October 1875, by which time the marriage already seems to have been on the rocks:

> She was a healthy, well-built country girl, whom the most critical must have called good looking, robust and ruddy, despite the toil of life in a boarding-house kitchen, but with a strangely thoughtful expression in her large dark eyes, as though she were ever watching the motions of Somebody who cast no shadow, and was invisible to all others. Spiritualists were wont to regard her as a strong 'medium', although she had a particular dislike of being so regarded. She had never learned to read or write, but possessed naturally a wonderful wealth of verbal description, a more than ordinarily vivid memory, and a gift of conversation which would have charmed an Italian *improvisatore*. These things we learned during an idle half hour passed one summer's evening in her company on the kitchen stairs; while the boarders lounged on the porch in the moonlight, and the hall lamp created flickering shadows along the varnished corridors, and the hungry rats held squeaking carnival in the dark dining-room. To the weird earnestness of the story-teller, the melody of her low, soft voice, and the enthralling charm of her conversation, we cannot attempt to do justice. . .[62]

Hearn loved a good story: his Japanese wife would also be a consummate story-teller, particularly of the supernatural variety. Mattie wove tales of ghostly happenings from her childhood on a farm in Bracken County, Kentucky. There were ghosts of suicides haunting their place of death, and a house where a 'Thing' gave her an horrific experience as she lay in bed, very similar to an experience which Hearn had had in childhood and would have again in the West Indies. No doubt there was also a strong sexual element in Hearn's rush to marry Mattie. He had written to Watkin that 'life without the embraces of woman, were naught but a goblin dream – too hideous to be endured'.[63] Watkin believed that he had married in a fit of sexual infatuation and tried beforehand to make him reconsider but found him impervious to advice. Later, he attributed the marriage to a desire to be loved: 'His sensitiveness of his personal defects was so deep, and the feeling that owing to them all doors were closed to him, so great, that it seemed to him the love of even one of earth's social outcasts was too great a boon to be cast aside.'[64]

Mattie Foley stated that Hearn was attacked in the press at the time of his marriage because she was coloured. He certainly showed enormous perseverance in overcoming the legal and other obstacles. Judge M.F. Wilson of Cincinnati later told George Gould that Hearn's application for a marriage licence had been turned down because the Ohio law then forbad interracial marriage.[65] Finding a minister to perform the ceremony was not easy but a black Episcopalian, John King, eventually agreed to do it. The marriage did not take place in church but in the home of a negress, Lottie Cleneay, on 14 June 1874. Hearn remembered it as 'a very cheerless affair; it was celebrated in a very queer place; the participants were very odd people; the celebrant was a curious character; the whole of the affair was an insult to Society. Society avenged it right speedily and might have done worse had she not been partly ignorant of the matter'.[66] The misery was probably compounded by Mattie Foley's prior knowledge of society's likely reaction. Mattie's attempt to secure Hearn's estate failed on the grounds that the marriage had been illegal though the court did accept that a marriage ceremony had taken place. She claimed that they were together until the autumn of 1877 when she left him, allegedly because of his morose, silent disposition and fastidiousness about dress and food.

Actually, the marriage, which Elizabeth Bisland attributed to 'a fantastic sense of duty', crumbled after a few months and the couple parted in 1875. Correspondence from Hearn to his old friend, Henry Watkin, who acted as an intermediary between the two after their separation, documented the sordid awfulness into which the relationship degenerated. In a lengthy letter, written sometime between 1875 and 1877, when Hearn had left Cincinnati, he told Watkin that he would always love Mattie no matter how low she fell. He felt he had been unjust in marrying her – lifting her up and letting her fall lower than ever. At this stage she had fallen on hard times, quarrelling with former friends and even drawing a razor on a woman. No one would give her lodgings because of her reputation for violence and viciousness. She was in debt. Hearn did not know if she was 'keeping company' with anyone else; that she did not sell herself was his main concern and he continued to agonise over how he might help to avert her complete 'ruin'.

Each day, little melancholy memories recurred of her innocent goodness, songs she had taught him, unavailing efforts to provide help when he needed it. He was haunted by the feeling that Mattie was looking at him or following him. He thought of little presents she had made him, a lock of hair she had sent, her despairing efforts just to speak to him again, and his answer having been to have her locked up by the police.[67] A few years later, when he had moved to New Orleans, Hearn was still tormented by remorse about Mattie. He claimed that he was as fond of her as ever and sent her money even when he was himself destitute. Things seem to have improved for her and she married a coloured man, John Kleintank, in 1880.

The relationship may have been dead but it was not buried. In his New Orleans period particularly, Hearn was always afraid that it would be resurrected to his detriment. Indeed, years after his death, a review of Nina Kennard's biography in the Cincinnati *Times-Star* stated that, 'as an Englishwoman', she could not measure the full depth of his social offence in marrying a 'mulatto woman'.[68] These depths could be gauged from the fact that eventually it cost Hearn his job and from a feature article which appeared in the Cincinnati *Tribune* in 1895 castigating him as a 'debauched Bohemian' and 'ribald traducer' whose marriage had represented 'contempt for existing notions'.[69] Ironically, by this time, Hearn himself had come around to these notions and blamed himself for the débâcle. He continued to be remarkably philosophical about what he termed his unfortunate experience in Cincinnati, deciding that it had not been love at all, only 'nature' at work.[70]

By the Mattie Foley episode, Hearn closely paralleled his father's marital experiences. Both of them married beautiful women, prone to violence, from different cultures, below them in education and intelligence. Both marriages failed and all involved remarried. Hearn's marriage to Mattie Foley was also a natural outcome of his views on women, which he did not subsequently recant or modify. In 1884, he wrote that he was attracted by anything which dealt with intermarriage between the races. Among the Northern races there was 'a magnificent type of womanhood' which 'you are afraid even to think of sex with'. Sex, marriage and this magnificence did not, for him, mix.[71]

Hearn's attitude towards women in general was a mixture of idealisation and superiority. He quoted with approval from the the old Sunday-school hymn that 'only man is vile: nature and Woman are unspeakably sweet'; a man might become wholly depraved but there was always something good in the heart of the worst of women.[72] At the same time, he believed firmly in male superiority: 'As a matter of stern physical fact' man was superior to woman 'morally as well as physically'.[73] He constantly strove for an independence which he saw as threatened by the social convention to which a man who wished for woman's society had to submit; when he had done so, he was 'forever buried in the mediocrity to which she belongs'.[74]

He complained to his Japanese students in the late 1890's that women were then being over-educated. The existence of intelligent women was but grudgingly acknowledged: 'The less intellectual, the more lovable. . .'[75] In his New Orleans period, when he might have been expected to have been reacting against the Mattie Foley experience, he was telling his friend, Mrs Marion Baker, that he would not care for intellectual companionship in a wife and would prefer a simple, quiet wife to look after his creature comfort.[76] His views never really changed. His Japanese wife testified that he preferred women of quiet disposition and bashful, downcast eyes. He was wont to compare Japanese and Western women, very much to the latter's disadvantage; he asked which was better, 'the childish, confiding, sweet Japanese girl – or, the superb, calculating, penetrating Occidental Cerce of our own more artificial society, with her enormous power for evil, and her limited capacity for good?'[77]

The notion that he could not relate to anything other than his social inferiors was, however, dispelled by his dalliance with Mrs Ellen Ricker Freeman, the wife of a doctor in Cincinnati. She was a cultured lady, conscious of her prominent position in local society, who became infatuated with him as he recovered from the Mattie Foley affair. She was twice his age and wealthy, with a husband and family. Struck by his sensitivity, she began to invite him to social occasions – piano recitals and the like – at her home. He had no intention of being integrated into this drawing-room culture and fended her off. Acutely aware of the impact of his marriage to Mattie Foley – the relationship with Mrs Freeman seems to have formed after it had broken up in 1875 – he referred to himself as 'ostracised, tabooed, outlawed'. Mrs Freeman knew of the marriage but blamed Watkin for not having prevented it.[78]

Quite what course the relationship followed is not clear. Apart from some references in her letters, such as his 'blood that beat so red in lips and heart',[79] there is no evidence that it took physical form though it would appear that she might have wished it to do so. If anything did pass between them, it would have been in the early stages. After that she is lovelorn, in hot pursuit of a man whose evasiveness fully justified a colleague's description of him in another context as 'feline'.[80] An element of deception, or at least concealment, however, was involved: Watkin was used as an intermediary. Through him letters were exchanged and secret messages passed.

Mrs Freeman had paid compliments to Hearn's literary abilities, how he was a beautiful butterfly compared to common moths such as herself, how his wings touched the heart of every lady as he spread them in the columns of the *Commercial*: '. . .you wait not for heart doors to open, you sail in mysteriously, and wing your way to suit your own sweet will'.[81] That was May 1876: the next month she was writing of wanting to sink her teeth into his hand, to bite him because he did not like her better.[82] It is this element which casts some doubt on what would otherwise be the most obvious explanation, that Hearn had responded initially with sympathy to a refined woman who offered cultured friendship. Mrs Freeman was in this respect one of the many people with whom Hearn carried on an intense correspondence. If this line of reasoning is followed, then Hearn became evasive when he realised the Mrs Freeman wanted a more intense friendship. She was accused by Watkin of strange and sickly sexual infatuation – 'or worse', whatever that might have meant – and sentimentality of the kind which should be 'spanked out of a seventeen-year-old schoolgirl'. Watkin anticipated trouble and warned her, after an 'exhibition of feeling', that he had retained evidence of her 'folly' which he would use if necessary.[83]

In October, when Mrs Freeman and her sister tried to call on Hearn, he refused to see them. She wrote to Watkin threatening to kill herself.[84] Her different moods were reflected in her handwriting, ranging from the rational and poetic in copperplate to wildly scrawled, hysterical notes. They might almost have been written by two different people. In November, she reported to Watkin that Hearn had accused her of lack of common sense. When she sent him a picture of herself in a low-cut dress, he displayed the iron in his nature which only emerged when his evasiveness in trying to shake off unwanted attentions had no effect. He wrote bluntly that she was 'not a handsome or even a tolerably good looking woman physically' and that her picture was 'horrible', 'unutterably coarse and gross and beefy' and 'simply unendurable'.[85]

This letter may have been a draft which was never sent but it does reveal Hearn's physical reaction to Mrs Freeman. Meanwhile, she became alarmed at a spreading knowledge of the affair, which she attributed to his indiscretion and asked him to return her letters. He may not have obliged because she approached Watkin late in November 1876 to use any means of getting them back, including buying them, adding a promise not to write to Hearn again. He must have succeeded as another note from her expressed gratitude and undertook to pay him. This seems to have been the end of the affair.[86]

It has been accepted up to now that, before he left for Japan, Hearn gave his correspondence with Mrs Freeman to his old friend, to dispose of them as he saw fit. The available evidence suggests that they stayed with Watkin after they came into his possession late in 1876. After Hearn's death, Henry Watkin allowed himself to be persuaded to give some of the letters up for publication. The published letters did not, however, give the whole story: Hearn's letters may have been publishable but those of Mrs Freeman, revealing her demented passion for the young reporter, were not.[87]

In the same period, and for many years afterwards, Hearn was also supposed to have corresponded with another woman friend, Countess Annetta Halliday Antona; these letters were published under the title, *Letters to a Pagan*, Hearn's pet name for her. By her account, she could not reciprocate his passionate feelings and fixed their friendship on a platonic plane. Whether it was, in fact, a grand passion cannot be ascertained for certain from the published letters. Overall, these are light-hearted, playful, humorous, with Hearn creating a quaint, mock-wicked persona which was not meant be taken too seriously.

These letters did, however, help to reinforce the romantic distortions surrounding Hearn's youth – fleeing from a monastery in Wales, still wearing his monk's garb, to London where he ruined a lovely young maid, and was 'cursed and driven out, penniless into the most degraded quarter', in which he endured further grotesque horrors before treading the 'borderline of despair' in New York.[88] Even while describing the beauties of Japan, he cannot resist telling her of being suddenly overcome by 'old savage longing for a gipsy life, for freedom from the bondage of civilization'.[89] Romantic regret for the lost paradise of the West Indies was also a pitch for maternal affection.[90] He praised her *High Noon on the Campagna* lavishly and suggested that she apply for the Chair of English language and literature which there was talk of creating at an Imperial Japanese university for women.[91] As she was then the mother of a family, nothing came of this impractical suggestion and no further letters were exchanged. The letters from the Tokyo period portray Hearn as a lonely man, needing the reassurance of old friends, and pleading not to be made to beg for affection that was freely given in the past.[92]

Hearn's close friends in Cincinnati in this period included fellow-journalists, Henry Krehbiel and Joseph Tunison, as well as the artist, Farny. According to Elizabeth Bisland, he threw all the ardour of youth, 'even beyond the usual intensity of young friendships' into these relationships.[93] Devotion to art was their common denominator. Tunison and Krehbiel were, like Hearn, journalists with artistic aspirations. Hearn's talent proved the most enduring of the four and we can see how he appeared to his friends then in Tunison's description: 'He was a wonderfully attractive personality,- full of quaint learning and a certain unworldly wisdom.'[94]

He, in turn, paid extravagant compliments to his friends' powers and promoted them whenever possible. In one article, Hearn described Krehbiel's desire to have Chinese music performed on authentic instruments by Chinese musicians. The intrepid reporter remembered seeing some such instruments which had been confiscated by the police and went to the Chinese laundry of the owner. In an atmosphere dense with opium smoke, the Chinese musicians were induced to play and Krehbiel, 'the handsome young Aryan', was 'flushed with the triumph of his art. . .'[95] Krehbiel was a stolid, conservative man and it may well have been Hearn's enthusiasm which carried this search for musical authenticity to an opium den. Hearn's carelessness about the nature of the locale may have given rise to later allegations − for which no reliable sources have ever been identified − that he had undergone a period of opium addiction. This is unlikely − his productivity was consistently too high for such a luxury − though he may have sampled it, together with milder drugs such as marijuana.

His irregular marriage made his position on the *Enquirer* impossible − he was asked to leave when news of it leaked out in mid-1875. It has since been alleged that pressure was put on Cockerill by a local politicians wanting to silence a troublesome critic[96] but it is not disputed that what was then seen by respectable white society as 'deplorable moral habits' was the ostensible reason at least for his dismissal.[97] Hearn's was too great a talent to be left unemployed in Cincinnati; he was hired by another newspaper, the *Commercial*, albeit at a lower salary. His last piece in the *Enquirer* was on 8 June 1974; his first for the *Commercial* was on 16 August of the same year. In this piece, 'Pariah People', about Bucktown, the vice quarter of Cincinnati, Hearn covered familiar ground. Woven into a seemingly straightforward tale of whores and thieves was a subtly defiant reference to his own situation. Of the two classes who inhabited Bucktown one was made up of those who had 'lost caste by miscegenation'. He noted acidly that as the violation of nature's laws − interracial marriage in Ohio then fell into that category − was believed to breed deformity and hideousness, so the people of Bucktown were supposed to be ugly or monstrously deformed. Yet, in reality, the multi-racial community contained many remarkably attractive people whose 'viciousness and harlotry' was less shocking than that of the more respectable quarters of Cincinnati. One pariah at least could answer back.[98]

His reporting from the night station for the *Commercial* was, however, noticeably more restrained than the drastic dispatches which had made his name at the *Enquirer*. The extremes of violence and eroticism were being muted in favour of a more sober view of actual conditions around him, though he could still turn the stomach. 'Balm of Gilead', a lengthy and sordid description of the turning of animal carcasses into fertiliser, was a return to a theme explored previously for the *Enquirer*.[99] 'Haceldama' was such a frightful description of cruelty and horror in a slaughter-house that even today one wonders how it was ever published. The more squeamish of his readers would probably have been appalled at his dreamy enthusiasm for drinking animal's blood, 'ruddy, vigorous, healthful life. . .No other earthly draught can rival such crimson cream. . .'[100]

In August 1876, Hearn witnessed the hanging of a criminal at Dayton, Ohio for the *Commercial*. Faced with the grim reality of judicial killing, he was sombre. The brutality of the murder which led to the execution had aroused strong feelings locally but Hearn did not respond to this mood. The facts of the case as he saw them were simply that a young, drunken lout had taken life and paid the penalty by a hundred days of mental torture and a hideous death. It was to be expected that Hearn would describe this hideous death in detail. What his readers may not have expected was the fair-mindedness which he applied to the condemned man and the tone of restrained, sober simplicity. He was learning that restraint could be an effective weapon in the arsenal of the horror writer. The sensitivity of the condemned man, James Murphy, and his capacity for suffering only added to the terrible effect; a criminal being ignorant, uneducated and unimaginative did not mean, Lafcadio told his readers, that he was incapable of feeling 'the torture of hideous suspense'.[101]

At the place of execution, Hearn managed to insinuate himself into a group of doctors to the rear of the scaffold and to take up a position immediately to the trap-door's left. The first attempt at execution failed when the rope broke and Murphy fell to the ground on his back. The intrepid reporter felt his pulse while musing that the unfortunate criminal probably thought he really was dead. Murphy then came to and nobody had the heart to answer his piteous demand to know what they intended to do with him. Hearn kept his hand on the boy's pulse and felt it 'quicken horribly' when the answer dawned on him. He kept his hand on the pulse after the second drop, when the rope did not break and felt it diminish to imperceptibility. After seventeen minutes, Murphy was declared dead. Hearn's total absorption in the ghastly ritual attracted the attention of some other journalists there:

> . . .after the doctor had pronounced life extinct. . .Hearn
> still lingered over the pale body under the scaffold, lifting
> the pulse to his ear, listening to the heart, and going over
> the body, inch by inch, eyes and nose in close contact, like
> a veritable gad-fly, his eyes alight with interest to detect a
> flicker of life that had been overlooked.[102]

Hearn's conclusion to the piece was quiet, in keeping with the restraint he had shown throughout. He returned half an hour later to view the body in its coffin and examined the dead face, no doubt with the intensity described above; the face was now still, '. . .as the face of a sleeper, calm and undisfigured. It was perhaps slightly swollen, but quite natural, and betrayed no evidence of pain. The rope had cut deeply in the flesh of the neck, and the very texture of the hemp was redly imprinted on the skin.'[103]

Late in the autumn of 1877, Hearn made what must have been a very difficult and courageous decision. He would abandon the secure job, friends and local fame of his situation in Cincinnati and travel south to New Orleans. The immediate cause was, according to Elizabeth Bisland, a quarrel with his superiors at the *Commercial* whom he believed had given him misleading information for an assignment.[104] This is unlikely, however, as he made an arrangement before his departure to send dispatches to the *Commercial* from New Orleans. Watkin wrote in a letter to the Cincinnati press in 1895 that Hearn had gone to New Orleans under the auspices of Messrs Halstead and Henderson of the *Commercial* who, with himself, had seen him off on his journey south.[105]

The explanation accepted by most biographers to date was that a description of the delights of the South by a newspaper colleague determined him to experience them at first hand. A variation of both of these stories was provided by Edwin Henderson, the city editor of the *Commercial*: Lafcadio had been so enchanted by a story he told of waking in Alabama among magnolias and mocking birds that he neglected an assignment he had been given to cover the agonising death of a boy from hydrophobia, normally a natural subject for his morbid talents, and announced to Henderson that he had lost his loyalty to the paper and intended to go south to New Orleans. His city editor understood and carried Lafcadio's bag onto the train at the Little Miami Depot a short while later. Colonel Fairfax, his future editor on the *Item* newspaper in New Orleans, believed that he had been sent south by a Northern newspaper to do a series of articles on the Returning Board. Yet another tale was that he had been smuggled out of Cincinnati by friends to frustrate his intention to marry a negress who had nursed him through a long illness as a mark of gratitude.[105a]

Hearn himself was somewhat more laconic: he later told Watkin that he had felt it was time to get out of Cincinnati when they began to call it the Paris of America.[106] It would also be in line with his belief that he could never settle down in one place:

> There is such a delightful pleasantness about the first relations with people in strange places – before you have made any rival, excited any ill will, incurred anybody's displeasure. Stay long enough in any one place and the illusion is over: you have to sift this society through the meshes of your nerves, and find perhaps one good friendship too large to pass through.[107]

Hearn, too, was utterly determined to put artistic success above all else and, as his work on the life of the levee had opened up the possibilities of the field of negro folklore, it would have been a logical step to travel further south. Then there must have been considerable attraction in a city whose Creole population still preserved the old French culture of North America. For a man immersed in French literature and, indeed, involved in the translation of it, this would have been a powerful magnet. Finally, the opportunity may have been welcome to put half a continent between himself and the distressing episodes of his marriage and the affair with Mrs Freeman; he had told her that it was 'quite nice to be an Ishmaelite for a time; but one gets weary of fighting with that Megatherium of Public Opinion'.[108]

CHAPTER THREE

NEW ORLEANS

My idea of perfect bliss would be ease and absolute quiet,-
silence, dreams, tepidness,- great quaint rooms overlooking
a street full of shadows and emptiness,- friends in the
evening, a pipe, a little philosophy, wandering under the
moon. . .And I feel that I am getting old – immemorially
old,– older than the moon. I ought never to have been
born in this century...because I live forever in dreams of
other centuries, and other faiths and other ethics,– dreams
rudely broken by the sound of cursing in the street below,
cursing in seven different languages. . .

Hearn to Henry Watkin, from New Orleans, 11 November 1882[1]

WHEN HEARN arrived in New Orleans 'into the tepid and
orange-scented air of the South' to find the city 'drowsing under
the violet and gold of a November morning', he was, he
afterwards admitted, prepared to idealise everything tropical he
encountered. His mind was full of stories of Southern writers.[2]
On 26 November, the readers of the *Commercial* were treated to
Hearn's initial impressions of New Orleans in 'At the Gate of the
Tropics'. The piece was strikingly similar in construction to the
later West Indian and Japanese essays, with a mix of impressions,
descriptions of architecture, commerce and ancient folklore. This
idealisation – the belief that he had found a paradise, beautiful
and sad – is confirmed by his letters of the time. He painted
idyllic scenes to Watkin, in an unsuccessful attempt to lure 'Dear
Old Dad' down to join him:

> Think of the times we could have,- delightful rooms with
> five large windows opening on piazzas shaded by banana

trees; dining at Chinese restaurants and being served by
Manila waitresses, with oblique eyes and skin like gold;
visiting sugar-cane plantations; scudding over to Cuba;
dying with the mere delight of laziness; laughing at cold and
smiling at the news of snow-storms a thousand miles away;
eating the cheapest food in the world,- and sinning the
sweetest of sins.³

Hearn loved the slow, anachronistic life of the Creole quarter
which had managed to preserve its ancient way of life in the
midst of the changes going on about it. Whereas the 'American
city' was bustling by nine-thirty or ten o'clock, 'the old French
town' was deserted: it did not begin business until the sun had
well warmed the streets. The two elements left each other alone.
The Creoles minded their own business and carried on their
ancient life-style, tolerating those who understood them and
abominating those who did not. After staying initially at 228
Baronne Street, he found a room among them in which his
fantasy could run riot:

> . . .it was vast enough for a Carnival ball. Five windows and
> glass doors open flush with the floor and rise to the ceilings.
> They open on two sides upon the piazza, whence I have a
> far view of tropical gardens and masses of buildings, half-
> ruined but still magnificent. The walls are tinted pale orange
> colour; green curtains drape the doors and windows; and
> the mantelpiece, surmounted by a long oval mirror of
> Venetian pattern, is of white marble veined like the bosom
> of a Naiad. In the centre of the huge apartment rises a bed
> as massive as a fortress, with tremendous columns of carved
> mahogany supporting a curtained canopy at the height of
> sixteen feet. It seems to touch the ceiling but it does not.
> There is no carpet on the floor, no pictures on the wall – a
> sense of something dead and lost fills the place with a gentle
> melancholy;- the breezes play fantastically with the pallid
> curtains, and the breath of flowers ascends into the chamber
> from the verdant gardens below. Oh, the silence of this
> house, the perfume, and the romance of it.⁴

He claimed that the house was haunted, though the presence
of ghosts did not worry him, as he had become so like one of
them himself in his habits! Hearn loved particularly the European
overtones of New Orleans' seedy elegance: 'Something of all that
was noble and true and brilliant in the almost forgotten life of the
dead South lives here still (its atmosphere is European; its tastes

are governed by European literature and the art culture of the Old World).' Outside was the real world of 1879 where '. . .roared the Iron Age, the angry waves of American traffic . . .within, it was the epoch of Spanish domination'.[4a] A beautiful Creole home had for him overtones of Venice or Florence; Hearn's imagination brought it all back to life, the carriages with their French coats of arms thundering under the archway where, in reality, there was only a wagon crumbling to pieces in a disused stable. In his mind, even the dog sleeping by the door dreamt of the dead South![5]

He believed at this stage that he would never leave New Orleans, except to go even further south, to the West Indies or South America. His eventual move, ten years later, was indeed to the West Indies. Mattie Foley presented an immediate sense of threat to this happiness. Within weeks of his arrival in New Orleans, he was writing to Krehbiel that he had 'got into good society' and hoped to 'redeem' himself socially.[6] He had no illusions about the catastrophe which his wife could wreak: 'You cannot imagine how utterly the news of that time would ruin me here. It were better that I had committed incest or forgery. The prejudice here is unutterably bitter, and bottomlessly deep.'[7]

His understanding of this prejudice was particularly acute as he was developing a growing political identification with the defeated South. On his way to New Orleans, he was delayed in Memphis, the end of his train journey, where he was to connect with a riverboat for the remainder of the journey. He eked out his savings on survival in a carpetless room in a grim old house on the waterfront of the 'dirty, ugly town'. While he was there, watching the comings and goings of the river traffic in frustration, he observed the funeral of a Confederate Civil War veteran, General Forrest. This provided the material for his first dispatch to the *Commercial*, under the pseudonym, Ozias Midwinter, a self-deprecatory reference to a Wilkie Collins character. By dwelling on the shady character of the general's business transactions and his reckless temper, the article may have contributed to the 'Republican' reputation he developed and which was to lead to difficulties in New Orleans.[8]

This, however, did not represent his real political direction and he probably managed to alienate both political extremes in his Ozias Midwinter dispatches. The second last of the letters, 'A

Romance of Bitterness', an unsympathetic portrayal of W.C.C. Claiborne, the first 'Carpet-bag' Governor of Louisiana, was hardly what his post-Civil War Northern audience wanted to read.[9] In fact, Hearn had enthusiastically reviewed an article on the Southern question in the *Commercial* in July 1877, before he had left Cincinnati by Charles Gayarré, a noted New Orleans historian who would become a personal friend.[10] It is interesting that Lafcadio was even then so positive about an expression of the old Southern, former slave-owners', viewpoint, an indication that he had become politically conservative even before he reached the South.

A second threat came from within, from his inability to curb his own enthusiasms and cater to the expectations of his audience. Because Hearn felt at home with the language – he remembered visiting children speaking Creole in the Ireland of his youth and its melody remained in his mind – he followed an arcane linguistic progression in the series for the *Commercial*: 'Les Criollos' was totally devoted to Creole dialect and 'The Curious Nomenclature of New Orleans Streets; Some Little Creole Songs' was exactly what the title implied. There was a progression in this direction in the subsequent Ozias Midwinter letters. The fourth, published on 10 December, was even looser in construction and contained within its compass descriptions of the old Spanish Cathedral, the Custom-house, the evils of the 'Radical carpet-baggers and scallywags', the beauty of New Orleans women, the city's French patois, with texts and a translation of a versified lampoon. It ended with a ghost story.[11]

He began to have problems getting published. While the early letters appeared in the *Commercial* within a few days, this one was datelined January but not published until 18 February 1878. It was a pattern of a mass-circulation publisher losing enthusiasm as Hearn lost himself in the remote depths of an alien culture which would be repeated in the West Indies and Japan. So Lafcadio's hope that his position as New Orleans correspondent of the *Commercial* would keep him afloat financially was proving to be misplaced. He confided to Krehbiel early on that he was barely making a living but imagined that this was a temporary hiccup and he would soon be earning enough to be comfortable. He was determined not to resume local newspaper work, with its gaslight and generally 'horrid' life; his ambition was to study and to write something better than the police news. He had plans for magazine essays which he hoped would make him independent.[12] His determination to escape the bounds of regular journalism may have accounted, in part at least, for the determinedly anti-popular content of the letters to the *Commercial*. Milton Bronner, who edited the letters for publication in 1907, commented that Hearn's perspective was that of a foreigner, 'with the dim-seeing eyes of a Dickens or a saucy Kipling rather than the clear-headed, clear-eyed American, or the adopted citizen, understanding this country and its people'.[13]

The crumbling of his relationship with the paper would have contributed to the mood of gloomy introspection in which Hearn wrote to Watkin in February 1878. He was conscious of the approach of his twenty-eight birthday – actually still four months away – with a feeling of having accomplished nothing in life, a situation for which he blamed himself, his 'loss of temper, impatience, extra-sensitiveness, betrayed and indulged instead of concealed. . .' He elaborated a theory which he re-iterated constantly in later years, that 'small people without great wills and great energies have no business trying to do much in this wonderful country; the successful men all appear to have gigantic shoulders and preponderant deportments.'[14] His own success over the years in no way detached him from this belief. Despite his romantic identification with the warm south, he found the reality of acclimatisation difficult. Shortly after his arrival he became ill with 'fever and bloody flux'. His weight was down to only ninety pounds from his usual one hundred and forty. His face was so thin that the bones were showing through and he feared that if he were to get yellow fever it would be the end.[15] He was totally down in June 1878 when he wrote to Watkin that he had been in New Orleans seven months and had not made a cent in the city.

His luck changed, however, in the middle of the month when, 'shabby and half-starved', he was taken on as an assistant editor of the *Item* newspaper, albeit at a much lesser salary than he had had at the *Commercial*. The *Item* was a modest paper which had been founded originally as a cooperative before being bought by Colonel John Fairfax. Hearn's physical appearance, particularly his injured eye, had immediately struck Fairfax though, when he got used to it, he noticed a refined face whose features were otherwise good. Lafcadio had the additional disadvantage when he presented himself for interview of being miserably dressed, with grimy hands and black nails; the grim winter of unemployment had taken its toll. More than his appearance, however, it was his political reputation which made Fairfax and his managing editor, Mark F. Bigney, hesitate before hiring him. The rumour that he had had to leave Memphis because of his violently Republican views was a serious disadvantage.

Fairfax, however, took pity on Hearn's half-starved appearance and his sensitivity about how 'the boys' had treated him because of his supposed Republican tendencies and took him on.[16] It is possible that the Colonel was impressed also by the fact that Lafcadio had already been published in the city: the New Orleans *Democrat* had printed a 'Poem written for the decoration of the soldiers' graves at Chalmette Cemetery' on 31 May. He continued to write for the *Democrat* while he was on the *Item*, with 32 pieces appearing up to 16 October 1881. He did a regular column, 'The Foreign Press', for it between May 1880 and December 1881.

Fairfax asked the young Irishman to dinner. The first time he came he was shy: he just sat and crumbled bread. But once he got over it he revealed himself to be a charming conversationalist and the dinner invitations became regular. The family became attached to him, so much so that the daughter of the house used to tease him.[17] He settled down to a pleasant life-style based on the easy-going, tolerant atmosphere which prevailed at the *Item*:

> Early in the morning I visit a restaurant, where. . .a heavy breakfast costs only about twenty-five cents. Then I slip down to the office, and rattle off a couple of leaders on literary or European matters and a few paragraphs based on telegraph news. This occupies about an hour. Then the country papers – half-French, half-English, – altogether barbarous, come in from all the wild, untamed parishes of Louisiana. Madly I seize the scissors and the paste-pot and construct a column of crop-notes. This occupies about half an hour. Then the New York dailies make their appearance. I devour their substance and take notes for the ensuing day's expression of opinion. And then the work is over, and the long golden afternoon welcomes me forth to enjoy its perfume and its laziness. It would be a delightful

existence without ambition or hope of better things.

He became optimistic about acclimatising to the debilitating heat of New Orleans though he added ironically that if it meant becoming a 'bundle of sharp bones and saddle-coloured parchment' he had no doubt that he would succeed.[18]

Lafcadio responded to this congenial atmosphere by producing an impressively prolific output over the next three years. Between June 1878 and November 1881, he contributed 337 pieces. He may not have escaped journalism entirely but, from this time on, he was never again a reporter. In New Orleans his work was translation, reviews, illustrations, editorials and non-editorial comment on the editorial page. There were 'Creole Sketches', illuminating various aspects of Creole life, and imaginative sketches called 'Fantastics', the first of which, 'All in White', appeared in the *Item* of 14 September 1879. Between the summer of 1878 and the winter of 1881, he contributed a column of book reviews, 'Our Book Table', and a column of advice for young people. He also drew a series of cartoons, whittled out with a pen-knife on the back of old wooden types, which appeared for more than six months, from 24 May to 10 December 1880. Accompanied by verses which he illustrated himself, they were the first newspaper cartoons in that part of the United States.

As an example of their effectiveness, Fairfax told the story of the 'Magazine Market' gang which ruled part of New Orleans in defiance of the police. By holding both parties up to ridicule, Hearn forced the police to act and break up the gang. Cartoons of similar topicality were about the Presidential election of 1880 and the failure of municipal officials to control yellow fever and other epidemics. Most, however, were about quaint local customs, foibles of human nature, and public nuisances such as the churl, the bore, the boy on 'The Unspeakable Velocipede', and were generally inspired by letters to the paper. The cartoons reflected Lafcadio's preference for the Creole life of the canal area to the uptown Americanised district, for the humble life of the landladies, booksellers, washerwomen and coloured clothes-pegs sellers, queer old men haunted by 'ghostesses', inhabitants of cemeteries, hoodlums, quacks and flower-sellers.[19]

Hearn's work for the *Item* was extraordinarily creative and varied. Within weeks of joining the paper, he was producing editorials which, if they were not always wholly original, showed that their author was aware of the most advanced contemporary thought. He foresaw England's eventual loss of commercial supremacy, for example, and the invention of a flying machine and other extraordinary things then deemed beyond the power of science. On 9 July 1878, he wrote an editorial on the effect of a partial disbandment of the German army which foreshadowed to a remarkable extent what actually did transpire after the First World War – the soldiers would find it hard to get work and would become 'gloomy, dissatisfied and desperate. They [would] listen to Communist harangues and join Communist clubs. The spectre of Socialism may then soar its head to a threatening height when supported by myriads fresh from the training of war.'[20]

A liberal approach was evident in his editorials on the treatment of criminals but some of his conclusions send shudders down twentieth-century spines. He began one editorial in February 1880 by putting forward the view that incarceration of criminals served no useful purpose; the idea that it could reform or improve professional criminals belonged to a 'less enlightened age'. However, he then went on to conclude that in the new age criminals would be removed from society by swift and painless death for the first infringement of any major ethical law. The ancients who slew weakly children were more sensible than contemporary society; in the future, people would question the utility of building prisons for criminals and asylums for idiots. The capacity to prolong life indefinitely by the development of medicine would have terrible consequences unless the superior had recourse to the destruction of the inferior.[21] Yet the same man could deplore the killing of mocking birds for their skins and commend those would did not have the courage to kill an ant or a spider.[22]

The disregard for the susceptibilities of his audience, which the young reporter had so carelessly displayed in Cincinnati, was again in evidence in New Orleans. His contempt for the middle class respectability which most of his readers probably possessed or aspired to was revealed in pieces such as 'That Parlour'. The parlour's furniture was used only 'on state occasions' and the young lady tortures the piano while the young men sit around torturing their brains trying to think of what to say when she is finished. The decor consists of 'frightful. . ."oil paintings" turned out. . .wholesale to the order of New York speculators, . . .[a] villainously featureless clock. . .[and] the abominable things in delft and plaster of Paris. . .'[23] It was probably precisely the people being mocked here who made up an element at least of the audience which Hearn had for the impressive series of translations which he produced for the *Item*, including works by Gautier, Zola, Daudet, Gerard De Nerval, Ricardo Palma, Flaubert, Armand and De Maupassant.

Hearn occupied a privileged position on the *Item*, probably a reason for the difficulties he had with fellow journalists, just as he had had in Cincinnati. He told Watkin of 'spite work' on the part of a writer on the New Orleans *Times* who had pirated his work and got a 'raking' for it.[24] Yet, as his literary ambitions deepened, he began to realise that the *Item* was a far from prestigious vehicle for his literary talents. His work had, however, made a positive impression in the right quarters and his luck was about to change.

In December 1881, the New Orleans *Democrat*, which Lafcadio had imagined was moribund,[25] merged with the New Orleans *Times* to form the *Times-Democrat*. The owners, who hoped to develop it into a paper which would rival the prestigious Eastern dailies, invited Lafcadio to join the editorial staff at $30 per week, a substantial increase on his salary on the *Item*, from which he resigned. He has sometimes been given the title of literary editor but that post was held, formally at any rate, by Marion Baker, brother of the editor, Page Baker.[26] Ten years later, surveying the literary side of the paper from the vantage point of Japan, he indulged in the retrospective revisionism which was habitual with him: '. . .the original poetry is all about love and despair. The stories are tales about enamoured swains and cruel beauties. The whole thing is now nauseating to me – yet I used to think it rather refined compared with other papers.'[27]

At the time, he did indeed see things differently. In March 1884, for example, he wrote to his friend William O'Connor of his perceived good fortune in finding a city where there was almost no literary competition and influential people who took an interest in his work and let him have things his own way.[28] Foremost among the people of influence who promoted him was the editor-in-chief of the *Times-Democrat*, Page Baker. Hearn later recalled him as the most lovable man he had ever met, an old-time Southerner, very tall and slight – 'an ideal Mephistopheles'. He was a man of immense force but a gentleman without superior in Hearn's experience.[29] Hearn loved him and the friendship never soured, not in Lafcadio's lifetime at any rate. Baker was the prototype of the aristocratic, natural gentleman who appealed so much to Hearn. Elizabeth Bisland was also from a genteel Southern background and, in Japan, his closest friends, Nishida and Chamberlain, were gentlemen of high social rank. Hearn's prejudices were essentially those of the transplanted rural gentry among whom he had passed his youth, which accepted the common people but eschewed the industrial middle classes. It is noteworthy that his friendships with essentially middle-class figures such as Krehbiel and Gould were not lasting.

Hearn was also encouraged by Marion Baker, though he was wary of his literary editor, thinking him selfish.[30] Other colleagues at the *Times-Democrat* such as Honoré Burthe, John Augustine and Charles Whitney, described by Elizabeth Bisland as representing 'the best impulse toward new growth among both the American and Creole members of the city's population', provided Lafcadio with an appreciative, sympathetic environment in which his work was able 'to expand along the natural line of his tastes and capabilities'.[31]

While in some respects Hearn was a pre-telegraph anachronism, he was also a pioneer, particularly in his use of a daily, mass-circulation newspaper as a vehicle for foreign language translations. The translations and literary editorials published in the *Times-Democrat* were on much the same French authors who had featured in his *Item* work: Gautier, Alphonse Daudet, Loti, Villiers de l'Isle Adam, Jules Lemaître, Octave Mirbeau, Hugo, Sacher Masoch and, especially, de Maupassant. Translation for Hearn was more than the mere transliteration of one language's literature to another: it also provided a channel for the expression of his particular interests, some of which might otherwise have seemed out of place in a newspaper.

They were a means, for example, of expressing his continued fascination with gore and horror in his New Orleans period, now that he was no longer on the police beat and dealing with it in the flesh. Good examples were Flaubert's 'The Crucified Lions', a description of the practice of the Carthaginian peasants of crucifying ferocious beasts[32] and 'The Secrets of the Scaffold', with its detailed account of decapitation by guillotine, by Compte de Villiers de l'Isle Adam.[33] 'The Story of Tse-I-La', also by Adam, combined his interests in horror and the Orient.[34] The Orient featured also in pieces such as 'The Shadow of the Light of Asia'.[35] He put forward, as early as 1882, a theory of ancient lives, which was to become almost obsessional in Japan.[36] 'Missionaries as Linguists' was a defence by Hearn of the work of Christian missionaries in the linguistic field in the Orient, ironic in view of his later opinions on the subject.[37]

With these and his original work he built up a small but appreciative audience which grew into a local clientele that followed his later career with warm interest. Indeed, Page Baker published some of his Japanese work in the *Times-Democrat* in 1892 and 1894. The easy-going atmosphere at the *Times-Democrat* can perhaps be gauged from the spoof editorial which Hearn foisted on his readers on April Fool's Day, 1882; it claimed that Edison had invented a fearsome electrical weapon with the force of 150,000,000,000 horses. The writer was supposed to have attended an experiment at which 43 sheep, horses and mules were roasted to perfection at a distance of five miles.[38]

On the serious side, Hearn showed that his political judgement was almost as far-sighted as his literary perception. He predicted, for example, that the world was not, as many then imagined, nearing the dawn of universal peace – 'there will be wars yet which will almost crack the earth's crust like an earthquake'. One can also detect the belief in the power of religion as a social and political force, that underlay his best work in Japan, in pieces such as the one on the rising in the Sudan in 1885, the nature of which he felt the politicians had only half understood: 'A few hard-won victories will not settle the country; – the tribes will resist bravely until extermination.' Heroes – 'call it fanaticism if you please' – would not be checked by disaster. Those who were religiously motivated might be dreamers 'but there are dreams that shake the world, and make men laugh in the face of death. . .'[39]

Hearn's self-imposed exile from the developments of the nineteenth century, his love of the doomed, pre-industrial cultures is evident in much of his Creole work. The figures at the Mardi Gras Ball, for example, in his eyes belonged 'to other ages' and he emphasises its distance from 'the prosaic life of the century'.[40] A book on ancient Greek civilisation set him dreaming that 'the beautiful dead world seemed to live again, in a luminous haze, in an Elysian glow'. The marble dreams of Greek statuary became lithe flesh but asked why he had evoked them: 'Ours was a world of light and of laughter, of loveliness and of love. Thine is smoke-darkened and sombre'.[41]

It is little wonder that, to the average citizen, Hearn appeared to be a bizarre character: a letter dated 17 December 1886 by an unknown writer described the marriage of the gruesome and the poetic elements which survived in Hearn's character from the 'Tan-Yard Murder' in Cincinnati to the final masterful horror stories of his Japanese days:

> His hobbies were fantastic. He knew all manner of odd things, dreadful things, uncanny things. He was purblind, and the shadow of a telegraph pole rose to him 'the shadow of a gigantic skeleton'. He studied Hoodooism [sic], witchcraft, etc. . .and knew all the horrible things about the old-time doings – frightful, barbaric, hideous punishments, etc.; and he knew some of the sweetest poetry in all tongues. I have always predicted some sort of prominence for the man, for he has undoubted genius, but it is, to use a favorite word of his own, orgiastic. He is a helpless sort of genius, and has great admiration for men who are 'practical and square'.[42]

Letters to Krehbiel and Watkin provided Hearn with a means of venting his dissatisfaction with journalism in the New Orleans period. This correspondence marks the beginning of a practice which Hearn maintained until his final years in Japan, that of writing long and frequent letters to close friends in which he committed his most intimate thoughts to paper. Sometimes he would dash off letters daily to a particular correspondent in what was effectively a lonely man's substitute for conversation. Many of these letters were conscious literary efforts – indeed, their sheer volume and intensity makes one wonder at the intellectual energy of a man who was also involved over the years in journalism, translation, teaching and writing.

His approach to these letters, as to anything which touched his art, was highly methodical and he did not hesitate to address virtually the same letter, or employ the same phrase, to different correspondents. He opened a letter to Krehbiel in 1881 with the phrase, 'Your letter rises before me as I write like a tablet of stone bearing a dead name. I see you standing beside me, I look into your eyes and press your hand and say nothing. . .'[43] Krehbiel took this as an expression of condolence on the recent death of his baby but Hearn's use of virtually the same phrase to Watkin over a year later indicates that it was merely a device used when he felt he had been tardy in replying to correspondence.

The letters to Krehbiel reveal a serious divergence of views on Hearn's literary efforts which became a factor in the eventual end of the friendship. Krehbiel was the first in a line of friends who themselves had literary aspirations and attempted to guide Hearn into different literary paths, a receipt for disaster as far as friendship was concerned. To him, the 'Fantastics' were repugnant and he tried to switch Hearn to classic subjects with historical backgrounds. As was the case a few years later when another morally earnest friend, George Gould, attempted to influence him in much the same way, Hearn complied in form but not in content. The result on this occasion was a story with a classical background but which Krehbiel classed as erotic and clearly disliked.

The relationship between the two men went steadily downhill from the time Hearn left Cincinnati until the final rupture took place on the eve of his departure for Japan. Hearn has been portrayed in previous biographies as a neurotically quarrelsome individual who inexplicably cut off close friends, Krehbiel being a prime example. Lafcadio was indeed highly sensitive and quick to take offence but the evidence available – admittedly mostly Hearn's own letters – give the impression that in Cincinnati the things which united them – youth, journalism, musical interest, literary ambition – forged close bonds of friendship. Later, in addition to the natural inertia which distance exercises on a friendship, changing circumstances emphasised the fundamental differences which divided them.

Even in these years though there were hints of the later parting of the ways. The veneer of deferring to Krehbiel's intellectual superiority was discarded when he was told by Lafcadio not to pontificate on art and literature; he testily told his friend not to judge everything by Gothic standards, caustically reminding him

that his ancestors had destroyed the marvels of Greek art. Hearn
was proud of living in a 'Latin' city and valued his contacts with
members of the races apparently detested by Krehbiel, a 'son of
Odin' in Lafcadio's phrase.[44]

While he was growing apart from some of his Cincinnati
acquaintances, Hearn's circle of friendship was being replenished
from new sources in New Orleans. Elizabeth Bisland, daughter
of a Louisiana landowner ruined by the Civil War, was impelled
by her admiration of a 'Fantastic' to arrange a meeting in the
winter of 1882. She made a deep impression on Hearn, as she did
on most people that she met. Hearn's friend, Ellwood Hendrick,
considered her the most beautiful woman he had ever seen due,
not to the classic regularity of her features, but to her
'magnificent presence that radiated beauty and charm'. Arriving
at a reception, the men would immediately flock to her.

To Hendrick, it appeared that she had recognised Hearn's
genius from the first and he in turn was 'always reverencing her
amazing beauty'.[45] Even in middle age, she struck Nina Kennard
as 'dainty and beautiful'. While there is no doubt that Hearn had
at least an aesthetic appreciation of Bisland's beauty, he
consistently denied that he found her 'voluptuously attractive'.
He wrote to Hendrick from Kobe in 1895 that he had been
'very, very much afraid of Queen Elizabeth's magic. I could
never tell you how much afraid of it I was. But the gods were
good to me'.[46]

The complexity of his feelings towards her was probably best
set out in a letter written in the early years of their friendship:

> The lady writer you enquire about is probably Miss Bessie
> Bisland, who writes the 'Bric-a-Brac' for T-D, reports
> Women's meetings, etc, and occasionally writes some
> superb poetry. . .She is really a genius poetically, needs only
> discipline and practice. . .Tall, fair-skinned, large black
> eyes, and dark hair: Some call her beautiful; others, pretty: I
> don't think her one or the other; but she is decidedly
> attractive, physically and intellectually. Otherwise she is
> selfish, unfeeling, hard, cunning, vindictive: a woman that
> will make an inferno in any husband's life, unless he have a
> character of tremendous force. . .A girl that reminds me of
> a hawk,- although her nose is not aquiline – a graceful
> creature of prey![47]

The self-proclaimed romantic was not devoid of hard-boiled

realism. At the same time, Hearn was probably being genuine when he expressed admiration for Bisland's pluck in tackling New York, where she went to work on *Cosmopolitan* magazine in the late 1880s, and her success there.[48]

Despite occasional criticism of his 'queer ways', she was steadfast in her championship of Hearn, on a personal level and in print, as well as introducing him to appreciative New York friends. There was a mild flirtatiousness in the correspondence between them – writing of a prospective visit to New York in April 1887, he is gallant in his doubt that they might not meet: 'I do not know whether I shall behold you; – you will be there, as here, a blossom dangerous to approach by reason of the unspeakable multitude of bees.'[49] At other times he playfully referred to himself as her chaperon but his insight into the less attractive side of her character was such that his disclaimer of serious interest may have been genuine.

Dr Rudolph Matas was another New Orleans friend with literary inclinations. Later to become an internationally-renowned surgeon, at the time he was a young man of twenty-three when, according to one account, he persuaded Charles Whitney of the *Times-Democrat* to introduce him to the author of 'those wonderful things – translations, weird sketches, and remarkable editorials', which had enchanted him. Hearn, in turn, was astonished to find that Matas knew him so well, so thoroughly had he absorbed his work. A fruitful relationship developed, with Matas providing medical knowledge, specifically on Arab medicine, which was included in Hearn's encyclopaedic interests. Material provided by Matas was used by Hearn in some of the books he produced in New Orleans.[50]

Lafcadio remembered Matas as 'a very dear friend, almost a brother', whom he predicted would turn out to be a great name in American medicine.[51] Matas's recollections of Hearn were somewhat more mixed: 'Both in taste and temperament he was morbid and in many respects abnormal'. Matas claimed he understood this better because of his knowledge of the pathology of such personalities and because Hearn revealed himself to him in a way which would have shocked others: the writer allegedly was obsessed with the notion of his own persecution, bitterly denouncing his enemies in frightful language, and inventing unheard-of tortures to punish 'plotters' against him. He had 'an almost feminine jealousy' and exaggerated sensitivity while at the same time being as gentle and tender-hearted as a woman and as passionately affectionate. Matas in turn warned his friend against consorting with prostitutes, advice which Hearn confessed to ignoring on occasion.[52]

The course of Hearn's friendship with George Washington Cable, the Southern writer, ran a course similar in many respects to that with Krehbiel. Like Krehbiel, Cable disapproved of the 'Fantastics' and hoped that Hearn would 'stop spinning spiderwebs and weave a fabric that would clothe facts and things and people and actual conditions'.[53] The two men did, however, have a fascination with Creole life in common though they had different attitudes to it. Though they ultimately fell out in 1884, the constancy of Hearn's literary judgement was such that he continued afterwards to respect Cable's writing.

Unlike Lafcadio though, Cable was not enamoured of the Creoles and his essentially Northern outlook – despite being a Southern Civil War veteran – alienated the Creoles who felt that they were being portrayed as racially inferior. Hearn was placed in a difficult position because, while he appreciated Cable's literary qualities, his fundamentally different attitude had won him the friendship of prominent Creoles. Indeed, as he became acquainted with the local intelligentsia, a clique of what were know as 'Hearn's admirers' formed. A call on Lafcadio became part of the pattern for visiting literary lions and he enjoyed what was perhaps the most sociable period of his life.[54]

A flavour of this can be gauged from his correspondence with Mrs Marion Baker, who wrote a sonnet inspired by his book, *Stray Leaves from Stray Literature*.[55] She remembered him as a character of strong contrasts, warm-hearted and affectionate but prone to distrustfulness, often suspecting friends of designs to slight or injure him. He could take offence inexplicably and was easily influenced against sincere well-wishers by mischief-makers: the 'last speaker' left a strong impression on him. Not a good judge of character, he would attribute subtlety to simple people and would work himself up into rages against those who had helped him materially. He was not happy and she sensed – wrongly, as it turned out – that he would not be 'good to tie to'. At that time he had a strongly sensual nature and 'made no pretence of leading an ideal life'. Yet, to Mrs Baker he could also be a charming companion and delightful conversationalist, one who never sought to dominate the proceedings. Those attracted by him were usually of strong personality, people who distinguished themselves later in life. In conversation he was far more humorous than appeared from his writings, enjoying a joke, giving a quiet chuckle when amused. She only heard him laugh heartily once, 'a loud wild, harsh scream like the laughter of a lunatic. . .'[56] Ellwood Hendrick, who got to know him a few years later, recalled him having a lively sense of humour, chuckling over a Rabelaisian joke provided it was not cruel or pornographic.[57]

Benjamin Forman, a New Orleans student who remembered him from this era, Mrs Baker, and Elizabeth Bisland agreed in their physical descriptions of Hearn at this time. He was short – about five feet, three inches – and strongly built with, according to Bisland, an 'almost feminine grace and lightness in his step and movements'. His small feet were shod in clumsy and neglected shoes – indeed, his whole dress was peculiar. His favourite coat – winter and summer – was a heavy blue chinchilla 'reefer' and the wide-rimmed hat which invariably accompanied it were a standing joke among his friends. The rest of his clothes were purchased for durability rather than appearance but his linen was always fresh and he had an innate physical cleanliness.[58]

Lafcadio imagined himself ugly and some agreed but Mrs Baker recalled a fine head with well-cut features and a handsome profile. Bisland described his head as remarkably beautiful and speculated that he must have been handsome before the accident to his eye which he instinctively shielded with his hand in company. His poor eyesight did not prevent him being able to detect the slightest change of expression in the faces of those to whom he was talking. Despite abnormal shyness, especially with strangers, he was not awkward in manner and would walk about 'pouring out a stream of brilliant talk in a soft, half-apologetic tone, with constant deference to the opinions of his companions'. Any idea advanced was received with respect, however much he might differ from it. Bisland could not imagine a wittier companion but his sensitivity was such that any expression of anger or harshness, any story of moral or physical pain, 'sent him quivering away'.[59]

Edward L. Tinker, in researching his book, *Lafcadio Hearn's*

American Days [1924], interviewed many in New Orleans who remembered Hearn. He described his subject's conversation as having 'a controlled fire of passion' and 'a strange compelling charm. . .his marvellous memory, that enabled him to quote anything he had ever read, illuminated his conversation with bits of the strangest and most unusual information; and his literary opinions were as vivid and continental as if he had just landed from Paris'.[60]

Perhaps the most extraordinary of these relationships was with the Irish landlady who took him under her wing, Mrs Margaret Courtney, and her brother, big, burly Dennis ('Denny') Corcoran, former deputy sheriff and ward politician. She lived on Gasquet Strret in an area of cheap boarding houses and ran a grocery shop on the side; Lafcadio rented his rooms from her in the 1880s. They became great friends – 'both being Irish', as she boasted – to a point where she could remonstrate with him over his lack of faith: 'Ah! and I pray God every night on my knees to make you a good Catholic, and you an Irishman, too!', to which Hearn would reply: 'I'm glad you pray your God for me. Don't stop.'[61] Sometimes he would eat his dinner alone with his cat and write all night – it was here that his books of the New Orleans period were written. Indeed, when *Stray Leaves from Strange Literature* was published in July 1884, he presented a copy to his landlady with the inscription: 'To my kindest friend, Mrs Margaret Courtney, whose unselfish care aided me not a little in obtaining the health necessary for study – the first printed copy is respectfully presented.'[62]

Denny Corcoran later recalled his memories of his nocturnal walks with Hearn, sitting in parks while the writer explained the meaning to him of the statues, 'de nooder de better. . .I don't know nuttin he was talki' about, but I loved him'. One source claimed that Hearn accompanied Denny, a hard man by all accounts, to opium dens and became an addict for a short time.[63] However, as Denny also 'remembered' having accompanied Lafcadio to the West Indies, and he most certainly did not, such claims should be treated with circumspection.[64] It is unlikely that such a fate could have befallen so prominent a person without it having been recorded by friends and enemies. There is a dreamlike quality to some of the 'Fantastics'' prose but Hearn's productivity in this period (nine books between 1882 and 1890 in addition to his journalism) would hardly have been possible for someone struggling with opium addiction. He may have experimented with the drug but if he were an addict, it must have been for a very short period indeed. It is possible that he told Denny of his experiences of opium dens in Cincinnati and that this became transmogrified into something much more dramatic.

CHAPTER FOUR

SOME CHINESE GHOSTS

LAFCADIO'S painstaking devotion to literature began to bear fruit in New Orleans. His first work to be published in book form was a reprint of 'A Louisiana Idyll' from the *Item* in *La Nouvelle Atala* by his friend, Adrian Rouquette, in New Orleans in 1879. Ironically, in view of Lafcadio's often fiercely anti-clerical attitudes, the work was published with the imprimatur of the 'Propagateur Catholique'. He was described as 'un remarquable Ecrivain anglian'.[1]

In 1967 one of Hearn's more obscure works, his Creole cookbook, *La Cuisine Creole*, was attractively re-published. The origin of the recipes may be a matter of conjecture; the style has a Hearnian sprinkling not normally found in works of this kind. Around the same time was published *Gombo Zhèbes*, a dictionary of Creole proverbs which was a compilation of over 350 proverbs selected from six Creole dialects – those of French Guyana, Haiti, New Orleans, Martinique, Mauritius and Trinidad. He had picked up the proverbs when studying the patois of the Louisiana negro, the local name of which is 'Gombo'. The bulk of work on the book, which he termed 'a mere compilation. . .from many unfamiliar sources', was done between 1881 and late 1883. He tried, unsuccessfully, to interest his future publisher, Houghton Mifflin of Boston, in it, claiming that he was not interested in profit, only in contributing to folklore.[2] Ultimately it was brought out by Will H. Coleman, the publisher of the cookbook, in New York, early in 1885.

It was, however, his growing mastery of French, enabling him to continue translating his literary idols into English, which was the key to his early literary work. While his declaration that he 'hated' English might be regarded as hyperbole, he did find French literature more interesting. He hoped to create in English 'a Latin style, modelled upon foreign masters, and rendered even more forcible by that element of strength which is the characteristic of Northern tongues'.[3] He later realised that it was impossible to replicate French literature in English but it was the attempt to do so which provided the impetus to Hearn's literary career in New Orleans.

Lafcadio was intensely aware of the Greek connection with French Romanticism – he believed, for example, that Gautier followed the 'Greek ideal. . .and sought the beautiful only'.[4] His translation of Gautier's *Avatar* was an attempt to render Gautier's 'engraved gemwork of words' into English. He was unable to find a publisher for it, however, and threw the manuscript away in disgust, raging at 'the self-styled Anglo-Saxon. . .damnable prudery' which was shocked by this 'innocent phantasy'.[5] A less determined man might have given up but Hearn still doggedly translated exotic verse which took him 'by the throat with the strangulation of pleasure'.[6] He persevered with Gautier and, after four years of rejection, managed to find a publisher in 1882 for a translation of six of his 'Fantastic Romances' using the story, *One of Cleopatra's Nights* as the title. He had, however, to contribute $150 to the publishing costs.

The gently sadistic, and mildly erotic, work of Gautier provided a perfect means for Hearn to bridge the bloodthirsty and occasionally erotic journalism of his Cincinnati period with the Romantic literary ambitions he was determined to pursue in New Orleans. Yet in terms of his ultimate literary destination – simply, direct prose – *Cleopatra* represented a retrograde step. The opening of the title story is, for example, suitably atmospheric but the bejewelled French Romantic prose tended to turn wooden in translation. Arch literary confections, such as '. . .and Sleep soon sprinkled his golden dust upon the beautiful eyes of Ptolemy's sister', come across as trite and contrived. Exaggerated literary effect requires conscious acts of concentration on the part of the reader, such as:

> Above the dark swarm of men no longer tower those
> Titanic colossi who bestrode the world in three paces, like
> the steeds of Homer; no more towers of Lylacq; no giant

Babel scaling the sky with its infinity of spirals; no temples immeasurable, builded with the fragments of quarried mountains; no kingly terraces to which successive ages and generations could each erect but one step, and from whence some dreamfully reclining prince might gaze on the face of the world as upon a map unfolded; no more of those extravagantly vast cities of cyclopaean edifices, inextricably piled upon one another, with their mighty circumvallations, their circuses roaring day and night, their reservoirs filled with ocean brine and peopled with whales and leviathans, their colossal stairways, their super-imposition of terraces, their tower-summits bathed in clouds, their giant palaces, their aqueducts, their multitude-vomiting gates, their shadowy necropoli.[7]

Perhaps the kindest review was that in the *Argonaut* by Jerome A. Hart, who became a correspondent of Hearn's. While criticising the book's literalism, he recognised that Hearn had few equals as a translator.[8] In a 1912 biography of Hearn, the Welsh poet, Edward Thomas, agreed with Hart about the quality of the translation but was also less enthusiastic about its literary merits, though he felt that a better translation was unlikely because a man capable of it would do original work. The style was Lafcadio's 'early prose, a cumbrous English stiffened with beauties which do not make it beautiful. It is unwieldy but not massive, hard without being firm, and it is not alive. It is not Gautier and not Hearn, yet the more imposing parts of it become parts of Hearn'.[9]

Yet there were positive aspects to the book, apart from its language, not allowed by Thomas, if it is put in the context of Lafcadio's long-term development: *Cleopatra* looks forward in some ways to the mature horror of Hearn's Japanese work. Elements of its subject matter – the casual horror of Cleopatra's murder of servants and lovers in the title story, and her studied indifference at the death of her would-be lover, Meiamoun, for example – was the stuff of which some of his best work would later be made. In any case, *Cleopatra* brought Lafcadio to the attention of a contemporary popular audience; the book sold well, particularly to railway travellers, even though Hearn later damned the publisher, Worthington, for an abominable, error-littered printing.[10]

The publication of *One of Cleopatra's Nights* spurred William Douglas O'Connor to begin corresponding with its author.

Eighteen years older than Hearn, O'Connor was a poet and short-story writer described by his friend, Walt Whitman, as 'a gallant, handsome, gay-hearted, fine-voiced, glowing-eyed man; lithe-moving on his feet, of healthy and magnetic atmosphere and presence, and the most welcome company in the world. . .'[11] O'Connor for his part found 'health and happiness' in being near 'the great Walt'. He believed Whitman to be one of the greatest literary figures of all time and was a passionate advocate of his work even though they had fallen out in 1872 over black voting rights.

There was an empathy of race between Hearn and himself; ten years after his death, Lafcadio wrote *apropos* O'Connor: 'I was wondering how much nationality has to do with these friendships. Is it only Irish or Latin people who make friends for friendship's sake?'[12] They disagreed, however, in their respective literary tastes: Whitman was to Hearn 'barbaric'.[13] Not alone was his approach the antithesis of Lafcadio's but he offended Hearn's essentially patrician instincts:

> . . .when the poet draws his speech not from pure nature, but from dwarfed nature as it exists in the factitious life of factory cities, I cannot admire. Some phrases [of Whitman's] jar upon one like fragments of coarse converse heard in passing street corners. I can admire the language of savages. . .but the language of everyday life of [the] working class in our civilized cities is unendurable.[14]

Social evolution, over which Hearn took issue with O'Connor's optimistic view of the future, was one of the staple topics in the voluminous and wide-ranging correspondence which the two men maintained up to O'Connor's death in 1889.[15] Hearn adopted a paternal tone towards the older man, advising him, for example, not to return to a government job – a 'terrible mill for grinding minds'.

In this period Hearn ruminated on his style and, indeed, his whole approach to literature in correspondence with his friends. He remained stubbornly romantic, insistent that he would 'always be more or less Arabesque – covering my whole edifice with intricate designs, serrating my arches, and engraving mysticisms above the portals'.[16] At the same time, he recognised the difficulties in such an approach:

> What troubles my style especially is ornamentation. An

ornamental style must be perfect or full of atrocious discords and incongruities; and perfect ornamentation requires slow artistic work – except in the case of men like Gautier, who never re-read a page, or worried himself about a proof. But I think I'll improve as I grow older.[17]

This was written as he corrected the page proofs of *Stray Leaves* in May 1884. He had already adopted a plan for literary study, concentrating on what he perceived would contribute to his future development. He wrote in 1883 that he only read books which powerfully impressed the imagination and contained 'novel, curious, potent imagery. . .When the soil of fancy is really well enriched with innumerable fallen leaves, the flowers of language grow spontaneously'. He looked to four elements especially to enrich his 'fancy': mythology, history, romance and poetry. In mythology he sought 'the most fantastic and sensuous'; in history and romance, 'the extraordinary, the monstrous, the terrible'; while poetry was the 'crystallization of all human desire about the impossible, the diamonds created by prodigious pressure of suffering'. Science was essential to the creative process as it furnished 'a wonderful and startling variety of images, symbols, and illustrations'. Hearn planned to give himself another five years of study, after which he felt he would have forged a good, or at least an impressive, style.[18] He was more-or-less right in his timetable: five years later he was about to embark for Japan where his mature style evolved.

The increasingly irksome trade of journalism was to be performed as mechanically as was necessary to preserve his reputation as a good workman; 'the sacred work of literature', on the other hand, required the utmost devotion, with every line being written out three times to start with, twice in pencil and then in ink. Such labours were complimented by the use of Roget's *Thesaurus* and etymological dictionaries in different languages: 'Such books give one that subtle sense of words to which much that startles in poetry and prose is due. Time develops the secret merit of work thus done. . .'[19] Independent corroboration of Lafcadio's painstaking methods of literary composition was provided by George Gould at a time when he was locked in mortal combat with Hearn's posthumous reputation:

Sometimes he would be able to write with comparative

ease a large number of sheets (of yellow paper – he could write on no other) in a day. At other times the words did not suit or fit, and he would rewrite a few pages scores of times.[20]

Interestingly enough, Lafcadio found that such unrelenting application, rather than restricting the imagination, freed it to wander in unexpected directions. He would sometimes work at a page for months and then be surprised at the result, feelings that his best work often emerged from the unconscious. Through such methods Hearn believed in the mid-1880s that he would realise his 'ancient dream of a poetical prose – compositions to satisfy an old Greek ear – like chants wrought in a huge measure wider than the widest line of Sanskrit composition, and just a little irregular, like Ocean-rhythm.'[21]

He believed that the artist must strive to create something novel: 'The ground of imagination may be enriched by new experience, new sights and sounds and perfumes; unfamiliar colours and forms and music; but the thing must produce a crop wholly different from the old'.[22] The emphasis on external stimuli rather than his own imagination is noteworthy, particularly as Hearn's later attempts at imaginative fiction would not now be remembered were it not for his other work. He was filling his brain with unfamiliar topics, believing that some day he would be able to use them in a new way. Knowing, as he said, that he was not a genius and that ordinary talent must be supplemented by 'curious study', he set out 'to woo the Muse of the Odd' and thereby attract attention. He devoted a huge amount of research to these esoteric subjects. In 1883, his indignation at being asked to cater to popular taste prompted him to define his literary aspirations: 'Fancy how I felt when asked (indirectly) by the "Century" to write something "SNAPPY" – even I, who am no specialist, and if anything of an artist only a word artist in embryo!'[22]

Curiously enough, it was through the medium of the despised newspaper, rather than his books, that he expressed his imagination in its purest form at this time. He was lucky that Colonel John Fairfax was enthusiastic about his attempts at imaginative work in the columns of the *Item*. Fairfax knew that his assistant really hated his routine work and needed occasionally to be prodded: 'But when he would write one of his own little fanciful things, out of his own head – dreams – he was always dreaming – why, then he would work like mad. And people noticed those little things of his somehow, for they were truly lovely, wonderful. "Fantastics" he called them.'[23]

The 'Fantastics' were Hearn's first really creative work to be published. They were slight, imaginative pieces, frequently in the form of reveries, which nevertheless often revealed a strong autobiographical basis. The genre gave him an opportunity to indulge his romanticism; he could proclaim his 'madness of longing for freedom' and a love for the gypsies whose wild blood allegedly made fever in his veins (an old conceit of the Hearn family). He could curse his bondage to civilisation, supposedly being isolated among a people not his own.[24] He could have had little idea of the extent to which the persona being created would, in time, come to be taken for his real character.

Through the 'Fantastics' Hearn expressed a philosophy which was to guide him for the rest of his life. He distanced himself from his contemporaries, the 'Beings' of the nineteenth century, to whose ranks he did not wish to belong. They had devoted themselves to the work of destruction and reconstruction; dreamers such as himself were, to them, an abomination.[25] As well as longings for his mother's welcoming South in the face of rejection by his father's cold North there were other aspirations evident in the 'Fantastics'; for a home and children, 'smiling faces, comfort, and a woman's friendship, the idea of something real to love and be loved by', which haunted him 'in hours of disgust with the world and weariness of its hollow mockeries'.[26] The ultimate form of escape was to disembody himself completely and fantasise about being a cloud, a wave, or an eagle; he imagined himself a flower, describing in detail the sensations of bees singing to him, before he is cut off and put in the hair of a dead woman.

The 'Fantastics' allowed him to explore a world of pure imagination, one which he said allowed him sufficient vagueness to hide the absence of detailed, technical knowledge.[27] He was firm – beneath a veneer of self-deprecation – in their defence: 'But I fancy the idea of the Fantastics is artistic. They are my impressions of the strange life of New Orleans. They are the dreams of a tropical city. There is one twin-idea running through them all – Love and Death.- And these figures embody the story of life here, as it impresses me.'[28] Krehbiel complained that the 'Fantastics' lacked purpose. Hearn seemed to concede the point but added significant qualifications; they had no purpose 'beyond the gratification of expressing a Thought which cries out within one's heart for utterance, and the pleasant fancy that a few kindred minds will dream over them, as upon pellets of green hascheesh. . .'[29]

Lafcadio's attempt to expand the boundaries of literary acceptability collided with reality when he presented his next translation, Flaubert's *La Tentation de Saint Antoine*; his publisher, Worthington, a 'Methodist of the antique type', had been much upset by the *Christian Observer*'s description of *Cleopatra* as 'stories of unbridled lust without the apology of natural passion. . .[which] reeked with the miasma of the brothel'.[30] That he was not enthusiastic about *La Tentation*, described by Hearn himself as 'one of the most exotically strange pieces of writing in any language and weird beyond description' is perhaps not surprising.[31] To escape the clutches of Worthington, Lafcadio again tried to interest Houghton Mifflin of Boston, but it was not published in his lifetime.[32] Sadly, a great deal of wasted effort went into this translation. In fact, the only books of French translation after *Cleopatra* published in his lifetime were a hack work written to relieve desperate financial circumstances on his return from the West Indies and a translation of Gautier's *Clarimond* published in New York in 1899. By that time he had come to regard *Cleopatra* as one of the 'sins' of his 'literary youth' though he remained convinced of the value of the original stories.

Notwithstanding these reverses, Hearn's career was progressing: the year after the publication of *One of Cleopatra's Nights*, at the age of thirty-three, he could write that he was in favour with Harper and Scribners, the publishers of two of the leading periodicals in the country.[33] Access to their magazines was crucial to developing a national audience and, as they paid well, represented a first step towards the realisation of a dream of independence from the drudgery of newspaper work and total concentration on literature. He was to find though that the larger stage imposed its own constraints. The small compass of a local newspaper allowed him the luxury of indulgence in his most esoteric interests and fantasies; the magazines had a much more clearly-defined sense of what their readership wanted and, while they were happy to accept his more orthodox work, he had difficulty when he tried to pursue his personal interests. In March 1884, he was moaning to his friend, William O'Connor:

> I think the magazines are simply inabordables. My experiences have been disheartening. 'Very good, very scholarly – but not the kind we want;'. . .'Highly interesting – sorry we have no room for it'. . .; 'I regret to say we cannot use it, but would advise you to send it to X'. . .; 'Deserves to be published; but unfortunately our rules exclude' etc. . . .[34]

He had hoped to contribute a 'strong line of colour on Oriental subjects' to the magazines but found that editorial policy excluded papers not of popular or immediate interest. Lesser magazines requested pieces on juicy Southern topics which he refused to do. He was adamant that he would never write anything 'magaziny'; each piece should be a chapter of a future book, copyrighted in advance.[35] When he listed his interests, the unreality of what he was attempting, even in the compass of literary magazines, became apparent: 'The Legends of the Saints of Islam, the traditions of the poets of the Desert, the stories of the Monteyemian or the Lone-martyrs of Arabia and the very peculiar Folklore of the Sahara tribes – or subjects almost unrepresented in English popular reading.'[36]

At the time he was writing this, Hearn was in fact celebrating the publication of just such Oriental material in his second book, *Stray Leaves from Strange Literature*. The previous September he had written to Krehbiel that he had almost completed a collection of Oriental stories – 'from all sorts of queer sources – the Sanskrit, Buddhist, Talmudic, Persian, Polynesian, Finnish literature, etc.' – which he would try to publish.[37] They were 'monstrous dreams, Oriental flowers transplanted and changed in color by the process'.[38] *Stray Leaves* actually suffered from the same stylistic immaturity as *Cleopatra*. The self-conscious striving after effect, the stilted use of archaic language, the set-piece descriptions, are all irritating – and yet the book clearly represents an advance over its predecessor. It is again translation, but this time not purely literal. The sources have cohered and become distinctly Hearnian; the familiar themes of love and death, frequently involving beautiful, celestial women, give the work an artistic unity that derived from the author. Hearn's reaction to his own work followed a lifelong pattern; he was upbeat when it was in preparation but quickly identified what appeared to be glaring faults once it came to fruition. He had not even finished the page proofs of *Stray Leaves* when he was telling Krehbiel that his 'poor little book' would show some journalistic weaknesses.[39] He was actually lucky that it was being published at all: the manuscript had been rejected by the publisher's reader when a letter of recommendation from Page Baker swayed the issue in his favour.[40] *Stray Leaves* was dedicated to his editor in gratitude. The publisher, Osgood, only accepted it on condition that Hearn would not receive royalties until the book had generated $1,000 for the firm and his later claims that he had made no money from it were probably correct but at least the reviews were an improvement on *Cleopatra*'s and the book helped to promote Hearn's growing reputation.

Hearn was astonished though to find himself confronted with cool, unapologetic plagiarism. R.H. Stoddard, a then-popular poet, published a blank verse 'poem' plagiarised, with minimal change, from *Stray Leaves*, in *Harper's Magazine* of October 1884. Hearn wrote in indignation to his publisher and, on 2 December 1884, they replied extricating themselves neatly by suggesting that he write a letter to Stoddard, not complaining but 'calling attention to his inadvertence'.[41] Hearn followed Osgood's advice. Whether or not he was being disingenuous, Stoddard's reply was disarmingly candid:

> You were correct in your belief that the inspiration of the Judgement of Solomon was drawn from your *Stray Leaves*. . .I recognised instinctively your imaginative additions to the original legend. You saw, of course, that I supplemented your material from other Eastern sources; precisely what these were I forgot now. . .I have since taken another poem from your *Stray Leaves*, the original of which you will recognise when I state its title − the Brahman's Son. I recognised in that as in the Judgement of Solomon, the brilliant editions [sic] of your Occidental talents; notably in the description of the sunset palace of the Gods I have followed your example in drawing upon my imagination. The poem I am speaking of will probably appear in the December number of Harper's Magazine. It gives me great pleasure to acknowledge my many obligations to your *Stray Leaves*, which were blown in my

direction last July. Make any use you please of this note. . .[42]

Stoddard was as good as his word: his second plagiarism was indeed published in the *Harper's Magazine* of October 1886. Hearn was reluctant to push matters with the Harpers who had been good to him – he had, for example, been paid $200 for some articles about a New Orleans 'Exposition' – and he was apprehensive about the effect of the arrival of a new editor with whom he had, as yet, no influence. The plagiarism nevertheless always rankled Hearn although he continued to correspond with Stoddard after this.

Stray Leaves represented a fundamental shift in Lafcadio's interest towards the Orient and this, in retrospect, was to be the turning point in his life. It would lead him within a few years to Japan and his most enduring work. While he had travelled psychologically south in Cincinnati, the mental journey changed direction to the east when he reached New Orleans. He was to go even further south after New Orleans, to the West Indies, but he did not find a culture of lasting challenge there. It was the Orientalism which became so marked in New Orleans which was to be the development of long-term significance. An interest in Japan had indeed manifested itself even in the early years in New Orleans: as early as June 1879 Lafcadio was writing excitedly to Watkin that he had wild theories about Japan, imagining that it would be a splendid field to work in.[43]

The 'Fantastics' provided a vehicle for Lafcadio's general fascination with the East. One such example appeared in the *Item* of 17 April 1880; it told how he and some others had been kept spellbound for hours by a stranger who told them of the Orient until only the host remained, 'dreaming of moons larger than ours, and fiercer summers; minarets white and keen, piercing a cloudless sky, and many-fountained pleasure-places of the East'.[44] Japan surfaced in a 'Fantastic' of 8 June 1881 where a traveller speaks of a Yokohama bath-house and the strange things he had seen there, 'until the memory of the recent vision mingled fantastically with recollections of the Japanese bathing house, and he sank back into another reverie, leaving the untasted cup of black coffee before him'.[45] The following month, the sight of a little Japanese fan in a street car prompted Hearn to ask where the Japanese got their exquisite taste for colour and tint-contrasts: '. . . is their sky so divinely blue? – are their sunsets so virginally carnation? – are the breasts of their maidens and the milky peaks of their mountains so white?'[46]

Together with *Stray Leaves*, *Some Chinese Ghosts*, published in 1887 – it was actually written some time earlier – provides conclusive evidence that his mind had turned to the Orient in New Orleans. In April 1886 he told O'Connor that he had a Chinese book, an attempt at poetic prose, with Ticknor. The publisher was more interested in getting Lafcadio to turn his hand to a novelette and the negative decision induced a nervous shock despite his efforts to be prepared. He turned yet again to Houghton Mifflin in May 1886, trying in vain to convince them that there was a growing interest in Oriental literature in Boston which would not be 'bored' by the book.[47] It was accepted, however, by another Boston publisher, Roberts Brothers, although their demands for the dropping of Oriental terms were 'particularly afflicting' to the writer.

Some Chinese Ghosts consisted of six stories from the Chinese, ostensibly translations but actually woven into a coherent whole by Hearn's style and his familiar themes of love and death. There is the beautiful Ko-Ngai who leapt into the white-hot lava of bell-metal to save her father's life. Oriental filial piety, which the author was to preach and practise later in Japan, was also represented in 'The Legend of Tchi-Niu', where Tong's selling of himself into slavery to pay his father's funeral expenses was rewarded by the celestial Tohi. Each of the stories represented months of study and hard work and Hearn regarded the 'literary finish' as better than *Stray Leaves*.

It was a work which divided the critics. Hearn himself described the book's notices as very contradictory outside New York and Boston: some said the stories were literal translations; others that:

> . . . they were fabrications, without any Chinese basis; others said the book was obscene; others called it 'exquisitely spiritual' – in short, the writers didn't seem to know what to make of it. Three lines in the *Atlantic* consoled me amply for naughty Western criticism.[48]

This last review, which appeared in the June 1887 issue of the *Atlantic Monthly*, called the book a 'rare flower that has the delightful surprise of the exotic. . .a mosaic such as a modern artificer might frame of antique marbles. . .' It even went as far as stating that Keats' treatment of the Lamia myth was coarse in comparison with 'The Story of Ming-Y' with its fine idyllic romanticism. It did, however, comment on the 'over-accented' mannerisms of the style and expressed the hope that, in future work, the author would develop in the direction of simplicity rather than artificiality.

Characteristically, Lafcadio was his own severest critic, describing *Some Chinese Ghosts* in 1898 as the early work of a man who had tried to understand the Far East from books and found that he could not, though he did not disown it entirely. If reprinted, he vowed not to change the text, only to preface it with an apology.[49] Perhaps he recognised that the book was a milestone on his own journey to the heart of Asia, the road which led from his identification of his mother's Greek inheritance to Japan. In 1876 he had written of being 'Oriental' by birth and blood.[50] The visit to the Chinese laundry with Krehbiel in Cincinnati in search of Chinese music had awakened in him 'fancies of a heart longing after the sight of pagoda towers, and of tea gardens, of serrated souls, of sluggish junks, and the eternal mourning of the Yang-tse-Kiary.'[51] Around this time he was 'enchanted' by Edwin Arnold's *Light of Asia* which 'perfumed' his mind 'as with the incense of a strangely new and beautiful worship'.[52]

The Japanese exhibit in the New Orleans Exposition of 1885 on which Hearn reported in *Harper's Weekly* and *Bazaar*, provided a fillip to his Eastern interests. He met Ichizo Hattori, the Japanese Government's representative in charge of the exhibition, a meeting that was to prove fateful in later years.[53] He was sufficiently impressed by a Japanese musician's treatise on the relationship of Japanese to ancient Greek art to send it to Krehbiel. He was particularly struck by the ability of Japanese art to suggest motion and was amazed by its animal forms. His later fascination with insects in Japan was foreshadowed by his delight in the bugs and reptiles printed on the Japanese cotton he saw in New Orleans. Silks depicting Mount Fuji inspired lyricism comparable to that evoked by the actual sight of the sacred mountain later in Japan.[54] His later unrestrained enthusiasm for Japanese culture was anticipated when he wrote, for example, of Japan's armourers having surpassed the world and bewailed his inability to afford Japanese artifacts. He was particularly anxious to come to terms with 'the phases of Japanese art – the esprit'.[55]

Years before the Exposition, he had developed the belief in the convergence of contemporary scientific philosophy and Oriental religious belief which would underpin his Japanese interpretative writings. Indeed, the roots of the attempt in Hearn's mature work to reconcile Far Eastern religion with 'scientific' evolutionary philosophy can be found in this period, an attempt which was to preoccupy Hearn for the rest of his life. As early as September 1880, he declared that the depths of German philosophy were shallow compared to the profound knowledge of the East, and that modern scientific research simply confirmed ancient Oriental beliefs.[56] In 1883 he wrote that 'Buddhism in some esoteric form may prove the religion of the future. . .I have the idea that the Right Man could now revolutionize the Occidental religious world by preaching the Oriental faith'. He asserted that the cycle of transmigration was proved by evolution and the tendency of contemporary philosophy was towards acceptance of Indian teaching that the visible was but an emanation of the Invisible, a delusion.[57] By 1886 he was examining Japanese Buddhism and ancestor worship, the contrast of which would provide the dynamic of his most considered work of Japanese interpretation.[58]

For the moment, however, Lafcadio was mainly concerned with the notion that the tenets of Buddhism were convertible into scientific truths through the transforming medium of evolutionary philosophy. The particular branch of evolutionary philosophy which he now espoused so enthusiastically was the teaching of Herbert Spencer whose 'disciple' he declared himself to be. As early as 1884, he referred to Spencer's *Sociology* as 'that giant-summary of all human knowledge, [in which] everything relating to the arts of life is considered comparatively and historically'.[59] Two years later, in a period of intense self-doubt, Lafcadio was advised to approach Spencer afresh by a close friend, Lieutenant Oscar Crosby, a young officer of great ability who moved in the same circles as himself. A philosophical metamorphosis resulted: in April 1886, he wrote to W.D. O'Connor:

> He [Spencer] has completely converted me away form all
> 'isms, or sympathies with 'isms: at the same time he has

filled me with the vague but omnipotent consolation of the Great Doubt. I can no longer give adhesion to the belief in human automatism,- and that primitive scepticism that imposes itself upon an indisciplined mind, has been eternally dissipated in my case. . .[60]

He concluded that, from the day he had finished the *First Principles*, 'this oceanic philosophy' opened up a new intellectual life for him.[61] Hearn attempted to convert his friends of the new all-embracing philosophical key to existence. Elizabeth Bisland was told that Spencer was slow but invaluable reading which systemised all knowledge; to have read him was to have 'digested the most nutritious portion of all human knowledge'.[62]

Lafcadio's initial respect for Spencer was partly a reflection of his regard for Crosby: his correspondence with Charles Washington Coleman, whom he tried to convert to Spencer's philosophy, reflected the intensity of his admiration for the Army engineer.[63] His relationship with Coleman developed at a time when his restlessness in New Orleans was turning his thoughts towards the West Indies. Coleman contacted him in 1886 about an article on the 'New Southern Literary Movement' which was published in the May 1887 issue of *Harper's Magazine* and a lively correspondence ensued. Hearn was almost obsequiously modest but on matters about which he cared, he could be devastatingly direct. At a time when he was piloting *Some Chinese Ghosts* through the page-proof stage, Lafcadio bluntly dismissed Coleman's views on Chinese beauty: 'They no more represent the finer type than the caricatures of Irishmen in *Harper's Weekly* represent the Irish University graduate or Irish colonels of a Light-Horse brigade', an indication that, while he generally kept his own counsel on the matter, Hearn was acutely critical of the nineteenth-century caricatures of his fellow countrymen.[64] Still, he came well out of the half page devoted to him towards the end of the article on the 'New Southern Literary Movement', the poetic prose of *Stray Leaves* and *Some Chinese Ghosts* attracting high praise.[65]

He was not, however, interested in Coleman's idea of a Southern magazine and, indeed, had had enough of New Orleans at this stage: 'I had hoped to find eternal summer in New Orleans. My hopes have been frost-burned; and as soon as my little book [*Some Chinese Ghosts*] comes out I am going to flee to

the West Indies,- to the tropics,- in search of light and caloric.'[66]
Hearn had always seen New Orleans as a staging post on a route
leading even further south. He had worked hard at Spanish and,
as early as 1879, he was planning to go to Havana. Even then, he
felt he had had his fill of the romance of New Orleans. The
finance for the trip was to have come from a restaurant venture
which was to give him the money to 'play the gipsy for a while
in strange lands'.[67] 'The Hard Times' or 'Five Cent' restaurant
was a success, so much so that the partner – 'a large and ferocious
man who kills people that disagree with their coffee'[68] –
absconded with the first few weeks takings leaving Hearn's
dreams of financial independence and Latin America shattered.
He had to face the fact of his continued dependence on
journalism but he still felt restless, particularly when Spanish ships
came in and he longed to sail away to see the quaint cities of the
Conquistadors. Meanwhile he felt his youth slipping away – the
'summer of life' had passed – and his hair was turning grey at
thirty. He complained that friendship was impossible in a
Southern city where men mocked 'at all that youth and faith
hold to be sacred'.[69] He recognised that he could have had fine
prospects if only he could content his restless soul in New
Orleans but therein lay the rub: he could not.

He longed for greater exoticism, for the 'Orient', and he
found the closest equivalent in the polychromic population of
the Gulf. The final spur to his leaving New Orleans – in June
1887 – was connected with a holiday he had taken three
summers previously. As early as 1883, inspired by Pierre Loti, he
determined to be a 'literary Columbus'; his wish came true the
following summer when, in the company of Elizabeth Bisland
and Marion Baker, he went on a holiday to Grande Isle, one of
the islands lying in the Gulf of Mexico, at the mouth of the
Mississippi river in the Bay of Barataria. Hearn thoroughly
enjoyed Grande Isle which was, in his words:

> An old-fashioned, drowsy, free-and-easy Creole watering-
> place in the Gulf – where there is an admirable beach,
> fishing extraordinary, and subjects innumerable for artistic
> studies – a hybrid population from all the ends of heaven,
> white, yellow, red, brown, cinnamon-colour, and tints of
> bronze and gold, Basques, Andalusians, Portuguese, Malays,
> Chinamen, etc.'[70]

There were no temptations, except the sea, in which he luxuriated, not having swum in it for fifteen years. He was an extraordinarily good swimmer who could outstrip the best of the islanders with ease. He was physically fit, having, as he wrote to Krehbiel, 'disciplined myself so well of late years, that I am no longer the puny little fellow you used to know'.[71] He found himself contrasting the pleasures of the sun and sea at Grande Isle with 'the dust and roar of New Orleans. . .the smell of ancient gutters instead of the sharp sweet scent of pure sea wind. . .'[72] He relaxed, bronzing his body in the sun and lazing in the water for hours at a time. He impressed those who met him as simple and natural, not at all anxious to show off, though the poetry and power of observation in his conversation did make an impression. He delighted in the seabirds on the beach and the alligators which could be watched in safety from the deck of the *Jon Weber*, the steamer which plied the route from New Orleans to the island.[73] Lafcadio returned in subsequent years. He kept in touch with Mrs Courtney, writing letters devoid of any striving for literary effect, which were all the more effective for that:

> The sea has become smooth again. At night it is all a blaze of fire. If you enter the water, circles of flame play around you, and when a fish passes it is like rubbing a match upon a wall. And the foam of the waves at night sparkles like tinder.[74]

If Hearn is to be believed, tree-frogs sang in his room at Krantz's hotel, part of the slave quarters in a former Creole plantation, while mud-daubers built nests above his bed and birds piped on his roof. He told Mrs Courtney about the other guests who caught his fancy. There was 'a very fine Irishman' called Conway who came with his family and he imagined that she would be tickled that one of his best friends was a priest, Father Kelly of Lake Charles, 'a little stumpy man, with a big beard, small grey eyes, and a hooked nose. He is a lively priest, – takes a drink like a man, swims like a fish, and smokes one of my pipes'.[75] The local fishermen took to him and he was all the time receiving invitations to take trips to 'queer places' along the coast, where he felt that he was absorbing literary raw material.

The only jarring note was Hearn's aversion to the presence of Jews among the guests and both to Mrs Courtney and Marion Baker he wrote some undeniably anti-Semitic letters.[76] The curious thing about these is that Hearn was a life-long admirer of the Jews – 'this phenomenal people' – an admiration which frequently surfaced in his journalism as well as private correspondence. He despised anti-Semitism as a product of envy and was a keen student of the Talmud. These views did not vary in the years when these racist letters were written: in April 1886, for example, he denounced the stereotyping of Jews in European literature as 'trash'. There is little doubt that Hearn was not innately anti-Semitic; the overwhelming burden of evidence is that he was a consistent champion of the Jews.[77] There is, therefore, no convincing explanation – there can be no excuse – for these letters except that he was indulging in an ingrained habit of pandering to the prejudices of his correspondents, though this may be unfair to the two people concerned.

In 1885, inspired by the previous summer's vacation at Grande Isle, Lafcadio decided to attempt what he dubbed his 'first serious effort at original work – a tiny volume of sketches in our Creole archipelago, at the skirts of the Gulf. I am seeking the Orient at home, among our Lascar and Chinese colonies,- and the Prehistoric in the characteristics of strange European settlers'.[78] He found his inspiration some distance west of Grande Isle where lay the remains of L'Île Dernière, a popular summer resort until its devastation by a storm on 10 August 1856. The story of the tragedy remained a vivid tradition along the coast where most had lost a friend or relative. On Lafcadio's return to New Orleans, he wrote a brief account of the storm, interlaced with poetic description of the magnificent nature of the Gulf. When published in the *Times-Democrat* it was so favourably received that he was encouraged to enlarge it into a book. Given Lafcadio's painstaking approach, progress on the book was slow. Firstly, there had to be more trips to Grande Isle to gather further material for the book, the plan of which he described as 'philosophical and pantheistic'. He was already so enamoured of the tropicality of the island and its tepid seas that he felt he would like to live there forever. It would appear from his correspondence that his heart was still set on Oriental work but he decided that fiction was the road to publishers' hearts and he would give it a try in a brief format, 'striving as much as possible after intense effects'.[79] This work did in any case have an Oriental flavour as the fishing people of Chénière Caminada, with whom he enjoyed chatting, were Malays.

By May 1887 the manuscript was with Henry Mills Alden, editor of the *Harper's Magazine* and Lafcadio was waiting anxiously to hear its fate. He was already fretting that its novelty covered 'a multitude of sins'.[80] Indeed it did. Still, despite glaring weaknesses of structure and characterisation, it proved highly successful with a Victorian audience which reacted favourably to the exoticism of the locale and characters, the sentimentality, and the set-piece descriptions of nature at its most magnificent. *Chita* was, in its author's words,

> . . .founded on the fact of a child saved from the Last Island disaster by some Louisiana fisher-folk, and brought up by them. Years after a Creole hunter recognised her, and reported her whereabouts to relatives. These, who were rich, determined to bring her up as young ladies are brought up in the South, and sent her to a convent. But she had lived the free healthy life of the coast and could not bear the convent;- she ran away from it, married a fisherman, and lives somewhere down there now – the mother of multitudinous children.[81]

Nearly twenty years later, when a storm of the magnitude described in *Chita* did, in fact, devastate Grande Isle, a female child was rescued by Manila fishermen and lived with them for some time, in much the same way as happened in *Chita*.

In addition to English, French and Spanish, Lafcadio demonstrated his mastery of Creole in *Chita*. Elizabeth Bisland noted that while his laborious study of the tongue spoken only by and to the negro servants in Louisiana may have seemed 'a work of supererogation' at the time, it was invaluable to him later in the West Indies where the patois had held its own alongside the French of the educated Creoles.[82] Without it, he could not have communicated with the common people, a communication so essential to his book of that period, *Two Years in the French West Indies*. Of more immediate importance was the fact that the success of *Chita* enabled him to realise his dream of penetrating further into the tropics and, in 1887, with a 'vague commission' from Harper,[83] he left New Orleans for the Windward Islands. The nature of the commission would later be a subject of dispute but certainly the $350 he was paid for the serial rights of his novel by *Harper's Magazine* in the spring of 1887 helped to make the trip feasible. He was thinking in terms of a short break at this time and imagined he would return to New Orleans: 'To make my home in the West Indies would be for me like making my home in Paradise: but I doubt if circumstances will ever enable me to make a permanent residence there, unless I should choose to see a situation as tutor or schoolmaster.'[84]

When he was unhappy in Yokohama, shortly after his arrival in Japan in the spring of 1890, he wrote to Joseph Harper that three years earlier he had abandoned a well-paid position and undertaken the literary work which resulted in *Two Years in the French West Indies* on the verbal advice of Mr Alden. Alden had convinced him, he claimed, that he could live by literary work alone, the first choice of which was to be given to Harper. He had had such unbounded faith in the editor that he had left his library behind and burned his boats behind him.[85]

Whatever the exact nature of the verbal dealings between Hearn and Alden, they took place after Lafcadio had left New Orleans as he met Alden for the first time in New York in late June 1887. Prior to the meeting, he had formed a high opinion of the editor; he wrote to Coleman on 4 March 1887: 'I owe him much. He first opened my eyes to the necessity of dealing with vital modern themes. He will have made me, to a certain extent, if I ever achieve success; and what he tells you about yourself, you should certainly believe.'[86] The evening he spent at Alden's home on 26 June 1887 confirmed these impressions. Everything was delightful; Alden made a most favourable impression and his daughter, Miss Annie, who became a correspondent of Hearn's, made him feel at ease.[87] Hearn and Alden did have much in common, both having overcome early obstacles − Alden had been a bobbin-boy in a cotton factory at the age of seven − to achieve positions of intellectual prominence. Alden was editor of *Harper's Magazine* from 1869 until his death in 1919.[88]

On the way to New York, Hearn called to see Henry Watkin in Cincinnati. 'Dear Old Dad' jumped and shouted for joy when his former protegé appeared and then cried as if his heart was breaking. Krehbiel met him at the depot in New York on his arrival in the first week in June 1887 and took him to his house on West 57th Street. Lafcadio was impressed by the 'beautiful home. . .dearest sweetest little wife and baby girl. . .'[89] Mrs Krehbiel made him feel comfortable. Lafcadio was fine tuning the style of *Chita* and consulted his friend, now music critic of the New York *Tribune*, about its musical allusions. Krehbiel was impressed by Hearn's endless polishing and re-polishing of his style. He would ask about the possible effect of the change of a word in a sentence which Krehbiel already thought as close to perfection as could be achieved, revealing 'a genius of patience like Beethoven'.[90] But Mrs Krehbiel was less impressed and the month Hearn spent in her home was not a success. She was frightened by the 'wild' abuse of his enemies and his non-respectable opinions. He smoked in bed and burned holes in the best sheets. Only her young daughter was happy with Hearn; with her he was gentle and held her entranced for hours at a time with tales of Greek heroes and Creole folklore.[91] It was not surprising that when Lafcadio returned to New York a few months later he found he could not make contact with the music critic of the *Tribune*.[92]

CHAPTER FIVE

TWO YEARS IN THE FRENCH WEST INDIES

ON 27 JUNE 1887, his thirty-seventh birthday, Lafcadio wrote to Coleman that he was about to sail for Trinidad and Demerara on board the steamer, *Barracouta*.[1] In June of the following year, he summarised his first experience of the West Indies:

> I went to Demerara and visited the lesser West Indies in July and August of last year – returned to New York after three months with some MS. – sold it – felt very unhappy at the idea of staying in New York, where I had good offers – suddenly made up my mind to go back to the tropics by the very same steamer that had brought me. I had no commission, resolved to trust to magazine-work.[2]

The manuscript in question was 'A Midsummer Trip to the Tropics', which was acquired by Alden for *Harper's Magazine*. It was published in 1890 as part of *Two Years in the French West Indies*, of which it formed nearly a quarter. The article was based on notes taken on a voyage of 3000 miles, lasting less than two months. The writing has a staccato, telegraphic quality of impressions jotted down in a notebook with, in his own words, 'sundry justifiable departures from simple note-making'.[3] While it lacks the smoothness of his best Japanese writing, there is at the same time a reaching towards the simplicity which characterised that later work.

Blended into a chronological account of his rapid progress from island to island through the tropics are the twin themes of the beauty and horror of tropical nature. The approach of another ship at sunset becomes a supernatural occurrence: the ship seems to be a phantom with rigging like something from a dream and 'cuts a cross upon the face of the moon'. There is 'spectral splendour', 'weird magnificence' and the sun, 'a monstrous disk', is inverted with connotation of blood as it 'crimsons'.[4] An element of eroticism occasionally intruded:

> In all these soft sleepy swayings, these caresses of wind and sobbings of waters, Nature seems to confess some passional mood. Passengers converse of pleasant tempting things,- tropical fruits, tropical beverages, tropical mountain-breezes, tropical women. . .It is time for dreams – those day-dreams that come gently as a mist, with ghostly realisation of hopes, desires, ambitions. . .

Lafcadio's sly humour compared the whispering of the sea to 'sounds as of articulate speech under the breath,- as of women telling secrets. . .'[5] The hints of his childhood, which had always been present in his American journalism, made an appearance; the blue-black of the sea is the colour 'that bewitches in certain Celtic eyes'.[6]

The man who allegedly drank blood in a Cincinnati slaughter-house liked to drop the fact that he had eaten worms in the West Indies; he told his readers casually that they tasted like fried almonds when cooked alive. Insect horror was a theme developed at length in his Japanese work. A related horror, that of the snake, gave Hearn the opportunity to convey at length his vision of the interdependence of life and death in tropical nature.[7] The description of the effect of a bite by a fer-de-lance, one of the deadliest serpents in the world, should make anyone heed his warnings not to stroll unguided in the forest:

> Necroses of the tissues is likely to set in: the flesh corrupts, falls from the bones sometimes in tatters; and the colors of its putrefaction simulate the hues of vegetable decay,- the ghastly grays and pinks and yellows of trunks rotting down into the dark soil which gave them birth. The human victim moulders as the trees moulder, crumbles and dissolves as crumbles the substance of the dead palms and balatas: the Death-of-the-Woods is upon him.[8]

The, literally, blow-by-blow account of the killing of the fer-de-lance by a cat which follows is almost light relief by contrast.

Even as he studied the physical beauty of the West Indian people, horror turned over in his mind. The sweet, baby Indian girl he imagines growing up into a beautiful woman with witchcraft in her eyes, and a smile with the power of life and death; jealousy would lead to a 'swirling flash of a cutlass blade; and a shrieking gathering of women about a headless corpse in the sun; and passing cityward, between armed and helmeted men, the vision of an Indian prisoner, blood-crimsoned, walking very steadily, very erect, with the solemnity of a judge, the dry bright gaze of an idol. . .'[9]

Despite the *leitmotif* of horror running through the 'Midsummer Trip', this short exposure to the tropics was long enough for their magic to take hold of Hearn. He had dreamt of them for years and a long letter to Elizabeth Bisland from Georgetown, Demerara, on 16 July 1887 showed that New Orleans now seemed not only dull by comparison but 'dead' and 'rotting'. St Pierre, Martinique, on the other hand, where he was to live for the next two months, he claimed to love as if it were a human being. He believed that he would do something novel with this most colourful of material but he was not yet sure what: the violence of the experiences had produced artistic indigestion. One memory that stayed with him for the rest of his life was the vivid blue of the tropical seas, 'a flaming azure that looked as if a million summer skies had been condensed into pure fluid color for the making of it'.[10]

Lafcadio returned to New York in September 1887. Relations with Krehbiel having cooled, he stayed at the United States Hotel, in a frenzy of preparation for his return to the tropics. Another visit to Alden helped to cement an increasingly confident relationship and, by paying $700 for the 'Midsummer Trip', Harper provided the wherewithal once again for his travels, even if he did immediately dissipate some of it on an expensive camera which his poor eyesight precluded ever being useful. A note to his old New Orleans friend, Matas, written on 29 September 1887, conveyed the mood of excited expectation as he prepared to set off again:

> I am going back to the tropics, – probably for many years. My venture has been more successful that I ever hoped; and I find myself able to abandon journalism, with all its pettinesses, cowardices, and selfishnesses, forever. I am able hereafter to devote myself to what you always said was my forte: the study of tropical Nature – God's Nature, – violent, splendid, nude, and pure. I never hoped for such

fortune. It has come unasked. I am almost afraid to think it's true. I am afraid to be happy!'[11]

A few days later, on 2 October 1887, he sailed again on the *Barracouta*. The tone of a letter of thanks written to the Captain as he prepared to disembark at St Pierre, Martinique, nine days later, indicated that Lafcadio's spirit of high good humour lasted the entire voyage.[12] He did not travel very far to settle down; he found lodgings within sight of the harbour and quickly adapted to the native life-style.[13] It was not long, however, before the initial 'enchantment' wore off and he started to find the dullness of colonial life 'indescribable and pitiable'.[14] The ladies did nothing but sit in dim rooms reading works of piety. They sent these to Hearn to read; he pretended to do so but found them insufferable. There were few whites and he heard English only when his friend, the New Orleans Creole, Testart, came to see him. He had learned enough Creole to get along but not perhaps enough to be completely at ease in it. He felt himself exiled and got 'tired of the eternal palms against the light, tired of the colors, tired of the shrieking tongue spoken around you, tired of hearing by night the mandibles of the great tropical insects devouring the few English books upon the table'.[15]

Still, he was sufficiently enchanted by Martinique for his original intention of staying a few months to stretch to two years. Nature in Martinique gripped his imagination but he found he had to stay indoors because of the heat, storms and snakes: 'A paradise this is – but a paradise of fire'.[16] His Irish genes simply could not take the climate. Another disillusionment was more predictable. How anyone with Lafcadio's ocular deficiencies could have imagined himself a successful photographer is a matter of no little pathos. There was indeed a pathetic element in the letters he wrote to Annie and her father describing his efforts. To Alden senior he confessed that the photographs taken to date were not good, and that he had been unable to master the instrument; views of palm trees were, for example, ruined by the heads being cut off![17] To Annie Alden he also admitted that he was not a success in this medium but blamed the camera – 'a fraud'.[18]

He encountered fraud of a different kind when he attempted to photograph the local canoe boys, *canotiers*, and induced 17 of them to cooperate with a promise of 10 cents each as a reward.

When the time came to pay, every boy in the neighbourhood joined in and it seemed that he had hundreds to pay off. He put the seventeen in a line, surrounded by a mob, and began paying down the line. As soon as one was paid, he ran to the other end of the line and became part of a circular process. Hearn ran but was pursued by the mob. He took refuge in a photographer's building which the mob attacked and the police had to be called to extricate him. That was the end of his career as a photographer and Lafcadio hired professionals for his later work.[19]

Hearn had, in any case, shifted his focus from reportage to original work within a month of arriving in Martinique for the second time. *Lys* was another attempt at imaginative fiction, dealing with the exposure of a tropical Creole girl to the cold North. It presented an opportunity to develop the North/South contrast which had occupied him mind over many years:

> . . .- grey sky of Odin,- bitter thy winds and spectral all thy colors! – they that dwell beneath thee know not the glory of Eternal Summer's green,- the azure splendor of southern day! – but thine are the lightnings of Thought illuminating for human eyes the interspaces between sun and sun. Thine the generations of might,- the strivers, the battlers,- the men who make Nature tame! – thine the domain of inspiration and achievement,- the larger heroisms, the vaster labors that endure, the higher knowledge, and all the witchcrafts of science!. . .[20]

In early December, the story was dispatched to Alden; the circumstances which had driven Lafcadio to what was for him phenomenally rapid work also dictated early payment. His ego took a severe beating when Alden rejected *Lys* in a manner which pulled no punches. The editor wondered if he had been too blunt but a chastened Hearn reassured him: 'Your letter was not at all harsh;- too kind, perhaps; and, as in most cases, opened my eyes. I saw at once the faults, and judged them probably as severely – no, more severely than you.' He berated himself for having attempted something outside his compass at a time when his health was not up to it; in future he would confine himself to short sketches.[21] He was so depressed that he wrote another letter to Alden telling him to destroy the manuscript but did not send it, remembering the editor's comment that it contained some material of value.[22] Eventually, he rewrote the story as plain, factual observation and it formed the final section of *Two Years in the French West Indies.*

Notwithstanding his meek acceptance of Alden's dismissal of *Lys*, Hearn did point out that his means were completely exhausted. He would stay on if he could earn his way; otherwise he would go elsewhere – Honduras, maybe. He asked Alden to examine the sketches soon and, if interested, send money by return steamer.[23] The differing perceptions of the nature of the trip, later to be the subject of much bitterness, are here plainly revealed. Alden thought he was sending a professional journalist, capable of work of literary merit, on a quick mission of a few months. Articles tailored to the magazine and suitable for collection as a book, were to follow quickly. Instead, he found that he had on his hands a painstaking artist who stayed two years and little of whose work was suitable for his periodical. Hearn's library, another divisive issue of the future, was also touched on in the letter. Hearn had left it in the care of Matas and he asked Alden to arrange for its transfer to his own keeping. As the library comprised over two thousand volumes, many of them weighty tomes, this was no small request but Alden complied. In return, he asked that Hearn send him a document which would give him claim to the books 'in extreme circumstances'.[24]

Hearn did not write to Alden from February to mid-April 1888 as he was seriously ill with fever. A recuperative spell in the mountains seems to have worked as he wrote again on 26 May that he was in 'splendid health'; the epidemic had now ceased in St Pierre though it was still raging on the other side of the island. He enclosed 'Les Blanchisseuses' which he thought would appeal to Alden;[25] it did not, however, appear in *Harper's Magazine*. His recuperation was buoyed by the publication of *Chita* in the April 1888 issue of the magazine. He wrote excitedly to Matas that it had been a great literary success, which he decided was determined, not by the press or the first impact on the public, but by the opinions of literary figures and these had been much more positive than anticipated.[26] The portents must have looked good for realising his dream of living by magazine work when 'A Midsummer Trip to the Tropics' followed in the July and August issues. In June 1888 he wrote to Gould that these would be followed in turn by brief West Indian sketches; those not suited to the magazine would be printed as a book.[27] However, apart from 'La Verette' the following October, *Harper's Magazine* published nothing further until 'Les Porteuses' appeared in July 1889. Indeed, when the contract for *Two Years in the French West Indies* was signed in October 1889, only four of the fourteen pieces which comprised it had been published in the magazine.[28]

While the success of *Chita* boosted Lafcadio's confidence, a long silence from Alden worried him deeply. By July he could endure it no longer and wrote irritably that he had not heard from his editor since February; he did not even know if his manuscripts had been received but he had earned only a hundred dollars in ten months. The theme of his poverty and difficult situation generally was developed at great length. He pleaded for help, to be given anything, even a job of translating, to allow him to work his way out of his predicament. He added a bitter postscript on the fruits of literary success: *Some Chinese Ghosts* had been critically acclaimed but the publisher could not sell 800 copies.[29]

Alden replied quickly. He had been busy with his own 'creative work', besides which not all the material submitted by Hearn had been suitable. Hearn responded with a gushing *mea culpa*, blaming the tropics for unnaturally inflaming his imagination and promising never to submit another 'extravagant paper', nothing along the lines of the 'absurdity' of *Lys*. He still seemed, however, to be under the impression that Alden would use his current West Indian work; he wrote confidently and made blithe demands of work which was never to be published in the magazine.[30] Lafcadio was prepared to eat humble pie and confess that Alden had made him see the faults in his work but he had difficulty suppressing his rage at the form the articles took when they did appear in the magazine. On 5 September 1888 he broached the subject diplomatically with Alden, expressing his worry at not being able to see the proofs and explaining that to him proofreading meant more than a rewriting: '. . .it is the finish, the polish, the correction of all the faults that cannot be judged in MS – MS is colorless, and vague. Print is positive and critical by itself'.[31]

Possibly in response to this letter, Alden sent 250 francs with the advice that Hearn return to New York. Lafcadio made it clear that returning to the United States would be difficult; the 250 francs would not suffice because of his obligations. He expressed disappointment with his work as it had appeared in

Harper's Magazine with thinly-veiled irony, given his real feelings on the subject: 'There is something wrong about it,- something that bewilders one. I have either lost some faculty, or am acquiring some new one, and I trust it will be the latter possibility which is to materialize.'[32] The poor quality of his published work continued to irk him and, in October 1888, he complained to Gould that it had been condensed and recondensed until it lost all originality.[33]

Finally, the dam burst and Hearn penned a direct statement of his feelings to the editor:

> I feel I cannot any longer endure the pain of seeing myself in print as somebody else. The whole 'style' of the composing room,- the changes,- the changes by omission and punctuation and reparagraphing and condensation,- destitutes [?] me of all personality – to an extent that discourages me utterly. No kindness and no money could help me to bear the torture of it. Assurance of personality is the one necessary stimulus to the duty of every true artistic striver. . .Take it away from him, and you kill him!
>
> Those papers – excepting *Chita*, – have not been me: they have scarcely been a suggestion.
>
> . . .[It] is like a block [?] of material only, to be hewn to fit an orifice! Illustrations that contradict the text; text abbreviated and made colorless. . .and the waiting of a long year to see this! And I have been working so hard to please you, and to please myself by polishing and coaxing into life another story!

He asked to be released from the obligation to give Alden first choice of his work, so that it might be published properly, whatever the financial implications.[34] The quarrel was somehow patched up but his feelings towards his publishers had irrevocably changed. He was still in a bind regarding publication and, therefore, income, pledged to an exclusive arrangement with a publisher who would not publish the bulk of his work and who delayed considerably anything which was published.

Notwithstanding this temporary, if pressing, problem, the West Indies did provide Hearn with the material for a significant work which was the prototype for his Japanese books. It was a miscellany, with even the individual chapters forming only a loose framework within which the author mixed observation, philosophy, autobiography, horror, story-telling and character sketches, with political, social and religious analysis. *Two Years in the French West Indies* was dedicated to Leopold Arnoux, a notary at St Pierre who had become a close friend. Much as Lafcadio might proclaim his preference for simple people, his friends in Martinique were, as elsewhere, of the educated and social elite. Arnoux he described as 'one of the aristocrats in this little world' as well 'a friend,- a rare friend, who lent me money to prevent my effects being seized, when no one else would credit me even for a cigar. . .'[35] Another member of the Creole elite who was of great help to Hearn was Doctor J.J.J. Cornilliac, a gentleman of the old regime whose magnificent collection of scholarly works was placed at his disposal. Testart, the New Orleans Creole who had settled in Martinique, was another educated friend with whom he could enjoy some intellectual stimulus.

The impact of the book came from stimulus of a different kind: in 'La Vérette', the coincidence of the smallpox plague with the Carnival was classic Hearn raw material, allowing the contrast of the colourful festival's wild celebration with the grim horror of the pestilence's devastation. There was, for example, young Pascaline Z-, one of the prettiest of the shop girls of Grande Rue, with a face never to be forgotten; but when the plague had done its work, even before the quick lime was poured on it, no features could be discerned, 'only a dark brown mass, like a fungus, too frightful to think about'.[36] Woven into this pantomime of colour and dreadfulness is a typically Hearnian tale of a mother being carried away by the plague, leaving her children orphaned; they were then cared for by a neighbour, leaving Lafcadio to marvel at the inherent goodness of this coloured population and made him doubt – for a moment anyway – the accepted theories of the natural egotism of mankind.

His attitude to the indigenous population was, however, strictly paternal. Hearn's reaction to meeting a member of the small white ruling element in predominantly black Trinidad – feeling 'the dignity of a white skin'[37] – is disconcerting to the modern reader. His views on the racial question in the West Indies were similar to those he had evolved in the southern United States, and were equally wrong. While, however, he imagined that the black race would die out in America, he believed that it would continue to expand in the West Indies, squeezing out the Indian population in the process. The emancipation of the slaves would in the future lead to 'universal blackness. . .perhaps to universal savagery'. This would be nature's retribution for the sins of past colonialism, 'for all the crimes and follies of three hundred years.'[38]

One theme which ran throughout the book was his admiration for the women of the island.[39] Indeed, the 'vigorous, graceful, healthy' bodies of the natives were naturally of interest to Hearn, with his predilection for the fit and muscular. At a tanning-yard where he was studying the workers' fine physiology, his attention was caught by a young mulatto with a faun's face wearing nothing but a cloth around his loins, displaying the most beautiful muscular development Lafcadio had ever seen. Children bathing were described with a blithe unawareness of homosexual innuendo:

> Young boys – yellow and brown little fellows – run in naked, and swim out to pointed rocks that jut up black above the bright water. They climb up one at a time to dive down. Poised for the leap upon the black lava crag, and against the blue light of the sky, each lithe figure, gilded by the morning sun, has a statuesqueness and a luminosity impossible to paint in words. These bodies seem to radiate color; and the azure light intensifies the hue: it is idyllic, incredible;- Coomans used paler colors in his Pompeiian studies, and his figures were never so symmetrical.[40]

The generally jaundiced view of the Martinique male is epitomised in 'Ye', Hearn's portrait of the typical 'mountain negro of the lazy kind' who is depicted as unable to adjust to emancipation from slavery. The nineteenth century, ironically given the epithet, 'enlightened', had abolished the old patriarchal power which had kept him 'strong and healthy on scanty fare' and scourged him 'into its own idea of righteousness'. Now he was free, as a citizen of the Republic, to vote, to work or to starve, to do evil and suffer for it; the only *Bon-Dié* he had ever had, the old Creole master, could not care for him now and he could not care for himself.[41]

The evils of 'French Radicalism' were elaborated even more in 'Un Reverant', in which the surprising object of Lafcadio's sympathy is the Roman Catholic Church. It had, he felt, been 'ungenerously' treated after the overthrow of the old colonial order. He was even favourably disposed towards the unaesthetic wayside shrines:

Yet there is a veiled poetry in these silent populations of plaster and wood and stone. They represent something older than the Middle Ages, older than Christianity, – something strangely distorted and transformed, it is true, but recognizably conserved by the Latin race from those antique years when every home had its beloved ghosts, when every wood or hill or spring had its gracious divinity, and the boundaries of all the fields were marked and guarded by statues of the gods.[42]

His imagination was gripped by Jean-Baptiste Labat, a Dominican who spent twelve years in Martinique, from 1693, whom Hearn concluded was one of the most extraordinary men of his time.[43] 'Un Reverant' ends with a long, lyrical reverie in which Hearn dreams of meeting Labat's ghost, returning to Martinique to find all his achievements negated. The Roman Catholic Church is seen as a creative and beneficial influence – the trees felled by the priest had been sawn 'in their primitive and inviolable beauty as if fresh from the Creator's touch in the morning of the world'; those being felled by Lafcadio's contemporaries were 'secular' and were pulled to the sea on a device known as a 'devil'.[44] This is not to say that Hearn regarded himself as a Catholic in any sense: there was a humorous dialogue with his *bonne* (housekeeper) in which she accuses him of being a Protestant because he tells her that the sky is only an appearance and he replies that he is neither a Catholic nor a Protestant.[45]

There was much in *Two Years in the French West Indies* which anticipated important elements of Hearn's Japanese work. The appreciation of Labat was paralleled by admiration of what the Jesuits had achieved in Japan. His description of climbing La Pelée, the highest peak in Martinique, could be contrasted directly with that of the ascent of Mount Fuji in *Exotics and Retrospectives*. Indeed, in 'La Pelée', he used the analogy of 'the landscape colors of a Japanese fan'[46] and wondered if a Creole artist could imitate Hokusai's 'Hundred Views of Fugisama' [sic].[47] The classification and enumeration in almost obsessively pedantic detail of, for example, the 400 mountains of Martinique or the designs and laws of colour contrasts of native costumes, foreshadowed a similar tendency in Japan.[48] He regretted the adoption of Western dress in Martinique as much as in Japan. Insects attracted his attention and his analysis of the 'true horror' of the centipede being 'due to the monstrosity of its movement' was similar to the theory of gothic horror resulting from 'monstrous movement' which he elaborated in Japan.[49] The story of a man lured to his death by a goblin who took the form of a beautiful woman in 'La Guiablesse' was precisely the kind of tale which found its way into the later Japanese books.[50]

There was, however, a fundamental difference of approach in the two periods. Whereas Hearn treated Japanese culture with respect, he was still the superior Western observer in Martinique. The belief in zombies, he allowed, possessed charm 'even for the civilized'[51] but local jewellery was 'semi-barbaric' and the food 'barbarous'.[52] He wrote of 'the apish grossness of African coast types'[53] and how, in Martinique, the Africans preferred their own 'ghastly beliefs' to Christianity.[54] The adjectives describing even the negro women he admired – 'artless', 'primitive', 'savage', 'serpentine' – were similarly pejorative.[55] His views on the abolition of slavery, already outlined, were reactionary even by the standards of the time.

The book was well received by his contemporaries. *The New York Times* said that there was no other writer who could have immersed himself 'in this languorous Creole life and tell so well about it. Trollope and Froude give you the hard, gritty facts, and Lafcadio Hearn the sentiment and poetry of this beautiful island'.[56] The New York *Herald* found that he

> . . at once takes every one with him into the true and natural atmosphere of the islands, introduces the inhabitants, describes their customs, looks backward a century or two, and soon has his reader entirely out of the world, and unwilling to return to the prosaic details of northern latitudes and work-a-day life.[57]

Equally complimentary was the New York *Sun*, which was to be vituperative about the author after his death. Now it found that *Two Years in the French West Indies* was the finest travel book in years. The reviews outside New York were no less enthusiastic. The *Boston Traveller* felt that it had to 'be reckoned among the most charming books of the year, and will take a deservedly high place in the field of literature of description and travel'. The *Chicago News* awarded it the accolade of being the most 'brilliant descriptive work. . .contributed to English literature in the last quarter of a century'.[58] Even Edward

Thomas, writing in 1912, modified the astringent view he had held of Hearn's work up to that point and declared that Lafcadio's descriptive skill had found a perfect outlet in *Two Years in the French West Indies*.[59]

The racial attitudes so much in evidence in *Two Years in the French West Indies* also underlay the story of *Youma*, a novelette which was written in Martinique at this time. It is the story of a poor nurse (Da) who is left with the responsibility for a rich Creole child. She risks her life to save the child from a snake, refuses to go with her lover for the sake of her charge and finally gives her life rather than abandon it in the course of the negro revolt. The willingness of the negroes to burn both alive was in line with the racial views expressed in *Two Years in the French West Indies*. Hearn maintained that the story was substantially true. The ruins of the old house where the denouement of the story took place were still to be seen in St Pierre. The girl had really died under the heroic circumstances described, refusing the help of the blacks. He might, he conceded, have idealised her, but not her act. An incident of a serpent had happened also but the heroine was a different person – in reality a plantation girl celebrated by the historian, Rufz de Lavison.[60]

Hearn described it to Alden as:

'. . .less fantastic than *Chita*, less psychological; but the facts, which are real have intrinsic color and strangeness enough to give it equal originality in other respects – and I think it ought to appeal to a larger audience. It is a tale of the negro-revolt of '48. If you are pleased, try to get me a good price for it.'

This Alden most assuredly did as the sum of $2000 which was paid for publication in the magazine was very substantial by the standards of the day.[61] It was actually written under wretched conditions in Martinique, near the scene described and under the cross with the black Christ which featured in it.

Into this tropical tale, Lafcadio managed to insert a flashback to his own childhood, in the form of his only memory of his mother. Youma, the heroine, has a fantasy of her mother:

Then she became aware of a face,- the face of a beautiful brown woman looking at her with black soft eyes. . .and lighted by a light that came from nowhere,- that was only a memory of some long-dead morning. . .They two were

walking somewhere she had been long ago. . .she felt the
guiding of her mother's hand as when a child. . .And. . .
there loomed again the vision of the English island. . .[62]

A similar image of his mother had featured in *Chita*. The child
is told her mother is dead yet she dreams of her at night and does
not believe she could have passed away 'since the sweet presence
came to her in dreams, bending and smiling over her, caressing
her, speaking to her,- sometimes gently chiding, but always
chiding with a kiss'.[63]

Youma was Hearn's last major work of fiction. It is generally
considered superior to *Chita* but it shares the same faults:
weakness of structure, imaginative inadequacy and a cloying
sentimentality at the heart of his romanticism. Indeed, it was the
last expression of this romanticism and the self-consciously
literary creations he had struggled over so laboriously since his
arrival in New Orleans. In *Two Years in the French West Indies* and
his Japanese work he returned to the skills he had learned in the
despised craft of journalism and created more enduring art.

In April 1889, Lafcadio's decided that it was time to take a
break from the tropics and return to the United States. On board
ship he fell into 'that sympathetic mood which the natural
emotion of leaving places and persons one has become fond of, is
apt to inspire'.[64] Now that he was going he seemed to
understand as never before the beauty of tropical nature, and
the simple charm of its life. Prophetically, he held in his hand a
Japanese paper fan with only a bamboo depicted on it:

> Trivial to my Northern friends this design might seem; but
> to me it causes a pleasure bordering on pain. . .I know so
> well what the artist means; and they could not know, unless
> they had seen bamboos. . .Beyond a doubt, the artist who
> dashed the design of this fan with his miraculous brush must
> have had a nearly similar experience. . .[65]

★   ★   ★

When he arrived in back in New York he had difficulty finding a
place in which to stay. He went first to Philadelphia, to George
Gould, with what were to prove fateful results. The tangled
relationship with Gould went back to New Orleans and the
West Indies. In Martinique, in particular, Hearn had been
afflicted by loneliness and it was little wonder that when George

M. Gould appeared to offer sympathetic understanding, he eagerly embraced it. The ensuing friendship became one of the most controversial in the history of literature.

Gould was 39, two years older than Hearn, when they first made contact in the spring of 1887. A graduate of Ohio Wesleyan University, Harvard Divinity School and Jefferson Medical College, Gould was attempting to combine a literary with a medical career and published widely in both fields. Impressed by Lafcadio's writings, the older man had letters forwarded and a friendship developed. Its pattern was established in the very early exchanges. In April 1887, before he had left New Orleans, in what appears to be a reply to the first overture of Gould's, Hearn expressed gratitude for the 'literary encouragement from an evidently strong source' and defined the aim of the author as 'touching that kindred something in another which the Christian calls Soul – the Pantheist, God – the philosopher, the Unknowable'. He felt that much of what Gould had said regarding the 'aesthetic symbolism of color' had been intuitively expressed in *Chita*, especially regarding the sacred importance of the colour blue.[66]

Gould had sent a pamphlet on the 'colour-sense' which Lafcadio had reviewed favourably in the *Times-Democrat* of 8 May 1887, relating it to the philosophy of Herbert Spencer.[67] Privately he expressed admiration of Gould's 'remarkable mind'. With typical modesty, he declared that he felt 'very small' when he compared his work with Gould's.[68] There were references to Gould's ambition to write a 'medical novel'[69] and subjects such as epics, on which Lafcadio could adopt an authoritative tone.[70] Perhaps because he was dealing with a doctor, there was a strong confessional thread running through Hearn's letters, admitting to such conditions as demophobia and 'a badly balanced nervous make-up'.[71] He would later have reason to regret this candour. When *Chita* was published at last in the magazine in April 1888, it resulted in Lafcadio receiving several appreciative letters from fellow authors. There was one from Gould which Lafcadio believed recognised 'what persons outside of literary circles very seldom think of, the cost of nervous energy involved. . .'[72] Indeed, Hearn was so impressed with this new source of friendship that he attempted to further Gould's literary career and sent some of his scientific work to Alden in the hope of getting it published.

Still, the basic temperamental disaccord which later divided the men so bitterly is evident in retrospect. When Gould sent a photograph of himself in August 1888 the revelation of personality in it made Hearn 'half afraid' of him.[73] Gould also crossed the invisible borderline at which friends incurred Lafcadio's displeasure with his literary advice. His suggestion that Hearn produce pot-boilers until he could gain more literary success and command higher prices was as close as anyone could come to mortal insult. The manner in which Lafcadio dismissed Gould's plot for a medical novel was a clear sign of irritation. Gould, with his reforming Christian zeal, sent a negative essay on Loti's sensuousness, no doubt to wean Lafcadio from his adherence to the French Romantic school, a particular *bête noire* of the doctor's. Hearn responded that such sensuousness seemed to him a 'splendid augury of the higher sensitiveness to come, in some future age of poets and writers'.[74]

When Hearn decided that he needed to get away from the tropical heat for a while and go to the United States 'to seek some vitality' he was without a place to stay there. He needed time and a place to shape his West Indian material for publication. A few years later he realised that he had been unable to finish the task until he saw 'the magical island again through regret, as though a summer haze', in circumstances removed from the soporific air of the West Indies.[75]

The home of George Gould seemed just the place. Two years previously, Gould had suggested that Lafcadio visit him in Philadelphia.[76] The itinerant writer now decided to avail himself of the offer and wrote a fateful letter virtually inviting himself to enjoy the doctor's hospitality.[77] Whether he was positively encouraged at this point we shall never know but he was obviously not discouraged and it was to Philadelphia that he went, when, pausing only briefly in New York on his return from the West Indies in May 1889, he had travelled on there. Hearn later claimed that his host had 'begged and prayed' him to spend the summer there and told him that even the mention of money would be considered an insult.[78]

J.M. Redway, a geographer who, according to Gould, was also a member of the household during Hearn's stay, disputed this claim; by his account, Hearn went to Philadelphia, was invited to visit the Goulds and accepted. When it transpired that he was without funds, he was allowed to remain for the summer.[79] This account has the air of polite unreality about it and runs counter to the tone of the previous correspondence between the two men. Besides, it is hard to accept that Redway really was a guest at Gould's home throughout the summer without having been once mentioned, even in passing, in Hearn's considerable correspondence from there. A far more plausible account came from Gould himself, written before the publication of Hearn's letters embittered him against his former friend; it was that once Lafcadio arrived at Gould's house it was agreed that he was free to stay indefinitely.[80]

Initially, things seem to have gone well. Hearn wrote to Elizabeth Bisland that his environment was so pleasant that he was sure of doing better work than was possible in New York, 'that frightful cyclone of electricity and machinery'.[81] To Alden he was similarly positive but there was a note of foreboding: 'The sensation is too pleasant to last, and like all other flashes of happiness gives me the idea I am having too good a time, and ought to sacrifice something to the gods.'[82] In view of Lafcadio's extraordinary sensitivity, Gould must have been making him feel very much at home to inspire such agreeable impressions. At the same time, Hearn did see that his situation in Philadelphia could not continue indefinitely and, by the end of June, was asking Alden to get him a job in New York: independence was necessary to the self-confidence upon which his work depended.[83]

He discovered that his host was occupied with 'writing a curious essay on Civilization and Vision,- a sort of Philosophy of Spectacles, – showing the effects of the reading habit and of industrial occupations of particular kinds upon the sight-sense of civilized man'.[84] Lafcadio suggested sending it to Alden, little suspecting that Gould was elaborating a theory relating eyesight to genius which would form part of a posthumous indictment of himself. Gould had other theories, one being that there was a tendency of the son to repeat his father's experiences at the same age. On this basis, he encouraged Lafcadio to visit the Greek islands, though to no avail.[85]

The zenith of Lafcadio's friendship with Gould seems to have been reached in the mid-summer of 1889, when he may, for a brief interval, have fallen under the doctor's spell. He told Alden that his friend had taught him enough to awaken him in an ethical way though he imagined that it would be several years before it percolated through to his work: 'How wonderfully a strong well-trained mind can expand a feebler and undisciplined one, when the teacher has pleasure and time to teach!' He believed he was 'growing' and sent the publisher extracts from one of Gould's pamphlets, supposedly characteristic of his 'strangely powerful and earnest' style.[86]

For once, the tables were turned and it was Hearn who was attempting to persuade the other man to write fiction, believing that Gould had the capacity to 'do something very beautiful' in that medium.[87] Hearn was sufficiently impressed that, unusually, he allowed himself to be influenced in what he wrote. Gould defined his aim as making Hearn choose a modern subject and treat it objectively, 'hoping that his exquisite literary art might overcome the obstinacy of his material, and bring him perhaps a cruder but a more needed and better recompensing audience'. He came to regard his efforts as 'a sorry blunder'.[88] The result was *Karma* and a fragment in Hearn's hand leaves no doubt about the extent of Gould's influence on it:

> I have followed out your thought through nearly everything. . .You have made the story: your beefsteaks and coffee and muffins made the thoughts of it; your bed gave me recuperation from the labour of it; and the spiritual sum you forced into me – despite much wreathing of tentacles – is its soul.[89]

Essentially, the story of an idealised woman forgiving a suitor whom she prevails upon to reveal that he had fathered a child by the wife of a friend, *Karma* suffered from the same sentimentality which marred Hearn's other attempts at fiction. Hearn defined its theme as sin resulting from failure to meet the duty of fatherhood: 'The moral enigma, complex in all its knottings, could only be severed by truth – at its touch the evil falls asunder.' The girl he conceived as 'one with ancestral puritan love of truth and right intensely alive in every fibre of her being – stern, but having cruelty only for righteousness'.[90] Both the character of the girl, and the notion of being spiritually re-born through facing up to past sins, reflected Gould's determination to morally reform Hearn. It is possible too, though that the resolution of the story – the black-eyed boy is claimed by his father and the puritanical lady character agrees to love both of them – represents a recurrence of the fantasy of being reclaimed by his father and Alicia Goslin.

Gould's influence did not last. While he was trying to wean his guest from Herbert Spencer's evolutionary philosophy and French Romanticism as part of his effort to give him a 'soul', Hearn started to send a series of weird, highly ironic letters to Gould, sending up his religiosity. One, written after the initial, improbable, influence of his host has worn off, was cast in a pseudo-Old Testament style:

> I have thy letter, O thou of enormous working capacity. . .for God (whose will be exalted!) hath numbered thee among those who find felicity in exceeding activity. Thou art indeed forty-one years old, by reckoning of time; but as thou art of the Giants this reckoning hath no significance for thee. Verily thou art but twenty-five years old. . .this soul of mine is slowly evaporating. . .The memory of Schopenhauer hath passed – and with its passing I find my only salvation in a return to the study of the Oceanic Majesty and Power and Greatness and Holiness and Omniscience of the mind of Herbert Spencer.[91]

Apparently oblivious to its savage irony, Gould quoted in his book, *Concerning Lafcadio Hearn*, a letter written by Hearn from the next room after one of his spiritual sessions, in which the doctor saw 'truth and pathos and keen self-knowledge' which his guest 'shyly shrank form speaking':

> You have almost made me believe what you do not believe yourself – that there are souls. I haven't any, I know; but I think you have – something electrical and luminous inside you that will walk about and see things always. Are you really – what I see of you – only an envelope of something subtler and perpetual?[92]

Gould omitted the two final paragraphs where Hearn was jocosely blasphemous at his and his wife's expense:

> 'Ruth' maketh progress; but I had to murder the 'Mother of God'. Anyhow the simile would have had a Catholic idolatrousness about it, so that I don't regret it. . .Mrs Gould moveth or reposeth in serenity – Jakey [Gould] fulfilith with becoming dignity the duties devolved upon him. I have consumed one plug of 'Quaker City' [a pun on

Philadelphia and a brand of tobacco]; but as the smoke spires up, the spiritual-sensualism of 'Ruth' becomes manifest.[93]

Other letters were even more savage. One told of an alleged experience in Martinique where a bat circled him and some friends. One friend, Arnoux, kept hitting it as it repeatedly came back; Arnoux said it was Hearn's *maîtresse* at St Pierre who was dead and had come looking for him:

> I did not think for a moment it was Gould. . .Then I caught it in my hat and it revealed its plain nature by burying its teeth in my fingers; and it would not let go and it squeaked and chippered like a ghost. I was almost mad enough to hurt it, but I tried to caress its head, which felt soft and nice. But it showed all its teeth and looked too ugly, and there was a musky smell of hell about it – so that I know, if it were anybody, the place with a capital 'P' where it came from.[94]

There are various versions of the events surrounding Hearn's departure for New York in October 1889. He wrote to Hendrick a year or two later that Gould told him his wife was jealous of his friends and did not want him about. His host gave him money – he was completely broke – and told him to go to New York where, he suggested, Harper might be willing to send him back to the tropics. He was then to return to Philadelphia and report to Gould. However, when he got to New York he found a letter there from the doctor telling him never to return.[95] This may be at least an exaggeration. Redway said that Hearn had been 'a great trial' to both the doctor and his wife but that his host had refused advice to get rid of him. He did not believe that Hearn had been forbidden to return; on the contrary, he recalled money for this purpose being sent to him.[96]

After Hearn's death, Gould claimed that Hearn had had 'nothing but the most demonstrative feelings of kindness and affection for both Mrs Gould and myself and we felt the same way for him. Indeed, we still feel so, despite, as we now learn, of his turning against us afterward'.[97] This was, to say the least, disingenuous and an earlier version of events by Gould gives a definite hint of impulsion to his guest's departure. He claimed that Hearn had exhausted the West Indian vein and could find no inspiration in American life so that he forced the thought of going to Japan on him, 'and against his will I almost drove him to undertake the journey'.[98] Hearn started for Japan but got only as far as New York from where he wrote: 'The last tentacle has been pulled out: the result I await with indifference. . .I therefore dream Buddhist dreams in this hurricane of steel and stone and steam – my new soul shining calmly as an electric light (visible to myself only) through the tempest.'[99] Once he had left, Gould did let him know that his presence had not occasioned universal joy in the household. Hearn replied from New York in the late autumn of 1889, albeit perhaps a little sarcastically, expressing his regret that he had not known 'how matters were at the house,- I should have gone away long before, rather than have caused you such trouble'.[100]

Mrs Gould, upset at now being excluded from her husband's correspondence with Hearn as well as by the memory of his visit, entered the lists herself. Hearn's cunning response reveals the outline at least of what she had written. He claimed that his letters to her husband had been forced, just to humour him. That morality played a part in Mrs Gould's disquiet was indicated by his explanation of why 'naughty Gooley' did not read his letters to her: probably, Lafcadio said, he had mentioned jokes of New York life, 'not very wicked' but not quite 'proper' – 'But men will do these things, sometimes!. . .' Lafcadio assured her that if she had opened and read the letter which she had not been allowed see, she would have saved herself any anxiety about the contents; indeed, she would have felt the 'utmost sympathy'. Nevertheless, Hearn did not reveal the subject-matter to her. Before signing off as her 'horrid, horrid, little friend', he did apologise for his disruption of the household, recognising that he had outstayed his welcome.[101]

After this letter had been dispatched, Lafcadio heard from Gould, asking him to write a placatory letter to his wife. Hearn replied:

> Her letter, however, was illuminated by yours, and as I know myself no match for a woman in diplomacy, I simply ask you to read it, and understand it. It strikes me that Mrs G. is very anxious to terminate our relations even in the matter of correspondence, and that we can accommodate her in this without any ill feeling.[102]

It was not, however, the end of the relationship. Hearn's

letters to Gould continued this send-up of the doctor's attempt to re-orient him spiritually as well as in the literal sense. Sexuality, at least in passive form, raised its head with Hearn's accusation that Gould had been jealous of his attention to Elizabeth Bisland: 'Don't! She is only a Phaenomenon [sic]. You gave me a soul. My soul is studying her soul. – You see what you have done. You are like Goddlemitey: you make a soul, and then send the soul to New York, where there is a Garden containing the Tree of the Knowledge of Good and Evil, and this condemns that soul to eternal damnation by the temptation proposed to it.' The sexual innuendo continued with a tale that he was walking down a street when he heard someone call out in Creole; he opened a door and found himself in a room of naked women. 'Imagine Joseph when someone caught his mantle, – having only one mantle, and not being able to afford to lose it.' The ending was even more taunting, with a reference to a broken heart: 'Don't write such postals. I live with religious people. They really think I have broken somebody's heart, and looked upon me all day yesterday with stern disapproval.'[103]

Some letters written to Gould from New York were simply masses of pseudo-medical/scientific nonsense. These would be followed by others which were perfectly normal accounts of his daily life. Still others contain allusions which remain obscure. In one case he told Gould that there was nothing unkind in his letter 'but there was a single word in it better left unsaid'. On this occasion he asked the doctor not to write to him or to expect him to write for a few months: he had no money, had much on his mind and was apt 'to do very stupid or very unkind things in an unlucky moment'.[104]

It is difficult to fathom Lafcadio's state of mind when he wrote these letters. To have no money and to be dependent on a friend's charity as one approaches one's fortieth birthday would make many people sensitive. Underneath the surface of humility, Hearn was a proud – and strong – character and in these letters he was perhaps exercising his only weapon, his literary skills, against an unsubtle attempt to 'reform' the whole basis of his existence.

★   ★   ★

When Lafcadio arrived in New York from Philadelphia, he

turned to Alice Wellington Rollins, an author and critic, and a friend of Elizabeth Bisland's, whose review of *Some Chinese Ghosts* in the March 1887 issue of *The Critic* had delighted Hearn. When Elizabeth Bisland brought Lafcadio to lunch with Mrs Rollins for the first time in the autumn of 1889 all went well. Because he knew Bisland well and found Mrs Rollins sympathetic, his habitual shyness vanished and he enthraled Mrs Rollins with brilliant conversation. Encouraged by this success with what appeared to be a literary lion, Mrs Rollins then invited him to dinner and asked some of her other friends to meet the remarkable *raconteur*. He eventually turned up an hour late, miserable and frightened, from the kitchen. He had been too exotic to be respectable in the eyes of the doorman who had insisted that he take the service elevator at the back of the building.[105]

Despite this reverse, a correspondence developed and, when Hearn arrived in New York from Philadelphia in October 1889, Mrs Rollins invited him to stay in the family apartment in the Navarro Buildings on West 59th Street. When Lafcadio did turn up, another embarrassing situation ensued: he had been expected to stay only a few days and even then Mrs Rollins' son had to give up his room to accommodate the indigent writer.

His next hope, of a room at 149 West 10th Street where his old Cincinnati colleague, Joseph Tunison, now on the *Tribune*'s editorial staff, had lodgings, fell through at the last minute: the room proved unobtainable 'at reasonable terms'. In any case, it had no work facilities and was 'cold enough to freeze in'.[106] Hearn returned despondent to the United States Hotel. Things seemed to go from bad to worse. *The New York Times* offered him occasional editorial work on French reviews but he found that he would have to wait for new works to appear and lost interest. Alden wanted him to write a half-dozen short stories but in the circumstances, where he felt that he could not even correct the proofs at the hotel, it was out of the question. He could do well in New York, he believed, with a 'lift' from 'some literary source' but it would take time and money. The latter in particular he had not got – he had just borrowed ten dollars from Alden.[107] When Lafcadio wrote of his adverse circumstances to Gould, the doctor replied with a 'brotherly letter' enclosing a cheque for twenty dollars. Perhaps alarmed by the advice in the letter, which may have urged him on to Japan, Hearn hastened to provide reassurance that he was much stronger in New York than Gould imagined and his future in it was 'plain sailing' if he could keep in good health; his embarrassment was temporary and, indeed, he was 'quite a lion' there.[108]

Things did look up. Joseph Tunison had been a friend for eighteen years and was, Lafcadio had written to Alden some time before, 'one of the noblest and most unassuming of men'.[109] Although he did not reciprocate Hearn's feelings of deep respect, Tunison invited him to stay at 149 West 10th Street. *Chita* was published in book form and the notices were good: in a review on 2 November 1889, the Boston *Evening Transcript* went as far as stating that Hearn could lay claim to the title of being an American Victor Hugo.[110] The author himself found that '*Chita* seems to be pleasing people'.[111]

There were new friendships. Among the other guests at Mrs Rollins' dinner party in March had been Ellwood Hendrick, a fire-insurance salesman who rented apartment space from Mrs Rollins. He later became a writer of works on chemistry aimed at the general reader and was curator of the Chandler Chemistry Museum at Columbia University for six years prior to his death in 1930. Seeing Lafcadio's distress, he took him away to a tavern where they fell into deep conversation. Hendrick, then aged 28, was suffering a deep personal crisis. A chemical enterprise which he had established had collapsed, shattering his youthful dreams. Any hope of distinction, of realising a sufficient level of ambition to make life itself worthwhile, seemed to have vanished. According to himself, he decided then and there that here was his opportunity, that if Lafcadio would let him cultivate his friendship he might yet make a go of things. He did not make his feelings explicit to Hearn but he felt that he sensed them and 'resolved to fan the almost extinct spark of ambition in his new companion. . .until it might burn again and warm his disappointed soul'. The next day they met again and much of the winter was spent in each other's company.

Hendrick's description of his new-found friend corresponds with those left by other friends of the era. Physically, 'he had a beautiful profile; he was about five feet three inches tall, but very well built, and he spoke in a gentle voice with the clear, beautiful enunciation peculiar to Dublin. He was rarely dogmatic; usually his comments were made by way of suggestion. And he was the shyest mortal I have ever met'. According to Hendrick, the blind eye was not offensive: 'it was smaller than his good eye which protruded somewhat; the iris was complete but the pupil was defective'. Harshness or cruelty alienated him and was, in Hendrick's view, responsible for the ending of some friendships. At their first meeting, Hearn told Hendrick that he liked to be among simple people, a statement which was accepted on trust, though it could hardly be said that his friends of the era – Hendrick himself, Bisland, Gould, Tunison – were actually simple even in the most basic sense of being uneducated. 'Simple' in this case seems to have been a term employed to exclude businessmen.

Similarly, at a time when he was preparing *Two Years in the French West Indies* for publication, with its eulogy of the Dominican priest, Père Labat, Lafcadio was convincing Hendrick of his fear of the Roman Catholic Church. The rationalisation was a claim that the Church remained 'vindictive to those who had abandoned her'. Extraordinarily, because it was out of character with everything we know about his views before and after his New York period, when he was with Hendrick he declared his preference for 'the Methodists with their love-feasts, their Free Grace and sudden conversions. . .' The only possible explanation of this ludicrous nonsense, assuming that Hendrick's memory was accurate – there is no support for it in the extensive correspondence between the two men – was that Lafcadio was in some way trying to please his new friend. Hendrick's attitude to Hearn had, on the other hand, distinctly religious overtones: 'He was indeed my father confessor. . .I verily believe that my despondent spirit was born again on the night. . .when I first met him. He had such great merit, such keen spiritual vision and understanding that I doubt I ever appreciated the full measure of his great gifts.'[112]

Hearn, meantime, was casting around for new sources of income. He wrote to the *Century Magazine* suggesting that he might do West Indian work for it, asking not to be judged by the *Harper's Magazine* articles; he would be willing to undertake five years work anywhere in the American tropics at a moment's notice.[113] Apparent financial need drove him to attempt one of his least distinguished books, a translation of Anatole France's *The*

Crime of Sylvestre Bonnard. In 1898 he wrote that it had been translated in ten days and published within two weeks of starting it, at the wish of the Harpers. He got $150 and no commission on sales.[114] For once, Lafcadio was too generous to Harper – he actually got $100 in full for the translation, plus $15 for the introduction. The production certainly was rapid. On 9 January 1890 he forwarded the last of the copy; by 25 January, he had received copies of the book. Relations with Harper were cordial and, for once, he was happy about the proofreading and looked forward to 'a charming success'.[115]

Any lingering traces of poverty were dispelled when Lafcadio received $2,000 for the serial rights of *Youma*, which appeared in *Harper's Magazine* in January and February 1890. Payment had taken place by the time the contract for the book was signed on 24 February 1890. The magnitude of the fee paid for the serial rights of *Youma* reflected its author's growing reputation.[116] The momentum was maintained when *Two Years in the French West Indies* appeared later in 1890 to enthusiastic reviews.[117]

Elizabeth Bisland loomed large on the horizon in the interval between the West Indies and Japan. She had just started editing a new magazine, *Cosmopolitan*, when he obliquely suggested that she might want to use 'a little gem of Loti's' but, fussy as ever, asked that he see a proof if it were used.[118] The attempt at literary collaboration led to a sharp letter of exasperation when Hearn sent *Karma* for possible use in the magazine and Bisland was not happy with it. He asked for it to be returned, complaining that she had found it too long and, when he had shortened it, found it too short.[119] He sensed her hesitation was due to something more fundamental than that form of the piece and suggested that he might submit some Martinique work on which he was then engaged.[120] 'A Study of Half-Breed Races in the West Indies', did indeed appear in the June 1890 issue of *Cosmopolitan* as did 'West Indian Society of Many Colorings' the following month. After Lafcadio's death, Gould claimed that, when *Karma* was not returned as soon as he expected, he had written Bisland an abusive letter though he allowed himself to be persuaded not to send it and *Karma* was returned a few days later. If the letter had been sent, Gould believed, it would have ended Bisland's friendship with him forever.[121]

Whether or not this would have been the case is a matter for speculation – Elizabeth Bisland was probably tougher and more level-headed than Gould gave her credit for. In any event, Hearn's friendship with her was at its most intense in this period, even if he did on occasion chide her for showing his letters to other people.[122] He was always enamoured of her charms, physical and intellectual, and yet there remained a reserve, a discordant glimpse of an element of her personality he found disturbing. He reported to Gould from New York that she kept a 'Southern salon' in which it was hard to talk to her through a ring of admirers: 'She is a witch – turning heads everywhere; but some of her best admirers are afraid of her.' One told Lafcadio he felt he was playing with 'a beautiful, dangerous leopard, which he loved for not biting him'. She had the effect on Hearn of 'hasheesh'; he could not remember the conversation after leaving her house, with his head in a whirl, bumping into people, being run over and losing his way, his 'sense of Orientalism being grievously disturbed. But I am not in love at all; – no such foolishness as that: I am only experiencing the sensation produced upon – alas! – hundreds of finer men that I'.

Perhaps as a sop to Gould – or it may have been irony – he told the doctor that she had confessed to him that she had no 'soul' yet but knew that she would be transformed by a spiritual awakening some day.[123] On another occasion he wrote to Gould that Bisland had a very strange face, 'mobile and changeful as water under light' so that nobody could tell exactly what she was like. He was beginning, he claimed, to think her a phantom made of millions of beautiful dead women's souls. At this stage he was struggling – unavailingly – to escape from his fascination with her. When he saw her he was enchanted; the next day, when the sensation had evaporated, he would resolve to stay away in future but succumb to invitations, rationalising that he would turn the situation into literature, though he does not appear to have attempted to do so.[124]

As he was packing to leave for Japan, on 7/8 March 1890, he wrote her what was probably his most direct statement of his complex feelings for her:

> . . .after looking at your portrait, I must tell you how sweet and infinitely good you. . . can be and how much I like you. . .I do not think you really know how sacred you are. . .it is because you do not know what is in you, who

are in you, that you say such strangely material things. And you yourself, by being, utterly contradict them all. I might say I love you – as we love those who are dead (the dead who still shape lives); but which or how many, of you I cannot say. One looks at me from your picture; but I have seen others, equally pleasing and less mysterious.[125]

Her picture remained on display in his study throughout his time in Japan, even after his marriage.

Among the items he decided to pack for the journey was a pair of shoes he had left at Krehbiel's home when he had stayed there in 1887. When he called the Krehbiels were away and the maid who answered the door refused to countenance the exotic stranger's request for the shoes. Lafcadio penned a letter of protest to his friend and intimated that if he wished to make contact before the departure for the Orient, he should take the initiative. Krehbiel replied: 'Dear Hearn: You can go to Japan or you can go to hell.' The former friends met once by chance after this episode; no words were exchanged.[126] The kindness of other friends was an antidote to the nastiness of the break with Krehbiel. Mrs Rollins, whose financial circumstances were not what they had been, gave a magnificent send-off, the memory of which still reverberated in his memory over five years later:

> Ah! Do you remember the storks, the Japanese storks, on the table at that farewell dinner in your Aladdin's palace in New York? Who could then have foreseen all that Japan and its storks were going to become for me. How pretty and lovable it all was![127]

There was a last evening spent with that 'divine person', Elizabeth Bisland, who 'made a little space of magnetic sunshine' as they 'sat by a fire of driftwood, and talked and dreamed about things'.[128] The faithful Ellwood Hendrick accompanied him to the Montreal train, on the first leg of the journey to Japan, in early March.

At Montreal, he descended to dreaded ice and snow. Of the subsequent train journey to Vancouver, Lafcadio wrote of his 'white memories of the mighty vision of that trip across country en route here, of the smoke of the engine, a beautiful, licaceous blue, rolling over the snow. . .'[129] The account of the trip, the production of which was a duty, was not the most inspired of Lafcadio's writing but he was genuinely impressed by the majesty of the Rockies, the sight of which was, he declared, worth the trip.[130] On St Patrick's Day, the *Abyssinia* set sail from Vancouver, bearing Hearn and his companion on his last – and greatest – voyage of discovery.

CHAPTER SIX

YOKOHAMA

> Here I am in the land of dreams,- surrounded by strange
> gods. I seem to have known and loved them before
> somewhere: I burn incense before them. I pass much of my
> time in the temples, trying to see into the heart of this
> mysterious people. In order to do so, I have to blend with
> them and become part of them: It is not easy. But I hope to
> learn the language; and if I do not, in spite of myself, settle
> here, you will see me again. If you do not, I shall be under
> the trees in some old Buddhist cemetery, with six laths
> above me, inscribed with prayers in an unknown tongue,
> and a queerly carved monument typifying those five
> elements into which we are supposed to melt away.
> Hearn from Yokohama, 25 November 1890.[1]

ON ST PATRICK'S DAY 1890, the odd-looking, 39-year old
Greek-Irishman set off for Japan from Vancouver. On 4 April he
stepped ashore from his ship, the *Abyssinia*, to the welcoming
chaos of Yokohama 'in the white sunshine of a perfect spring
day'. Here he found himself:

> . . .suddenly in a world where everything is upon a smaller
> and daintier scale. . .a world of lesser and seemingly kindlier
> beings, all smiling at you as if to wish you well,- a world
> where all movement is slow and soft, and voices are
> hushed,- a world where land, life, and sky are unlike all that
> one has known elsewhere,- this is surely the realization, for
> imaginations nourished with English folklore, of the old
> dream of a World of Elves.[2]

Hearn recorded his first impressions of Japan in two essays,
'My First Day in the Orient', published in his first Japanese book,

and 'In Yokohama', published in his second. 'In Yokohama' was meant to add perspective, to be a form of revisionism in relation to the earlier essay. Even though he admitted that it was the product of notes made in the first few weeks in Japan,[3] by the title of the essay, 'My First Day in the Orient', and the style in which it was written, Hearn gave the impression that it was record of a magic first day; that he had barely landed and dumped his baggage with 'Carey the Mulatto', who ran the European Hotel in Yokohama, before he set off on his breathless round of discovery with Cha, his *jinrikisha* runner. Later he had the time to imbibe the 'atmosphere of sailors and sealers and mates and masters of small craft – in a salty medium full of water-dogs'[4] at the hotel but, on that first day, he had time only to explore this wonderful new world, grudging himself even the time to eat.

Lafcadio claimed he had neglected advice to write down his first impressions as soon as possible. He was warned that they were evanescent and, once lost, would never return.[5] But there was so much to experience in 'the sun-steeped ways of the wonderful Japanese city' that first day that he would not stay indoors and write them down, having time only to jot down hasty notes as he whirled from one temple to another. Yet he did manage to recreate the experience in magnificent detail in the essay, 'My First Day in the Orient'. In reality, Lafcadio stayed indoors at least part of that first day, writing letters to important contacts.[6] Like his accounts of his own life, Lafcadio crafted a coherent literary sketch, with a marvellously spontaneous feel, out of this first contact with Japan. It was, in fact, an artifice, a composite of the experiences of the first few weeks there. It was written later, when he had long left Yokohama, with the purpose of recreating for his reader the sensation of arrival in this new culture. It was not meant to be the literal truth, though it did create the impression of being so.

The omens were good from the beginning. This was, after all, something for which he had been preparing for years. Here were 'Hokusai's own figures walking about in straw rain-coats, and immense mushroom-shaped hats of straw, and straw sandals. . .'[7] In the midst of all this wonder, Hearn was overwhelmed by a flashback to the horror of his childhood; he experienced 'a sensation of dream and doubt' precipitated by the curved roofs, the dragons and Chinese grotesqueries of temple carvings.

Suddenly, they seemed not new, but like objects from dreams, stirring long-lost memories of picture-books in a long-ago Dublin home. That night he had a nightmare of Chinese ideographs coming to life with the monstrous movement of insects – these recurring visions of the monstrous movement of inanimate objects were a legacy of his formative years. He dreamt he was being taken through luminous streets in a phantom *jinrikisha*, running on soundless wheels.[8] Thus the thread of horror – something which was deeply rooted in his childhood and permeated all his adult thoughts – had insinuated itself into even one of the most pleasurable days of his life.

In his waking hours, however, he was overwhelmed by the wonder of this new civilisation. He wrote to the famous figure of Ernest Fenollosa, the great Japanologist, breathless with the delights of Japan:

> I wonder whether the Elder Egypt had equal power to enchant strangers? The intense delight of all this to see – the delicious ghostliness of it,- is the sense of being in a world of mysteries and Gods all ALIVE,- closer to you than neighbours,- real, comprehensible, beautiful beyond description. After having lived ten or twelve years with archaeology, the effect on me is so queer that I sometimes think I am dreaming it all.[9]

Here, for the first time, he was encountering in the flesh the world of classical antiquity, that world which he ceaselessly studied since its beauty first burst upon him in adolescence. Perhaps unconsciously, it was also a link with his Greek mother, that wondrous being who haunted his dreams and sent him wandering the world in search of her or her image, a quest doomed to failure. To his American friend, Tunison, he wrote from Yokohama of how Japanese art was 'surprisingly Greek' and of the similarity of their legends to the Hellenic myths. He speculated on how Greek art might have filtered through from the Greek kingdoms of India to ancient Japan.[10] He retained a keen interest in parallels between ancient Greek society and that of Japan: it was a major theme in the posthumously published *Japan, an Attempt at Interpretation*, considered by some to have been Hearn's masterpiece.

But his Hellenic enthusiasm carried within it a virulent strain which was to infect his most ambitious writing on Japan. In many respects, Hearn is astonishingly modern: much of what he wrote on Japan is only now becoming apparent to the West; some of it indeed, is probably still too advanced for easy acceptance. In one respect, though, he was very much a man of his time – his acceptance of evolutionary philosophy in its most extreme forms led him to conclude, despite clear evidence to the contrary, that the similarity of Japan to the social forms of the antique world meant that it was, in evolutional terms, thousands of years behind the West. Hearn was able to see through, and dismiss, contemporary Western imperialism but he was unable to break free of its philosophical constraints. This was in spite of the fact that, at the same time, initial contact with Japan led him to write to Elizabeth Bisland that by contrast with this wonderful new world, Westerners were barbarians and to express a longing to be reincarnated as a Japanese baby, so that he could 'see and feel the world as beautifully as a Japanese brain does'.[11]

Still, it was his interest in this philosophy, and his attempt to reconcile it with Buddhism, which had impelled him to look eastward in the first place. Here was the Buddhism he had studied in lonely hours in a boarding house in New Orleans – the student-priest the first temple he visits on that first, magic, day in Yokohama is impressed and moved to ask if he is a Buddhist:

> 'Are you a Christian?'
> And I answer truthfully:- 'No.'
> 'Are you a Buddhist?'
> 'Not exactly.'
> 'Why do you make offerings if you do not believe in Buddha?'
> 'I revere the beauty of his teaching, and the faith of those who follow it.'[12]

The depth of his interest in Buddhism before he came to Japan was made evident in his essay, 'In Yokohama', written five years after his stay there. It is an account of a trip to a small temple in Yokohama with Akira, his student guide and interpreter, where he converses at great length with a venerable old Buddhist priest. The conversation makes clear the extent to which Lafcadio had immersed himself in Buddhist philosophy and his unceasing exploration of the three great questions of life: the Whence, the Whither, and the Why of existence. The answers he had found in Buddhist books, although better than others, were still incomplete. He told the old priest that life in the West was more difficult to live and, as a result, Westerners were more troubled by the mystery of the world.[13] That unfavourable contrast of the two cultures remained constant with Hearn, and was not shaken by any disillusion over the years.

Another belief, rooted in Buddhism, that contemporary society represented a vast accumulation of former lives, that the dead exercised a subtle but decisive influence on the living, was also evident from the beginning. This would be one of the major themes of *Japan: an Attempt at Interpretation*. Now, as he travelled through Yokohama, he mused on this interaction of the living and the dead:

> The idea whose symbol has perished will reappear again in other creations,- perhaps after the passing of a century,- modified, indeed, yet recognisably of kin to the thought of the past. And every artist is a ghostly worker. Not by years of groping and sacrifice does he find his highest expression; the sacrificial past is within him; his art is an inheritance; his fingers are guided by the dead in the delineation of a flying bird, of the vapors of mountains, of the colors of the morning and the evening, of the shape of branches and the spring burst of flowers: generations of skilled workers have given him their cunning, and revive in the wonder of his drawing. What was conscious effort in the beginning became unconscious in later centuries,-becomes almost automatic in the living man,-becomes the art instinctive.[14]

Some fundamental aspects of Lafcadio's views on Japan were therefore being formed immediately on his arrival, most importantly on religion. His initial impression was that he was encountering a popular Buddhism, a new reality to juxtaposition with what he has gleaned from his reading:

> The religion seized my emotions at once, and absorbed them. I am steeped in Buddhism, a Buddhism totally unlike that of books – something infinitely tender, touching, naif, beautiful. I mingle with crowds of pilgrims at the great shrines; I ring the great bells; and burn incense-rods before the great smiling gods. My study is confined to the popular religion, so far, and its relation to popular character and art.[15]

This emphasis on the popular, from a man of essentially

125

aristocratic sympathies, was to dictate the shape of his vision of Japan.

It was not, however, Buddhism, the religion so long studied and now embraced with rapture, which would have the greatest effect on Hearn in Japan. Shinto, which was to become the cornerstone of his interpretation of Japan, was dismissed at the beginning: he sees a small temple but having 'read so much about the disappointing vacuity of Shinto temples' he finds a grove of cherry-trees in blossom 'infinitely more interesting' and promptly transfers his attention to its 'dazzling mist'.[16]

Hearn was an elusive, ambiguous personality who himself propagated much of the later misconceptions which have obdurately clung to his reputation. Within a few years, and with characteristic revisionism, he himself disowned his initial impressions as the madness of first love.[17] It is not surprising, therefore, that a belief gained general acceptance that his initial reaction to Japan was overwhelmingly romantic, a mistake he only corrected, in disillusionment, at the end of his life with *Japan: an Attempt at Interpretation*. One can indeed find passages in 'My First Day in the Orient', his account of his arrival in Yokohama, to support this:

> It is with the delicious surprise of the first journey through Japanese streets. . .that one first receives the real sensation of being in the Orient, in this Far East so much read of, so long dreamed of. . .There is a romance even in the first full consciousness of this rather commonplace fact; but for me this consciousness is transfigured inexpressibly by the divine beauty of the day. There is some charm unutterable in the morning air, cool with the coolness of Japanese spring and wind-waves from the snowy cone of Fuji; a charm perhaps due rather to softest lucidity than to any positive tone,–an atmospheric limpidity extraordinary, with only a suggestion of blue in it, through which the most distant objects appear focused with amazing sharpness. The sun is only pleasantly warm; the *jinrikisha*, or *kuruma*, is the most cosy little vehicle imaginable; and the street-vistas, as seen above the dancing white mushroom-shaped hat of my sandaled runner, have an allurement of which I fancy that I could never weary.
> Elfish everything seems; for everything as well as everybody is small, and queer, and mysterious. . .[18]

Passages such as this might appear to support the misconception that Hearn had swung from early infatuation with Japan to later disillusionment. Five years later he himself wrote of how, in that early period in Yokohama, he had fallen for the 'beautiful illusion of Japan' which by then was supposed to have 'totally faded' so that he could then 'see the Far East without its glamour'.[19] Statements such as this served to support the view put forward in the novel, *Kimono*, [1921], by John Paris, a pseudonym used by the distinguished British diplomat, Frank Ashton-Gwatkin, who had spent years in Japan, that Hearn's books are 'opium' which form visions of a land which never existed, where everything is 'kind, gentle, small, neat, artistic and spotlessly clean'; where men became gods by an easy process of nature – 'the reverse of our own poor vexed continent where the monstrous and the hideous multiply daily'; Hearn was a poet who imagined that if he could learn the language and Japanese customs, he would find out what was 'hidden' in Japan; but he learned nothing of the heart and mind of the Japanese until his later, disillusioned years when he wrote *Japan: an Attempt at Interpretation*.[20]

In fact, Lafcadio did not describe a fairyland in his books and the ideas contained in *an Attempt* can be seen developing in his previous works. He was thinking of leaving Japan, as he continued to do right up to his death, almost as soon as he arrived in Yokohama. While he was there, he asked both 'Pagan'[21] and Elizabeth Bisland, to help find him a position in the United States.[22] He complained about officialdom, the high cost of living in Yokohama, his inability to get out of Japan or to find employment.[23]

Yet, in the last year of his life, he was as vehemently pro-Japanese over the Russo-Japanese War as he had been over the earlier war with China and he remained as opposed as he had ever been to the spread of foreign influence in Japan.[24] Reality grated on Lafcadio's nerves in Japan as it did everywhere else, particularly when it took official form;[25] the common people he loved by contrast: 'What I love in Japan is the Japanese – the poor simple humanity of the country. It is divine. There is nothing in this world approaching the naive charm of them.'[26] That opinion never changed.

Indeed, the complexity of Lafcadio's reaction to Japan is present from the very beginning, even if it is subtle rather than overt. Whatever he may have thought later, 'My First Day in the Orient', is not all fairyland. A major theme of Hearn's later Japanese work was sounded on that first day: the magic of everyday life in Japan is juxtaposed with the sinister and stealthy march of Western modernisation: 'The illusion is only broken by the occasional passing of a tall foreigner, and by divers shop-signs bearing announcements in absurd attempts at English.'[27] At the second temple he visited, Hearn noted the signs in English forbidding injury of the trees, necessitated by the activities of foreign tourists.[28] The foreign buildings he passes are castigated as 'costly' and 'ugly'.[29]

A related, but more positive, insight was the happy co-existence of the new and the old in Japan:

> . . .an electric bell in some tea-house with an Oriental riddle of text pasted beside the ivory button; a shop of American sewing-machines next to the shop of a maker of Buddhist images; the establishment of a photographer beside the establishment of a manufacturer of straw sandals: all these present no striking incongruities, for each sample of Occidental innovation is set into an Oriental frame that seems adaptable to any picture.[30]

He had noted something which he would develop into one of his most important perceptions about Japan, that it was assimilative, not imitative, that it took only what it needed from the West and transformed the borrowing into something new and indigenous. On the first day he decided merely to note this discovery and made a conscious decision to concentrate on the traditional, the wonder of which was more than enough to absorb his attention.[31]

In his account of Yokohama, Hearn gave his reader no inkling of the drama which rocked his own circumstances there. Firstly there was the sudden disappointment of what appeared to be a new and promising friendship. When he had been only five days in Japan, he was encouraged in his belief that teaching could provide a basic income while he pursued his study of Japan by an English teacher, C.H. Hinton, headmaster of the Victoria Public School in Yokohama.[32] The headmaster had a pupil, Edward B. Clarke, later a professor at Kyoto Imperial University, who recalled that Hinton was enthusiastic about one of Hearn's magazine pieces, 'Rabyah's Last Ride'. When he discovered that its author was in Japan, he offered the hospitality of his home until Hearn got work. Clarke wrote an account of how he became Lafcadio's first – and only – foreign pupil in Japan

Hinton impressed on Clarke the great privilege of being coached by a famous writer. For the first lesson, Clarke prepared a composition in which he let his imagination run riot. Hearn approached his task of tutor earnestly and worked as laboriously on this schoolboy rubbish as if it were his own. Oblivious to everything, even his young companion, he re-wrote, half a dozen times or more, each sentence until it reached a state of minimal satisfaction. After a few weeks, Clarke was shattered to be told that his lessons were at an end.[33] Hinton and Hearn had fallen out; Lafcadio later claimed that he had been brutally turned out of the house because Hinton's wife could not stand his defective eye.[34] He returned, a sad man, it would seem, to Carey's little hotel, at No. 93 Yamashita-cho.

At the same time, the years of discord with his publisher, Harper, finally burst into the open and caused a rupture which was dramatic even by Lafcadio's standards. In his first day in Japan, he had described succinctly his relationship with his publisher: they were, he claimed, interested in publishing his material but otherwise were not aiding his Japanese venture; the risks are all his own. At this stage, he was, however, optimistic that he could earn a fair income from magazine work for Harper.[35]

To fully understand the complexity of his current relationship with his publisher, it is necessary to go back a few months to New York, where Lafcadio had become friendly with William Patten, art director at Harper. Hearn had been in touch with him over the years and was grateful that his own very specific ideas on illustration, far from being rejected, actually seemed to be welcome. Shared interests led to friendly correspondence. Patten had ideas on the kind of material Lafcadio should attempt – in 1887, before he had left New Orleans, he had guided him towards Louisiana's Creole 'Gulf-life'.[36]

When Hearn returned to New York in 1889, it was natural that they should get together. Both were keen Orientalists and bibliophiles. Hearn appreciated Patten's kindness in lending him rare and costly books. He could, for example, share with the art director his enthusiasm about Basil Hall Chamberlain's translation of the classic Japanese text, the *Kojiki*, and discourse on esoteric subjects such as the importance of 'the ethnological study of Ainu [Japanese aborigines] influences in the formation of Japanese myths and language'.[37]

The idea of a trip to Japan by Hearn was developed in conversation between the two men. In an undated letter to Patten, Lafcadio set out his ideas on the subject:

> In attempting a book upon a country so well trodden as Japan, I could not hope. . .to discover totally new things, but only to consider things in a totally new way. . .I would put as much life and color especially into such a book, as I could, and attempt to interpret the former rather through vivid sensation given to the reader, than by any accounts of explanations such as may be found in other writers. . . Such a book would therefore be essentially a volume of Sketches – brief for the most part,- each one reflecting a peculiar phase of life.[38]

The format suggested was, of course, the one which had proved so successful for *Two Years in the French West Indies*. It was his determination, already evident here, to look at things in a totally new way, which was to make him such a great interpreter of Japan.

Patten then approached Henry Alden, the editor at Harper, to lend his support to the project. Alden agreed in a letter devoid of any specific commitment:

> The idea of a Japanese trip – involving sufficient time to secure careful studies of the country and the people – to be undertaken by Lafcadio Hearn and C.D. Weldon, has naturally my cordial sympathy as an editor and I sincerely hope that your plan may succeed. . . Those who have read Mr Hearn's wonderful romance, *Chita*, and his 'Midsummer Trip to the West Indies' [sic], know that there is no writer of English so capable as he of fully appreciating and of adequately portraying with the utmost charm and felicity every shade. . .of the life of strange peoples. The result of close studies by him in Japan will be a revelation to all readers. . . .With best wishes for the perfect success of the undertaking. . .[39]

The C.D. Weldon referred to was an artist at Harper. From the context of the letter, the idea of his accompanying Hearn seems to have been Patten's. No doubt he thought that the artist's interest in Japan would make him an ideal companion for

Hearn. He could hardly have been more wrong. Lafcadio's initial reaction to Weldon was negative; however, he suppressed his doubts and wrote cheerfully to Patten on 3 February 1890 that he had passed the previous Sunday evening with Weldon, who seemed 'to be in every way a splendid fellow; and I believe we shall be in thorough sympathy artistically, which you know is the all-important sensitive, and trenchant point in undertakings of this kind. My previous doubts in this regard have ceased to exist'.[40] Despite the happy note, this had an ominous ring: Lafcadio's attempts to feign liking people he really deeply disliked were seldom successful – his loathing usually surfaced eventually in vigorous fashion. Patten also involved himself in arrangements for the trip – these, too, were to boomerang.

William Van Horne, President of the Canadian Pacific Railroad Company and Steamship Lines, was a lover of the Orient who had been favourably impressed by *Some Chinese Ghosts*, and it was to him that Patten turned, successfully, to help finance the expedition. He not only agreed to provide transport for the writer and artist from Montreal to Japan but gave each of them $250 in expenses. The *quid pro quo* was to be a favourable account of the journey from a pen whose capacity Van Horne knew and respected.[41]

While Patten's arrangement with Canadian Pacific covered the cost of the journey, living and working in Japan for the extended period Lafcadio had in mind would require a guaranteed source of continuing income. His experience with Harper while he had been in the West Indies was not reassuring and Hearn decided to face the issue squarely. He wrote to Patten, probably in January or February 1890 – the letter is undated – that nothing could be decided until Harper made an official commitment: 'No verbal arrangement could settle it for me, as the agreement to work from one to two years without pecuniary profit, will involve some points which can only be covered by contract.'[40]

Such arrangements were the province of Alden, not Patten, and, on 12 February 1890, Lafcadio wrote him a frank statement of his views, concluding that the conditions under which he was going were grossly unfair.[43] The reply pointed out to Hearn that Harper were not underwriting the expedition and would use only such material as suited their purpose. The terms on which material would be accepted, artistic and financial, were detailed. The decision on whether or not to proceed was left to Hearn, though Alden informally advised him to do so. Lafcadio decided in favour but without the exuberant expectation with which he had started out for the West Indies.[44]

In an autobiographical fragment, Hearn later wrote:

> Went to Japan against my will,- simply because it was either that or a return to journalism. Journalism allows little time for literary study or work of the durable sort;- so I chose Japan. Stranded. Found employ as teacher – and the story ends.[45]

Even allowing for the element of self-pitying distortion which runs through these later attempts at autobiography, there was probably an essential basis of truth in this statement. He had exhausted the potential of the West Indies and was exhausted himself by them. He was determined not to return to New Orleans and journalism. He hated New York and, in any case, his fitful attempts to make a living there had not been very successful. He was unhappy about the lack of substance in the Japanese arrangements but there was, quite simply, no palatable alternative. He decided to go ahead.

The first shot in the rupture with his publisher came in a letter written by Hearn to Patten from Yokohama, asking for the second CPRR instalment to be paid separately to him. A postscript added the cause of the injury in Lafcadio's mind: he had been ignored in Montreal by a Mr McNicoll of CPRR and Weldon had not honoured the agreed arrangements.[46] The artist now became a hate figure, '. . .an ignorant brute and unbearably disagreeable. . .'[47]

The break-up was effected by a series of vituperative, recriminatory letters. Hearn detailed various annoyances to the owner, Henry Harper – one letter ran to over thirteen pages – and enclosed extracts from a letter by Alden, his editor, stating that, while the firm was in no way responsible for the 'Japanese enterprise', it could avail itself of the literary results. He concluded that if there were no obligations on one side, there were none on the other – 'But I feel under an obligation to tell you,- as represented by Mr Alden,- to go to the Devil!'[48] Harper got Canadian Pacific to convey to Hearn their desire to show 'conciliatory disposition'. His response was sustained, scatological invective:

. . .liars,- and losers of MSS,- employers of lying clerks and hypocritical, thieving editors, and artists whose artistic ability consists in farting sixty-seven times to the minute,- scallywags, scoundrels, swindlers, sons of bitches;-

Pisspots-with-the-handles-broken-off-and-the-bottom-knocked-out,- ignoramuses with the souls of slime composed of seventeen different kinds of shit,- Know by these presents there exists human beings who do not care a cuntful of cold piss for 'their own interests', if it is indeed to their own interests to deal with liars, scoundrels, thieves, and sons of bitches. Know also that there exists one particular individual, whose name is at the end of these words, whom all the money of all the States of America and Mexico could not induce to contribute one line to your infernally vulgar beastly goodey's-Lady's-Book-Magazine,- you miserable beggarly buggerly cowardly rascally boorish brutal sons of bitches. Please understand that your resentment has for me less than the value of a bottled fart, and your bank-account less consequence than a wooden shithouse struck by lightning.[49]

Another letter returned his contracts; he wanted no more contact, not even to receive royalties: 'This ends everything – positively, irredeemably, everlastingly.'[50]

Around this time, Weldon met Lafcadio in the street and was told of the row with Harper. In a letter of 7 May 1890, he gave Patten his view of the writer, brooding irrationally and childishly on imagined wrongs. Weldon did mention one factor which would not have improved anyone's spirits: it had rained incessantly in the weeks since their arrival, a piquant contrast with the literary image of sunshine created by Hearn. He attributed much of Hearn's pique to a belief that Matthew Arnold was to produce some articles on Japan for a fee of $2,000. Though the artist blamed Hearn for his own low productivity, he was nevertheless critical of Harper's lack of attention to the arrangements before they had left New York.[51]

Alden wrote to Hearn in an effort, not so much at conciliation, as comprehension. He protested that he had been his friend, appreciating his genius and sharing his enthusiasms: 'I have become sufficiently attached to you to feel all the pain which a friend can feel to find his friendship has been wholly & from the first not only misunderstood but construed into hostility.'[52] Hearn was not, however, swayed by the judicious rationality of Alden. While Harper insisted on paying Lafcadio his due through his London agent,[53] he was serious in his determination to have nothing further to do with them.[54] It was a not inconsiderable gesture on his part: excluding the $150 he was paid for 'A Winter's Journey to Japan' when it appeared in the magazine, his book sales for the period 5 March 1890 to 10 September 1890 netted him $402.06 for *Chita*, *Two Years in the French West Indies* and *Youma*.[55]

Lafcadio wrote to his friend, Joseph Tunison, telling of his break with Harper. Tunison, horrified by the implications of what he considered a rash act – the prospect of having the wanderer return for another prolonged stay at his New York apartment may also have played a role – dispatched a letter on 4 July 1890 to Alden in which he revealed the ambiguous nature of his feelings for Hearn:

> This letter is a plea for Hearn, though I fear his case is past pleading for. I understand from Mr Ratten some weeks ago that Hearn had fallen into one of his obstinate fits and had made himself unpleasant, not to use a harsher term. I inferred, at once, that I should never hear from him again, knowing so well his lack of reason and his dependence on his temper for guidance. However, I was wrong on that point because a letter came at last a couple of days ago. It is interesting, for the reason, as it seems to me, reading between the lines, to indicate that the bottom of his discontent and ill-temper. . .was his feeling that the task of doing justice to Japan after a few months' observation, merely, was for him impossible. He declares that he finds the language very difficult, fears that he may have to stay there all his life and is certain that he can not write a book on Japan in less than five years, and he adds in a burst of melancholy, very blue indeed, that he almost deems his life a failure. Perhaps, he has already written all these things to you. But I think I am correct in my inference, which tallies, also, with his indecision before he started when he seemed to presage failure. From the point of view of utility, this, of course, does not change Hearn's responsibility nor relieve him of blame; but from another point of view, that of genius in a state bordering on paralysis, when it feels that all its wonted powers are crippled for the time being, he is really an object of compassion. I hope you will be indulgent to my boldness in writing of the matter; but I feel, in spite of myself an affection for Hearn, an affection almost as eccentric as he is.[56]

A few months earlier, in March 1890, another deeply ambiguous friend of Hearn's, George Gould, had also written to Alden, who must have wondered at this stage if he were a publisher or psychiatrist. Gould had seen in a newspaper that Lafcadio had gone to Japan:

> This I hoped for his sake would come to pass, but he acted in such a crazy and unaccountable manner to me that I can hardly credit him with sanity. . . Have you his books still,- I mean his library at your house? I have his letter to you requesting you to give them to me; this was to have been done before he should leave the United States. Do you wish to keep them, and did he say anything to you concerning their transfer to my keeping? I suspect from many things he has told me that you have also found him a strange fellow. His long stay at my house, my much befriending, and considerable money loaned him lends a strangeness to his marvellous ingratitude that 'genius' can hardly explain. But the ingratitude puzzles me less than the wonderful contradictions and psychological conundrums that his every act arouses. You have known him longer; can you explain some of them?[57]

Gould's letter to Alden raised the tangled – and still unclear – matter of the transfer of Hearn's library from Alden to Gould. The transfer was Hearn's idea. He appears to have begun the process before leaving New York. Having got Alden to pay the cost of transferring the library from Matas, he now told Alden to transfer it to Gould who was to dispose of it to clear his debts.[57a] These supposedly dated from the period Lafcadio had spent at the doctor's house.

In Yokohama, Hearn was so engrossed with his row with Harper that he seems to have forgotten the manner of his parting from George Gould in Philadelphia the previous summer. Their initial warm friendship may have dried up but Lafcadio had left his valuable library with Alden and his priority now was to remove it from the execrated editor. He decided that Gould would be the instrument to wrest the library away and, on 30 April 1890, he concocted a promissory note to convince Alden that he owed $500 to Gould. In lieu of ready money he gave his library to the doctor and instructed Alden to deliver the books to him.[58] Lafcadio was impulsively generous to Gould: 'Either sell them, take out what is due you, and send me the balance;- or keep the whole collection and send me whatever you can freely give or lend on them. I leave the matter entirely in your hands.'[59] Hearn followed up quickly with another letter urging Gould to act at once: 'You will strike him at a time when he dare not refuse. . .there is no knowing whether he will try to be trickey [sic]. . .Once you get the books into your hands,- remember, they are yours, if you wish, to do as you please with. What you may think proper to do afterwards in my case is a totally different matter.' The letter was signed in the old, affectionate 'Hearney boy' manner.[60]

After Hearn's death, Gould claimed that neither he nor Alden wanted or had any interest in the books.[61] The sharp tone with which Hearn began asking for various works from the library to be sent to him, once the transfer had been effected, charted his change of heart towards the library's new possessor.[62] Within a short time, there was a complete break. Lafcadio's version was that Gould had moved to take possession of the library as soon as he left for Japan, without waiting for word from him and had then broken off relations.[63] Gould denied this.[64] Whatever the truth of the matter, Lafcadio broke irretrievably both with his publishers and with Gould when he was in Yokohama. He burned his bridges with the two previously important sources of support.

The episode raises all sorts of questions about Lafcadio's state of mind in Yokohama, not to mention his judgement of his former friends and contacts. While he afterwards bathed the early period in Yokohama in glorious light, in both his first and second Japanese books, we know that the weather was foul and his personal and professional life was being rocked by the bitterest disputes in a life marked by more than its fair share of fallings out. The break with Harper showed how his heart ruled his head. A cooler temperament would have delayed any final rupture until some alternative was lined up. Perhaps he sensed that he was about to embark on a cultural discovery whose success would obviate the problems of publication, in book form at least. Still it was the end of his emotional involvement with a publisher; henceforth it would be a cold business affair, even if it would still be liable to conflagrations.

Quite what role his heart played in the relationship with Gould is an intriguing question. Firstly he was asking Gould to be his loyal ally against Alden, seemingly oblivious of the letters written a few months previously terminating the relationship. Then there was the fact of Mrs Gould's concern about what passed between the two men and the secretiveness of their correspondence. Did Hearn think, for example, that he had some hold over Gould, one that would compel the doctor to do his bidding, come what may? Notwithstanding the savagery of Hearn's treatment of him, Gould remained loyal for the rest of Hearn's life, even writing a 'loving' letter of reconciliation a few years later.[65] After Hearn's death he flew to the defence of his reputation, until the publication of unfavourable material caused him to write the bitterest of denunciations.

If Hearn was impulsive in his dealings with Gould and Alden, he pursued a very different tack in his approach to Basil Hall Chamberlain, the Englishman who was, incredibly, Professor of Japanese at Tokyo University, and would be an invaluable source of influence for him over the next few years.

When Hearn first wrote to Chamberlain, on his first day in Yokohama, he thought that he would need to stay several years to do justice to the country. He asked Chamberlain about getting work in Japan – a post of English tutor to a family perhaps – so that he could learn the language.[66] Chamberlain's reply was immediate and positive, though he must have referred to him as an American as Hearn denied this, pointing to his British citizenship. In the same letter, he told Chamberlain about Ichizo Hattori who was then Vice-Minister of Education; Hearn had met him a few years previously at the New Orleans 'Exposition' and believed he would have 'a kindly remembrance' of him.[67]

He later claimed that he had got his first teaching position, at Matsue, through the goodwill of Hattori. He made no mention of the role played by Chamberlain, but by then the friendship had ended and Hearn perhaps did not wish to recall being indebted to him.[68] This post began with the school year, in September 1890, at a salary of $100 per month. By accepting this position, Lafcadio became part of the government machinery which was transforming Japan into a modern power, a process he decried, while accepting its inevitability. An irony inherent in Lafcadio's dislike of Japanese officialdom was the fact that he was himself an employee of the Japanese Government throughout most of the time he spent in Japan.

CHAPTER SEVEN

MATSUE

> I believe that the period here [Matsue] will be one of the happiest, as I am sure it will be intellectually one of the most productive of my life.[1]

THE LAFCADIO HEARN who arrived in Matsue on 30 August 1890, just two days before he was due to take up his teaching post, was a very different figure who had landed in Yokohama a few months before. Now at least he was going to have an assured income and not be dependent on the caprice of publishers, infuriating at the best of times but intolerable when magnified by distance. Although he may not have yet fully realised it, he could hardly have chosen a better place, at a better time, for his exploration of Japan.

Japan itself was in the throes of the Meiji revolution, the dramatic change in Japanese polity sparked by Western intervention. The downfall of the Shogunate which precipitated the headlong rush to Westernisation had taken place only a generation previously. Japan had witnessed the humiliation of its traditional great teacher, China, by the supposed 'barbarians' and realised that only by emulating Western methods and achieving great power status could its own position in the world be safeguarded. The newly-restored Meiji Emperor set the agenda in his 'Charter Oath' of 1868 by decreeing that knowledge should be sought from all over the world to strengthen Japanese capability.

Initially Japan could only start to catch up by recruiting Westerners to teach them the know-how which had been

excluded by the hermetic seal of the Shogun's xenophobia. Thus
it was that Japanese policy dictated that foreigners such as
Lafcadio Hearn should be given the positions which would allow
them to transmit their knowledge to the Emperor's 'reawakened'
subjects. Hearn's pupils would form part of the new bureaucratic
and academic elite which would propel Japan so vigorously into
the twentieth century. He would do his duty in aiding this
process, but his heart was not in it; rather, cultured reactionary
that he was, he would embrace the old order, and campaign
passionately for its preservation, just as the scholars and the
writers were doing back in Ireland.

As seems to be inevitable in all such revolutions, the initial
enthusiasm for change caused an indiscriminate reaction against
the entire culture of the old order. As Hearn traversed Japan to
reach his new post in August 1890, he went from east to west,
from the treaty port of Yokohama with its Westerners and its
Westernisation, to the heart of old Japan, a remote corner where
the Meiji changes had been slow in percolating through. No
contemporary Japanese, any more than Hearn himself, could
have dreamt of the unique role he would play in helping to
preserve the antique Japanese culture he found there.

Matsue at that time was a quaint, historical city with a
population of 35,000. The surrounding hills were distinguished
by evergreens, temples and shrines. The city was divided by two
rivers and numerous canals, crowned by hump-backed little
bridges. There were three distinct quarters; temples to the south-
east and the old samurai districts formed the tips of a crescent
around a core of shops. It was dominated by an ancient fortress –
the Oshiroyama – 'a vast and sinister shape, all iron-grey, rising
against the sky from a cyclopean foundation of stone. . .a
veritable architectural dragon, made up of magnificent monstrosities. . .'[2]

Hearn's school term began on 2 September 1890. His duties
were to teach English at the Jinjo-Chugakko or Ordinary Middle
School and, less frequently, at the Shihan-Gakko or the Normal
School. His pupils were adolescent boys and he was a success
from the start. Serious, dedicated and highly organised, he won
the confidence and respect of his pupils. To the Western mind,
this probably appears easy. Nothing could be further from the
truth. Hearn found that each school was 'an earnest, spirited little

republic' in which the teachers could keep their positions only if they were deemed adequate by their students and would be 'deposed by a revolutionary movement whenever found wanting'.[3]

The Normal School was a State institution designed to produce teachers and the discipline was severe. Hearn did not like it. He was not, technically, on the staff, his services being lent by the Middle School where he spent most of his time. His relationships with the Normal School students was formally correct: they were forbidden to pay social calls on their teachers' homes. With the Chugakko students, by contrast, he was able to encourage a more informal relationship, that of elder brother rather than teacher. He also preferred its dingy teachers' quarters, where he was seated beside a sympathetic fellow-teacher, Nishida, to the greater comfort at the Normal School.

Hearn's pleasure in his students shines out of his writing. He encouraged their frequent afternoon visits, when they all squatted happily on the floor of his small study, taking tea and cakes. The students opened their hearts and minds to him, speaking of things they thought would interest him, but avoiding the subjects of school; to come to learn from the teacher in his home would have been 'unjust'. They delighted in his garden, inspected his books and pictures and brought along some of their own. But what they came for most of all was the 'the sympathy of pure good-will: the simple pleasure of being quite comfortable with a friend'.[4] This was a novelty for the boys as much as for Hearn – they had vivid memories of an English Christian clergyman who had discounted their customs as ignorant savagery.

On his first day, he met the Governor of the Izumo region, Koteda, who utterly captivated him. Towards the end of his life, Lafcadio came to believe that the kindness shown to him in Matsue was the result of official edict.[5] If so, it would have come from Koteda. A dedicated conservationist, practitioner of the traditional Japanese arts and one of the finest swordsmen of the era, he was seen to favour Lafcadio and all Izumo took its cue from him. The new teacher, therefore, was treated as an honoured guest by the local population.[6]

In the autumn, Lafcadio moved out of the Tomitaya Inn, where he stayed initially, to a fine house, fronting the lake, with views overlooking a stretch of beautiful blue water and mountains.[7] He had left the Inn in high dudgeon when the owner refused his offer of medical aid to save a daughter's sight. His feelings on the subject remained so strong that when a new neighbour came to his house and mentioned that he was a friend of the innkeeper, he was abruptly dismissed by Hearn. This, at any rate, was the story told by his wife after his death when she was cataloguing the embarrassments this strangest of foreigners inflicted upon her.[8] A more likely cause of the move might have been his impending marriage.

This marriage was a lightning affair: he was hardly four months in Matsue when it took place, in January 1891. He must have been introduced to his future wife shortly after his arrival in Matsue as he was musing on the possibility of becoming a Japanese citizen as early as December 1890,[9] a step which he only considered in the context of his wife's welfare. He had clung stubbornly to the citizenship of his birth over the two decades in America and finally renounced it only with the greatest reluctance. In other words, his sense of identity remained closely bound up with his formative years in Ireland and Britain, something he came to recognise overtly a few years later.

On the surface, it was an unlikely affair, this one-eyed, forty-year-old foreigner marrying the daughter of a traditional samurai family, eighteen years his junior. They could not even converse. While Lafcadio was a prolific correspondent at this time, his letters contain no glimmer of insight in this most personal of concerns. His seemingly personal letters to his American correspondents were, in fact, extensions of the romantic persona he had created. He bitched about Japan but gave no clue that he was about to settle down there. It might be imagined that he was being cynical in entering into marriage but he knew that this was no 'Madame Butterfly'; he was giving a lifetime commitment – his consideration of Japanese citizenship beforehand, and his attitude ever after, is proof of that. He wrote of his discovery of Japan at great, sometimes wearisome, length to Chamberlain but equally never touched on the subject to him. Indeed, it was one topic on which Hearn never ventured into print, in contrast to his earlier, failed, marriage in Cincinnati.

From a Japanese perspective, there is little mystery. The

introduction to his future bride – match-making would be a better term – came about through Sentaro Nishida, the Middle School teacher who became his dearest Japanese friend. Nishida influenced Lafcadio's life profoundly, not just in the personal sense, but also in the literary sense for he gave him much of the material for his book, *Glimpses of Unfamiliar Japan*. His future wife's family – Koizumi – had been connected with Nishida's as lesser samurai in the feudal era. Nishida's mother had grown up in the Koizumi household before the Meiji restoration had brought about the downfall of the feudal system and ruined the fortunes of many samurai families such as the Koizumis.

Japanese custom allowed Nishida to assume a parental role in arranging a suitable match for Lafcadio and this dovetailed neatly with economic reality: on an income of 200 yen a month from teaching – quite apart from his not inconsiderable income from writing – Hearn was affluent. The Koizumis had declined into poverty. Imbued with the true aristocratic spirit, they were unwilling to adapt to the mundane requirements of earning a living in the new world of Meiji Japan. Marrying Hearn repaired the family fortunes: in addition to Setsuko (Setsu) and her parents, there was her adopted grandfather and three servants, all of whom he took under his wing.

Perhaps the reason was crudely sensual: after all, Hearn never concealed this side of his nature. Indeed we know that, prior to his marriage, he continued his old habit of resorting to prostitutes for his pleasures. He was very frank on the subject, even to the point of admitting that he had not been 'extremely particular in those times'. It seems, however, that he was careful not to compromise himself too much in Matsue circles and only used whores from the large cities of Kyoto and Osaka.[10] The difficulty with this explanation is that, while opinions on Setsuko's appearance differ sharply, she was not good-looking in any conventional sense and Hearn, his physical blemish notwithstanding, applied his aesthetic sensitivity to women's physiology. The reaction of the early Hearn biographer, Nina Kennard, who met her on a trip to Japan in 1909 was particularly negative – and distinctly bitchy!:

> Mrs Koizumi could never have been, even according to Japanese ideas, good-looking; it was difficult to reconcile this subdued, sad-faced, Quaker-like person with Hearn's

description. . .of the little lady whom he dressed up like a queen, and who nourished dreams of 'beautiful things to be bought for the adornment of her person'. But the face had a pleasing expression of gentle, sensible honesty. Had it not been for the arched eyebrows, oblique eyes and elaborate coiffure,- the usual erection worn by her country-women,- she might have been a dignified, well-mannered house-keeper in a large English establishment.[11]

A Japanese biographer, Noguchi, by contrast, described her as a 'delightfully beautiful woman', although this seems to have been more to do with the 'sweetness of [her] old samurai heart' than Setsu's physical beauty.[12] This suggests that she had remarkable presence; indeed, Basil Hall Chamberlain, who was struck by her 'nobility', considered her the most remarkable woman he had ever met.[13]

The picture painted later by Kazuo, their eldest son, is probably an accurate one of the relationship between his parents, even if it betrays signs of bias against his mother:

Father always said that he had the best wife in the world. Not in the sense that she was a pretty, smart, or obedient wife. . .he never forgot that he was deformed, and that made him all the more kind and sympathetic. . . At times her hysteria was bad and her selfish nature became very noticeable, but these he tried to overlook by considering her fine qualities. . . sewing and cooking were left with grandmother. Mother would tell him old stories or read something to him, and he praised her as the best wife in the world.[14]

Perhaps the best view came from Lafcadio himself. He believed that a marriage of strong opposites made the best match: '. . .the two characters unite, like two elements in chemistry, to form a peculiar but effective combination'.[15]

At this stage, Mrs Hearn spoke no English and he had little Japanese. He refused to teach her English, an unacceptable act of Westernisation. They developed a 'mutual' special Japanese, dubbed *Hearn san kotoba* [Hearn's language], through which they seem to have been able to get along.[16] This raises the thorny question of Hearn's Japanese, one which has never been satisfactorily resolved. According to Papellier, a doctor who attended him a few years later in Kobe, his knowledge of the Japanese vernacular even then was very poor and he concluded that Hearn's knowledge of Japan had been gained through interpreters.[17] This inability in the language was attested by a number of contemporaries, Japanese and Western. His wife agreed that his Japanese was poor as did Kazuo, who said that he only began to learn the language at the same time as himself, in 1900.[18] Professor Foxwell, later a colleague at Tokyo University, recalled an unsuccessful attempt by Lafcadio to introduce his wife in Japanese, though he could handle the basics such as asking for food. Foxwell was equally struck by Mrs Hearn's lack of English.[19] The final word on the subject should perhaps rest with Yone Noguchi, a Japanese academic who produced a book on Hearn; the reliability of Hearn's books had, he noted, been doubted by some on account of his lack of facility in Japanese but they did not contain even a single Japanese misspelling.[20]

His marriage gave Hearn an extended household, and he revelled in its hierarchical nature. He was back again, for the first time in almost thirty years, in a structure of domesticity, with its servants and its protocol, akin to the one he had grown up in under Mrs Brenane in Dublin.

The rehabilitation of the Koizumis was completed in the early summer of 1891 when Lafcadio and the household moved to what he described as 'nearly the nicest house in town'.[21] It was a fourteen-roomed, secluded *katchiu-yashiki*, a feudal samurai residence. The large gateway would have been manned by armed retainers in olden times. Broad verandas overlooked an impressive garden on three sides. When he returned home weary from teaching, he put on a Japanese robe and squatted on the verandahs, contemplating the glories of the ancient garden. The sounds of the city, the bustling, new, modernising Japan, were excluded:

> There is a charm of quaintness in the very air, a faint sense of something viewless and sweet all about one; perhaps the gentle haunting of dead ladies who looked like the ladies of the old picture-books, and who lived here when all this was new. Even in the summer light – touching the gray strange shapes of stone, thrilling through the foliage of the long-loved trees – there is the tenderness of phantom caress. These are the gardens of the past. The future will know them only as dreams, creations of a forgotten art, whose charm no genius may reproduce.[22]

By the time he moved to this house, Lafcadio had become a

local celebrity. He gave lectures through an interpreter which were then published. To speak to a Japanese audience was delightful: 'One look at all those placid smiling faces reassures the most shrinking soul at once.'[23] Every week or so the local Matsue paper carried an article about him. 'The foreigner's' every act was a subject for comment.

Hearn, however, was never completely happy. The gripes which had started in Yokohama continued in Matsue. He complained of money worries and poor health. While he had no excuse for pleading poverty, he did indeed have to contend with ill-health. It was largely a matter of the weather which, by January 1891, he was describing as 'diabolical', with constant temperature changes, snow and seemingly perpetual rain.[24] Inadequately heated, the houses seemed 'cold as cattle barns'. He developed severe lung trouble and feared that a few more winters there would be the end of him.[25]

He began to find fault with the Japanese themselves, complaining of a lack of depth in their character[26] and of 'a granite wall, impassable. . .between the Occident and the Orient'.[27] He was finding literary work difficult, blaming it on a lack of strong emotion, or inspirational thrills. He also claimed – untruthfully – that all his other American correspondents had dropped him. His 'soul', he said, urged him to save money and go home, or back to the West Indies.[28]

He had an accurate premonition that the East would keep him 'bespelled forever'; indeed, when he had left Harper's premises in New York, he had felt unconsciously that he would never return to the West. But now in Matsue a sense of loneliness set in; he complained to 'Pagan': 'I am here in exile, as it were, amid a neutral people, everything gray and misty, I who respond to color with every emotion of my being.'[29] A contributory factor may have been his effort to fit into the mainstream of Japanese life by the adoption of a Japanese diet. In the summer of 1891, unable to recuperate fully from his winter illness on Japanese food, he had to admit defeat and return to Western fare. He was much ashamed but laid the blame on his ancestors: '. . .the ferocious, wolfish hereditary instincts and tendencies of boreal mankind'.[30]

He later admitted in print that, living in the interior, he had need of Occidental individuality; he longed 'for the sharp, erratic inequalities of Western life, with its larger joys and pains and more comprehensive sympathies'. Still, he tried to console himself that this was a passing phenomenon; the intellectual inadequacies of interior life were more than compensated for by its social charm; the Japanese were, he told himself, still the best people in the world to live among.[31] Indeed, when his old friend and benefactor, Mrs Rollins, paid a visit to Japan and wrote from Yokohama suggesting that he visit her there, he did not jump at the chance of congenial Western company but excused himself on the grounds of passport difficulties. He boasted that he was now living as a Japanese and was so Oriental in his outlook that he regarded his fellow Occidentals as 'Barbarians'.[32]

With the passing of the harsh winter, he was able to resume his travels. In April, he went with Nishida to a settlement at the southern end of Matsue which was shunned by ordinary Japanese because its inhabitants were *yama-no-mono*, pariahs who performed functions considered unclean. When schools closed in July and August, Lafcadio spent the two months' holiday travelling with his wife, indulging his love of swimming along the bays of the Izumo coast. His travels yielded a good deal of literary material which formed the basis of some chapters of *Glimpses of Unfamiliar Japan*. The extraordinarily irregular landscapes reminded him of Chamberlain's view that Japan's mission was to teach the Occident the value of irregularity, 'Nature's greatest charm'.[33]

Although it was not published until 1894, *Glimpses of Unfamiliar Japan* was essentially a work of Hearn's Matsue period. He lived there for just over a year, September 1890 to November 1891. The book opens with 'My First Day in the Orient' and ends with 'Sayonara!', the story of his departure from Matsue and the 'Province of the Gods'. In between, was sandwiched the largest work Hearn ever attempted – seven hundred pages in the modern paperback version; it was originally published in two volumes.

The format was the one he had successfully pioneered with *Two Years in the French West Indies*, a collection of essays which mixed autobiography, story-telling, scholarship, travel and various other elements with greater and lesser degrees of success. Now, however, he had a much more substantial theme than the West Indies had provided, the transition of Japan from feudalism to modernity. While there was a great deal of affection for the old Japan, and much of the old anecdotal, rambling style of before, Hearn now had a hard core of meaning to impart and his essential realism shone through in his handling of the Meiji transformation; Japan had to modernise if it was to retain its national independence: 'No doubt that change of civilization forced upon Japan by Christian bayonets, for the holy motive of gain, may yet save the empire from perils greater than those of the late social disintegration. . .'[34]

An outstanding essay in *Glimpses*, 'The Japanese Smile', was part of the small percentage of the work not a product of Matsue. A trip to Kobe in 1893, where he heard English spoken again by Englishmen after having lived in a Japanese environment for three years, set him pondering the problem of mutual comprehension between East and West. The reactions of an accompanying Japanese friend made him realise that:

> If the Japanese are puzzled by English gravity, the English are, to say the least, equally puzzled by Japanese levity. The Japanese speak of the 'angry faces' of the foreigners. The foreigners speak with strong contempt of the Japanese smile: they suspect it to signify insincerity; indeed, some declare it cannot possibly signify anything else. Only a few of the more observant have recognised it as an enigma worth studying.

They did not realise that a mien of happiness must always be presented to the outside world whatever one's true feelings; even with a breaking heart, a brave smile is to be maintained.[35]

To Hearn, much of Western personality was masked aggression, a type of individuality that had not yet emerged in Japan. With his pessimistic belief in evolutionary certainty, he thought that the Japanese smile was due to vanish as ancient Greek culture had done. Japan would then '. . .regret the forgotten capacity for simple pleasures, the lost sense of the pure joy of life, the old loving divine intimacy with nature, the marvellous dead art which reflected it. . .Perhaps she will wonder most of all at the faces of the ancient gods, because their smile was once the likeness of her own'.[36] As usual when he relied on Herbert Spencer rather than on his own powers, Hearn has been proved mistaken: the Japanese smile has not vanished. He was, however, optimistic that Japan would be able to assimilate Western culture without losing her collective individuality. He took it as a hopeful sign that the Japanese were able to distinguish between the West's material superiority and its moral weakness.[37]

Hearn had never been comfortable with the type of Western, urban, industrialised, society he had found in London and Cincinnati but this full-blooded denunciation was something new. His new-found confidence in openly denouncing the West, and its entire value-system, came from the discovery of a new religion, one to which he never aspired to truly belong. When his pupils in Matsue told him of the imperialistic dismissal of their culture by other foreign teachers, Lafcadio's reaction was ardently nationalistic: their highest duty was, he told them, to honour the Emperor and to be ready to sacrifice their lives for Japan.[38]

This nationalism was something new for Hearn: he had never exhibited any feelings for anyone's nationalism in his life before. In Japan, it was closely connected to his discovery of Shinto, the indigenous Japanese religion. His journey to Matsue from Yokohama in August 1890 was in a sense his farewell to Buddhism, the religion he had studied so intensively before coming to Japan and which had occupied his interest during the months at Yokohama. It was ironic, in the circumstances, that he should have been accompanied by the Buddhist monk, Akira. As the journey to Matsue progressed, Lafcadio noticed how the manifestations of Buddhism declined while those of Shinto correspondingly increased; it got to a point where he looked in vain for the Buddhas.[39] What was to become a major component in his view of Japan was manifesting itself in the countryside as he passed.

Buddhism was now displaced by Shinto as his main object of study. He continued to have an intellectual interest in Buddhism and the possibilities of its reconciliation with evolutionary philosophy but it survived mainly in his interpretation of Japan as an illustration of the ultimate fate of foreign accretions to the native core of Japaneseness. The fact that Buddhism's influence could be measured in thousands of years only served to underline the drama of this point. Shinto, by contrast, represented the very essence of that Japaneseness which he spent the rest of his life illuminating.

In his first month in Matsue, Hearn paid a visit to Kitzuki, a most venerable Shinto shrine near the city. Armed with a letter of introduction, he was received by Senke Takamori, whose family had been in charge of the great temple from time immemorial, in the inner shrine of the chief deity. He was the first European ever granted this privilege.[40] Hearn was awed by the occasion; it consolidated what he had seen on his journey from Yokohama and prompted his most fundamental – and lasting conclusion – about Japan:

> To see Kitzuki is to see the living centre of Shinto, and to feel the life-pulse of the ancient faith, throbbing as mightily in this nineteenth century as ever in that unknown past. . .Buddhism, changing form or slowly decaying through the centuries, might seem doomed to pass away at last from this Japan to which it came only as an alien faith; but Shinto, unchanging and vitally unchanged, still remains all dominant in the land of its birth, and only seems to gain in power and dignity with time. . . Shinto extends a welcome to Western science, but remains the irresistible opponent of Western religion; and the foreign zealots who would strive against it are astounded to find the power that foils their uttermost efforts indefinable as magnetism and invulnerable as air.[41]

This was no passing fancy: it would develop and mingle with his other seminal influences, the classical world, evolutionary philosophy, Roman Catholicism, and folklore, to inform his considered view of Japan.

There was personal material in *Glimpses* too, not all of it straightforward. He presented a gently ironic thumbnail sketch of Elizabeth Bisland, as the lady of many and changing souls.[42] His favourite elements of horror and humour were blended in 'Of Ghosts and Goblins', and provided links back to his previous American and West Indian work, as well as forward to the masterly horror of his later Japanese books. It was the story of a beautiful girl whose strange test caused all her suitors to flee except a poor samurai. The test consisted of following her to an ancient cemetery where she signalled him to wait by a fresh grave. She digs down until she reaches a coffin and tears off the lid, revealing the corpse of a child inside:

> With goblin gestures she wrung an arm from the body, wrenched it in twain, and, squatting down, began to

devour the upper half. Then, flinging to her lover the other half, she cried to him, 'Eat, if thou lovest me! this is what I eat!'

Not even for a single instant did he hesitate. He squatted down upon the other side of the grave, and ate the half of the arm, and said, '*Kekko degozarimasu! mo sukoshi chodai*' ['It is excellent: I pray you give me a little more'] For that arm was made of the best kwashi [Japanese confectionery] that Saikyo could produce. Then the girl sprang to her feet with a burst of laughter, and cried: 'You only, of all my brave suitors, did not run away! And I wanted a husband who could not fear. I will marry you; I can love you: you are a *man*!'[43]

Despite the eventual length of *Glimpses*, Lafcadio confided to Chamberlain in November 1893 that, for every page written, as many as ten were suppressed. He also revealed the agonised process of multiple revision involved. He would begin simply by arranging notes and hurriedly writing down the most interesting ideas. The next day he corrected the manuscript. The following day he re-wrote again; this usually yielded an improvement but not the definitive version. Then he began the final copy which would be done twice. Lafcadio knew the work was finally finished by a sort of focusing which happened when the first impression returned even more strongly after the whole process had been completed and the length cut in half. He remarked that this approach to writing was akin to spiritualism – 'Just move the pen, and the ghosts do the writing'.[44] He still managed to average one hundred and fifty pages per month this way. His journalistic training revealed itself in the keeping of note-books – classified and indexed – in which he jotted down every sensation or idea which struck him.[45]

Basil Hall Chamberlain may have been responsible for putting Lafcadio in touch with the new publishers, Houghton Mifflin & Company of Boston, to whom fifteen hundred pages of manuscript – which Hearn regarded as merely scratching the surface – were now dispatched. They published the *Atlantic Monthly*, edited by Horace E. Scudder, in which some of Hearn's work appeared before being published in book form. The connection always remained on a businesslike, professional level; Lafcadio never attempted to form with Scudder the intimate relationship he had had with Alden of Harper. Scudder did find himself in the same position as Alden, being inundated with a mass of material in which Hearn was pursuing his own enthusiasms rather than writing specifically for – or catering to the limitations of – magazine audiences. Ultimately, only six of the 27 pieces in *Glimpses* were published in the *Atlantic Monthly* and the ratio declined further with future books.

When 'Bon-Odori', one of the terser pieces, was rejected Lafcadio wrote to Scudder in August 1891 asking that he be relieved of his promise to give first choice of everything he wrote to the firm. He enquired if Scudder saw them being publishing as a book and would he agree to prior publication in the New Orleans *Times-Democrat*? If Scudder did not want other manuscripts, they could be placed elsewhere.[46] Not that Lafcadio had complete confidence in the material himself: he asked that his work be judged by later rather than earlier manuscripts because it was only then, after a year-and-a-half, that he felt he was beginning to know something of Japan – 'the most difficult of all civilized countries to know, and one in which first impressions are most deceptive'.[47]

Lafcadio was reassured by Scudder's reply and agreed to leave the manuscripts with Scudder until there was enough to make a good volume. He claimed to have had lucrative offers from other quarters '. . .but for one who wishes to do sincere work, the financial side of literature is something to be considered only as a last resort'.[48] On other occasions, however, his response to Scudder's editorial suggestions was trenchant; sometimes it appeared that Houghton, Mifflin would go the way of Harper as, for example, when he swore that he would prefer his material not be published '. . .than appear in a shape which would defeat its original purpose – to convey a general character and feeling'.[49] Yet Lafcadio was himself aware of the problem of bulk: he admitted to Scudder that he was 'grievously tormented by the accumulation of new material' which he did not know how to use.[50]

When *Glimpses of Unfamiliar Japan* was eventually published, Hearn was pleased with the reaction which it evoked. He was sent about fifty notices of the book and judged the overall tone to have been positive. He remarked acutely that a mixture of blame and praise usually meant literary success as indeed it did in this case; a third edition was printed by January 1895. He grudgingly admitted that he would make some money out of it.

Basil Hall Chamberlain was delighted with the book: 'Take it altogether, your accuracy of detail seems to me almost as wonderful as your beauty of style.'[51] When Hearn started to gripe, Chamberlain replied: 'How can you expect to hit the public taste better than you have done already? Surely the success of *Glimpses* has been absolute.'[52] In later years, as was his wont, Hearn turned against the book, telling Mitchell McDonald in 1898 that when he wanted to feel properly humble he read about half a page of *Glimpses*.

While Hearn was first satiating his artistic appetites with the wonders of Japan, he had not neglected the practical side of things and set about using an introduction to Basil Hall Chamberlain he had got from William Patten of Harper. Lafcadio had read the Englishman's works in Patten's library and Chamberlain, in turn, had read and commented favourably on *Some Chinese Ghosts*. Hearn could hardly have had a more influential contact. Chamberlain had been born at Portsmouth, England, the son of a Vice-Admiral and was just a few years younger than himself. His grandfather, Captain Basil Hall, had been a pioneering Orientalist who, in command of *HMS Lyra*, had visited Great Loochoo in 1816 and had been the first to describe it to a European audience, an interest which his grandson continued when he visited there in 1893 and delivered a lecture on the subject to the Asiatic Society of Japan. Houston Stewart Chamberlain, his younger brother, was the son-in-law of Richard Wagner and author of *Foundations of the Nineteenth Century*, a work which profoundly influenced the Nazis.

Basil Hall's brilliance took a more benevolent turn. He lived in Japan from 1873 until ill-health forced him to leave in 1911. A master of the Japanese language and calligraphy, he was Emeritus Professor of Philology and Japanese at the Imperial University of Tokyo, then, as now, Japan's pre-eminent institution of higher learning. His works ranged over the Ainu, the mysterious aborigines of Japan; a translation of *Kojiki*, the earliest history of Japan; and, *Things Japanese*, which is still considered worthy of publication, though tainted by a patronising attitude in parts.

At Kitzuki, Akira had mentioned Lafcadio's friendship with Basil Hall Chamberlain to the priest and they had made it clear that they held the Englishman in the highest respect.[53] Chamberlain asked Hearn's help in getting something from

Kitzuki and invited his comments on *Things Japanese*, then being prepared for its second edition. Lafcadio begged him to change the dismissive tone of the chapter on Japanese music[54] which contained phrases such as: 'Music, if that beautiful word must be allowed to fall so low as to denote the strummings and squealings of Orientals' and '. . .the effect of Japanese music is, not to soothe, but to exasperate beyond all endurance the European breast'.[55] Chamberlain, however, would not relent and these comments were preserved in subsequent editions.

This exchange shows a divergence of outlook which was at least a factor in the eventual rupture between the two. For all his erudition and love of Japan, Chamberlain was in some respects a conventional Victorian at heart. From a twentieth-century perspective, Lafcadio was the more enlightened. The break was, however, a few years away; in the meantime, they developed a close friendship. Lafcadio was invited to contribute to *A Handbook for Travellers in Japan*, a new edition of which was then being prepared by Chamberlain and his friend, W.B. Mason. Some of the material he submitted was used and Chamberlain showed great generosity of spirit by preserving it in future editions, after his friendship with Lafcadio had ended.[56]

Of more immediate concern was Chamberlain's role of intermediary in securing a new teaching post for Hearn in Kumamoto, on the southernmost island of Japan, Kyushu. Hearn felt that his health could not stand another Matsue winter and so his friend set about getting him a position in a congenially warm climate. When Chamberlain wrote to Lafcadio on 4 October 1891 conveying the offer of Mr Kano, Director of the Kumamoto Koto Chugakko (Higher Middle School), he begged him not to lightly reject it. The conditions of the post of English teacher were advantageous: a salary of $200 per month with a house supplied if he wanted it.[57] Maximum tuition would be five hours per day, with none on Sundays. Hearn gilded the lily when he wrote to his old editor, Page Baker, saying that he had been 'promoted' to a better-paying position in Kumamoto.[58]

Lafcadio was not disappointed in the send-off he was given by his pupils and fellow teachers at Matsue. His colleagues banded together to buy him a pair of ancient and no doubt extremely valuable vases. The students of the Jinjo-Chugakko gave him a sword made when the *daimyo* still exercised power in Matsue. After the presentation of the sword, addresses of farewell were made in the college assembly hall. The students told him he had been one of 'the best and most benevolent teachers' they had ever had.[59]

Hearn's return address provides an insight into the extent to which he had become imbued with the spirit of Shinto, including the 'holy' wish of dying for the Emperor. He exhorted his students to retain this 'beautiful sense of duty' and to continue to respect the faith of their ancestors in language which anticipated the blood-sacrifice psychology of Patrick Pearse, leader of the 1916 Rising in Dublin:

> But however much the life of new Japan may change about you, however much your own thoughts may change with the times, never suffer that noble wish. . .to pass away from your souls. Keep it burning there, clear and pure as the flame of the little lamp that glows before your household shrine.

He did balance this by telling them that living for their country would be no less noble than dying for it.[60]

Lafcadio was agreeably surprised when the students of the Normal School, whom he had taught only for a few hours in the week, gave him a banquet at which the captain of each class read a farewell address. They sang their college songs and the Japanese version of *Auld Lang Syne* before escorting him back to his home. Despite an outbreak of Asiatic Cholera which carried off some of the pupils and forced the schools to close, on his day of departure Hearn was given a terrific send-off at the wharf by an assembly of teachers and 200 students. Masanobu Otani, a favourite pupil who had made the farewell address on behalf of the Jinjo-Chugakko, later verified that the scene on the wharf had happened as Lafcadio described it, on 26 October 1891.[61]

CHAPTER EIGHT

KUMAMOTO

ON 14 NOVEMBER 1891, just after his arrival in Kumamoto, Hearn was upbeat about both his personal and literary prospects. He expected to stay five years in a post with better conditions and double the salary he had been getting in Matsue. His first reaction to the school was surprise at the magnificence of the buildings. He formed a good impression of the students and felt he had established a good initial rapport.[1]

Even as he was being positive about the school, he could not work up any enthusiasm for Kumamoto itself. He was, however, barely a month there when a rumour that the college was to close for economy reasons threw his world into turmoil. He gave it sufficient credence to tell Scudder to send all his mail care of James Beale, manager of the *Japan Daily Mail* newspaper in Yokohama.[2] Uncertainty about his position was to haunt him until he resigned three years later and could have done nothing to help him settle in his new situation. There were some French and English speakers among the 28 teachers, but he found that his fellow teachers never spoke to him. He went and returned to college alone, with no 'mental company' but his books. He did not dine during his lunch-break but went to an old cemetery behind the college where his company consisted of a statue of Buddha whose opinion he would ask on the 'vanity' of all school activity; the Buddha, not surprisingly, would just look sad.[3] This statue inspired the 'The Stone Buddha' chapter in Hearn's second Japan book, *Out of the East*, in which he mused on the ill-effects of the Westernisation of Japan. The Kumamoto teachers were portrayed as the hollow men of the new generation.[4]

155

Within a few weeks, indeed, Hearn was venting his spleen against Kumamoto in no uncertain terms: it was '. . .devilishly ugly and commonplace – an enormous, half-Europeanized garrison town, full of soldiers'. To American friends he vowed he would leave the country were it not for the nine dependants – his wife, her mother and father, her adopted mother, her father's father, servants and a Buddhist student – who tied him down. 'A respectable person' could not allow such a community to grow up around him and then break it up.[5] The respectable notions of Mrs Brenane's drawing-room were mingling with filial piety, that reverence for parents and ancestors basic to Oriental society.

His filial piety was practically tested when, for example, after he had rented a house, his wife's grandfather, who was over 80, active and unfailingly elegant though poverty-stricken, looked around and selected the best room for himself.[6] Lafcadio was irritated by his deafness and silence though he appreciated the old man's queer tales of the past. Not that he was enthused by the neat but uncharming house they had found: the garden was not pretty and the rent, at eleven dollars, was three times what he had paid in Matsue. One wonders if there was any connection here with the realities of marital existence: we know that, in later years, Setsuko refused to humour his taste for spooky old houses. Domestic life had further complications: due to his 'cunning and foolishness', one servant had to be discharged.[7]

Family life did, however, have its compensations. He was the head of a house of a dozen people to whom he was '. . .life and food'; when he went home in the evening he entered his '. . .little smiling world of old ways and thoughts and courtesies;- where all is soft and gentle as something seen in sleep. . .It has become Me. When I am pleased, it laughs; when I don't feel jolly, everything is silent. . .it is a moral force, perpetually appealing to conscience'.[8]

In Kumamoto Hearn settled down to a life-style as close as he could come to the Japanese. Although he had had to abandon an exclusively Japanese diet, he still ate Japanese food once a day; in the morning and evening he indulged in '. . .beef-steak, bread and Bass's Ale'. Otherwise, he wore Japanese clothes in the house and lived mostly on the floor. In the evening, he enjoyed a Japanese bath. For amusement, he had Japanese theatre and newspapers, street-festivals, visits of friends, occasional pilgrimages to curious places and the delight of Japanese shopping. Lafcadio found himself at the centre of accustomed solicitude. When he got even a little sick, prayers were offered to the Gods for him by the family and little vows of self-denial made.[9]

Lafcadio seems to have overcome his principled objections to Setsu acquiring English, as he was attempting to teach her the language in a 'fast memory' system in early 1893.[10] Nothing came of it so communication must have continued in Hearn's pidgin Japanese. Language was not the only difficulty. In her *Reminiscences*, Mrs Hearn recounted the tale of going to a tiny mountain village in the Higo province with Lafcadio while they were living in Kumamoto. She was terrified in the filthy inn where they were forced to spend the night and fancied that the aged creature who showed them to their room was 'a Devil woman'. She found her husband's failure to be upset completely bizarre.[11]

Her diplomacy, however, now played an important part in keeping Hearn on an even keel and preventing, in particular, any precipitate break with his publishers. When asked to mail his letters, she would keep them in a drawer as a hedge against his tendency to write letters:

> . . .of a very warm coloring in spite of himself, since his blood boiled unnecessarily for any slight matter, and that he felt awfully sorry afterward for writing it. 'Did you mail my letter? Not yet? I am so glad,' he would say when she gave back the letter which he had asked her to mail, and he was then found, Mrs Hearn said, tearing it to pieces.[12]

Hearn himself provided collaboration of this, telling Chamberlain how she had noticed he was in a bad mood before writing a letter to Houghton Mifflin. So she 'posted it in a drawer' and asked him a few days later if he would not have liked to withheld some of the correspondence: 'You see she understands me very well'.[13]

In September 1892, Hearn returned to Kumamoto after having travelled several thousand miles by steamer and kuruma. He had explored the Oki islands off Japan's west coast, among the remotest and least known parts of Japan. Foreign warships had touched at Saigo, the largest, but no foreigners, except naval officers, had ever set foot on Oki soil. In other islands he visited, no foreigner had ever been seen. He spent three weeks on different islands and, on the return journey, crossed Japan for the third time, taking a new route. Hearn's imagination had been fired in advance by Nishida, who had actually visited the islands and knew that, contrary to popular misconception, they were highly civilised. He found there legends and lore of various kinds and unexpected beauty. He realised that the blazing foreground colours of the traditional *ehon*, Japanese picture books, which puzzled foreigners, represented 'chromatic extravaganzas' which did indeed flare in Japanese nature for very brief periods.[14]

Even in these remote islands, the nineteenth century was intruding and Hearn regretted it. However, even he found the scene at remote Urago, where crowds blockaded the streets around his hotel to catch a glimpse of the first foreigner to set foot in the place, unpleasant. Wherever he went, he drew the population, totally silent, after him '. . .with a pattering of geta like the sound of surf moving shingle'.[15] After three days, he fled.

Lafcadio was delighted to have been able to arrange a meeting with Nishida at Mionoseki and to allow him the use of his house in Kumamoto. He had maintained contact with Nishida who continued to provide information on obtuse topics. Nishida, in turn, used Hearn to enquire about the origin of the Ainu names from Basil Hall Chamberlain. In putting the request, Lafcadio described his friend as '. . .a dear fellow, and [he] deserves pains. Though dying of consumption, he is always writing to me and telling me curious things'.[16]

At Mionoseki, Hearn was also keeping an eye on his 'stolen boy'. This was a young child with whom Setsu and himself had fallen in love at Oki and persuaded to come with them. The fact that he was of samurai stock but was now reduced to working as a hotel servant for people who had formerly been retainers to his family would have touched particularly Setsu, whose family had experienced a similar fall from nobility to poverty. To Lafcadio it might have seemed an opportunity of redressing one of the casualties of modernisation.

The child, Kumagae Masayoshi, was treated like an adopted son. Hearn, however, found his interaction with the family difficult to understand. He discovered it was not in accordance with custom to pet him, with the result that he was barely able to establish any communication; the boy remained under the control of the women of the house. A perfect code of etiquette was established between him and all in the house according to degree and rank.[17] Even the elaborate protocol of the Japanese household was unable to sustain the experiment, however, and by mid-1893, the Hearn family could no longer cope with what appeared to be a little devil in their midst and Masayoshi had to be sent back to Oki, after he had given 'a world of trouble'.[18]

In December 1892, the family moved to Tsuboi, Nishihor-ibata 35, having found there 'a pretty house, with a pretty garden – surrounded by cemeteries and images of Gods'.[19] While the lure of a warmer climate had been a major factor in Hearn's decision to accept a position in Kumamoto, he found the first winter colder than he had expected or could tolerate. In spite of his enthusiasm for traditional Japan, he found he could not endure the cold even with an *hibachi* (a copper-lined box filled with glowing charcoal, then the universal means of heating in Japan) and had his study turned into a 'glass box' with a Western stove for warmth.[20]

While he was savouring the pleasures of his new house, Lafcadio was thrown into uncertainty again, just as had happened the previous December, by a proposition before the Diet to abolish three High Schools, including the Fifth at Kumamoto. He declared to Nishida that he would not stay after the summer of 1893 whatever happened. It was too risky; working for the Government was like building on quicksand – a strong man was needed 'to smash up the whole crew of squabblers, and make a respectable despotism'.[21] Much as he had pined for the old pre-Civil War South in the United States, Hearn indulged in nostalgia for the Japan of the Shoguns, neither of which he had experienced directly.

The common people were the least altered by the change in society and government and these were his particular theme. He wrote to Chamberlain in January 1893 that he loved the Japanese people more and more the more he knew them but, conversely detested '. . .the frank selfishness, the apathetic vanity, the shallow vulgar scepticism of the New Japan, the New Japan that prates its contempt about Tempo times, and ridicules the dear old men of the pre-Meiji era, and that never smiles, having a heart as hollow and bitter as a dried lemon'.[22]

In these early days in Kumamoto, Hearn was unhappy too about the quality of his literary work, being 'haunted' by the 'phantoms' of his earlier papers which he now wanted returned for revision. His unhappiness was fuelled by a feeling that he was 'fizzled out' mentally. This was not really true but he was going through a difficult transitional period. In Matsue, the inspiration had flowed for *Glimpses of Unfamiliar Japan*. Now he was struggling to evolve a different style in its more analytical successor, *Out of the East*. At the same time, he was experiencing a less pleasant aspect of Japan in Kumamoto compared with Matsue: '. . .the peasants and the lower classes drink and fight and beat their wives and make me mad to think that I wrote all the Japanese were angels. . .' His first impressions of Japan now began to dry up and now there was only a dead grind though he could see that the result was valuable. He was still worried, though, by the absence of feeling, '. . .the want of something to stir one profoundly when his knowledge of the country is sufficient to prevent illusion. And it won't come. I'm afraid it will never come any more'.[23] A few months later, there was a *cri de coeur* to Chamberlain that he was in 'literary despair'. The editor of a magazine had offered him almost any terms for a Japanese novel of three hundred pages or so but he did not feel confident of being able to produce even a single sketch which would portray 'the truth about the inside of an Oriental brain'.[24]

Lafcadio's spirits had been dampened further early in 1893 by the departure of Mr Kano, the Director of his school, who had been appointed to the post of Counsellor in the Education Department. He had always been kind to Hearn, who, at this stage, found him an '. . .extraordinary man, and a fine gentleman. . .he alone made Kumamoto seem tolerable for a considerable time'.[25] Kano was indeed a many-faceted individual and, particularly, an authority on *jiujutsu*, which came to fascinate Lafcadio though his high opinion of the educationalist did not last long.

In the midst of this gloom, Lafcadio was surprised to find that he enjoyed a certain standing in Kumamoto. When, in January 1893, a distinguished Buddhist scholar, Inouye, gave a public address at Governor Matsudaira's request, he pronounced 'eulogies' on Hearn: 'I seem to be tolerably popular with the Kumamoto folk,- though I'm not much of a favorite with the teachers in Daigo K.C'.[26] His assessment of his pupils was even less positive: each new generation of students seemed more sullen and less courteous than the preceding – 'I don't much love them. They are very, very queer in Kyushu'. The old Izumo boys still wrote to him but those of Kumamoto seldom said goodbye before leaving for Tokyo.

They, on the other hand, were much more positive about him: Katsumi Kuroita, one of his Kumamoto students, recorded that his fame as a writer '. . .incited our delightful curiosity and strange respect'. They were impressed by his kindness and 'seeming wrapped in silence' He lectured in easily-grasped, clear and simple language; they were not awed as they had been by previous teachers. Kuroita confirmed Hearn's own assessment of the initial low quality of the student body; he credited him, however, with having 'worked a magic' on them. Lafcadio gave Latin lessons but English was his main focus: he began with Chaucer and finished with George Eliot. For composition, he simply asked the students to write of their experiences; they were probably unaware that their contributions would be perused for its potential as raw material in his Japanese studies. As Edward Clarke had found at Yokohama, Hearn devoted great attention to each composition and wrote an individual criticism of it, as well as correcting the grammar. The boys marked their appreciation by sending a congratulatory deputation to him at the end of the school year, something which had not happened previously.[27]

Even George Gould seemed to be coming round: in April 1893, Hearn sought Ellwood Hendrick's advice when the Philadelphia doctor had sent a 'loving' letter, asking him if he wanted his books back. Lafcadio was unsure whether Gould's approach was 'really a generous impulse or a fraud'. He finally replied to Gould asking him to sell the books, keep what was owed and send on the balance. The doctor did nothing.[28]

Hearn was in fine form when he wrote to Chamberlain on 27 June 1893, his forty-third birthday, declaring that he was stronger now than when he was thirty, with at least twenty years more literary work in him.[29] Some weeks earlier, visits from Percival Lowell and Basil Hall Chamberlain had assuaged his feelings of isolation and brought home to Hearn his consolidating position among Orientalists. Lowell was described enthusiastically by Lafcadio on the eve of his visit as a lucky man, with 'wonderful genius, strength, youth, and plenty of money', who could afford to spend six months of each year in the East.[30] A few weeks later, Hearn was adopting a much more confident posture towards Lowell, telling Chamberlain that he was wasting his talent in newspaper controversy.[31] Then there was the discovery that Josiah Conder, an authority on Japanese gardens and flower-arrangement, had included 'a kindly reference' to Hearn in his latest book.[32]

But it was the visit of Basil Hall Chamberlain in the spring which gave him most pleasure, bonding a friendship hitherto based on correspondence. Even with Chamberlain though, a growing confidence in his position as a Japanologist was evident. There was a note of gloating as he corrected the Professor on a point about a Japanese deity[33] while, at the same time, he deprecated his own earlier work. He sent Chamberlain a copy of *Chita* with the comment that it was 'terribly overdone'. Chamberlain, on the other hand, was delighted with it.[34]

Chamberlain was less positive about some of Lafcadio's current work. He disagreed with Hearn's use of Japanese words which he believed should be reserved for concepts for which there was no English equivalent. He also defended foreign sailors against Lafcadio's uncomplimentary comments.[35] Hearn pointed out that his observations on the sailors were based on police reports in the *Japan Daily Mail*. He adopted some of Chamberlain's 'strictures and suggestions' while stubbornly retaining Japanese words; he defended their use in a passage worthy of Dylan Thomas: 'For me words have colour, form, character; they have faces, ports, manners, eccentricities;- they have tints, tones, personalities. That they are unintelligible makes no difference at all.'[36]

A number of factors combined around this time to make Hearn reassess the core of his experiences and values. Firstly, two family links were forged with the renewal of correspondence with his brother, James, and with his half-sister, Minnie Charlotte Atkinson. Two years previously, just before he left the United States for ever, he had been contacted by his long-lost brother, James D. Hearn. They had been in the same country for many years, and quite close to each other, unbeknown to both.[37]

James, too, had had an eventful life, though in a different way to Lafcadio. He had come over to America initially in 1871, at the age of sixteen. Part of his luggage had been lost in the Great

Fire of Chicago, while en route to friends in Wisconsin in the market-gardening business, for whom he then worked for five years. At the age of 21, he went back to England, intending to go to India to start in the tea industry with the son of Dr Stewart, whose school he had attended in England. The latter had had the idea that he should first gain knowledge of tobacco-growing in the United States. When young Stewart died, James abandoned tobacco-growing and bought a one-third interest in a mill at Gibsonburg, Ohio, with money he had received from 'home'. The source of this money, whether it was from the Hearn family, was not specified. He had to give up milling on health grounds and went into farming but failed in this. Lafcadio had been in Ohio at the same time, working in Cincinnati, but the two had been unaware of their proximity to each other.

After Lafcadio had returned from the West Indies, James saw his name in a Cleveland newspaper and wrote to him. His brother's unsigned reply had all the grace and enthusiasm of a tax query and consisted mainly of a series of questions intended to test his correspondent's *bone fides*.[38] He was convinced by the photograph of their father which James forwarded as proof of their relationship and replied eagerly, explaining the peremptory note of his first response as a reaction to previous hoaxes from supposed relatives. When James sent photographs of his wife and baby, Lafcadio showed that delight in lineage which was part of his psychological make-up. He outlined to James his sole memory of his mother, the one he worked into both *Chita* and *Youma*.[39]

The other scraps of recollection of his parents, or what he had heard about them, followed: his father's stabbing by his mother's brother, his fateful visit to Alicia Crawford, who became his second wife, his alienation from Mrs Brenane and, indeed, Lafcadio's own sparse relationship with a taciturn, feared father who allegedly had never addressed him. He recalled Miss Butcher, his mother's interpreter, without giving any hint of knowing the evil role she was alleged by Nina Kennard to have played in his parents' break-up. James was less enamoured of the memory of their mother, who seemed to him to have irresponsibly abandoned them in their infancy but Lafcadio would hear none of it.[40]

Lafcadio wrote to his brother that he felt he had two souls, one 'the spirit of mutiny' and the other 'pride and persistence', each pulling in different directions. The latter had 'had little power to use the reins' before he was thirty (he claimed to have had a nervous breakdown sometime before then). Notwithstanding his preference for his mother, one wonders if he did not consciously identify 'the spirit of mutiny' with his mother's psycho-inheritance and that of 'pride and resistance' with his father's 'rigid, grim face and steel-steady eyes'.[41] That certainly was his brother's view; he wrote later to their half-sister that their 'dark, passionate Greek mother's blood had a taint in it' and he believed that whatever manliness he had come from their father.[42]

James would have liked to have met his brother and offered to pay his expenses to Ohio but Lafcadio had other plans. His last letter was written in haste the day before he left for Japan. He apologised for being unable to make the trip to Ohio but declared himself 'a slave of contracts and opportunities'. There may have been a note of irritation on the subject of 'Lafcadio', as his brother would have remembered him as 'Patrick': 'It was a mistake to suppose my name 'assumed': it is the name my mother gave me. Patricio I dropped from the time of my arrival in this country.'[43] This latter point was not, of course true; he had continued to be 'Paddy Hearn' for some years after his arrival in the United States.

The correspondence with James revived in 1892. James had encountered a traveller from the Orient who painted a lurid picture of a Japan sunk in heathenism. Lafcadio set out to disabuse him. In answer to some of James' questions, he also made his own position clear:

> No, I do not belong to any society, and I am not a Mason. I do not believe in any form of religion on this earth or outside of it. When I was in the Northern States of America, I was a believer in Republicanism, because I was young. When I had lived 5 years in the South I believed in Democracy. Politics, like religions and manners, have their reason for being in different conditions of society and different necessities.[44]

The essence of Lafcadio's interest was, however, their parents and he was savagely critical of his brother for not having made a greater effort to find out more about them, to a point where he wrote a letter which terminated the correspondence:

What most astounds me is that you never heard, or never tried to find out anything about mother. I tried. I thought also you would surely know; and I had a Spanish friend in Paris hunting for Uncle Dick, to get his address. He knew all about it. The Elwoods of Dublin, I think, knew about it; but both are dead. The best way to find out would be through army sources, and Sister in London might help in that. Perhaps there are officers still living, who were in the 76th (now 2nd Battalion West Riding) at the same time as father. They might know. It would be really worthwhile to learn about our own history. Perhaps we should learn amazingly curious things.[45]

In the contradictory way common to such outbursts, Lafcadio still expressed the belief that they would see each other. They never did. While the tenor of his correspondence with James was otherwise cordial, he later gave a very twisted account to his son, Kazuo, who was led to believe that his father had:

. . .only one brother on this earth, named James. To him father wrote an affectionate letter from the bottom of his heart, and sent it off. In reply he expected to get a warm, affectionate reply, but was disappointed in having him take advantage of his soft words and, in an unfeeling way, try to take advantage of him. Father was disgusted with him, [and] so left his brother without seeing him.[46]

As James passed out of his life, Minnie Charlotte, one of his father's three daughters by his second wife, entered. She was the second of the three children born to her father in India (on 27 July 1859) and the last to attempt communication with the half-brother whose reputation was beginning to percolate through to the circles in which the Hearns mixed. As Nina Kennard has pointed out, public interest in Japan was developing and the works of eminent Japanologists such as Chamberlain and Satow were becoming standard.[47] There was a craze for 'Japaneserie' in Britain in the last twenty years of the nineteenth century, leading up to the Anglo-Japanese Alliance of 1902.[48] Hearn's magazine contributions and, even more likely, the newspaper syndication organised by Page Baker, which included England, naturally attracted attention. It is not surprising that the Hearns, with their literary and artistic tradition, should have been among those impressed.

Minnie Charlotte, now married to a Mr Buckley Atkinson in

Portadown, may have been the first of the three sisters to receive an answer because she was apparently able to provide news of Elizabeth Bisland's marriage; Bisland lived in London for a time but how Minnie Atkinson knew her remains a mystery. Much of the correspondence between Lafcadio and Mrs Atkinson during his stay in Kumamoto was paralleled by that with Basil Hall Chamberlain – it was an old habit of his to write virtually identical letters to more than one correspondent. The letters to Mrs Atkinson were, however, distinguished by a keen interest in the Hearn family and a tender regard for her and her children. In his second letter, he confessed that he knew little of his relations, so her letter had interested him in 'a peculiar way, apart from its amiable charm'.[49]

Setsu, good politician that she was, entered into the spirit of the correspondence and 'stole' Minnie's picture, framed it and hung it in the *Toko*, the household's 'second Holy place'. He became ever more eager, saying he would like to see her, to find out what the 'angel' in her heart was like. His insecurity surfaced when he warned her to make her children love him in advance because, if they saw him without being prepared, they would be afraid of his 'ugly face' – his photo showed only half; 'the other is not pleasant, I assure you: like the moon, I show only one side of myself'.[50]

These exchanges had a much deeper effect on Lafcadio than the surface would indicate: he told Chamberlain that they made his soul turn 'not sky-blue, but indigo' because they made him realise how isolated he was 'even in the midst of an amiable population'. He also revealed his private ambiguity about his Irish relations, combined with fascination with the connection between India, his father and his father's second family. He had only recently discovered that his father had been in the West Indies; he himself had had the sensation when he was there of having seen it all before. He imagined that he would experience even stronger sensations in India. His tone to Chamberlain about his half-sisters was caustic: he would give ten years of his life for one in India while they could '. . .blaspheme the Gods at being obliged to live in such a blasted country'.[51]

As these feelings eddied within Hearn, he discovered that Setsuko was pregnant. He, whose life was still so profoundly influenced by his dead parents, was to become a parent himself.

In the weeks leading up to the birth, he returned to explore his own childhood – the golden years, this time – in 'a sort of reverie',[52] which was published as 'The Dream of a Summer-Day'. The 'Dream' is a short gem of poetic prose in which Lafcadio fuses the tale of Urashima, the young fisherman who is taken to the palace of the Dragon King of the Sea (a place of eternal youth, similar to the Irish legend of *Tir na nOg*) with a flashback to an enchanted memory of his own childhood and Mrs Elwood, an aunt he had loved dearly:

> I have a memory of a place and a magical time in which the Sun and the Moon were larger and brighter than now. Whether it was of this life or of some life before I cannot tell. But I know the sky was very much more blue, and nearer to the world,- almost as it seems to become above the masts of a steamer steaming into equatorial summer. The sea was alive, and used to talk,- and the Wind made me cry for joy when it touched me. Once or twice during the other years, in divine days lived among the peaks, I have dreamed just for a moment that the same wind was blowing,- but it was only a remembrance.
>
> Also in that place the clouds were wonderful, and of colors for which there are no names at all,- colors that used to make me hungry and thirsty. I remember, too, that the days were ever so much longer than these days,- and that every day there were new wonders and new pleasures for me. And all that country and time were softly ruled by One who thought only of ways to make me happy. Sometimes I would refuse to be made happy, and that always caused her pain, although she was divine;- and I remember that I tried very hard to be sorry. When day was done, and there fell the great hush of the light before moonrise, she would tell me stories that made me tingle from head to foot with pleasure. I have never heard any other story half so beautiful. And when the pleasure became too great, she would sing a weird little song which always brought sleep. At last there came a parting day; and she wept, and told me of a charm she had given that I must never, never lose, because it would keep me young, and give me power to return. But I never returned. And the years went; and one day I knew that I had lost the charm, and had become ridiculously old.[53]

Around this time, Lafcadio went to Tokyo to stay at Chamberlain's house at 19 Akasaka Daimachi, a visit which stirred other happy childhood memories. Chamberlain himself was away at Miyanoshita but had given his guest the run of his home. Hearn was delighted with what he found – a beautiful house, a magnificent library and Mr Toda, an English-speaking servant who attended punctiliously to his wants. It transported him back across the years to the opulence of Mrs Brenane's home in Dublin, which he translated to England for Chamberlain's benefit:

> And besides, there are memories of England which bring back visions of my boyhood – suggestions no American home furnishes. The English crest on silver plate, – the delicious little castors,- the 'homey' arrangement of articles. . .all created for me a sort of revival of old, old, and very intimate impressions. Therefore, I suppose, some ghosts of very long ago came soundlessly about me once or twice in twilight time,- portraits of another era, forgotten for thirty-five years, faintly shaped themselves for me in the dusk before the lighting of the lamp. In thought I sat again upon the floor of a house which no longer exists, and shot at armies of tin soldiers with cannon charged with dried peas.[54]

There were other ghosts, from the dark side of childhood's legacy; one night he dreamt of robbers:

> . . .who became transformed into something nameless and awful. I did not see them – only felt them. Something entered the house; and the stairs groaned under a hideous weight: I wanted to rise, but could not. It was coming, coming. I suddenly awoke; and felt the whole house shaking. Imagine the momentary sensation.[55]

It was only an earthquake.

While Lafcadio was being transported back to his childhood memories, the attention of the household was concentrated on his first-born child. The day after Kazuo's birth, in November 1893, Lafcadio wrote to Ellwood Hendrick expressing feelings of awe at the sacredness of maternity, mixed with humility and gratitude. There were other feelings, too complex to define: '. . .perhaps an echo in a man's heart of all the sensations felt by all the fathers and mothers of his race at a similar instant in the past'. He was already formulating his views on Kazuo's upbringing:

> The little man will wear sandals and dress like a Japanese, and become a good Buddhist if he lives long enough. He

will not have to go to church, and listen to stupid sermons,
and be perpetually tormented by absurd conventions.[56]
Unlike his father, he would not be made miserable by
Christianity.

The birth of Kazuo made acute in Hearn's mind the question
of his citizenship. He had tried several times since going to
Kumamoto to have Setsu legally registered as his wife and always
got the answer that it was a very difficult matter which, in Japan,
indicates a considerably greater degree of difficulty than it does in
the West. Within a week or so of Kazuo's birth, he tried to
register him and was told that, as both parties came from Matsue,
they should make a statement of marriage to the Matsue
authorities while being told cryptically at the same time: 'The
law is difficult for you'. He found that if he wished his son to
remain a Japanese citizen, he should be registered in his mother's
name only; if registered in his father's name, he became a
foreigner. Hearn wanted Kazuo to be a Japanese citizen and
believed that he himself could become a citizen by direct
application to the Government but the old fear of a salary
reduction still restrained him. He had seen discouraging
precedents.[57]

There was, though, the consolation that in these three years he
produced what was arguably his finest book. Notwithstanding his
claim of lack of inspiration there, *Out of the East* was as surely a
product of Kumamoto as *Glimpses of Unfamiliar Japan* was of
Matsue. A slim volume compared to its predecessor, it was tauter
and more analytical. This had been his objective. He had
informed Nishida in August 1893 that he was writing:

> . . .another book on Japan, of a different kind. . .I am
> trying to write little stories illustrating the beautiful side of
> the Japanese character – not of feudal times, but of today. I
> try to get ideas about the thoughts of children, and actions
> of the common people,- peasants, servants, labourers. For
> the people are the tree,- root, trunk and branches: the
> cultivated class are only the flower.

If Nishida heard of 'anything noble, or beautiful, or touching,
or brave in common life during the next two years', he was to be
informed.[58] All Hearn's friends, such as Chamberlain and Mason,
were asked to contribute information in this way. As far back as
November 1891, when his former Matsue pupil, Masanobu

Otani, wrote offering to find out about Shinto for him, Hearn replied asking a series of specific questions. This is the first evidence of his using students as researchers, something he was to do a good deal later.[59]

By late September 1894, he had sent off the final paper for *Out of the East* which had been limited to 70,000 words, presumably to avoid the mushrooming which had afflicted *Glimpses of Unfamiliar Japan*. The volume began with 'The Dream of a Summer Day' which contained, as had already been noted, a flashback to an idyllic memory of a childhood experience in Ireland. 'With Kyushu Students', the second essay, was an unflattering, if fair, account of his teaching experiences and its contrast with 'From the Diary of an English Teacher' is the contrast of his happiness in Matsue with his unhappiness in Kumamoto. The change of tone from *Glimpses* was again emphasised in the next essay, 'At Hakata' which opens with a very negative account of travelling in Japan. With the jolting of the *karuma* making reading impossible, the passenger is confined to gazing at the monotonous scenery. Hearn asks himself how many times he must see the same Kyushu landscape 'deploring the absence of the wonderful'.[60]

The following month, March 1894, Lafcadio wrote to a former Matsue pupil, Ochiai, who had been ostracised by his schoolmates and turned to his old teacher for advice. Hearn counselled him not to feel anger against those who had shunned him – they had done so because he had offended their 'national sentiment,- that jealous love of country with which every man is born. . .' This prompted Hearn to recall the Mattie Foley incident in his own life and the complete change in his perspective showed just how conservative the former defier of convention had become:

> I was too young then to understand. There were other moral questions, much larger than those I had been arguing about, which really caused the whole trouble. The people did not know how to express them very well; they only felt them. After some years I discovered that I was quite mistaken – that I was under a delusion. I had been opposing a great national and social principle without knowing it. And if my best friends had not got angry with me, I could not have learned the truth so well,- because there are many things that are hard to explain, and can only be fully taught

by experience.[61]

A more radical and fundamental change of attitude was apparent in 'Of the Eternal Feminine' in *Out of the East*. Nine years before its composition, in March 1884, Hearn had written to W.D. O'Connor a long defence of indulgence in the 'mad excess of love': love was the creator of great thoughts and great deeds; all history was illuminated by the 'Eternal Feminine'.[62] Ironically enough, it was the sight of an old copy of the *Times-Democrat*, on which he was working when he wrote this, which set him thinking in Japan of the contrasting sexual attitudes of Japan and the West.[63] He sketched out his ideas first in a series of letters to Chamberlain and Ellwood Hendrick. To Chamberlain, he wrote:

> . . .it occurred to me that certain peculiarities of the art of both hemispheres can only be explained by the absence or presence of the dominant sexual idea. Not only must the Japanese remain quite blind to all in our literature, art, etc., created by that idea; but we ourselves must suffer aesthetically by the necessarily one-sided character of our own art − or aesthetic development.[64]

Hendrick must have been surprised when the erstwhile Bohemian wrote in April 1893 that Western man lived in a 'musky atmosphere of desire', that everything in the West was aimed at 'stimulating, exaggerating and exacerbating the thought of sex'. The Oriental was shocked by Western art − he would see it for what it was, an 'artificial stimulus to dangerous senses'. It seemed to Hearn 'almost disgusting'.[65] This theme was developed at length in 'Of the Eternal Feminine'. When completed, it moved Basil Hall Chamberlain, who was not given to flattery, to comment:

> 'The Eternal Feminine' seemed to me yesterday when re-read, as it had when read first, quite the best thing ever written on Japan. There is more of truth and insight in its first few pages than in whole volumes by even such men as Lowell, let alone the Arnolds and the lesser fry of book-mongers.[66]

In February 1894, a visit to a *jiujutsu* school gave Hearn an idea for reforming the educational system. Here was the old samurai school system, 'severely simple, healthy, lovable, romantic'; could not all schools be based on it? The great mistake for Japan was to have built Western 'monstrosities of brick, and destroyed the Oriental relation of pupil to teacher'.[67] Lafcadio was enormously impressed with the *jiujutsu* teacher, Arima Sumihito, a handsome cynic who spoke English perfectly. His musing on *jiujutsu*, which he translated as 'to conquer by yielding', inspired one of the finest chapters in *Out of the East*. It provided him with a graphic means of illustrating fundamental differences between East and West and illuminating a secret of Japanese success.

'*Jiujutsu*' was a major essay in *Out of the East*. The concept of irregularity, which Lafcadio had borrowed from Chamberlain, now fused with his observations of the martial arts' form: whereas the Occidental mind appeared to work in straight lines, that of the Oriental worked 'in wonderful curves and circles'. Hearn believed that only an Oriental mind could have elaborated the theory of never opposing force by force but, instead, of using an opponent's own strength to defeat him. A generation before, foreigners might well have assumed that Japan would adopt, not just the industry, science and technology of the West but also its religious convictions. It would have been logical to believe that Japan would be opened to foreign settlement and capital. But such beliefs were based on ignorance of Japanese capacity, foresight and 'of its immemorial spirit of independence.' Nobody suspected that Japan was practising *jiujutsu*.[68]

In practice, Japan had taken from the West 'the highest results only' of industry, applied science, economic, financial and legal experience and shaped them to her own needs. She had adopted nothing for purely imitative reasons and taken only what would increase her strength. Hearn then made a point which is absolutely critical to any understanding of Japan but which is, even today, but dimly understood: 'Those who imagine Japanese to be merely imitative also imagine them to be savages. As a fact, they are assimilative and adoptive only, and that to a degree of genius.'[69]

In '*Jiujutsu*', Hearn gave religion a fundamental role in the life of the nation. It was, he believed, much more than a dogma about the supernatural; it was a synthesis of the whole ethical experience of the race and no nation could afford to voluntarily abandon the faith identified with its ethical life. The great success of Buddhism was its ability to incorporate alien faiths whereas

Islam and Christianity were, by contrast, essentially intolerant. In Japan, Buddhism was able to co-exist with the indigenous Shinto. To introduce Christianity to an Oriental country necessitated the destruction, not just of its native faith, but of its social system as well.[70] This conviction remained a fundamental tenet of Hearn's philosophy in relation to Japan until he died.

Hearn's style in *Out of the East* continued to be a fusion of the factual and the philosophical, the anecdotal and the analytical. 'The Stone Buddha', for example, reveals the lonely lunch-hours spent in the cemetery behind the school but is, at the same time, an attempt at synthesis of Buddhist and scientific thought. There was an element of public *mea culpa* for the perceived shortcomings of *Glimpses* in this second Japanese work. 'In Yokohama' contained a confession of what he felt had been a maturing process in coming to terms with the country:

> The beautiful illusion of Japan, the almost weird charm that comes with one's first entrance into her magical atmosphere, had, indeed, stayed with me very long, but had faded out at last. I had learned to see the Far East without its glamour. And I had mourned not a little for the sensations of the past.[71]

While Hearn was perhaps using poetic licence to exaggerate the extent of his early illusions, there was indeed a harder note in *Out of the East*. Where he had idealised Japanese women in his first book, he now saw that under the submissive sweetness of the Japanese woman 'there exists possibilities of hardness absolutely inconceivable without ocular evidence'. She could forgive a thousand times but if subjected to deliberate malice, 'there may suddenly appear in that frail-seeming woman an incredible courage, an appalling, measured, tireless purpose of honest vengeance'.[72]

He had determined that he would now write stories of real Japanese life and 'The Red Bridal' was such an attempt.[73] Nina Kennard was told by Dr Papellier, a doctor who attended Hearn in Kobe in 1895, that he had once shown the writer a report in the *Kobe Chronicle* describing the suicide of a demi-mondaine and her lover in a railway tunnel; the incident supposedly formed the basis of 'The Red Bridal', which Papellier claimed distorted the real facts of the case.[74] This, however, was simply not true as

Hearn dispatched the story to Scudder under cover of a letter of 14 November 1893, well before he went to Kobe.[75] It was a superbly crafted tale of the double suicide of a couple who die under an express train: '. . .the wheels passed through both,- cutting evenly, like enormous shears'. Chamberlain liked the story, which Lafcadio described as '. . .an awfully dangerous experiment. . .'[76]

The theme of love suicide, with its background of cruel calculation of social forces which had thwarted the young couple's desires, marked a further contrast with *Glimpses*. Similarly, 'Yuko', the tale of a girl who takes her own life in an act of national atonement, shows an awareness of the deeper currents stirring in Japanese society. While Hearn clearly admired Yuko's heroism, he saw other forces at work:

> For this people, like its own Shinto gods, has various souls: it has it *Nigi-mi-tama* and its *Ara-mi-tama*, its Gentle and its Rough Spirit. The Gentle Spirit seeks only to make reparation; but the Rough Spirit demands expiation. And now through the darkening atmosphere of the popular life, everywhere is felt the strange thrilling of these opposite impulses, as of two electricities.[77]

The coincidence of his unhappy personal circumstances and his darkening artistic vision of Japan were temporarily obliterated when Lafcadio set off from Kumamoto, on 10 July 1894, to meet at last in the flesh his long-time correspondent, W.B. Mason. On board ship, he had felt afraid, coming out of the long years' solitude when 'a sudden sense of the civilization I had been so long decrying and arguing against, and vainly rebelling against, came upon me crushingly'.[78] Within a few hours, Lafcadio was with Mason and his family in Yokohama. He felt immediately that he was amongst friends. There was now a great surge of joy to be back within a Western atmosphere; he declared that he had misjudged the open ports. Now he waxed lyrical about the expatriates who had given up their home countries 'for the pure love of duty' and wanted to study '. . .this excited Western life. . .and tell all the beautiful things that are in it'.[79] But Lafcadio was also engaged in the serious business of 'feeling pulses' in Yokohama, scouting for prospects of employment there, as a reaction to the uncertainty of his position in Kumamoto.[80]

1.

Lafcadio Hearn and Mitchell McDonald, Yokohama 1901

2.

3.

Lafcadio Hearn aged about eight with
Mrs Sarah Brenane (Dublin, late 1850s)

Lafcadio Hearn at Ushaw College, Durham,
aged about 13

4. Interior of Ushaw College, Durham, in the 1860s

5.

48 Lower Gardiner Street
Dublin, where Lafcadio
Hearn and his mother, Rosa
Antonia, lived with Mrs Eliza-
beth Hearn (grandmother) on
arrival in Ireland in 1852

6.

8.

Charles Bush Hearn (Hearn's father),
1818–1886

Lafcadio Hearn *ca.* 1873

9.

7.

10.

Elizabeth Bisland *ca.* 1890

House of Mrs Courtney with whom Hearn lodged in
New Orleans

Lafcadio Hearn, Kumamoto, 1891

The Hearn house in Matsue

13.

Lafcadio Hearn with colleagues and pupils of the Matsue Ordinary Middle School, 18 July 1891

14.

Lafcadio Hearn with colleagues and pupils in Kumamoto, 1894

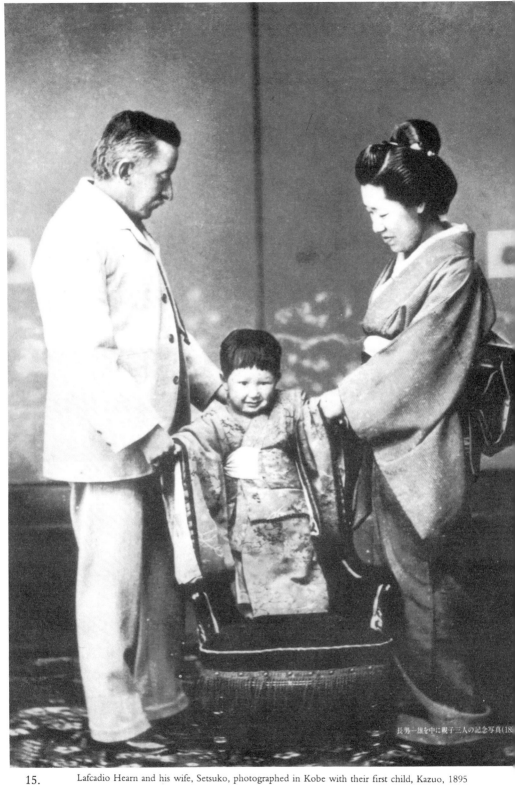

長男一雄を中に親子三人の記念写真(18

15.   Lafcadio Hearn and his wife, Setsuko, photographed in Kobe with their first child, Kazuo, 1895

17. Yone Naguchi   18. Masanobu Otani   19. Basil Hall Chamberlain   20. Nobushige Amenori

21.

Lafcadio Hearn, 1895

16.

James Daniel Hearn, Lafcadio's younger
half-brother

22.

Minnie Charlotte Hearn (LH's half-sister)

23.   Lafcadio Hearn photographed in Ueno Park, Tokyo, 19 September 1904, the week before his death

On his way from Shinbashi Station in central Tokyo to Chamberlain's house at Akasaka, Lafcadio called to see Hasegawa, the publisher of a Japanese fairy-tale series. Shortly beforehand Hasegawa had asked Chamberlain for an introduction to Hearn. The professor wisely decided to consult the writer first, setting out the conditions under which Hasegawa operated: he paid $20 per tale, with only one being taken on at a time as the illustrations had to evolve gradually between the publisher, author and artist.[81] Hearn liked Hasegawa immediately and gave him two stories.[82] It was the beginning of a fruitful collaboration which lasted until Lafcadio's death. Here was a publisher whose approach – meticulous, painstaking and aesthetically sensitive – was the same as his own, so that the altercations which marked his relations with the large-scale, commercial publishers did not mar this relationship. The series was easily the most beautifully-produced work of Hearn's to be published in his lifetime.

On this journey, Lafcadio discovered from an official that he was much more popular with his Kumamoto students than he had imagined. This confirmed his own impression that he had been winning them over.[83] He was also more accepted in his locality; the people of the street now came to his house on festive occasions.[84] But even such happy integration could not completely dispel the restless ambiguity which, even in the best days, pervaded Hearn's attitude towards Kumamoto. On 16 May 1894, he confessed to Chamberlain that he was 'getting rather hungry' for the open ports. It might be preferable to live in an obscure village where the old ways prevailed but his family did not share his taste for 'out-of-the-way nooks and corners'.[85]

At this time Hearn was probably more preoccupied by major – and threatening – political developments. In the spring of 1894 the outbreak of the Sino-Japanese War was only weeks away. The man who had beaten the drum of Japanese nationalism was having to live with its less pleasant side. He who, in 1893, had denounced the idea of opening up Japan to mixed residence as 'sheer wickedness. . .a monstrous crime'[86] was now feeling 'the power of anti-foreign reaction'; he was sometimes subjected to a 'sudden hiss of hatred' by passers-by and was convinced that foreigners like himself in the interior of the country would be in difficulties if the political situation developed as he anticipated.[87]

The previous July he could take satisfaction in having saved

$3,500;[88] by June 1894, the political uncertainties, allied to a drop in the exchange rate and the birth of Kazuo were making him anxious about money.[89] Worst of all, he had now come to the conclusion that his position at work had become untenable. On 8 June 1894, he confided to Chamberlain: 'Well, I'm ashamed to acknowledge it; but I am beaten. I would go tomorrow if I could get a man to jump right into my place. Nerves worn out. Today I am sick with a fever – caused by suppressed anger.' He asked his friend to let him know if he heard of any nice post going. At this time, he also made enquiries in Yokohama about prospects in journalism.[90]

A letter was penned to Mr Kano, the former headmaster of the school, but was held back because Lafcadio did not now trust him sufficiently. Hearn believed that a teacher had hidden in a grave to listen to his conversation with a student: 'It is madness – I am in a lunatic asylum.'[91] Two days later, he could stand no more; he dismissed his class and went home to compose his letter of resignation. He tore it up, however, and went instead to the house of Sakurai, the headmaster. He had confidence in this civilised, French-educated man, and Hearn conversed with him guardedly, not mentioning names, but simply setting out his unhappy experiences. The headmaster tried to reassure him that he was liked and that his not being asked to renew his contract was merely an oversight. Hearn responded that he was no longer interested in staying, only in leaving on good terms.

Sakurai promised to talk to the director on his return and Hearn felt some hope as the director also disliked his enemy, Mr Sakuma, and felt that a way might be found to get rid of him.[92] Sakuma was a fellow teacher in the English Department who was, Lafcadio believed, in league with the missionaries. He further believed that the lines of intrigue connected both Kumamoto and the *Mombusho* (Education Department). He saw Sakuma as playing a double game:

> . . .for he carried information about missionary work to Tokyo. He forced out of the school several better men than himself; and his cleverness at this sort of intrigue is very great. Now it strikes me that he was the chief party in the matter – at all events, after three years, I could not possibly live in the school with him any longer at any salary.[93]

Hearn did admit that he had no proof of these suspicions as

only the headmaster would talk to him. This isolation from his fellow teachers was undoubtedly a major cause of the difficulties in which he found himself: as a foreigner among the Japanese he felt terribly alone and a *go-ishi* (pawn).[94]

Hearn's suspicions extended to Mr Kano, the school's previous director, whom he had formerly liked. He now found Kano:

> . . .not kind at all. He denied many things I knew to be true; and came to the house chiefly for information as to how the Sendai and Kagoshima posts had been offered me. He left suddenly and abruptly,- and I felt quite convinced from his conversation that I had been got rid of with his approval.[95]

An interesting comment on all this was provided by Sanki Ichikawa who, as Professor of English at Tokyo University, edited a collection of Hearn's letters and writings in 1925: 'Some kind of intrigue is always going on in a Japanese school, office, or company. The trouble with Hearn was that he always thought that such intrigue was directed against him.'[96] Ichikawa's comment is probably the most judicious approach to the whole tangled, unhappy affair. He conceded the likelihood of intrigue having gone on. Hearn was doubly vulnerable, being isolated and a foreigner. It was a situation which might have affected the nerves of someone without his sensitivity. Also, he was an avowed enemy of the missionaries and it is not unreasonable to suppose that they would have used any influence they had to cause him discomfiture.

Lafcadio was deeply and lastingly hurt by the incident. A year later, in July 1895, he still felt disgusted at his treatment in Kumamoto and was '. . .inclined to dislike all Japanese – except my old Izumo friends. I answer no more letters, and refuse to see any more Jap[an]ese visitors'.[97] This squalid episode led to the ending of Lafcadio's sojourn in Kumamoto where he was, at best, intermittently content. His anger also turned inward and he wrote bitter letters of self-reproach to foreign friends in which he traduced himself as a chronic failure, and a fraud. Self-hatred mingled with bitterness when he wrote of himself in April 1894:

> Your ancestors were not religious people: you lack constitutional morality. That's why you are poor, and unsuccessful, and void of mental balance, and an exile in

Japan. You know you cannot be happy in an English moral community. You are a fraud – a vile Latin – a vicious French-hearted scallywag.[98]

By August 1894, he found that to write the very name Kumamoto was disagreeable: 'The old sensation of nervous lonesomeness enveloped me just like a black atmosphere after my return, and stays with me.'[99] By the following month, he was reporting that the whole household was fed up with Kumamoto and anxious to leave.[100] He himself was thinking of returning to the United States. Sometime in the later summer or autumn of 1894 Lafcadio wrote to Page Baker of the *Times-Democrat* asking if he could arrange a position for him in the United States. Had this request come to anything, it would probably have separated Lafcadio from his family. In the USA, he wanted to go south of the Mason and Dixon Line but felt he could not take his family there. South America, on the other hand, might, he imagined, be more possible, if Page Baker could get him something there in the field of education.[101] In September, he wrote to Watkin: 'I am almost sure I shall have to seek America again. If that happens, I shall see you or die. All now is doubt and confusion.'[102] However, the confusion rapidly dissolved and the trauma of separation from his family proved unnecessary as a newspaper job in Kobe materialised and he moved there with his family, in October 1894.

CHAPTER NINE

KOBE

WHEN ROBERT YOUNG, founder of the *Kobe Chronicle*, an English-language newspaper in one of the more congenial open ports, heard that Hearn wished to quit teaching in Kumamoto, he offered him a job. Young, a vigorous Scot, had been producing and publishing the daily paper with the sole help of his wife but now needed Hearn, with his journalistic talent and experience, to shoulder the editorial responsibilities. Always anxious about money, Lafcadio was unimpressed by the salary of one hundred dollars per month but accepted the job out of desperation.[1] Having anticipated misery, he was pleasantly surprised to find it the most agreeable position he had ever had in his life. Young and himself took to each other immediately and were in sympathy on the issues of the day.[2] He was treated, not as an employee but as 'a directing spirit' in the office and as a brother outside it. Young did, however, have to exercise at least a degree of diplomacy to keep matters on an even keel. He told Nina Kennard years later of an incident at his house when Lafcadio walked away from their dinner table and would not return because another guest had dissented from his opinion.[3]

Young did, however, get full value from his editorial writer at the *Kobe Chronicle*, and Lafcadio fulfilled his commitment to write daily editorials, contributing 47 to the newspaper in all between 11 October and 14 December 1894, when his failing eyesight forced him to resign. The Sino-Japanese War, which had begun the previous summer and continued until the following April, was the natural focus of his attention. He had supported Japan in the war from the beginning, describing it in September 1894 as the '. . .last huge effort of the race for national independence' by a nation 'under the steady torturing pressure of our industrial civilization – being robbed every year by unjust treaties'.[4] To all his correspondents, including Page Baker and Watkin, he expressed confidence, rightly as it turned out, in eventual Japanese victory. He held the view that everything Japan had worked for since the beginning of Meiji, her efforts to leave behind her feudal past and create a modern society, might be gloriously realised by military triumph and she might be able to win, not just a place among the great powers, but take a higher rank among them than had ever been deemed possible.[5]

He did, at the same time, have his doubts: the war might leave Japan independent of foreign interference but he had grave reservations about the possible long-term effects of victory on the Japanese body politic; though the ordinary people were still good, he saw a growing process of corruption within the upper classes.[6] In a sense Hearn was right. Victory strengthened the ruling oligarchy and began a process of military domination within it which helped to lead eventually to the disasters of the Second World War.[7]

Hearn also foresaw that the Japanese war effort would be followed by a strong anti-foreign reaction. Foreigners would be forced out in another 20 or 30 years and foreign commercial interests reduced to agencies: 'A system of small persecutions will be inaugurated and maintained to drive away all the foreigners who can be driven away.'[8] By the time of 'The Triple Intervention' of April 1895, he had the unpleasant sensation of being reviled as a foreigner in the streets of Kobe.

The politically-generated turbulence which Lafcadio's relationship with his friend Basil Hall Chamberlain now suffered must have added salt to the wounds. It sprang from their being diametrically opposed on the merits of the Anglo-Japanese Treaty of 1894, which abolished the – to Japan – unequal clauses of the previous treaty between the two countries. Chamberlain expressed his outrage at what he saw as a British diplomatic humiliation and confidently expected his friend to feel likewise. He was bewildered when he found that Lafcadio supported the treaty and wrote angrily:

But surely these are not the lines on which to judge a treaty between a great Western state and that two-penny half-penny Brummagem imitation of one which these frock-coated officials have made of Japan. . .But that you, YOU, who have over again expressed your adverse opinion about these officials should champion their cause, is to me inexplicable, except on the supposition that you confuse them and Old Japan.[9]

Chamberlain missed the point. He failed to see that Hearn was not championing the cause of the Japanese officials but, despite his dislike of them, recognised that they were promoting the national interest. Chamberlain revealed himself in this exchange as a conventional imperialist who not alone misunderstood Hearn but had underestimated the developing strength of Japan and Britain's farsighted diplomacy in allying itself with this rising new power, which was to be dramatically justified by Japan's defeat of Russia within a few years. Chamberlain, who was a friend of H. Rider Haggard's family, seems to have been caught up in imperialist illusions of a type associated with Haggard's novels. It is a curious contrast, this, between the distinguished professor who was immersed in Japanese scholarship of the highest order and yet failed to understand Japanese policy while Hearn, the relative newcomer whose knowledge of the language was rudimentary, emerges as the clear-sighted, *modern* figure.

Perhaps sensing this, Hearn quickly changed his tone towards Chamberlain. Gone was the old reverential deference and, in its place, an ironic contempt for Chamberlain's inability to be 'scientific'.[10] He even allowed himself a vicious – and unfounded – outburst of vituperation against Chamberlain whom he accused of colluding against him. In a letter to Chamberlain, he expressed his bitterness that the Professor had done nothing to help while he suffered in Kumamoto, accusing Chamberlain indeed of having revelled in his discomfiture. Incongruously, Hearn ended the letter by inviting Chamberlain to visit him:

Still, if you pass Kobe after I am settled here, I shall expect a call. In another fortnight all will be arranged; and I shall be well able to make you cosy with us.[11]

Later, Lafcadio admitted to being hypersensitive and baffled by friends who were differently 'soul-toned', but it was due to Chamberlain's capacity for friendship that the relationship between the two men continued. He displayed his loyalty to Hearn by being instrumental in obtaining a professorship for him at Tokyo University within two years.

Hearn, for his part, demonstrated the complexity of the relationship by rushing to Chamberlain's defence when he was attacked in print. The June 1895 issue of the *Atlantic Monthly* carried a joint review of *Glimpses* and *Out of the East* by an anonymous reviewer who was, Hearn was convinced, Ernest Fenollosa. It was positive, though in precisely the way which Lafcadio most resented: his 'genius' was variously defined in terms of poetry and painting. While criticising Lafcadio's architectonic powers – the chapters had 'little organic unity' and 'no scientific aim or philosophical grasp' to round them into form – tribute was paid to his 'sympathy and exquisiteness of touch'. The influence of Japanese restraint was contrasted with the voluptuousness of his West Indian sketches. If the reviewer really was Fenollosa, he showed no false modesty by claiming that it was he who had introduced Hearn to the work of Hokusai and Hiroshige. If Hearn was damned with faint praise, no such compunction operated in the case of Basil Hall Chamberlain. His *Things Japanese* was not ostensibly under review but was nonetheless condemned as '. . .cynical, unfeeling, blind to all higher meaning of Oriental life and light, sour and self-conscious, like much of English comment on alien standards'.[12]

Hearn was furious. He wrote immediately to Scudder, editor of the *Atlantic Monthly*, denouncing Fenollosa as '. . .a pseudo-litterateur and a spiritualist quack. . . a theosophical, fraudulent, malicious person. . .' Lafcadio has been depicted as unreasonable in his dealings with publishers but this letter, though angry, was far from irrational. He listed the various criticisms made in the review and asked Scudder to say if they were true. He then dwelled on their contradictions. For once, he was not suspicious as to motive; he believed that Fenollosa had been asked to do the review under the mistaken impression that he was a close friend.[13]

Lafcadio's correspondence with Chamberlain picked up again, but even so contained within it the seeds of the final falling-out. Chamberlain made the cardinal error of attempting to alter, not just Hearn's style – he was willing to make grudging concessions on that – but his approach to writing; this was one sin Lafcadio never forgave. The Professor, in his academic, fussy fashion, admonished his friend over his misuse of 'shall' and 'will'. This, he suggested, may have been an American influence which he attributed to the 'Irish invasion' of the United States, a back-handed putting-down of Hearn's origins. He decided to send a 'corrected' copy of *Glimpses* back to its author. Hearn responded by saying that tone to him was everything; the word nothing. He was guided by euphony and felt:

> . . .angry with conventional forms of language of which I cannot understand the real spirit. . .I am 'colour-blind' to the values you assert; and I suspect that the majority of the English-speaking races – the raw people – are also blind thereunto. It is the people, after all, who make the language in the end, and in the direction of least resistance.[14]

Lafcadio seemed to climb down somewhat on the question of 'shall' and 'will' – the technically correct use of which frequently divides the Irish from the English! – but he was adamant he would not accept Chamberlain's strictures that he write with 'justice and temperateness'; that would mean writing as if he were Chamberlain.[15] On top of this, the bluff, straight-talking Englishmen remarked, with cavalier insensitivity, that Hearn would never be a ladies' man, referring to the deformity of his eye. Lafcadio was hurt to the quick but did not remonstrate; the wound probably went too deep for that and he was immersed in difficulties of a much more pressing nature.[16]

In December 1894, Hearn suffered a dramatic deterioration in his vision and was compelled to end his brief but enjoyable period at the *Chronicle*. He was fortunate in being attended by Dr Papellier, an oculist who was also an admirer of his work and had, indeed, translated *Chita* into German.[17] Papellier diagnosed that his patient had reached a critical stage. There was no sight in his left eye and the right was inflamed by neuritis. To avoid blindness, Papellier insisted on a total break from work and a period of recuperation in a darkened room. It was late January before the worst was over and even then the symptoms persisted. At that point, Lafcadio had to bow to the inevitable and withdrew from his post on the newspaper.

Setsu had been delighted by Kobe. Having been 'petted and helped and invited about' by the Youngs, she quickly came to love the busy, modern atmosphere of the city, not sharing her husband's predilection for archaic, rural, Japan. She had her mother and father with her for company, as well as two female servants and a male relative. Now her grandfather and another relative had to be sent back to Matsue, because Lafcadio and herself felt they could not afford to maintain so large a household on a reduced income.[18]

They had actually always adopted a frugal approach in Kobe, as if knowing that it was just another stop on a journey which would end somewhere else. They had considered building a permanent home in Kobe at the beginning to house their extended Japanese family but instead rented a scantily furnished house with a foreign upstairs and a Japanese downstairs. They practised an 'almost penurious' life-style, for the year and a half that he remained out of work in Kobe. Hearn was fairly accurate when he told Page Baker in April 1895 that he had little prospect of getting anything for a year or so; he would have to try to live by literature, 'a very stingy stepmother'.[19] A number of factors conspired to cushion what might have been desperate circumstances. The *Atlantic Monthly* provided an outlet for some of his articles. The timing of the publication of his first and second Japanese books could hardly have been more fortuitous. Together with his salary, they ensured sufficient income to enable Lafcadio to add to his savings, held in Setsu's name.[20] His situation was therefore far from desperate even if its uncertainty compelled him to be frugal until he moved to Tokyo in 1896.

Setsu, in consultation with the other members of her family, was probably the guiding spirit in this, fulfilling the Japanese woman's dominant role in the home. The decision to send her relatives back to Matsue, for example, is unlikely to have been initiated by Lafcadio. The building up of savings, adding to her security, was probably a happy coincidence of character between Lafcadio and herself, he being an inveterate worrier about money and saver and she being the possessor of the sound Japanese instinct to save with an eye to the future. At home, she was the directing spirit – even if she seldom appeared – or so it seemed to strangers like Dr Papellier; most of the work, at any rate, was done by others. Her husband's food, partly Japanese and partly Western, was brought in from a restaurant; her mother prepared the food for the rest of the family and a servant girl looked to Lafcadio's general needs. He always dressed cleanly and neatly,

Japanese-style at home. Papellier remembered him as a fluent conversationalist who smoked but drank little.[21]

His career in journalism over, Hearn began to cast around for an alternative means of income. He sought Chamberlain's advice, apparently suggesting the possibility of an editorial post elsewhere or a teaching job overseas. The Professor replied, sensibly, that if he was not fit for one post in journalism, he would hardly be fit for another; no teaching vacancy was then available though one would probably turn up in time and, anyway, his responsibility to his Japanese wife and child dictated remaining in Japan.[22] Subsequently, Page Baker, his former editor in New Orleans, responded to Lafcadio's distress signals by offering him a job but Hearn realised that Chamberlain was right and he turned it down.[23]

Hearn's initial reaction to Kobe, an open port, had been one of relief to be again among 'clean-souled Englishmen'. Though he was later to describe Kobe as a city of 'bargaining, struggling, and money-grabbing', he was now in a mood for a savage reaction against his experiences in the interior of Japan. Brooding over the treatment he had received at Kumamoto, he castigated the notion that an outsider could become a Japanese – not that he had ever really imagined he could – or to find true sympathy with the people as a whole: 'How foolish the foreigner who believes he can understand the Japanese'.[24]

At the same time, his confidence in his superiority as an interpreter of Japan was on the rise. Corresponding with Scudder, the editor of the *Atlantic Monthly*, Hearn revealed a strong awareness of his own worth, in contrast to his distrust of Ernest Fenellosa:

> That he is an authority on Japanese art,- out of which he made a fortune,- is unquestionable. I have no reason to doubt his knowledge of that. . .But I doubt his intellectual sincerity, his spirit of fairness, and the sense in him of scruple as to his use of that knowledge. . .[25]

In a letter of 20 August, 1895, Lafcadio went as far as to state that Scudder had not understood that he was a pioneer and that nobody knew more about the interior of Japan '. . .except a certain Jesuit father who looks at the matter from the 15th century point of view'. Hearn provided a succinct, clear-eyed definition of his own position relative to the others working in the same field:

> The difference between myself and other writers on Japan is simply that I have become practically a Japanese – in all but knowledge of the language; while other writers remain foreigners, looking from outside at riddles which cannot be read except from the inside. There is no one competent to criticize me from the point of view you suggest, because there is no one who has been able to assume that point of view among writers on Japan. . .You see how conceited I am; but my conceit is based on facts.[26]

Earlier in 1895, with his own first two Japanese books under his belt, Lafcadio's confidence in his position of preeminence, his awareness that nobody possessed his credentials for writing about the real Japan, was already evident in his reaction when Percival Lowell's *Occult Japan* was sent to him for review. He was not impressed by a work which, it seemed to him, had been written to make Japan and its popular beliefs seem ridiculous.[27]

However, while Hearn may have realised the importance of his practical interpretation of Japanese culture, his critics continued to restrict his work to the realm of poetic appreciation[28] and failed to understand his analysis of both Western and Japanese social systems. The depth of this analysis was demonstrated by his third Japanese book, *Kokoro*, roughly translated by Hearn as 'the heart of things'. While the book does contain instances of Hearn's approach to Japanese high culture, symbolised potently in the ancient capital of Kyoto, his writing tended to focus almost exclusively upon the customs and folklore of the common people of Japan. Even in the essay, 'From a Travelling Diary', where he describes two of the great Kyoto buildings, the Dai-Kioku-Den and the Higashi Hongwanji, the conclusions he draws are practical rather than poetic. To Hearn, the buildings reflected the future and suggested, prophetically, that the recrudescence of nationalism which they exemplified would lead to 'an era of great wealth' for Japan.[29]

It would be more accurate to think of Hearn as inspired by bustling Kobe rather than the 'archaic' Kyoto. Moving from the quiet homogeneity of Kumomoto to the mixed Western/ Japanese environment of Kobe jolted him into an examination of the relative merits and future developments of the two cultures. His respite from total immersion in Japanese society gave him the necessary perspective to digest and assimilate that experience. In the major *Kokoro* essay, 'The Genius of Japanese Civilization',[30] Hearn began with a view of the two cultures with which his Western readers would be comfortable. Compared with the West, Japan's intellectual or emotional life was dainty but small. A Gothic cathedral is compared to a Shinto temple; Verdi and Wagner with a *geisha* performance; a European epic with a Japanese poem; European architecture with the 'frail wooden streets of Japan'. Between the two, he argues, there was an incalculable difference in '. . .emotional volume. . .imaginative power. . .artistic synthesis'. Then follows a sudden contrast. The enormity of a Western city was 'hard, grim, dumb'; it was mathematical power applied to utilitarian ends. Buddhism, which taught men that life was an illusion, also taught them how to seize its fleeting impressions and interpret them in relation to the 'highest truth'. In illustrating the poetic instability of Japanese culture, Lafcadio crafted impressive prose-poetry which was all the more effective for being more disciplined than previously:

> In the flushed splendor of the blossom-bursts of spring, in the coming and going of the cicadæ, in the dying crimson of autumn foliage, in the ghostly beauty of snow, in the delusive motion of wave or cloud, they saw old parables of perpetual meaning. Even their calamities – fire, flood, earthquake, pestilence – interpreted to them unceasingly the doctrine of the eternal Vanishing.

Beneath this poetry was a hard core of meaning which has hardly begun to penetrate the West. Even today, many Occidentals would have difficulty accepting that the Western 'common worker' was less free than his Japanese counterpart, though they are now aware of Japan's 'capacity to threaten Western manufacturers'. In the 1950s and 60s, when Japanese products were synonymous with cheapness, it would have been difficult to give credence to the prediction made in another essay, 'From a Travelling Diary', that there was no reason why in the future Japan should depend on low-cost production:

> I think she may rely more securely upon her superiority in art and good taste. The art-genius of a people may have a special value against which all competition by cheap labour is vain.[31]

Hearn saw that Japan's place in the world would be better

secured by 'commercial conquest' rather than military prowess. The displacement of the foreign economic interests in Japan would prove even more significant than victory over China in establishing 'Japan's real place among nations'.[32]

Watching the interaction of Japanese and Westerners in Kobe made Hearn aware of the nature of the racial gulf separating the two peoples. He also observed the exploitation of the Westerner by the native people of the port. The critical edge which had been detectable in his journalism, as when he complained of travellers landing at Yokohama being at the mercy of 'sharpers', was now evident in Kokoro. In 'A Glimpse of Tendencies', he wrote of how the average Japanese would prefer to work 15 hours a day for one of his own countrymen than eight hours a day for a foreigner paying higher wages.[33] Not that his views on imperialism had changed: in Kokoro he was withering about the Western masses who imagined a divine connection between military power and Christianity and the sermons which implied 'divine justification for political robberies, and heavenly inspiration for the invention of high explosives'.[34] Hearn was pointing to Japanese ways of resisting Western economic domination, particularly their ability to put national interests before those of the individual, which continue to be relevant.

However, Hearn's judgement was by no means infallible. When Lafcadio indulged in his weakness for Spencer he got it wrong. In a chapter of Kokoro, 'The Idea of Preëxistence', Hearn was concerned with an idea which had preoccupied him since New Orleans: the 'singular accord' between Buddhism and modern science which he believed was especially evident in 'that domain of psychology whereof Herbert Spencer has been the greatest of all explorers'. The influence of Spencer led him to make a prediction which has since been proved completely wrong – that scientific education in Japan could not '. . .immediately raise the average of practical intelligence to the Western level. The common capacity must remain lower for generations'.[36]

The pace of Lafcadio's work did not slacken. If Glimpses was the book of Matsue and Out of the East that of Kumamoto, Kobe inspired two works, Gleanings in Buddha Fields, as well as Kokoro. While Gleanings was not finished or published until 1897, after Hearn had moved to Tokyo, it was essentially a work of Kobe.

Two of the essays, 'Notes on a Trip to Kyoto' and 'In Osaka' were products of visits to these cities which were within striking distance of Kobe. Even these essays, although they do contain descriptions of Japan's most distinguished cultural centre and bustling commercial heart respectively, were marked by a growing process of internalisation in Hearn's work. If *Glimpses* had recorded his discovery of Japan and *Out of the East* coming to terms with it, *Kokoro* was, significantly, sub-titled 'Hints and Echoes of Japanese Inner Life'. *Gleanings* was sub-titled 'Studies of Hand and Soul in the Far East'.

Given the essay format employed by Hearn, it was natural that there was unevenness of tone and content. *Gleanings*, like all his Japanese books except *Japan: An Attempt at Interpretation*, was composed of a number of essays on diverse topics, some major and others slight, all of them characterised by a lack of structure. Various essays which comprised the book began to appear in the *Atlantic Monthly* in the second half of 1896, just as Lafcadio moved from Kobe to Tokyo. 'About Faces in Japanese Art' was published in the *Atlantic Monthly* in August 1896, followed by 'Dust' in November and 'A Living God' in December. Contrary to what Hearn had hoped, *Gleanings* did not prove to be significantly lighter, either in tone or in length, than its predecessor, though the inevitable horror was now so much more subtle than that with which he had churned the stomachs of his Cincinnati readers over breakfast.

The major themes did carry through from his previous books: the contrast of East and West, to the latter's detriment, was dwelt on at great length in 'About Faces in Japanese Art', one of Lafcadio's outstanding works.[37] He described it to Nishida as a defence of Japanese methods of drawing but it was a great deal more than that.[38] In portraying landscape, Hearn contended that the Japanese artist gave the general character, not a wearisome mass of detail but recreated the feeling of what he had seen. The same was true of his representation of the human figure and face; the general type was given, not the personal trait. Facial expression was rendered by typical, not individual, characteristics, as was the case with the conventional masks of ancient Greek actors:

> A common Japanese drawing leaves much to the imagination,- nay, irresistibly stimulates it,- and never

189

betrays effort. Everything in a common European engraving is detailed and individualized. Everything in a Japanese drawing is impersonal and suggestive. The former reveals no law: it is a study of particularities. The latter invariably teaches something of law, and suppresses particularities except in their relation to law.

Hearn saw it as an indictment of Greek, and hence Western, art that it expressed the aspiration towards the divinely beautiful and wise, whereas Japanese art reflected the simple joy of existence.

The theme of art carried through to another chapter of *Gleanings*, 'In Osaka', where Hearn waxed lyrical about the illustrations in the *Asahi Shimbun* newspaper. It might have been expected that he would have abominated Osaka, the commercial and industrial hub of Japan but the reverse was the case; its 'sober and sensible conservatism' delighted him.[39] He had gone there chiefly to see its temples and came away impressed by the happy co-existence of traditional Japan and the busy modernity he found there. This great city moved him to contradict much of the pessimism about the future of Japanese civilisation to which he had hitherto been prone. It was not true, he declared, that Old Japan was rapidly disappearing: 'Many curious and beautiful things have vanished; but Old Japan survives in art, in faith, in customs and habits, in the hearts and the homes of the people: it may be found everywhere by those who know how to look for it. . .'[40] If the ghost of Hearn were to hover over modern Japan, it might well be satisfied with this prescience.

Hearn demonstrated that his sense of fantasy was intact in 'A Living God', the story of Hamaguchi Gohei, a farmer who was declared a god in his own lifetime. The preface was very much along the lines of his New Orleans 'Fantastics', a vivid hallucination of what it would be like to be a god:

> I should be only a vibration,- a motion invisible as of ether or of magnetism; though able sometimes to shape me a shadow-body, in the likeness of my former visible self, when I should wish to make apparition.
>
> As air to the bird, as water to the fish, so would all substance be permeable to the essence of me. I should pass at will through the walls of my dwelling to swim in the long gold bath of a sunbeam, to thrill in the heart of a flower, to ride on the neck of a dragon-fly.[41]

The fantasy may well have been an escape from the more mundane domestic matters which mired him down in the real world. He fought – and lost – a personal battle with Setsuko on the subject of further children. Despite, or perhaps because of, his absorption in Kazuo he was not anxious to have more but family pressure forced him to give in. He outlined the circumstances to Ellwood Hendrick on 12 November 1895:

> Alas! I am going to have another child – and it might be a girl!? I think I told you of my old resolution not to have any more children. But the family – the mother, grandmother, grandfather, etc., etc. – who rule a Japanese home, you know,- wouldn't have it so. They said there must be two – or people would think it strange; and they said that if Kajiwo died, it would kill his mother if there were no other little brother or sister to live for. So now there will be another – by the will of the Gods, say the old folks:- perhaps so! not by mine.[42]

Lafcadio's attitude may have been influenced by the fact that, according to Nina Kennard, sclerosis of the arteries and other symptoms of heart failure made him aware, in the autumn of 1895, of the approach of death.

Also, surrounded by the nationalistic feelings unleashed by the Sino-Japanese War, he was acutely aware of the prejudice against the children of mixed race and how uncomfortable a home Japan could be for them; it was in fact this by-product of xenophobia which, his friend Ellwood Hendrick believed, finally determined Lafcadio to become a Japanese citizen.[43] It was certainly a factor, in addition to his family's refusal to consider becoming British citizens and thus losing their power of holding property in Japan. At the same time, he expressed a fear that his Irish relations could claim his estate after his death: 'I have a wife, of course, but relatives also to contest it. (They turned up only after it appeared I was getting to be a successful author).'[44] On the face of it, this was quite unfair. The two relatives with whom he corresponded in Japan – his brother, James, and half-sister, Mrs Atkinson, were both in touch with him long before *Glimpses* was published. If it was a reference to Hestia Austin, a relative who had written, comparing his work to his uncle, Richard's, pictures,[45] then to infer posthumous litigation from her charming note would seem fanciful. Still, with the memory of his great-aunt's ruin by an adventurer, Henry Molyneux, emblazoned in his memory, it is not surprising that he wanted to take no chances, though he also saw that the process of acquiring Japanese citizenship would not benefit him, and would be troublesome and costly.

As a preliminary to his 'adoption by marriage with a Japanese', Lafcadio had to renounce his allegiance to the British sovereign and take an oath of allegiance to the Emperor of Japan. This must have been difficult for Hearn as he had proudly maintained the citizenship of his birth through almost two decades in the United States and a further nine years of peripatetic wandering since then but he complied in July 1896. He was adopted into his wife's family and changed his name. First of all it was to have been to Inagaki Yakumo.[46] 'Yakumo' meant 'eight clouds' and was the first part of the most ancient poem extant in the Japanese language (the whole story is to be found in 'Yaegaki-Jinja' in *Glimpses*). It was also an poetic alternative for Izumo, 'the Place of Issuing of Clouds'.[47] When his new name became official in 1896, it was in the form, Koizumi Yakumo, the former being, of course, his wife's family name which, in Japanese, comes first before the given name. The reason for the seeming confusion with the family name, Inagaki, lay in the prevalence of adoption in Japan. Setsu had been adopted by the Inagaki family when young and was later re-adopted by her own family. It must have been mooted that he would take her former adopted name before it was finally decided that he would take the Koizumi surname.

The negotiations on citizenship were paralleled by other negotiations with Tokyo University. Basil Hall Chamberlain forwarded a letter on 7 December 1895 from Professor Toyama, Director of the Literature College at Tokyo University, offering Hearn the position of Professor of English Language and Literature. The salary was to be 350 yen per month for a total of about six hours work per day. He had the option of an unfurnished house provided free or forty yen per month rent allowance. In the context of the time, these were very generous terms. Chamberlain believed that Lafcadio's change of nationality need not affect this figure though it did, in fact, become a complicating factor. Lafcadio was to be responsible only to Toyama, a member of the Japanese House of Peers, whom Chamberlain found 'perfectly straightforward, reasonable, and easy-tempered'. Chamberlain added diplomatically that the students would be lucky to get Hearn while, at the same time, the title of Professor '. . .might be no bad ornament to your title-pages, notwithstanding the fact mentioned by Toyama and admitted by all, that you can stand on your own merits'. He was adamant that the initiative had not come from him but from the university authorities themselves, though naturally his portrayal of his friend was not 'unalloyed abuse'.[48] He must, however, have briefed Toyama on Hearn's sensitivities, as the Director knew of his difficulties in Kumamoto and his commitment to evolutionary philosophy.[49]

In April, Professor Toyama informed Lafcadio that the Diet had given permission to engage a foreign professor for the Chair of English Language and Literature at the University. Unaware that it was already a *fait accompli*, he suggested that Hearn's mooted change of nationality made a preliminary contract advisable before it was effected. The term of the contract was from 10 September 1896 to 31 July 1899. Lafcadio immediately informed Toyama that he was already a Japanese citizen; the latter replied on 10 April that this raised a difficulty but one he was determined to surmount. Toyama was as good as his word and Lafcadio did indeed assume the post.

His last months in Kobe were happy. In June the family returned to Izumo for a holiday. They went first to Matsue where Lafcadio nostalgically revisited his old school and his former house. His friends gave a banquet in his honour but he realised that 'a place once loved and deserted' could not be revisited with impunity; the lost charm, he felt, was something which had evaporated out of his own life. July and August were spent in the Izumo seaside resorts of Mionoseki and Sakai. At Mionoseki, 'very sleepy and quiet by day' but at night 'one of the noisiest and merriest little havens of Western Japan', Lafcadio slipped easily into a routine of sea bathing and relaxation. Lafcadio liked to observe the diversions of the seamen of Old Japan in Mionoseki, where 'marvellously large sums' were paid to geishas and tavern-keepers; but here also he saw the 'apparition' of a modern Japanese man-of-war which symbolised the intrusion of the New Japan into this idyllic backwater.[50] Now he felt himself about to be drawn into the vortex of this new Japan, Tokyo, 'the great capital so long dreaded'. There was a painful last parting from Nishida and then the Koizumi family started back to Kobe to pack for what Lafcadio hoped would be a short few years of money-making in Tokyo before retiring back to Izumo.

For once, Hearn was not fleeing from his present situation in search of more congenial surroundings. In his last letter to his half-sister, Minnie Atkinson, he said: 'We have a cosy little home in Kobe and Kobe is pretty.' He never again communicated with her. She tried to get some illumination from Beale of the *Japan Daily Mail* in Yokohama whose office was used as a forwarding address when Hearn was in transit. He was able to reassure her that her half-brother was in good health and conjectured that he was too busy to reply. She continued to write, only to find the empty envelopes returned to her, with no word from Hearn on them. Mrs Atkinson herself could think of no plausible explanation. Nina Kennard speculated that his longing to return to the West, 'to hold communion with those of his own race', was such that it was interfering with his literary work and made him determined to cut off the correspondence.[51] However, his last letter was warm and affectionate and not a likely prelude to the end of a close friendship. The sending back of empty envelopes was not characteristic of Hearn. One explanation might be that the later letters never reached Hearn but were instead intercepted by someone else. Setsu, for example, might have sent back the empty envelopes as a signal to Minnie to abandon any further attempts at communication. Elaborate diplomacy is a feature of the Japanese family and Mrs Koizumi was able and determined.

Her husband had become a Japanese citizen and had thus firmly jumped down on the Japanese side of the fence. Setsuko, had one child and was expecting another. Not just she, but her entire family was dependent on Lafcadio's income. She was in no position to become a 'Madame Butterfly'. On the other hand, Hearn was unsettled. Since the birth of Kazuo, he had talked of taking the child abroad, a step which would have meant leaving the rest of the family behind. Minnie Atkinson, who clearly had some useful connections, was promoting posts and publishing opportunities in England. The staple fare with his other correspondents was primarily intellectual: with his half-sister, it was tender and familiar, the exchanging of children's photographs, the sending of fairy tales. She was a bond, a bridge to a shared world of childhood, one to which he was growing ever closer, one which Setsuko could never hope to understand. Lafcadio's approach to the lucrative Tokyo post was short-term; he was determined to find Tokyo hell: she was enthralled at the prospect of the metropolis and determined they would settle happily there.

CHAPTER TEN

TOKYO

LAFCADIO HEARN in Tokyo could be presented in many lights. It was the most productive period of his life in terms of literary output yet he did not significantly expand his vision. A publicly known figure, the centre of a growing and devoted family, he became increasingly isolated and introspective. A passionate supporter of Japan in her war with Russia, he longed to leave the country. Physically and, if his wife is to be believed, mentally in decline, he produced his most ambitious intellectual work. He shunned society, yet could be the best of company.

Not the least of these contradictions was that, within weeks of taking up his post at Tokyo University, he felt that an element of comradeship had developed between himself and three other professors, based on their Roman Catholic backgrounds. Despite his professed fear of the Jesuits, it was Emile Heck, the Professor of French, who made the most profound impact. Hearn liked the Jesuit's 'delicious irony': and they were both amused by the ecclesiastical inspiration of the university architecture. They had in common a contempt of religion as convention, scorn of the missionaries and appreciation of Japanese religion. Hearn was also attracted by Inoue Tetsujiro, an anti-Christian philosopher who lectured on Buddhism and Von Koeber, the charming Russian Professor of Philosophy.[1]

As he found his feet at Tokyo University, Hearn added the greatest contradiction of them all by quietly severing his connection with the man who had been instrumental in getting him the job, Basil Hall Chamberlain. The two men each blamed the other's intellectual rigidity as the cause of their estrangement.

Its exact cause will never be known; what is certain is that their friendship faded for good. According to Kazuo, Hearn continued to love and respect Chamberlain and always impressed on his son his erstwhile friend's greatness as a scholar. He put a different complexion on the affair when he claimed – wrongly – in 1901 that his friendship with Chamberlain had ended in 1894: 'He is not so friendly with me at present. . .you have to think his thoughts to get on with him, and believe me, you can trust no one. . .'[2] Crusty and irascible the Emeritus Professor of Philology and Japanese might have been, but he was not intolerant in the sense implied by Hearn.

Chamberlain was philosophical, feeling that Hearn himself suffered most from these ruptures of friendship: 'He was much to be pitied – always wishing to love, and discovering each time that his love had been misplaced.'[3] Bisland believed that in his later years in Japan, when he knew that his health was failing, he dropped all 'burdens' which might interfere with his work. This was partly true in the last six years or so but it was hardly a factor in this case as Hearn was then making new friends on the staff of Tokyo University.

One of these was Professor Ernest Foxwell, who made Hearn's acquaintance just as he recovered from smallpox; his face was as red as beetroot but Hearn hardly seemed to notice. Paradoxically, in view of his break with Chamberlain, Foxwell found '. . .the same wide tolerance of mind ran through all his thoughts and actions. . .He seemed to me. . .the most natural, unaffected, companionable person I had ever come across'. He thought Hearn was extraordinarily gentle, more so than a woman, though he looked intensely male. Although he seemed at home in Japan, Foxwell found him essentially European.[4] The friendship was casual:

> We simply ate and drank and smoked, and in fact behaved as 'slackers'. We delighted in the air, the sunshine, the babies, the flowers, and especially in the China shops, common shops selling half-penny teapots; we were fascinated by the common crowded streets, or still more crowded canals,- and so on.[5]

Lafcadio described Foxwell as '. . .a rare fine type of Englishman – at once sympathetic and severely scientific – a fine companion and a broad strong thinker'.[6] He was, however, a blunt character, so perhaps it was as well that Lafcadio and he avoided the burning questions of the day. That may help account for the fact that their friendship was never marred by differences of opinion; Foxwell, in fact, believed that it would have been impossible, such was the tolerant nature of Hearn's character. This is diametrically opposed to Chamberlain's view: it may be accounted for by the much less deep friendship with Foxwell. Hearn's 'quiet mastery of every sentence' impressed Foxwell. His mastery of diverse subjects impressed others in Japan. Mason told Kennard that, when an argument on Browning started one evening at his house, Hearn was able to verify his statement by repeating numerous passages from various Browning poems in a soft, musical voice. A member of the Maple Club in Tokyo also told a story of a discussion on Napoleon at the Club in the course of which someone made a statement which irked Lafcadio:

> '. . .the insignificant figure with prominent eyes bent forward and poured forth a flood of information on the subject under discussion so fluent, so accurate that the assembled company listened in amazement.'[7]

Excursions to Foxwell's room at the Metropole Hotel became frequent as Hearn came to relax in his company; indeed, it seemed to his host that he was often reluctant to leave. On one occasion, Foxwell was entertaining the thoroughly Westernised son of the last Tokugawa Shogun who showed no rancour against the New Japan; their host was amused by the contrast with Hearn, who had not suffered by the transition, but was nonetheless deeply resentful of it. When Hearn wished to offer hospitality in return, he would invite Foxwell to a foreign hotel where he clearly enjoyed himself over a good lunch and cigars, keeping off deep subjects and not taking life too seriously.[8]

Hearn did enjoy good company in these years. When business took him to Yokohama there were dinners with his friend, the Japanese poet, Nobushige Amenomori, and Bledloe, the United States' Consul. The connection with Bledloe was through Mitchell McDonald who, as a Paymaster in the US Navy, was also an employee of the United States Government. Following the falling-off with Chamberlain, it was McDonald who was Hearn's closest friend for the rest of his life. *Glimpses* had been jointly dedicated to them both. Lafcadio had carried a letter of introduction from Elizabeth Bisland to the Paymaster when he travelled to Japan in 1890. As McDonald was based at Yokohama, Lafcadio's move to Tokyo naturally facilitated the development of their friendship.

There is a photograph extant of Hearn and McDonald together. It is a formal, posed affair in a photographer's studio. The American is a solid, handsome man, with mutton-chop whiskers and a steady, confident look. A greying Hearn stands behind, a slight, sensitive figure with a hand over one eye, which was already in shadow, and the other, good eye cast downwards. His fine, sensitive face would clearly have been handsome but for the disfigurement of the eye. The picture tells the story of the relationship between the two men. McDonald, the hearty man of the world, who combined a keen business brain with literary interests, would descend like a whirlwind on the reclusive writer and drag him away to meals of steak and wine and exhilarating conversation.

There were others in the circle such as C.H.H.Hall, the retired U.S. Navy doctor to whom *Exotics and Retrospectives* was dedicated 'in constant friendship'. But after he had been exposed to the company to such men, Hearn felt that he wanted to return to the United States, the world whence they had all come, and escape the awfulness of Japanese Government service; he seems to have forgotten the circumstances under which he had left what was once again an enchanted land through the refractive lens of memory.

Like other friends before him, McDonald believed he could convince Hearn to earn a healthy income from fiction. For a while, Hearn carried on the pretence that they could collaborate in producing this fiction. His acute critical sense had long ago told him that he could not succeed in this medium, on his own terms at any rate. Still, it was some time before he practised his own form of *jiujutsu* when, after seeming to yield, he finally floored the other party: in a letter that was friendly in tone, Lafcadio firmly rejected the line McDonald had been plugging and with which he had appeared for a while to be toying: it had been tried before and failed; no Western writer could make a success of it. Fiction had to come from the life familiar to the reader, and his Occidental readership was not interested in the remote life of the Orient.[9] Whether Ellwood Hendrick was fired with similar and simultaneous ambitions for Hearn by coincidence or whether Lafcadio had reported McDonald's ideas to him is not clear but he, too, attempted to convince the writer to put his talents to more lucrative use. He was told that '. . .the beautifully milled dollars and exquisitely engraved notes you talk of will stay in the pockets of practical people'.[10]

Hearn was also very firm in brushing aside McDonald's suggestion that he invest his savings in business under the Paymaster's advice but he did throw out a subsidiary idea which actually developed into something else. Lafcadio told his friend that the greatest favour he could do him would be to take his business affairs off his hands. He delighted in the thought of his formidable friend making publishers 'fork over'. What began as playful speculation became a reality when the two next got together in March 1898. Lafcadio went down to Yokohama early on a Friday afternoon and stayed the weekend. He made over power of attorney to McDonald and, 'for value received', assigned to him '. . .all of my right, title and interest in and to all accounts, debts, dues, royalties, commissions, profits, moneys, goods and chattels whatsoever now or hereafter due, owing, payable or coming to. . .' him from Harper and Houghton Mifflin. McDonald was given the power to deal with all related questions. The document was witnessed by John F. Gowey, the US Consul-General in Yokohama, who often joined in the conviviality when Hearn came down to the seaport.[11] To dislike the diplomat was, he said, impossible. Like McDonald, he had literary interests.

In granting McDonald power of attorney, Hearn was facing the reality that his estate necessitated it. His colleague, Foxwell, noted that he had a double income with his university salary and his literary income. He felt that Hearn's concern about money was a result of feeling that there was nobody on whom he could rely in time of need, that he had to have a cushion to fall back on.[12] Hearn must have thoroughly compartmentalised his friends if Foxwell remained ignorant of his closeness to McDonald. He was also unaware of the fact that care over money was an ingrained characteristic of Lafcadio's, only accentuated by a fear of the fragility of his position in Japan. Foxwell's surprise at Hearn's ease in the foreign-style hotels which they used would indicate that he was unaware of the convivial excursions to Yokohama. He may have imagined that he alone was drawing his colleague out of his seclusion.

Hearn was, however, highly selective in his friendships, as Ernest Fenollosa was to discover. Blithely unaware of the bitter denunciation he had suffered at the hand of Hearn over his suspected authorship of the attack on Chamberlain, he tried to coax friendship out of the fellow authority on Japan. There was some contact between them: the 'Mountain of Skulls', a legend told to Hearn by Fenollosa, was crafted into the brief, but highly effective opening of *In Ghostly Japan*. Later, he sent on a piece from his forthcoming volume, *Exotics and Retrospectives* to the Fenollosas and got an enthusiastic letter in return from Mrs Fenollosa.

Indeed, Hearn visited the Fenellosa's home in the spring of 1898 and made a profound impression on both of them. Ernest first spent an hour with Hearn alone, after which he 'came bounding upstairs his face radiant and cried, "Oh, he is splendid. I love him. . .It is a delight to see such a man".' Mrs Fenollosa, while conscious of the 'terrible defect' of Lafcadio's blind eye, was captivated by the 'irresistible charm' of 'his beautiful voice' and, as her guest's 'shy spirit' crept 'more from its fragile shell', ceased 'to care for anything material'. There were, however, subterranean tensions: as Hearn waxed eloquent on Spencer and Buddhism, the Fenollosas kept silent on their disagreement with his ideas but it is possible that his sensitive antennae would have picked this up. A false picture has been presented in Fenellosa's biography of a cosy relationship between Hearn and himself, with both of them portrayed as good friends, enjoying each other's company and loving the same beauties of Japanese art.[12a]

In reality, Lafcadio's letters to the Fenollosas became letters of regret. Regret that he had not been there when the Professor and his wife had called, regret that he did not share their taste in art. This probably was the kernel of their divergence. In 1885, for example, Fenollosa had dismissed the plebeian art of Japanese prints with aristocratic hauteur and, while he had progressed to writing the catalogues for the first ever exhibitions of common prints to be held in Japan in 1898 and 1900, it is clear from Hearn's letters that he saw a fundamental divide between them on the issue (which related, not just to art, but to Japanese society in general).

His letters to Fenellosa progressed from the formal courtesy with which Hearn habitually used to extricate himself from unwanted attentions to a blunt statement that he could not afford the time away from work which social intercourse required. Fenollosa and his wife once called twice to Lafcadio's home, hoping to inveigle him into coming to a *Ukioy-e* exhibition. On each occasion he was out, or at least so he said. There was a note of reprimand when he wrote that it would have been better for the Fenollosas to have written in advance; even if he had been free, he would not have gone, preferring modern colour prints and having no desire to 'learn better'; if he did acquire better taste, he would be less happy with cheap things. Here he made a remark which was illuminating in the context of his failure to became fluent in Japanese: once you began to learn the meaning of Chinese characters on shop-fronts, 'the magical charm – the charm of mystery – evaporates'.[13]

A short time later, he delivered the effective *coup de grâce* to the friendship, saying that he had decided not to visit the Fenollosas' home again for the foreseeable future. Friends were more dangerous than his enemies; the latter spitefully attempted to keep him from social situations and unwittingly helped him maintain the isolation essential to his work. Friends spoke beautifully of his work, believed in it, said they wanted more of it but would destroy it by breaking his 'habits of industry'. Each one wanted only a little time but the sum total had to be reckoned in terms of the significance of work undone, particularly now that 'the Scythe' was 'sharpening within vision'. He had, therefore, to disappear as far as the Fenollosas were concerned.[14]

While Hearn's treatment of Fenollosa may have seemed shabby, he did demonstrate his integrity in the way he fulfilled his obligations towards Tokyo University. It would have been understandable if a man so preoccupied with his literary output had treated his university post as a sinecure. The reverse was the case. He was deeply concerned with the structure and the content of his lectures and all sources agree on his impact as a lecturer. His long years of teaching in Matsue and Kumamoto had given him a keen understanding of Japanese students and so he was able to tailor his lectures to their thoughts and feelings. He did not need a prepared text: a little memorandum with names and dates, plus some reference works for quotations were sufficient. He then extemporised slowly, allowing the students to take down each word. The blackboard was used for illustration. A student later recalled how,

> . . .like the music of running water the sentences flowed from his lips. . .Gradually the subject matter under discussion held us enthraled. . .[15]

Professor Foxwell corroborated what might otherwise have seemed a somewhat flowery exaggeration. He once went into Hearn's lecture room and found,

> . . .his students. . .all in tears. . .a rare event for a Japanese. . .Hearn had been reading some very simple English poem; and there was the effect. His relations with his students were most affectionate at the university. . .[16]

Lafcadio soon realised that if he allowed himself to become immersed in the routine life of a professor, his own work would become impossible. He also learned a salutary lesson in the *realpolitik* of university life early on when a meeting was held to decide that fate of the German Professor of History. He had not liked the man but he was startled by the manner in which his professed friends deserted him when they saw how things were going. He decided there and then not to expect any love from his foreign colleagues; the Japanese at least were more frank.[17] He knew that he could be a target himself but was reasonably secure in the belief that his appointment was based on Japanese policy, the primary purpose of which was, he suspected, to encourage him to write books on Japan. He felt he was being hurried.

He did, however, have time for his old Izumo and Kumamoto pupils, some of whom were now successful in the professions. Masanobu Otani, one of the Matsue pupils who had featured in *Glimpses of Unfamiliar Japan*, entered Tokyo University at the same time as Lafcadio took up his position there. Otani was the first caller to his old teacher's temporary home in Tokyo in September 1896; six days later he agreed to become his literary assistant. Hearn set out in writing the arrangement under which Otani was to work for him: every month he would be given a subject for which he would be paid. If it was not good, it would be returned and payment withheld until it was brought up to standard. The arrangement would continue from month to month only if Otani was satisfactory and useful; if not, Hearn told him loftily, there were others at the university who would take his place.[18]

The arrangement began in January 1897. The first subject was a Japanese policeman's life; the second, the lives of priests and nuns. In February Hearn asked Otani to produce a collection of students' poems as his March project. He drew exclusively on the material provided, the seventeen-syllable Japanese *haiku* format, in the 'Bits of Poetry' chapter of *In Ghostly Japan*. Hearn set out detailed divisions and subdivisions for Otani; the following examples on sculpture in Buddhist cemeteries illustrate very well the painstaking exactitude of his approach to research:

> I-Inscriptions upon Sutpa.
> A list of these inscriptions (1) in Chinese characters, separately;- (2) in Romaji under the Chinese characters;- (3) in literal English under the Romaji;-(4) explanatory. (Some reference should be made to sect usage. Group if possible under respective sects – Shinshiu, Zenshiu, Tendai, Shingon, etc.)
> II – Inscriptions upon Haka.
> Arrange similarly. Group sects if possible.
> III – Sculptures – Carvings of Buddhist Symbols in Use by the Different Sects,- Swastika, Lotos, etc., but only Sculptures in Graveyards.[19]

The material provided formed the basis for the 'Literature of the Dead' chapter of *Exotics and Retrospectives*. Lafcadio, though usually kind and paternalistic, was capable of being a hard taskmaster. He would praise what he thought was good but be blunt when he was not satisfied. At the same time, he was concerned for the welfare of Otani, lightening the load as exams approached, and worrying about his health.

The Koizumi family moved to Tokyo from Kobe on 27 August 1896. Houses were provided by the university but Lafcadio wanted to live as far away as possible. The house he found, at Tomihisa-cho, certainly fulfilled the requirement: it was an hour's journey by *jinrikisha* from the university. His initial preference had been for a 'ghostly' old house but he deferred to Setsu's emphatic aversion and settled instead for 'a large bald utilitarian house'.[20] Five years later, in a burst of self-pity, he claimed that he was 'living in a Japanese rat-trap of a house, no garden, no ancient shrines. . .'[21] There was, in fact, a small garden and excellent views of the neighbouring Kobudera Buddhist temple in whose grounds he ruminated.

The house in Ushigome became a magnet for Matsue relatives who wanted to come to the capital for job-hunting or sight-seeing. The manner in which they had treated Setsu as a girl was the basis on which they were made welcome. Those who failed this test were turned out. Lafcadio acted as the peacemaker when a nephew of Kazuo's grandmother who had lived with them for several months passed the police exams without anyone being aware what he was up to. It seems to have been Lafcadio though who ejected a Matsue relative who tried to stay at Ushigome after having sold the family's burial plot at Matsue. Hearn was also very cautious about having a much-married niece by adoption of Kazuo's grandmother to stay, for fear of gossip.[22]

Lafcadio had visited the Tokyo Club when he had stayed at Chamberlain's house in Tokyo in 1894. Though he had liked it, he felt he could never accustom himself to that kind of life:

'It has occasional high value for me: just a dip into its atmosphere. But were I to live in the capital, I should try to live very quietly – just as I have been doing.'[23]

With some deviations, notably with Mitchell McDonald, Hearn adhered to such a life-style in his seven years in Tokyo. There seems to have been elements of both mutual antipathy and ambiguity in his relations with the foreign element in Tokyo. Ernest Foxwell portrayed a 'hopeless feud' between Hearn and the foreign residents, particularly with the women, who would not allow so much as his name to cross their doorsteps. Foxwell regarded Hearn's declarations of absolute indifference to Western women as protesting too much. You could see, he believed, by his face and by listening to his talk that he was '. . .the very man who required the society of women of his own race. That man was repulsed and treated harshly by European women. . .'[24]

Foxwell was sure that Lafcadio's intellectual and conversational abilities would have made him welcome in Tokyo's cultivated and cosmopolitan diplomatic society. He had indeed shown in the past – in New Orleans, for example – an ability to be lionised but whether he would have been happy attempting to straddle his Japanese domestic world and this society is open to question. His Western interlocutors, in turn, might have been less than at ease with Hearn's trenchant opinions on matters political, social and racial. In any case, the diplomatic society's 'assumption of superiority over the Japanese' and 'subjection to feminine influence' meant that Lafcadio, in his own words, avoided it 'like hell'.

The birth of Iwao, Lafcadio's second son, towards the end of 1896, consolidated his commitment to his Japanese family and made it even more unlikely that he would seek to engage himself with foreign society in Tokyo. He told 'Mama-San' (Setsu) that she did not belong to herself any more; henceforth she would belong to the children. He did not seem to realise how true this was of himself also and still entertained hopes of going abroad with Kazuo, though the realisation that these were chimerical slowly dawned on him in his last years. It was probably a need for some tangible affirmation of that now elusive Western world that made him write to the J.B.Stetson Hat Company of Philadelphia enquiring if they could send him Stetsons, which he had worn in the United States.[25] It is hard to imagine even one of Hearn's lack of sartorial elegance combining a Stetson with his habitual Japanese clothing! A side product of this request was a correspondence with a Mr Gullman, who replied on behalf of Stetson.

'Detestable' Tokyo was allowed few redeeming features in his correspondence at this time. The foreign embassy quarter 'looking like a well-painted American suburb' alternated with 'indescribable squalor', green pleasantness, a park 'full of really weird beauty, the shadows all black as ink', with urbanisation and 'hideous' military barracks. He told Setsu it would be much better to leave Tokyo and live in the country on a much smaller salary and have peace of mind. She replied that he would only have peace of mind when he became a Buddha; with patience he could at least be independent.[26] The weather might be vile and Ushigome unlovely but Setsu was happy fixing up the new home. As he put it to Ellwood Hendrick, the charm of Japanese life had fled away into the 'luminous globule' of domestic existence. That was the rub. Left to his own devices, he could depart to pastures new, as he had always done but with a family it was different: 'Were I but myself, instead of being many, I should fly to savage lands and live upon bananas and guava-jelly.'[27]

The closest he came to finding such a state of idyllic

primitivism was in Yaidzu, a remote fishing village which was discovered by a sort of methodical accident. As soon as the first academic year had been completed at the University, Lafcadio and the family set off on a holiday to the fashionable summer resort of Maizaka. It proved to be exactly what Hearn was trying to escape from in Tokyo and he wanted to leave immediately. Setsu persuaded him to stay overnight and to take the train eastward next day, stopping at each station in an attempt to find a place which appealed to him. She may have regretted her inspiration because by this process they discovered Yaidzu, a small, unvarnished fishing village. Hearn fell in love immediately with its simplicity and with the pounding sea which thundered as vigorously as that at Tramore did in his memory. He was equally taken with the character of Otokichi, the local fisherman whose 'guest apartment' constituted the available accommodation. Setsu and Kazuo were appalled by the smells, the dirty mats, the fleas and the low ceilings. Lafcadio told them not to look at the worst side of things: surely the pleasure of contemplating the great sea was sufficient?

For Setsu, it was not. Whereas Kazuo came to appreciate the simple virtues of the Otokichi family, the good food and even the upstairs living room with its picture window running the length of the room, she stayed behind in subsequent years, coming to join the rest of the family when the vacation was almost over. Most summers after that Lafcadio brought the children to Yaidzu. In Kazuo's description, he:

> . . .laid aside his individuality and become like any ordinary person, wearing a *yukata* (summer dress) all day, and going out in *zori* (straw sandals). Everywhere he was cheerfully greeted and he responded in the same manner to young and old. Everyone addressed him as 'Sensei'. He jumped naked into the sea, and walked a great deal.[28]

At Yaidzu he was able to relax. His normal obsession with work was put aside except in respect of the unfortunate Kazuo, whose tuition by his father continued throughout the holidays. He wrote to Setsu every day simple letters with comic illustrations.

When she did come, she would observe her husband down on the 'billow-washed' shore, mingling with and even joining in the singing of the unkempt local children. He did not permit his own children any prejudice against them. Indeed, on one occasion when he considered that Kazuo had shown discourtesy by reading a book while a fisherman's son was telling a story, Lafcadio made him go afterwards to the boy's house to apologise. Always the lover of a good story, he would encourage the children to come back to the Otokichis and happily listen to their tales. He, in turn, regaled all, including the Otokichi family, with his skill as a story-teller, notwithstanding the limits of his poor Japanese.

The villagers were amazed by the ability of their distinguished guest in the water, where he would remain for hours at a time. They used to say that the *sensai* (a Japanese term of respect, perhaps best translated as 'master') had been born from the water. His ability to float was to them strangest of all and they were amused when only his head, toes and *taiko no hara* (drum-belly) could be seen from the shore. Incredibly, his incessant smoking extended even to the water and Otokichi would see his cigar flashing like a firefly at an unusual distance. The Otokichis regarded him as a *Hotoke Sama*, a Lord Buddha, who had come to save the family. He used to pay twice or three times the rent asked by Otokichi who regarded it as a *zense no yakusoku* ('destiny of the last life appointed') that Hearn had taken a fancy to his home.[29]

Otokichi described Yaidzu as being 'one family'; to Hearn it was the best fishing village in the world. He once attempted to show his gratitude by restoring an old statue of Jizo, the sea-pacifying divinity in the form of a child which had always been an especial favourite of his. Work had already started when a letter arrived from Setsu in Tokyo vetoing the project. Lafcadio complied but pointed out that Jizo was not, as she seemed to think, a graveyard statue but 'the savior [sic] of seas and sailors. The Jizo is crying even now. . .*Gomen, gomen*: [forgive me!] The Jizo idol is shedding stone tears'. The letter was illustrated by a drawing of Jizo crying stone tears. Mrs Hearn found out afterwards that he had been right about the function of his Jizo.[30] Otikichi was most surprised by the deference shown by Lafcadio to Setsu in this instance. As soon as her letter was received, he obediently gave the project up at once: 'I never saw a man like *Sensei Sama* who listened [as] gently to his wife', Otikichi commented later. He also followed Lafcadio's tuition of Kazuo with keen interest. He thought him a bit too severe, though he could also be kindness itself.[31]

Part of the attraction of Yaidzu for Hearn was its magnificent seaward view, '. . .a jagged blue range of peaks crowding sharply into the horizon, like prodigious amethysts,- and beyond them, to the left, the glorious spectre of Fuji, towering enormously above everything'.[32] Adzukizawa, a former Matsue pupil whose adopted name was now Fujisaki, visited Lafcadio in Yaidzu in 1897 and together they planned a climb of Mount Fuji. The ascent was made on 25 August 1897. Given the grandeur of the subject, Hearn's account of the climb is sparsely matter-of-fact. There is description but it is muted in comparison to what he had lavished on lesser subjects.[32] There is horror, but it, too, is muted. When he had climbed to the summit of La Pelée, in the French West Indies, the previous decade, he had mused on the 'awful antiquity' of the scene he was surveying and was filled with melancholy that all this beauty would endure after his death.[33] At that time death represented finality; now it was a stage in an eternal process. He had not found faith in the meantime, but he had found certainty.

CHAPTER ELEVEN

ANCESTRAL VOICES

The thought that one's strength is the strength of one's ancestors – of a host innumerable and ancient as the race has its consolation.[1]

THROUGHOUT his mature work, Lafcadio's mind constantly flashes back to his childhood, to memories idyllic and horrific. Idyllically, he was the '. . .pampered heir to wealth and luxury. . .What very happy times those were! – they gave no augury of the years of nightmare to follow'.[2] Yet in those years the seeds of nightmare too were sown; the roots of Hearn's masterful horror anchored around a lonely and impressionable childhood. He was also capable of writing: 'With me all the past is a blur – except the pain of it.'[3]

In approaching Hearn's childhood, it is necessary to bear in mind that, not alone was he recalling events across a gap of up to fifty years but he was steeped in romanticism and Gothic horror which he magnified with a powerful imagination. He was also prone to self-pity; in his letters particularly, where he often angled for sympathy, the distortions were sometimes grotesque. Hearn himself was aware of the problem: he once told his Japanese students that no man really understood himself well enough to be able to tell the truth about himself.[4] Later, towards the end of his life, he wrote that, looking back over it, he realised he could remember nothing agreeable – since boyhood he had tried to forget disagreeable things and in the process had made no effort to remember the agreeable.[5] In fact, he recognised that he had spoken with more than one voice; when recalling the scattered memories of his boyhood, it seemed as if a much more artificial self were constantly trying to speak instead of his real self, with consequent incongruities.[6]

To really understand the tangled web of passion, madness, deceit and cruelty which shaped these tortured memories, it is necessary to go back to the mid-nineteenth century, when Europe was in the throes of revolutionary upheaval. On a Greek island, sometime between late 1848 and mid-1849, an Irishman and a Greek beauty were entwined in their own drama. The Irishman, a serving officer in the British Army was, according to the testimony of his son, set upon by an inhabitant of the island of Cerigo (now Kythira), where he was stationed, 'terribly stabbed and left for dead'.[7] Due to the tender nursing of his girl-friend, whose brother was the alleged assailant, he recovered and continued on a distinguished military career.

Like so many autobiographical fragments from the pen of Lafcadio Hearn, this story may well be apocryphal, though the known facts lend it credence. The officer in question was Charles Bush Hearn, then serving as Assistant Surgeon with the 45th Regiment of Foot (the Nottinghamshire) of the British Army, the rank at which he had joined on 15 April 1842[8] and which he held when he left Gibraltar for the Ionian Islands exactly three years later. He was following a well-worn path for Irish doctors joining the British Army in that era; indeed, nine out of a total of eleven surgeons who served in his regiment between 1852 and 1867 were Irish.[9] In his first three years on the Greek islands, Hearn was stationed at Zante, Ithaca and Corfu. In 1848, the simmering Greek hostility to British rule flamed into rebellion on the island of Cephalonia. There was trouble also on Cerigo and his regiment was transferred there in April 1848.

On Cerigo, Charles Bush Hearn became passionately involved with Rosa Antonia Cassimati whose family was prominent in the tight-knit society of that remote, poor island. She was an attractive, illiterate woman of twenty-five when they met: Lafcadio Hearn later remembered her '. . .dark, brown and beautiful face, with large brown eyes like a wild deer's'.[10]

Charles Hearn has been described as '. . .good-looking, clever, a smart officer, handling sword or guitar with equal dexterity, singing an Irish or Italian lovesong with a melodious tenor voice. . .gifted with all the qualifications for the cultivation of a young girl's fancy, and, by all accounts, he never allowed these qualifications to deteriorate for want of use'. An illustration of his gallant ardour was found in an Irish country house earlier this century in the form of a poem addressed to a beautiful heiress. The poem, which was dispatched from Correagh, the Hearn residence in County Westmeath, consisted of about six stanzas, beginning:

> Dearest and nearest to my heart,
> Thou art fairer than the silver moon,
> And I trust to see thee soon.

and ending:

> Adieu, sweet maid! my heart still bleeds with love
> And evermore will beat for thee![11]

Initially, the strong mutual physical attraction of Charles and Rosa triumphed over the formidable obstacles to their romance. The *pukka* ethos of the British officer corps would not have favoured romantic involvement with a 'native' and, on Rosa's side, Charles Bush Hearn would have been seen as an interloper in a traditional society where marriage had important economic as well as social ramifications. Additionally, he was part of the British garrison, enforcing resented alien domination.

Matters, however, took their own course and, late in 1848, Rosa became pregnant by Hearn. It was presumably at this point that the attack on Charles by Rosa's brother, if it actually took place, happened. The birth of their child, christened George Robert, on 24 July 1849, found Charles and Rosa still unmarried. His regiment had been ordered to proceed from Cerigo to Santa Maura, nowadays Lefkas. One can only speculate as to why they did not get married earlier, particularly as Rosa left her family on Cerigo to accompany Charles to his new station. The most likely explanation, in view of his later conduct, was a reluctance on Charles' part to face up to the long-term difficulties, social, religious, familial and professional, which his formal betrothal to Rosa would pose. The involvement with Rosa may well have been a 'fling' which went disastrously wrong when she became pregnant.

They did, however, get married on 25 November 1849, in the Greek Orthodox Church, of which Rosa was a fervent adherent. He was 31 and she was 26. Charles, a member of the Protestant Church of Ireland, a sister denomination to the Church of

England, may or may not have been aware when he went through the ceremony that it would not be recognised as binding in English law, the loophole he later used to obtain a divorce. A spur to marriage was probably Charles' promotion to Staff Surgeon, Second Class, in November 1849, following which he was instructed to proceed back to England. The couple may also have been influenced to marry by the fact that Rosa was already two months pregnant with their second child (Lafcadio) when the ceremony took place. The officiating clergyman was the Reverend Neofotisto Calafati 'of the Greek Church' and the witnesses were a Dr Giovanni Cavadias and a 'Sig.or' Stamati Logoteti, both obviously local men; it is noticeable that none of Charles's colleagues appear from the record to have acted in any capacity at the ceremony.[12]

On 27 February 1850 Charles left Lefkas in compliance with his orders to return to headquarters and was posted to the West Indies with the First (Royal) Regiment of Foot.[13] Rosa remained behind. From that point onwards, they were seldom together. Rosa's pregnancy may have been the reason for the separation only a few months after the wedding but Charles' decision not to report his marriage to the War Office (in effect, not inform his superiors) was an ominous harbinger of its eventual failure. In fact, he did not tell the War Office until almost three years after the event, in July 1852. When he did, he pleaded 'domestic afflictions' as one of the reasons for the delay; it can only be assumed that he was referring to difficulties with Rosa, something he may have assumed his superiors in London were already aware of due to the form of shorthand employed.[14]

Four months later, Rosa gave birth to her second son. He was baptised eleven days afterwards in the Greek Orthodox Church and given the names Patrick, in honour of the land of his father's birth, and Lafcadio, derived from Lefkas. George Robert, Rosa's first child, died on 17 August 1850, a traumatic experience for her, exacerbated by having to endure it alone. The following month, Charles Bush Hearn proceeded, sans wife and child, to the West Indies, from where he did not return until 1853. Years afterwards, Lafcadio Hearn claimed that, without knowing his father (he may have been unaware that his grandfather had also served there)[15] had been posted in the West Indies, they had induced 'the queerest, ghostliest sensation of having seen it all before. I think I should experience even stranger sensations in India!' (where his father had also been stationed).[16]

Rosa was alone with Patrick Lafcadio for almost a further two years. In mid-1852, arrangements were made for them to travel to her in-laws in Ireland. Whether these were instigated by her husband is not known, but the issue is open to doubt. It is possible that Charles' family in Ireland learned of the existence of a seemingly abandoned wife and child on a Greek island and decided that they should be brought to Ireland. Throughout his Irish childhood, Lafcadio was cared for by a great-aunt, Mrs Justin, 'Sally', Brenane, a wealthy convert to Roman Catholicism. If the testimony of her niece, Lizzie Hardy, is accurate, it was Mrs Brenane's idea to bring Rosa and Lafcadio to Ireland in the first place. When she heard that Charles Hearn had married a member of the Greek Church, which she confused with the Roman Catholic, she insisted on Rosa coming to Ireland immediately.[17] This aligns with the fact that Rosa travelled to Dublin two years before Charles was expected back. If, however, it was the case, it raises disturbing questions about Charles' attitude to his marriage. On the other hand, it must be open to doubt that a woman of Mrs Brenane's class would have confused the Greek Orthodox Church with Roman Catholicism.

The delay in reporting it to his superiors, until almost exactly the date his wife and child were due to arrive in Dublin, might point to a belated attempt to regularise a situation which was in any case about to become a *fait accompli*. Dublin in that era was a small, intimate city in which news – and gossip – travelled fast. The Anglo-Irish circle of the Hearns was tight-knit and it would have been unlikely that the arrival of Charles' Greek wife and exotically dressed child would long have remained unknown to the military authorities.

Lafcadio Hearn left Greece, never to return, in 1852, when he was only two but he always strongly identified with his Greek background. In his thirties, he wrote in New Orleans: 'Being of a meridional race myself, a Greek, I *feel* with the Latin race than with the Anglo-Saxon. . .'[18] His mother attempted to instill her native faith into him: one of his few memories of her was her voice telling him each night to cross his fingers in Greek Orthodox fashion and repeat Greek prayers. She made three wounds in her children as babies to ensure God's protection 'according to her childish faith'.[19] Her influence was too short-lived to be effective but it may have played a part in estranging him from a life-long adherence to the religion into which he was adopted, Roman Catholicism.

Rosa could have had little idea of the complexity of the social situation she was entering into when she landed with her young son at Dublin on 1 August 1852. In later life, Patrick Lafcadio wrote to his brother that they were descended from 'good stock' on both sides of the family.[20] Certainly his father would have regarded this as no understatement. Charles Bush Hearn was the product of generations of social position and education. A graduate, like his own father and many antecedent members of his family, of Trinity College, Dublin, he combined the impeccably respectable professions of medicine and the army. Following his graduation with a B.A. from Trinity in 1839, he studied medicine at the Royal College of Surgeons in Dublin. He qualified as a doctor three years later, before joining the British Army in 1842.[21]

His father had been a Lieutenant Colonel, a Justice of the Peace and High Sheriff in County Westmeath where his family were landowners. His grandfather, too, had been an officer and his great-grandfather the Church of Ireland Archdeacon of Cashel. The Venerable Daniel Hearn (1693-1766), was clearly a substantial figure in the Protestant ruling elite of the era. It is with him that the family of Lafcadio Hearn emerges into recorded history. He did not, as previous biographers of Lafcadio Hearn have maintained, migrate from England to Ireland in 1713, accompanying a Lord Lieutenant, Lionel, Duke of Dorset, to Ireland as a private chaplain.[22] This tale seems to have been a mixture of invention, ignorance and family grandiosity.[23] Daniel Hearn, in fact, graduated from Trinity College, Dublin after four years' study there in 1713,[24] so he was clearly Irish and, in any event, the Duke did not land in Ireland until 1735, when Hearn was already at the zenith of this career.[25] Daniel's sister was married to a Lieutenant Colonel in Ireland, a further indication of the family's established social position in the country at the time.[26] There is no need to attempt to establish a migration of the Hearns to Ireland; while the surname is commonly found in England and some Irish people bearing it may be of English decent, it is also indigenous in Ireland.

215

The Venerable Daniel Hearn was Archdeacon of Cashel, in the southern Irish province of Munster, from 1728 until his death in 1766, a position which would have provided a healthy source of income.[27] It is unlikely, however, that he ever lived near the source of this income – senior Church of Ireland clerics who did so in that era would have been considered eccentric, to put it mildly[27a] – and he probably spent a comfortable life as a resident of St Stephen's Green, in the centre of Dublin, where he was also Rector of the fashionable St Anne's Church in nearby Dawson Street. He was buried there, among various other people of 'rank and distinction'.[28] He married well and was sufficiently wealthy to have left a will.[29] Although he did leave a considerable estate on his death in 1766, it did not, as has also been accepted by previous biography, include the lands later occupied by his descendants in County Westmeath, supposedly a reward from the Duke of Dorset; these were acquired much later through judicious marriage by his grandson.

The extraordinary fecundity of his line diluted his inheritance: Daniel Hearn had seven children by his second marriage and his eldest son, Robert Thomas, had thirteen from his two marriages. Between them, father and son established a pattern of service to Church and Army which was continued by their descendants. Robert Thomas was a Lieutenant in the 14th Dragoons and no fewer than five of his six children by his second marriage pursued military careers. The exception, William Edward, graduated with a B.A. from Trinity College in 1805 and became a clergyman. He, in turn, was the father to the Hon. William Edward Hearn, A.M., LL.D, a very distinguished academic. By marrying Rose Le Fanu, herself the daughter of a clergyman, he joined two Irish families which produced leading Victorian horror writers.

The clerical tradition continued in this branch of the family: a descendant in the present century was a Church of Ireland bishop.[30] Though they may not have been possessed of great means by the standards of the upper classes of the time, the Hearns were highly respectable. In the late nineteenth century, a confirmation of arms stated that the armorial bearings of 'Per pale gules and azure a chevron between three herons argent crest' had been proved to have been long borne by prescription by the family. This confirmation was to yet another clergyman, a great, great grandson of the Venerable Daniel Hearn and a first cousin to Lafcadio.[31]

Notwithstanding his many children, Robert Thomas Hearn, son of the Archdeacon, was able to send his eldest son, Daniel James, to Trinity College, from which he graduated with a B.A. in November 1789, and the Kings Inns, where he qualified as a barrister in 1792. His memorial of admission as a barrister certified that both of his parents were Protestants; he was required to take an oath before graduation 'to prevent the further Growth of Popery', which he duly did on 26 November 1792. In the King Inns' papers, Robert Thomas is described as being of Scarlet in the Isle of Man and Knockballymore in County Fermanagh.[32] In the Trinity records his profession is listed as *Centurio*. Daniel James was a 'pensioner' at Trinity College. Pensioners were children of parents of moderate income who paid a fixed sum annually; they ranked above 'sizars', who were allowed free education, and below 'fellow commoners', who paid double fees.[33]

Daniel James did not practise as a barrister but followed his father's military profession, rising to become Lieutenant Colonel of the 43rd Regiment of Light Infantry which he commanded at the battle of Vitoria in the Napoleonic Wars. He had previously been posted in the West Indies and was a veteran of various campaigns, including that in Denmark where he served under Wellington and took part in the siege of Copenhagen. As well as a wandering existence, he shared with his famous grandson a marked linguistic ability, being fluent in French and with a fair knowledge of Italian and Spanish.[34] In 1815, retired from the Army, he married Elizabeth, daughter of Richard Holmes, of Streamstown in County Westmeath and Prospect in Kings County, as it was then called.[35] The Holmes were a distinguished literary and legal family. Dr John Arbuthnot, of Alexander Pope's *Epistle* and Queen Anne's doctor, was a great-uncle of Elizabeth.

Richard Holmes made generous provision for his third daughter. The marriage settlement of 11 January 1815 granted 361 plantation acres of generally arable land[36] at Correagh, Ballyfadine, Kilbeg, Ardbally and part of Kilgarvine Bog in Moycashel, County Westmeath to trustees for the use of Daniel J. Hearn for his life and, after his death, to Elizabeth. She was to get £300 per annum, with power of appointment to her husband.[37] The land was in the parish of Ardnurcher, or

Horseleap, so called after the legendary feat of the Norman knight, Hugh de Lacy, in leaping over a castle drawbridge to escape pursuers. Grimmer historical echoes are suggested by the name Ardnurcher, in Gaelic *Ard-an-orchor*, or 'the fort of the slaughter'.[38] It was a frontier post of the Pale, the irreducible core of English-controlled territory in Ireland over the centuries.

Daniel Hearn continued to hold a small amount of property in County Fermanagh,[39] but Correagh now became the focus of his family's life. The Hearns were not grand in the scale of the local gentry: their house was whitewashed and 'quaint'[40] rather than imposing and was not one of the principle seats of the area.[41] Still, they were ranked with the 'gentry and clergy' in *Pigot's Directory* of 1824 and there is no doubting the respect which Colonel Daniel Hearn commanded. It was probably the Colonel whom Nina Kennard, an early Hearn biographer, had in mind when she described the Hearns as '. . .members of the Irish Protestant squirearchy, leaders of religious movements, presiding with great vigour at Church meetings and Parochial functions. . .'[42] Daniel Hearn acted as chairman of local vestry meetings which approved tithe agreements, the tax which was then paid by the entire population to the minority but State-established Church of Ireland.[43] In 1828, he was appointed High Sheriff of County Westmeath.

Even though he did not marry until he was 47, Daniel and Elizabeth had eight children, one of whom, Charles Bush, the eldest son, was the father of Lafcadio Hearn. In a legal document of 1860, one of the children, Anne, is differentiated from the others by having the phrase 'also one of the children of Daniel James Hearn' inserted in parenthesis after her name.[44] Whether or not she was an illegitimate child regularised by adoption into the family is not clear. Elizabeth Hearn maintained a house in her name only from the 1820s at Fairview Avenue in Dublin, so she may have lived apart from her husband.[45] Daniel Hearn may have possessed the same wayward, passionate sexuality which was to wreak such havoc in the lives of his son and grandson. Elizabeth Hearn was still at Fairview Avenue twenty years later. By then she was a widow, Daniel James having died in 1837. For some years in the 1840s she shared the Fairview house with her younger sister, Sarah Brenane, also a widow.[46] More than herself, Sarah was to play a vital role in caring for Elizabeth's exotic daughter-in-law and grandson, Patrick Lafcadio, when they arrived in Ireland in 1852.

They came accompanied by Charles's younger brother, the painter, Richard Holmes Hearn. In much the same way as Lafcadio would later rebel against the constraints of the English language and attempt to create a new literary style based on French romanticism, Richard, in common with many other nineteenth-century Irish artists, saw Paris rather than London as the source of artistic education and inspiration. In fact, he trained at the same prestigious Thomas Couture teaching studio there as his better-known Irish contemporary, Nathaniel Hone who, like him, also gravitated to the Barbizon group of painters.[46a] Richard was an intimate friend of Millet, one of the Barbizon's leading figures. The determination of the Barbizon school to paint from nature, in rebellion against the then-prevailing classical tradition, would surely have been approved of by his nephew. Indeed, further parallels occur in the chapter on Jean Paul Laurens that Richard contributed to a book on various artists published in 1891 in which he determined that the crowning lesson of Lauren's art was the respect the new order should assume towards the old, a conclusion which would be echoed in Lafcadio's Japanese work.[46b]

He also shared his temperament with Lafcadio: although the warmest and most gentle-hearted of men, argument could make him quite irrational, a trait inherited by his distinguished nephew. In later life, Lafcadio remembered his big beard, and a boxwood top he had given him. Mrs Brenane was prejudiced against him by some tale she had heard about his life in Paris.[47] In later years he became a 'snoozer', never progressing from sketches to a finished picture. He died unmarried in 1890.[48] It was he who engaged a Miss Butcher, an English companion who was supposed to teach Rosa English and prepare her for life in Dublin; Miss Butcher was to play a much more sinister role in the life of her 'lady'.

It seems that Charles was apprehensive about his mother's reception of his wife and child. In the event, according to Hearn family tradition, she 'warmly welcomed' Rosa and Patrick Lafcadio to her large, old-fashioned terraced house at 48 Lower Gardiner Street.[49] The house did not actually belong to Elizabeth; it was rented by her son-in-law, Henry Colclough

Stephens. Henry Stephens was a rising solicitor and there was then a great concentration of lawyers and other professionals in the street. In fact, they shared the house with a doctor who does not seem to have been a relation.[50] Considering Mrs Hearn's position as a virtual guest of her son-in-law in a house they do not appear to have had to themselves and the whole family's position in the restricted world of professional Dublin, Rosa's arrival could hardly have added to their comfort. Nevertheless, the diary of Susan Hearn, Lafcadio's spinster grand-aunt, records the arrival with a note of kindly, if tentative, optimism: 'Rosa we are all inclined to love, and her little son is an interesting darling child. . .May Almighty God bless and prosper the whole arrangement.'[51] Susan, who lived nearby, was a sister of Daniel James Hearn. She had the literary aspirations which ran in the family and was the author of an unpublished novel, *Felicia*, which, interestingly enough, shared the same defects of sentimentality and architectonic inadequacy as the later attempts at imaginative fiction of her more illustrious great-nephew.

Forty years afterwards, Lizzie Hardy described Rosa as a '. . .large, stout woman with fine dark eyes and hair, very passionate temper when roused, of an indolent disposition and as she only spoke broken English it was not easy to converse with [her]'.[52] This agrees with the description gleaned from the Hearns by Nina Kennard; Rosa '. . .was handsome. . .with beautiful eyes, but ill-tempered and unrestrained, sometimes even violent. Musical but too indolent to cultivate the gift, clever, but absolutely uneducated'. She spent her time lying on a sofa, '. . .complaining of the dullness of her surroundings, the climate of Ireland, of the impossibility of learning the language. To her children [*sic*] she was capricious and tyrannical. . .'[53] Whether or not Rosa had, as Nina Kennard claimed, an inherited predisposition to insanity, she had begun to reveal symptoms of mental illness. Before her husband returned from the West Indies in October 1853, she attempted to throw herself out of a window. Fits of silence and depression alternated with outbursts of violence, to such an extent that she had to be forcibly restrained.[54]

Kennard states that, on his return from the West Indies, Charles found that his wife had lost her beauty. Miss Butcher, who had impressed Susan Hearn as a 'nice young person', was an important factor, not just in the strained relations which developed between Rosa and the Hearn family, but also in the marital difficulties which she experienced with Charles.[55] More serious, however, was Rosa's deteriorating mental condition; Susan Hearn's diary gives an account of a pathetic and terrible scene the night after Charles' arrival back in Dublin: 'Charles, his wife, and little boy, dined with us in Gardiner's Place [sic], all well and happy. That night we were plunged into deep affliction by the sudden and dangerous illness of Rosa, Charles's wife. She still continues ill, but hopes are entertained of her recovery.' After this, the entry in the diary breaks off abruptly.[56] Rosa recovered and passed a long convalescence in Dundrum, the site of a large mental asylum, after which she set up her own home in a house near Portobello Barracks in Rathmines, a Dublin suburb. Kate Ronane, an Irish nursemaid, was hired for Lafcadio though her duties also seem to have included coping with the violence of Rosa's mental attacks.

In March 1854, only six months after his return to Dublin, Charles Hearn departed, this time for the Crimean War. Rosa was pregnant again. She left for Greece in the summer, supposedly to visit her relations but she did not return. Lafcadio Hearn never saw his mother again.

In the circumstances, he was fortunate that he was cared for by his great-aunt, Mrs Sarah Brenane, a sister of his grandmother. The Holmes, like the Hearns, were strict Protestants but Sarah had braved the taboo to marry a Roman Catholic. Not that Captain Justin Brenane, whom she married in 1823, lacked for social consequence. A Justice of the Peace and a large landowner, his residence at 'Kiltrea-house' was the first of the principle seats of the parish of Monart, two miles north-west of Enniscorthy, County Wexford.[57] When she was widowed, Sarah leased the land and went to live with her sister in Dublin.[58] It was believed in the family that it was a great blow to the Holmes when the youngest daughter married a Roman Catholic but Sarah and her sister, Elizabeth, continued to have a good relationship. It was also part of family lore that the Hearns had trained their parrot to say, 'have you seen the priest', when Mrs Brenane called.[59] This may be apocryphal: if not, it is indicative of a very relaxed attitude on Sarah's part to her adopted religion, contrary to what has previously been believed.

Mrs Brenane has been described as '. . .a noteworthy figure, always dressed in marvellous, quaint-shaped, black silk gowns. Not a speck of dust was allowed to touch these garments; a large holland sheet being invariably laid on the seat of the carriage, and wrapped round her by the footman, when she went for her daily drive'.[60] She shared the Fairview house with Elizabeth and Elizabeth's painter son, Richard, until 1848/9, when she moved out to a house at 1 Martello-terrace, Merrion, in the parish of Donnybrook, two-and-a half miles south of the centre of Dublin. Sarah was an inveterate lover of the sea and the terrace consisted of mainly small houses, most of which were let in the summer to sea-bathers attracted by the smooth and firm strand.[61] She remained there until 1851, when she moved to 21 Leinster Square in Rathmines. She was at this address for about two years, until she moved to 3 Prince Arthur Terrace, also in Rathmines. She went from there to 73 Upper Leeson Street in 1855/6, where she remained for seven or eight years. She moved to England at this point but may have retained houses in Dublin at 4 Sandycove Avenue from 1863 to 1866/7 and at 2 Osborne Terrace for a brief period in 1866/7.[62] Following the pattern of the time, Mrs Brenane, like the Hearns, did not own the houses in which she lived. It was the fact that they were rented which explains the constant moving from one address to another.

The houses at Upper Leeson Street, Prince Arthur Terrace and Leinster Square, were all in the township of Rathmines, which was two miles south of the centre of Dublin, and had a population of three thousand. Twenty years previously it had been an insignificant hamlet; by the 1850s its main artery was a mile-and-a-half-long line of elegant buildings, intersected by numerous terraces and separated from the city at Portobello by the Grand Canal. At Portobello also was the Artillery and Cavalry Barracks, which would have been familiar to Charles Bush Hearn.[63]

Mrs Brenane took the four-year-old Patrick Lafcadio into her care when his mother left for Greece in 1854. More than forty years later, as he struggled to impose coherence on the fragments of memory, he recalled the solemn, wealthy home he had shared with her at Upper Leeson Street. By day, it was richly and sombrely furnished. On the floor, there were soft, expensive, patternless carpets. The walls were covered in heavy arabesque paper. The furniture was large-scale and old fashioned, with enormous four-pillared beds of solid mahogany, surrounded with curtains, so high from the floor that a little set of steps was needed to reach them. Also of solid mahogany were the tables and chairs, sideboards, wardrobes and cabinets, which impressed themselves on his memory as having been immense. Young Patrick Lafcadio's attention was drawn to the feet shaped like claws, complete with talons. It was not cheerful during the day but in the evening, when the lamps were lit and the window shutters closed, it was charming; the curtains and draperies which had seemed dull by day became 'a luxurious cavern of color'.[64]

One incident he remembered provides a vignette of a very different world from the hell he depicted when he was struggling to create a romantic persona for himself as a young man in the United States. He cried loudly in a fashionable gathering at the effect of an air played on the piano. Everyone tried to coax him to say what the matter was but he could not. Retrospectively, he came to believe that the emotions stirred were not of himself but of previous lives. On the occasion he lied and said he was thinking of a dead uncle. He was petted and given cake, and marvelled at his own ability to deceive.[65]

Lafcadio learned to read at an early age and this was his delight, though characteristically it was 'mixed with near terror'. There were illustrated books designed to promote good conduct, in which bad or dirty boys who disobeyed their parents suffered terrible fates, falling from roofs, being drowned, having their noses cut off or their tongues pulled out. Boys who swallowed orange seeds had trees grow out of their stomachs. More happily, he had his own picture books, gifts from visitors and others. These included the classic fairy tales, and stories about animals and natural history. He also had letters from his father in India, written in block capitals because he could not yet read handwriting, full of wonderful tales about tigers and serpents. He had a huge model of Noah's Ark, Swiss toys of all sorts and, befitting the martial tradition of his forbears, armies of soldiers with batteries of cannon. Years later, he would become quite sentimental at the memory of these toys:

> But of those mysterious toys which so strangely charmed the imagination of the child the fate has ever remained a mystery to the memory of man. You cannot tell whether

the broken trunk of the wooden elephant, which you tried so vainly to repair with disappointed tears, was ever mended; or what became of the tin locomotive which was so ruthlessly torn apart in order to find out what made it 'click-clack' inside or the battalions of lead soldiers, or the bronze cannon which shot off peas, or the wooden swords and other mockeries of war, or the building blocks which possessed secrets so hard to find out. Who knows what became of them? What foolish little trifles they were and yet what pleasure they gave, and what power ever their recollection has upon you today! The ghost of the wooden elephant with the broken trunk may after all affect the regularity of the pulse for an instant. That broken trunk, ridiculous as it may seem, can still stir up memories, which you dare not laugh at. You know you dare not laugh at them. What a beautiful time of life that was, and how golden the hours before we first learned that life is a struggle and that passions are playthings for children of a larger growth – in short, before we had 'become as gods knowing both good and evil', as Mephistopheles mockingly observes.[65a]

Young Patrick Lafcadio could hardly be described in the circumstances as deprived or neglected but he did find fault with his situation as a world '. . .wholly without ideals. Of nature or beauty I knew and felt nothing. My world was in rooms looking out upon dull streets and a dismal garden'.[66] Mrs Brenane's house in Leeson Street was actually situated in a area of pleasant, tree-lined roads and streets.

The real misery was psychological. In 1846, before he went to Greece, Charles Bush Hearn had fallen in love with a Dublin beauty, 'the pocket Venus', Alicia Goslin. It was believed that he had become engaged to her before he went abroad. He nearly went out of his mind when her letters dried up and a fellow officer told him she had married the worthy figure of Judge Arthur Crawford. Passing through London on his way back from the Crimea in 1856, an officer friend asked him to drop a travelling rug off at a certain house; the butler showed him upstairs to the drawing room where the door was opened by none other than Alicia, now widowed and again available.[67] Patrick Lafcadio was an unwitting witness to the intrigue which followed. When his father returned to Dublin, he took his six-year-old son for a walk, which was not in any event a comfortable experience:

. . .he never laughed, so I was afraid of him. He bought me
cakes. It was a day of sun, with rain clouds above the roofs,
but no rain. I was in petticoats. We walked a long way.
Father stopped at a flight of stone steps before a tall
house. . .a lady came to meet us. . .she seemed to me
lovely beyond anything I had ever seen before. She stooped
down and kissed me. I think I can feel the touch of her
hand still. Then I found myself in possession of a toy gun
and picture book she had given me. On the way home,
father bought me some plum cakes, and told me never to
say anything to 'Auntie' about our visit. I can't remember
whether I told or not. But 'Auntie' found it out. She was so
angry that I was frightened. She confiscated the gun and the
picture book, in which I remember there was a picture of
David killing Goliath. Auntie didn't tell me why she was so
angry for more than ten years after.[68]

Auntie's anger did not deter Charles. He was granted leave of
absence from the Army from mid-September 1856 until July
1857, the first month for 'Private Affairs' and then on the
grounds of 'Ill Health'. Firstly, he had his marriage annulled.
According to Mrs Brenane's niece, the divorce was agreed
between Charles and Rosa, though Lafcadio Hearn was
apparently told by Mrs Brenane that his father had obtained it
on a dubious technicality. It seems likely that it was agreed, given
the fact that Rosa never returned from Greece, where she
subsequently remarried. Mrs Brenane may have wished to ensure
that Lafcadio thought well of his mother by placing all the blame
on his father and shielding him from the shattering reality that he
had been abandoned by both parents. Divorce was in any case
anathema in that era, particularly in the solidly respectable world
of the Holmes and the Hearns and Mrs Brenane would probably
have been more forgiving of an illiterate foreigner than one from
her own social background. Her 'strict upbringing and strong
belief in self-discipline' did not make her sympathetic to her
nephew's behaviour.[69]

In July 1857, Charles married Alicia Crawford, just a month
before he departed for India with his regiment.[70] He went as a
decorated veteran of the Crimean War,[71] accompanied by his
wife who, in contrast to the hapless Rosa, would not have raised
any eyebrows among his fellow officers. He was a successful
soldier but the ten remaining years of his life were dogged by
misfortune. In India, Charles and Alicia had three daughters.

Then, in the intense heat of the autumn of 1861, Alicia, who had been in poor health, had a still-born child. She seemed to be making a slow recovery but, one afternoon, when Charles returned home, he found Alicia on the verandah, apparently asleep. When he bent over her he found that she was dead, with a letter from her mother-in-law, Elizabeth Hearn, clutched in her hand.[72]

James Daniel, the third and last son of Charles and Rosa Hearn, had been born just after his mother's return to Greece, in August 1854. When Rosa remarried, she dispatched James back to his Irish relatives. This has been rationalised in some previous Hearn biography on the grounds that her second husband was supposed to have stipulated that he would not care for the children of her first marriage, but it is hard not to see the abandonment of her children, whatever the circumstances, as an unnatural act of either selfishness or mental incapacity. Rosa had four more children by her second husband. Her mental condition worsened, however, and she spent the last ten years of her life in the National Mental Asylum on Corfu, before her death in December 1882, at the age of 59.[73]

Mrs Brenane paid Rosa's fare back to Greece in 1854. She was so angered by Charles Bush's divorce and remarriage that she refused even to look at his picture. Now her vexation extended to James. He was taken from his nurse at Liverpool and baptised. This time there was no concession to the child's Greek lineage; he was called after his paternal grandfather and sent to live with Dr Stewart, on old Scotsman, who had a boarding school at Alton, Hampshire, England, until he was sixteen.[74] Mrs Brenane vowed that James and Patrick Lafcadio would never be together and Lafcadio saw him only once: he was playing with toy soldiers when a little boy with big eyes was introduced to him as his brother. James seized some of the soldiers; Lafcadio took them back, beat him, and threw him down the stairs. He never met his brother again.

A fascination with Greek culture, which Lafcadio regarded as his maternal inheritance, coexisted with the haunting presence of his mother throughout his life. In an incident in Japan, a Chikanobu print, 'The Spirit of the Cherry Tree', released a flood of memory of this haunting. Though she is not explicitly identified as such, it concerned his mother. She was the beautiful shape bending above his rest as a child. Her apparitions cause 'breathless delight' and 'sadness inexpressible'. Her visits filled him 'with rash desire to wander over the world in search of something like her', a quest doomed to failure. Beneath a thin veil of philosophy, here is a key to Lafcadio's restless wanderings, a search for an enchanted land where he could find the 'eternal haunter' and retain the 'luminous moment [when] all the tides of your being set and surge to her with a longing for which there is not any word'.

In reality, he always found that 'the sun had gloomed, the colors of the world turned grey'.[75] This was not surprising, as the violence of his mother's mental illness must have traumatised his infant years. The clearly autobiographical 'Gipsy's Story', published in New Orleans when he was in his early thirties, is probably an accurate summary of his memories:

> Of my mother. . .I knew her little when a child; I only remember her in memories vague as dreams, and perhaps in dreams also. For there are years of childhood so mingled with dreams that we cannot discern through memory the shadow from the substance. But in those times I was forever haunted by a voice that spoke a tongue only familiar to me in after years, and by a face I do not ever remember to have kissed.

His mother's face is ' clear, dark' with 'liquidly black' eyes. She was bending over him in his sleep with 'something savage even in the tenderness of the great luminous eyes. . .and this dark dream-face filled me with strange love and fear'. This may have been the source of the fear which entered his psyche in childhood and fuelled the terror of his adult writing. It certainly predated, and probably inspired, the nightmares which blighted his years with Mrs Brenane.

The 'Gypsy's Story' continues with an allusion to his father's second wife and children: 'And the strange beauty of the falcon face, that haunted me forever, chilled my heart to the sun-haired maidens who sought our home, fair like tall idols of ivory and gold.' Here may be the seed of Lafcadio's life-long rejection of the cold north, home of the fair maidens who had wrecked his child's home, and concomitant identification with his mother's sunny south. The conclusion of the 'Gypsy's Story' is idyllic: 'a tall girl, lithe as a palm, swarthy as Egypt' appears, points to an encampment and tells him that the gypsies have been waiting for him for years: 'For thy mother was of my people; and thou who hast sucked her breasts mayst not live with the pale children of another race. . .thou wilt leave riches, pleasures, horses, and the life of cities for thy heart's sake; and I will be thy sister.'[76] The rejections of cities was another life-long obsession. The gypsy fantasy was a pathetic reversal of reality: his mother never reclaimed him and he was rejected by his father and step-mother, not vice-versa.

The adult Hearn's idealisation of women in general and mothers in particular could be seen as a reaction to the mother he had hardly known. Take, for example, the following passages from one of his Tokyo books:

> . . .we know of nothing else, in all the range of human experience, so sacred as mother-love,- nothing so well deserving the name of divine. Mother-love alone could have enabled the delicate life of thought to unfold and to endure upon the rind of this wretched little planet: only through that supreme unfeelingness could the nobler emotions ever have found strength to blossom in the brains of man;- only by help of mother-love could the higher forms of trust in the Unseen ever have been called into existence. . .[77]

The single memory he actually had of his mother bending over his bed was a recurrent theme of his adult writing, although the reality of the incident was a little different from the tender idealisations. One day, when she bent over him, he gave way to a childish impulse to slap her face. The result was immediate and severe chastisement. He remembered both crying and feeling that he deserved what he got.[78]

In a passage much quoted by previous biographers, Hearn dissociated himself from his father and credited his mother with all his worthwhile attributes.

> The soul in me is not of him. Whatever there is of good in me. . .came from that dark race-soul of which we know so little. My love of right, my hate of wrong, my admiration for what is beautiful or true: my capacity for faith in man or woman;- my sensitiveness to artistic things, which gives me whatever little success I have – even that language-power whose physical sign is in the large eyes of both of us,- came from Her.

> What if there is a 'skeleton in our closet'? Did he not
> make it? I think only of her. I have thought only of her, and
> of you, as imagining her possibly, all my life – rarely of him.
> It is the mother who makes us, makes at least all that makes
> the nobler man; not his strength or powers of calculation,
> but his heart and power to love. And I would rather have
> her portrait than a fortune.

Yet there was a note of uncertainty here. He was responding
to a criticism from his brother who was staunchly of the opposite
opinion about the respective merits of their parents and Lafcadio
was being defensive:

> With regard to what you say about mother's treatment of us
> – I must tell you that, even as a child, I used *to wonder at it*.
> But my old grandaunt and others – the old family servants
> especially – would say to me: 'Don't believe anything about
> your mother; she loved you all as much as any mother
> could do; she could not help herself'.[79]

The summary of traits inherited from his mother contained in
an earlier letter to an American friend is considerably less
flattering: 'My mother, who couldn't speak a word of English,
gave me large, beautiful eyes, at birth, an ill-temper, often
unrestrained and violent, and an inherited predisposition to
insanity.' He contrasted the hereditary, educated, scepticism of
his father's side of the family with the reverential tendencies of
his mother: '. . .she believed in the Oriental Catholicism – the
Byzantine fashion of Christianity which produced such hideous
madonnas and idiotic saints in stained glass'.[80]

Lafcadio knew his father little better than his mother. The only
possible contact could have been during his father's brief sojourns
in Ireland, October 1853 to March 1854 and July 1856 to August
1857. After that he departed for India, never to return. Lizzie
Hardy met Charles when he came back from Greece and
remembered him making fond remarks about his son.[81] Lafcadio
recalled seeing his father four or five times, usually in a military
setting. Once he was playing with his nurse when the sound of
galloping horses was heard behind. The nurse laughed and lifted
him up so that he could call to his father who was passing in a
military formation. His father took him from the nurse. On
horseback with him, with a great body of mounted soldiers
following behind, he imagined he was a general. It was the only
time he was glad to be with his father and felt him to be good.[82]

Another time he was taken to a mess dinner where he crawled about under the table, pinching the striped legs of the red-coated soldiers.

If an autobiographical fragment, written by Hearn in Japan, is to be believed, one of the few contacts between father and son ended in tragedy. When he was about the age of seven, his father was using a Turkish scimitar in the garden one day, slicing effortlessly through the branches of trees. Young Patrick Lafcadio decided to have a go and gashed his left knee. The wound needed surgical treatment; it healed slowly and there were complications. A tendon contracted so that the leg could not be straightened. Abscesses developed on various parts of his body and it was feared that he might not live. The treatment caused horrible pain; he remained for months in bed, 'under torture'. The doctor insisted that he be kept at the seaside for a couple of years, where he was cared for by a doctor friend of Mrs Brenane's. In the two years that it took him to recover, he was helpless, unable to move without assistance. Every day he was wheeled to the beach in a perambulator and given a sea bath. He had no pleasures except reading, and being told stories by those kind enough to talk to him.[83]

Even if this incident did happen, Hearn's penchant for exaggeration may have translated months, or even weeks, into years. It is likely that he would have recuperated at Tramore, the seaside resort in south-eastern Ireland where he spent many childhood holidays. It was there that Lafcadio met his father for the last time:

> We took a walk by the sea. It was a very hot day; and father had become bald then; and when he took off his hat I saw that the top of his head was all covered with little drops of water. He said: 'She is very angry; she will never forgive me.' She was Auntie. I never saw him again.[84]

Auntie made sure that no correspondence developed between father and son. When Charles Bush Hearn wrote from India, his son never replied: Auntie did not exactly forbid it but neither did she encourage it and he was lazy.

His father died of Indian fever on board ship at Suez on his way back from India on 21 November 1866. He was 48. His three daughters – Elizabeth Sarah Maude, Minnie Charlotte, and Posey Gertrude (Lillah), then eight, seven and six – by his second marriage were given homes by various members of the family.[85] One of them later went to stay at Michigan with Lafcadio's younger brother, James Daniel, known as 'Jim'. The other two married; Minnie Charlotte to Buckley Atkinson, a lawyer in Portadown in the north of Ireland.[86] She was the one who became a correspondent of Lafcadio in his Japanese years.

Lafcadio could have had little inkling of the wretchedness of the circumstances in which his father died. Charles had first of all been effectively dispossessed by his mother. In 1843 she had appointed him to the family lands in Westmeath but had reserved the power to revoke and, in 1860, she exercised this power. He was now appointed only to a share with five of her other children and, unlike some of the others, no money was settled on him.[87] Even more seriously, he was being pursued by Mrs Brenane through the courts for the recovery of an outstanding loan at the time of his death.[88]

The memories Charles Bush bequeathed to his son were far from kind. His father's picture, with its grim face and steely eyes, produced a sense of aversion; he liked to think that there was nothing of his father in him, physically or mentally.[89] However, his devoted friend and first biographer, Elizabeth Bisland, believed this was a mistaken prejudice, for the children of Charles Bush's second marriage bore '. . .the most striking likeness to the older half-brother, having the same dark skins, delicate, aquiline profiles, eyes deeply set in arched orbits, and short, supple, well-knit figures'.[90] Nina Kennard also noted with some amusement that the dark tint in his physiology, which he was so convinced was part of his mother's exotic inheritance, was present in the Hearn line.[91] It would have been the psychological rather than the physical affinities, though, which mattered to Lafcadio. Here his perceptions were indeed more complex. He recognised that at least some of his artistic attributes – an aptitude for drawing and a great love of music (its imagery was recurrent in his writings) – came from his father.[92] He also recognised that he had inherited, temperamentally at any rate, a great deal from his paternal line: what he saw as a lack of force and a softness of soul, a strange mixture of weakness and firmness. The firm side of his nature he saw as '. . .an uncontrollable resistance in particular directions – guided by feeling mostly, and not always in the direction most suited to my interest'.[93]

He prized the photo of their father which his half-sister had given him and wished that they could have talked about him and their experiences in India. In his thirties, when his long-lost brother sent him a photo of their father, Lafcadio was very keen to have it copied. Later, in Japan, he was anxious to get whatever information he could about both parents.[94] At the age of thirty, he wrote of believing that he was influenced by hereditary memories of his father. In the story, a doctor is holding forth on the phenomenon of hereditary memories; Hearn says he dreams of places he has never been. The doctor asks if his parents were ever in India: he replies that his father was. The doctor explains this by 'hereditary impressions' made on an English traveller in India through the medium of sight and sound, having been inherited by his children who, having never seen the Orient, would nevertheless be forever haunted by visions of the Far East.[95]

What is striking about this piece, written ten years before Hearn went to Japan, is that he was indeed forever haunted by visions of the Far East, where he spent the last fourteen years of his life. Prior to that, he spent two years in the West Indies, where his father had served before he went to the East. The reference in this story to his father being English is a typically Hearnian touch. It was partly that, in New Orleans particularly, he camouflaged himself as English, partly that he transmogrified his childhood reminiscences to other settings and partly that, to him, 'England, Ireland and Scotland mean(t) the same thing.'[96]

Overall, Lafcadio's attitude to his father was remarkably charitable, considering how he had been treated. In fact, he seems to have forgiven his father while still a young man if a passage, written when Hearn was 23, is any indication. As a Cincinnati reporter, he went to investigate a medium. He was clearly cynical but then an exchange took place, supposedly with the spirit of his dead father. He asked the spirit its name; the reply was 'Charles Bush H-'. The spirit then claimed: 'I am your father, P-'. – Hearn was still called Patrick or, more usually, Paddy, at this stage. The spirit asked forgiveness for having wronged him. When the son replied that he did not consider he had been so wronged, the medium intervened:

> 'It would be better not to contradict the spirit,' interrupted the medium, 'until it has explained matters.'

I do not wish to contradict the spirit in the sense you imply,' answered the reporter. 'I thoroughly understand the circumstances alluded to; but I wish to explain that I have long since ceased to consider it a wrong done me.'[97]

Mrs Brenane was not so forgiving. Lafcadio, a clever and darkly handsome child, was a great favourite of hers, to the extent that she became jealous if he stayed away from her for any length of time. She was obviously much involved with Lafcadio from the time he arrived in Ireland. Before Charles Bush Hearn left for India in 1857, it was agreed that she would educate him as a Roman Catholic and provide for him, which was generally taken to mean that he would be one, at least, of her heirs.

CHAPTER TWELVE

TERROR IN THE DARK

L A F C A D I O had complained to Hendrick that it was difficult to think of art 'in the dead waste and muddle of this mess', the streets of Tokyo. Yet these streets did provide much of the inspiration for the book which was then in incubation, *Exotics and Retrospectives*. Specifically, the inspiration for the chapter, 'Insect Musicians', the first of many essays he was to write on insects, came from a visit in 1897 to a little-known part of Tokyo, all ablaze with lanterns thirty feet high and painted with weird devices. His attention was caught by the insect-sellers and he bought a number of insects, reflecting that only a poetical people could have '. . .imagined the luxury of buying summer voices to make for them the illusion of nature where there is only dust and mud'.[1]

Lafcadio observed that few sense impressions remained longer with the traveller than sounds in a strange country. This was particularly so in Japan with insects and, to a lesser extent, with frogs. Their proliferation in the streets may have disgusted him, but the Japanese's appreciation of their aesthetic qualities made the frogs worthy of a separate chapter in *Exotics and Retrospectives*. Because there was rice everywhere in Japan, so also were there frogs:

> Hushed only during the later autumn and brief winter, with the first awakening of spring waken all the voices of the marsh-lands,- the infinite bubbling chorus that might be taken for the speech of the quickening soil itself. And the universal mystery of life seems to thrill with a peculiar melancholy in that vast utterance. . .[2]

Frogs were a favourite subject of Japanese poetry, particularly and, to Western minds, peculiarly, love poetry. Yet this poetry ignored the coldness and clamminess of the frog because, Lafcadio believed, Japanese poetry ignored the qualities of sensation in favour of the aesthetic: it represented the healthiest and happiest attitude towards nature. By contrast, it was possible that Occidentals shrank from natural impressions by reason of a 'morbid tactual sensibility'. By accepting nature as she is, the Japanese discovered beauty where Westerners found only loathsome insects, stones, and frogs.[3]

Together with 'Fuji-no-Yama', an account of his climb of that world-famous mountain, and 'The Literature of the Dead', these chapters on insects and frogs represented a welcome infusion of Tokyo-inspired freshness into a work which had been simmering in Lafcadio' brain for some years. He had written to his publisher as far back as December 1894 outlining his plan for the book:

> It will be entirely psychological, and will deal, I fancy, only with a number of common sensations and emotions from the standpoint of evolutional inheritance as a basic idea. You have now, I think, papers on the childish fear of darkness, upon First Impressions (better called Super-imposition), upon the sensation of blue, upon one sort of musical emotion, upon a palm-tree, etc. You will receive by this, or next mail, a paper on the thrill caused by human touch. Well, here is just a suggestion – sight, hearing, smell, touch, should furnish each a subject. 'Parfum de Jeunesse' might be the title of a future paper, 'Red' the subject of another. The whole to be called thoughts about feelings, etc.[4]

Hearn did adhere to this plan and chapters were written on 'Parfum de Jeunesse' and 'A Red Sunset'. It was slow work, though: over two years later the book was still only half-finished. This was partly because Lafcadio did not wish to strain either his muse or his eyes. His plan was to '. . ."feed up",- read queer things, digest them, and wait. . .'; and then to try to write something 'quite astonishing'.[5] At this stage he was flush with the confidence which often preceded publication but seldom outlasted it.

The ten slight, philosophical essays which made up the 'retrospectives' element of the book, on which Lafcadio worked so hard, turned out to be less successful than the six 'Tokyo' essays which made up its 'exotics' element but they are of immense biographical interest for the manner in which they hark back to his childhood and the West Indies. As might be expected, horror made appearances in the book, sometimes subtly and sometimes overtly. 'Vespertina Cognitio', based on the hauntings which came in the stupefaction of a West Indian siesta, was one of his horrific masterpieces. But beneath the descriptive mastery and philosophical earnestness, there was a deeper purpose: to understand the fears of childhood. It is clear in the essay that he had as a child suffered a fear of the supernatural by night and day, the horror of which was so intense that he believed it would have been fatal if it had been prolonged beyond a few seconds. It was a 'prenatal, ancestral fear'; the training of the mind under civilisation was directed towards its conquest. It could be suppressed but not eliminated, an interesting concept given the seepage of horror into most of Hearn's work.[6] He now attempted to rationalise the similarity of an horrific dream which he had experienced in the West Indies to a shape which had disturbed his sleep in childhood by asking if the 'human organic memory' did not hold records of pain from former lives.[7]

Hearn had been drafting, in fragmentary fashion, some elements of his autobiography. The more he worked on it, the further it departed from pure autobiography and eventually he abandoned the project altogether. Fragments of the material were reworked and appeared in various forms in his later books. 'In a Pair of Eyes' dealt with adolescence, that 'sudden awakening from the long soul-sleep of childhood'. Much the same thing happened with two other Tokyo pieces, 'Gothic Horror' and 'Nightmare-Touch', which had also been quarried from childhood. Philosophically, the works were linked by an attempt to demonstrate that certain human sensations could be explained 'evolutionally'. In 'Gothic Horror' it was the terror inspired by the architecture of the church where he was taken to Mass by Mrs Brenane in Dublin. He realised it was the 'wizened and pointed shapes' of the windows which were the source of his distress. He linked the goblins which haunted his dreams with Gothic architecture. He identified the points, into which doors, windows, aisles, roofs and everything else in this form tapered, as the specific focus of his fear:

Even though built by hands of men, it had ceased to be a
mass of dead stone: it is infused with Something that thinks
and threatens;- it has become a shadowing malevolence, a
multiple goblinry, a monstrous fetish![8]

★   ★   ★

The answer to his childhood puzzle came in the tropics where
the movement of the giant palm trees suggested to him that what
he had felt as child had been 'a horror of monstrous motion'. He
recognised that it must have been due to an old memory of the
childhood church, revived by the sight of the giant palms rising
into the gloom. As he looked up at them, his mental picture
blurred and the trees distorted into the Gothic church of
childhood vision; he saw the architrave 'elbow upward in each of
the spaces between the pillars, and curve and point itself into a
range of prodigious arches;- and again the sombre thrill
descended upon me'; the giant palms had reproduced that old
mixed sense of religious awe and delight, 'shadowed by a queer
disquiet'. The child had associated goblins and Gothic churches,
the profane with the Christian. But now he realised that there
was yet another element, crucial to his future development: the
aesthetic, 'and this, in its general mass, might be termed the sense
of terrible beauty' (Hearn's anticipation of Yeats' famous phrase
seems to have escaped notice up to now).[9]

Although he died when the cinema was in its infancy, there is
a distinct cinematic aspect to this piece, as there is with much of
Hearn's horror writing with flash-backs, distortions, sudden stark
images, and so on. It tells us more about its author than it does
about Gothic architecture: from his tropical phase onwards, he
was infusing inanimate objects with the horror of monstrous
motion. There is also the link with his adult self in his
observation that part of his childhood distress was caused by 'the
silent manipulation of power' in Gothic architecture which was
not 'natural'.[10] Here is a clue to the origin of the adult Hearn's
philosophical rejection of nineteenth-century Western society,
particularly the life of its cities: they shared with the terrifying
Gothic forms the horror of not being natural. His adult life was a
long journey from industrial society back to the naturalness of
traditional society. He was now closeting himself away from the
unnaturalness of contemporary Tokyo to immerse himself in

disentangling these dim childhood memories.

In one essay, 'Nightmare-Touch', he detailed at thrilling length the hauntings which terrified him in his room at Mrs Brenane's; he remembered a little five-year-old, referred to only as 'the Child', (more affectionate, however, in Irish usage than Hearn made it sound) and condemned to sleep alone in the Dublin house:

> The room was narrow, but very high, and, in spite of one tall window, very gloomy. It contained a fire-place wherein no fire was ever kindled; and the Child suspected that the chimney was haunted.
>
> A law was made that no light should be left in the Child's Room at night,- simply because the Child was afraid of the dark. His fear of the dark was judged to be a mental disorder requiring severe treatment. But the treatment aggravated the disorder. Previously I had been accustomed to sleep in a well-lighted room, with a nurse to take care of me. I thought that I should die of fright when sentenced to lie alone in the dark, and – what seemed to me abominably cruel – actually locked into my room, the most dismal in the house. Night after night when I had been warmly tucked into bed the lamp was removed; the key clicked in the lock; the protecting light and the footsteps of my guardian receded together. Then the agony of fear would come upon me. Something in the black air would seem to gather and grow – (I thought that I could hear it grow)- till I had to scream. Screaming regularly brought punishment; but it also brought back the light, which more than consoled for the punishment. This fact being at last found out, orders were given to pay no further heed to the screams of the Child.
>
> Why was I thus insanely afraid? Partly because the dark had always been peopled for me with shapes of terror. So far back as memory extended, I had suffered from ugly dreams; and when aroused from them I could always see the forms dreamed of, lurking in the shadows of the room. They would soon fade out; but for several months they would appear like tangible realities. And they were always the same figures. . .sometimes, without any preface of dreams, I used to see them at twilight-time,- following me about from room to room, or reaching long dim hands after me, from story to story, up through the interspaces of the deep stairways.
>
> I had complained of these haunters only to be told that I must never speak of them, and that they did not exist. I had

complained to everybody in the house; and everybody in the house had told me the very same thing. But there was the evidence of my eyes! The denial of that evidence I could explain only in two ways:- Either the shapes were afraid of big people, and showed themselves to me alone, because I was little and weak; or else the entire household had agreed, for some ghastly reason, to say what was not true. This latter theory seemed to me the more probable one, because I had several times perceived the shapes when I was not unattended;- and the consequent appearance of secrecy frightened me scarcely less than the visions did. Why was I forbidden to talk about what I saw, and even heard,- on creaking stairways,- behind waving curtains?

'Nothing will hurt you',- this was the merciless answer to all my pleadings not to be left alone at night. But the haunters did hurt me. Only – they would wait until after I had fallen asleep, and so into their power,- for they possessed occult means of preventing me from rising or moving or crying out.

Needless to comment upon the policy of locking me up alone with these fears in a black room. Unutterably was I tormented in that room – for years! Therefore I felt relatively happy when sent away at last to a children's boarding-school where the haunters very seldom ventured to show themselves.[11]

Perhaps his fear of the dark was regarded as a mental disorder because his great-aunt, Mrs Brenane, feared a recurrence of his mother's mental illness in Lafcadio and determined on drastic, if typically Victorian, remedies. If an episode in *Chita* when the little girl is taught to swim is autobigraphical, then a similarly muscular approach may have been adopted to conquering his terror of the sea, described as possessing malevolent power in the child's mind; if so, the treatment left him with outstanding swimming ability, as it did Chita.[114]

This was the longest of the autobiographical essays, parts I and II of which were a sort of catharsis, with part III an attempt to explain the mystery of the shock of the touch of the haunters, to interpret the intensity of the thrill. As part of his hypothesis, he put forward a theory of the unconscious '. . .that profundities of Self,- abysses never reached by any ray from the life of sun,- are strangely stirred in slumber, and that out of their blackness immediately responds a shuddering of memory, measureless even by millions of years'. The main part of his hypothesis was that the

239

sensation of 'dream-seizure' had its origins in the limited consciousness of man's evolutional ancestors. They would have dreamt of falling victim to predators. As the brain evolved, so did its capacity to intensify the 'dream-fear'. In parallel, heredity was accumulating and transmitting to future generations 'the summed experience of the life of sleep'. Over time, religious belief added a superstructure to this primaeval sub-structure. So the shock of touch was a 'point of dream contact with the total race-experience of shadowy seizure'.[12] His application of evolutionary philosophy to this ancient pain can be seen as a futile attempt to contain the hurt within the comforting framework he had chosen to impose on his life. Privately, he probed his memories in drafts of an autobiography; publicly he scattered hints, recollection and analysis throughout the books he wrote in Tokyo.

He had probed some of this before: much the same tale was told in a piece, 'Unwilling Spirits', which Hearn wrote for the Cincinnati *Enquirer* when he was 23 and much closer in time to the events described. Here his account of the terrors of Mrs Brenane's house was leavened with a sardonic humour missing from the later recollection. It also gives the impression that the whipping for howling in fear was a once-off event:

> The reporter had once been a Spiritualist when he was very young. That is – he used to believe in ghosts. He can yet remember a great, gloomy house where his youthful days were spent, whose walls were hung with dim-looking portraits of deceased ancestors, dressed in quaint fashions long since dead, as those who wore them, and where the rooms were filled with massive old-fashioned furniture ornamented with grotesque carving. He used to think that the house was peopled with goblins. Hideous faces seemed to peep at him from behind the window curtains, and nightmare shapes to crouch in all the dark corners, and ghostly footfalls to echo upon the stairs and shadowy hands to clutch at him when he went up to bed of dark evenings. He remembers how awfully afraid he used to be in the dark and how he would put his head under the bedclothes, and howl in an agony of fear. But he remembers how somebody who heard him yelling one night came into the room with a candle in one hand, and a strap in the other, and how well, how a very unpleasant combination of circumstances compelled him to change his opinions concerning ghosts and ghostness [sic] and from that

eventful night he ceased to hold heterodox sentiments upon the subject of ghostology.[13]

Similar recollections were triggered in the West Indies, on which Hearn now began to muse. He had stayed at a West Indian lodging-house and went to sleep at night with a servant in the room; after midnight he felt the uneasiness which for him preceded nightmare. It developed into terror when he found that he could not cry out. Then he heard a step on the stairs, '. . .a muffled heaviness; and the real nightmare began,- the horror of the ghastly magnetism that held voice and limb,- the hopeless will – struggle against dumbness and impotence'. The step approached his room. Soundlessly the locked door opened '. . .and the Thing entered, bending as it came,- a thing robed,- feminine,- reaching to the roof,- not to be looked at! A floor-plank creaked as It neared the bed;- and then – with a frantic effort- I woke, bathed in sweat; my heart beating as if it were going to burst'.

He heard long nightmare moanings that seemed to answer each other from two rooms below. Then his guide, sleeping nearby also began to moan, 'hoarsely, hideously'. Hearn cried out and they both sat up, the guide fumbling for his cutlass. The moaners continued moaning and there were sudden screams, with bare feet running and the sounds of lamps being lighted. There was a general clamour of frightened voices. Hearn rose, and groped for the matches; the noises ceased. His servants had been aware of it also. He later rationalised that changes of temperature warping the wood had produced the sounds. That left unexplained the similarity of the dreams of the guide and himself. What they had experienced was familiar in West Indian superstition; but the shape in Hearn's dream was also one which '. . .used to vex my sleep in childhood,- a phantom created for me by the impression of a certain horrible Celtic story which ought not to have been told to any child blessed, or cursed, with an imagination'.[14]

On another occasion, an incident in a Japanese village triggers recollections of infant lullabies and the sea, the sound of which was forever etched in his consciousness at Tramore. He remembered an Irish folk-saying that any dream may be remembered if the dreamer, once awake, does not scratch his head in a effort to recall it. Hearn had a dream at Hamamura in

Japan, of 'a broad pale paved place' where a woman was seated at the base of a great, grey pedestal. She began a soft wailing chant in a voice that seemed to come 'through distance of years' and memories revived of an Irish lullaby. Originally he had thought that the woman was Japanese; then her hair fell down and began '. . .crawling with swift blue ripplings to and fro. . .' Suddenly, he became aware that the ripplings were far away, and the woman was gone: 'There was only the sea, blue-billowing to the verge of heaven, with long slow flashings of soundless surf'. For Hearn, the sea was always connected with terror, a sign that loneliness pursued him on his seaside holidays as a child: on this occasion, he found himself thinking of the vague terror with which he had listened, as a child, to the voice of the sea. In later years, on different coasts in different parts of the world, the sound of surf had always revived that old emotion of childhood.[15]

CHAPTER THIRTEEN

DEVIL'S BOY

BEING A WEALTHY LADY of leisure, Mrs Brenane took frequent holidays, accompanied by the young Patrick Lafcadio. In Japan, Lafcadio could remember living at Clontarf, North Dublin, when he was a very small boy.[1] As Clontarf is on the coast, he may have been there for holidays. His grand-aunt would have been familiar with the area from the time she shared a house with her sister at nearby Fairview Avenue. But it was Tramore, a seaside resort in south-eastern Ireland, noted by contemporaries for its fine, long beach, spacious hotel and comfortable lodging-houses, which was her particular favourite. Communications with the city of Waterford were good and it was a favourite summer resort for the people of the nearby counties.[2] Mrs Brenane had probably formed the habit of going to Tramore when her late husband was alive and they lived in the adjoining county of Wexford. She may have had contact with the many Roman Catholic Hearns in the area, especially now that she had a young Catholic Hearn under her care. This was a connection which would later prove fatal to Lafcadio's financial prospects.

He also claimed to have been at Bangor in North Wales, where he later remembered a private museum of South Pacific and Chinese curiosities, owned no doubt by a friend of Mrs Brenane's, who diverted his young visitor by striking a Chinese gong for him.[3] There is, however, also a Bangor in Northern Ireland, a seaside holiday resort, and it is at least possible that the name presented Hearn with one of his easiest transmogrifications from Ireland to Britain. Correcting the fallacy believed by early biographers – broadcast by Hearn himself – that he had been taken to Wales when he was about seven and seldom saw Ireland after that, Nina Kennard says it was due to his 'sensitive, capricious genius' transplanting 'his imaginings to a more congenial atmosphere' because Ireland was connected with unhappy memories.[4] However, it is equally, or more, likely that he made the change because the rarefied environment of privilege he had known in Ireland, with its expectation of a life of genteel leisure, formed an intolerable contrast with the unhappy circumstances he experienced later in life.

Some of Hearn's happiest memories concerned the Elwoods, owners of a beautiful estate on Lough Corrib in County Mayo, in the West of Ireland. Catherine Frances, elder sister of Lafcadio's father, had married into the family. She survives in Kennard's description as '. . .a most delightful and clever person, beloved by her children and all her family connections, especially by her aunt, Mrs Brenane, who was often in the habit of stopping at the Elwoods' place with her adopted son'.[5] Captain Thomas Elwood was a magistrate in County Mayo[6] and his residence at Strand Hill was the finest of the 'gentlemen's seats' in the area.[7] The family fortune derived in large part from the town of Cong, which they virtually owned.[8] A contemporary source noted a contrast between the spectacularly beautiful scenery of the parish of Cong and the town, '. . .a dingy, dismal, disorderly, starved collection of squalid cabins, with few, very few points of relief'.[9]

Lafcadio Hearn later corresponded extensively with an American, Ellwood Hendrick, and wondered if there was a connection through the Elwoods: 'Perhaps we are related. The Irish Elwoods, my relations, were army-men for generations. They were rather too fond of revelry and earthy living: one, a subaltern, looked to me so beautiful in his uniform that I adored him as a boy. . .'[10] This may have been his cousin, Frank Elwood, 'Ensign in the Army' whom Hearn somewhat inconsistently told his half-sister he disliked because he used to pinch him as a child.[11] His childhood relationship was much closer with another Elwood boy, Robert, a jolly extrovert, with a fine singing voice. A kind and good friend, Robert was a rumbustious rebel at school who remained undeterred by the teacher's use of the whip: 'But he was not such a tough, savage boy as he seemed to be. He was a handsome youth with bushy, golden hair, with red cheeks like an apple, and with big blue eyes.'[12]

In Japan, Hearn's mind flashed back to a 'glowing glorious August day' when he was seven and looking with Robert for fairy rings – the island of Innisduras in Lough Corrib had the ruins of four[13] – when an old harper – Dan Fitzpatrick of Cong, a well-known character in the locality – arrives and begins to sing Thomas Moore's *Believe me, if all those endearing young charms*. Young Patrick Lafcadio is shocked 'with a new sensation of formidable vulgarity' because he regards it as intolerable that the unkempt old harper should sing the song he had heard sung 'by the lips of the dearest and fairest being in my little world', his aunt, Catherine Elwood, who was renowned for her performance of Moore's melodies. But his anger at Dan Fitzpatrick lasts only a moment:

> With the utterance of the syllables 'to-day', that deep, grim voice suddenly breaks into a quivering tenderness indescribable;- then, marvellously changing, it mellows into tones sonorous and rich as the notes of a great organ,- while a sensation unlike anything ever felt before takes me by the throat. . .What witchcraft has he learned? what secret has he found – this scowling man of the road?. . . Oh! is there anyone else in the whole world who can sing like that?. . .And the form of the singer flickers and dims;- and the house, and the lawn, and all the visible shapes of things tremble and swim before me. Yet instinctively I fear that man;- I almost hate him; and I feel myself flushing with anger and shame because of his power to move me thus. . .'
>
> 'He made you cry', Robert compassionately observes, to my further confusion,- as the harper strides away, richer by a gift of sixpence taken without thanks. . .'But I think he must be a gipsy. Gipsies are bad people – and they are wizards. . .Let us go back to the wood'.
>
> We climb again to the pines, and there squat down upon the sun-flecked grass, and look over town and sea. But we do not play as before: the spell of the wizard is strong upon us both. . .'Perhaps he is a goblin', I venture at last, 'or a fairy?' 'No', says Robert,- 'only a gipsy. But that is nearly as bad. They steal children, you know. . .'
>
> 'What shall we do if he comes up here?' I gasp, in sudden terror at the lonesomeness of our situation.
>
> 'Oh, he wouldn't dare', answers Robert – 'not by daylight, you know. . .'[14]

Lafcadio was clearly a great favourite of Mrs Brenane's at this stage: an old family servant remembers him following her around like a lap-dog.[15] One can well imagine an elderly woman being deeply affected by the child as described by Mrs Weatherall, one of his step-mother's daughters by her first marriage: '. . .a more uncanny, odd-looking little creature than Patrick Lafcadio it would be difficult to imagine'. The first time she saw him, when he was about five, he had '. . .long, lanky hair hung on either side of his face, and his prominent, myopic eyes gave him a sort of dreamy, absent look. In his arms he tightly clasped a doll, as if terrified that some one might take it from him'.[16] Another relation remembered him more charitably as being near-sighted, very fond of drawing and '. . .very tender and careful of me as a little child.'[17]

By his own account, he was quite a handful for the old lady to manage: 'I was. . .wilful beyond all reason, and an incarnation of the spirit of contrariness. . .I was the perfect imp'.[18]

Even if there was an apocryphal element in the anecdotes he related to his Japanese family, it is clear that Mrs Brenane must have been severely taxed by her charge. He claimed, for example, that when he was petted on the head by a lady caller on his great-aunt, whom he disliked as a flatterer, he slapped her face and ran away and hid. There were other tales of visitors spiked by needles he had hidden in chairs and having their dresses ruined by bottles of ink balanced on tops of doors. Cake was given to him as a bribe to eat meat; the cake would be devoured while the meat was hidden, to be detected in time only by putrefaction. His claim that he rushed out to kiss passing pretty girls sounds romantic in more senses than one. 'Then all the mothers of the girls were mad with me; and my poor grandmother [great-aunt] made it her work to go around saying *Gomen, gomen* [beg your pardon, beg your pardon]. How naughty I was!' He tortured the cook by cutting off her prize cabbages. When the knife was hidden, he made a new one himself and attacked the neighbour's cabbages. He noticed that people stopped calling him by his pet name and a distinct lack of enthusiasm when Mrs Brenane, as was her wont, took him on her calls on friends. People used to say that this 'Devil's boy' would be fit only for a prison when he grew older.[19]

Due partly to some of his own more extravagant statements

246

and partly to the prejudices of his early biographers, a myth developed that Hearn's childhood was tortured by excessive religiosity on Mrs Brenane's part. Yet his own autobiographical fragments present a radically different picture. One version states:

> For some reason which I do not know, I had long been left alone on the subject of religion. It was understood that I was to be brought up as a Catholic, but my relative supposed no doubt that there was plenty of time,- also, perhaps, that my mother had taught me enough for a child to know.'[20]

This does not make sense considering the very early age at which he had been abandoned by his mother. Also, anything she would have taught him would have been of the Greek Orthodox faith. Lafcadio himself probably realised this himself; a later, more polished version says simply: 'But of religion I knew almost nothing. The old lady who had adopted me intended that I should be brought up a Roman Catholic; but she had not yet attempted to give me any definite religious instruction.[21]

He had been taught a few prayers but repeated them parrot-like. He had been taken, without knowing why, to church and given pictures, the meaning of which he did not know. There was a Greek icon of the Virgin and Child in his room – he thought the Virgin represented his mother and the Child himself. He repeated the phrase about the Father, Son and Holy Ghost without being aware of who they were. He then speculated that he was allowed to remain ignorant of dogma so long because he was a nervous child – those around him were forbidden to tell him ghost or fairy stories – but this carries little conviction. The inescapable conclusion, which Hearn probably did not want to face because it conflicted with the legend he was propagating, is that Mrs Brenane simply was not a lady of strong religious convictions.

He claimed that, unlike other children, he did not ask questions about the ultimate meaning of things, being too preoccupied by his own 'dreams and shadows', about which he was forbidden to talk. The one element of religion which did interest him was the Holy Ghost: he was unable to reconcile the notion of the unspeakable horror of ghosts with that of holiness. He ended up with the vague notion that the Holy Ghost was a white ghost who would not make faces at him if he behaved himself! However, the term, ghost, was so charged for him that he refused to allow his suspicions to be allayed.

This state of infantile ignorance was altered by a privileged visitor, said to be a cousin, who stayed each winter at the Brenane household. A young girl, emanating sorrow, dressed always in black, young Patrick Lafcadio never saw her laugh or smile. She was kind to him but was so sombre that he was never comfortable with her. There is a difference in emphasis in his treatment of her in the two versions of his draft autobiography. In the later version, he 'feared to approach her' and she indulged in exhortations about being obedient, good and pleasing God, which he detested as he felt he was being found fault with and pitied. He once got fed-up and asked why he should please God more than anyone else; this produced a horrified reaction from his 'cousin' who then gave him a blood-curdling lecture on the horrors of hell. He hated her so intensely for having brought this new terror into his life that he hoped she would die.

The earlier draft also includes the lecture on hell, but the circumstances are otherwise different. It is more convincing as a child's behaviour and gives the impression of being an honest attempt to set down what he remembered, before it was polished up for possible publication. In this, his 'cousin' was in the habit of telling him what was right and wrong, without young Patrick Lafcadio being able to understand why. One day, when she spoke yet again about displeasing God, he asked her who God really was. A look of horror came over her face. He had been sitting on the floor at her feet:

> She stooped and lifted me upon her knees; and after looking all about the room, fixed her eyes on mine with such curiousness that I was frightened. Then she asked:-
> 'My child, is it really possible you do not know who God is?'
> I remembered answering
> - 'No'.
> 'God- who made the world, the beautiful sky, the trees, the birds – you do not know this?'
> - 'No'.
> 'Do you not know that God made you and your father and mother and everybody,- and I who am talking to you?'
> - 'No'.
> 'Do you not know about heaven and hell,- and that God made you in order that you should be happy in heaven if

you are good?'
- 'No'

The rest of the conversation has faded out of my mind – all except the words – '. . .and be sent to hell, to be buried alive in fire for ever and ever – always burning, burning, burning, always – never forgiven, never. Think of the pain of fire – to burn forever and ever'.

This picture of the universe gave me a shock that probably preserved it in memory. I can still see the face of the speaker as she said those words – the horror upon it,- the pain,- and then she burst into tears. I do not know why, we kissed each other; and I remember nothing more of that day.

But somehow or other from that time, I never liked my so-called cousin as before. She was kinder to me than any other being; but I felt an instinctive resentment towards her because of what she had told me. It seemed monstrous, ugly, wicked. She became for me a person who thinks horrible things. My world had been horrible enough before. She made it worse. I did not doubt what she said, and yet I was angry because she had said it. After she went away in [the] spring I hoped she would never come back again.

She did indeed come back, the first time under 'curious circumstances'. Lafcadio went upstairs one autumn evening and saw her pass from her own room to the one next door. He could not see her face. He called out her name but she did not answer. He followed her into the room. She went to the other side of the bed and looked towards him. She had no face, only a pale blur. In the same instant, the figure disappeared and he was alone in the room. So great was his panic to escape that he fell headlong down the stairs. When picked up and questioned, he was afraid to say what he had seen.

The next month she returned in the flesh, bringing presents of toys. She caressed him fondly, took him out for a walk and bought him 'a multitude of things'. They passed a pleasant day together. Next day he heard she was sick; she died in the room from which he fancied he had seen her ghoulish form pass. She left her money to a convent and her books to him. It was a bequest he learned in time to value: Plutarch, Pope, Locke, Byron, Scott, Edgeworth and many others. Curiously, there was nothing religious in the collection. Patrick Lafcadio was left to muse on the mystery of the girl whose name he could not even remember in later years (in the previously published version she is called 'Jane'):

> . . .her secret sorrow, her religious fear, her strange habit of
> living in convents [in the other draft she wants to become a
> nun but cannot for reasons he is told he is too young to
> understand] and withal aversion to becoming a nun, her
> love for me – all these I have never been able to learn. . .I
> should have loved her and often reproved myself that I
> could not. The reason I could not was that she had first
> taught me religious fear. It is not easy to love those who
> make the world uglier for us.

These fragments[22] are by far the fullest account of the
influence of religion in Hearn's upbringing. The picture which
emerges is the antithesis of the generally accepted view that he
was subjected to intolerable compulsion by a grand-aunt whose
Roman Catholicism had all the zeal of the convert. The Greek
icon on the wall of his room does not point to sectarian rigidity
on her part. Even his 'cousin', who has been portrayed as having
had a traumatic effect on him, appears to have been a kindly,
widely-read, and well-intentioned woman whose reaction to his
declaration of ignorance about God was, by Victorian standards,
relatively restrained.

Yet Hearn was also capable of writing, around the same time,
that '. . .the medieval creed. . .as it had been taught to me in the
weakness of my sickly childhood. . .seemed to me the very
religion of ugliness and hate'.[23] Any attempt to explain this
contradiction must be speculative, based on very incomplete
information. A possible explanation is that Hearn became quite
religious at some point in his youth and that this was a factor in
his later reaction.

It is possible, too, that the apparent contradiction might be
explained by differing experiences at home and at school.
Whatever about Mrs Brenane's regime, there is no doubting the
rigour of the religiosity to which he was subjected when he was
sent to an English Roman Catholic public school, Ushaw, in
1863, at the age of thirteen. The choice of a school in England
was logical now that Mrs Brenane herself had moved there. This
was precipitated by the growing involvement of Mrs Brenane
with a Henry Hearn Molyneux (1840-1906).[24] Ironically, an
institution called the 'Molyneux Blind Asylum' was situated at
the back of her house at Upper Leeson Street and Henry could

hardly have wreaked more havoc had he been an inmate of that institution![25]

The Roman Catholic branch of the Hearns were substantial landowners in County Waterford and had produced their own share of prominent personalities, such as the Rev. Thomas Hearn, involved in founding the Cathedral and Catholic College in Waterford, as well as introducing the first of the Conventual Orders into that part of Ireland. Although they appear to have grown up in England both Molyneux and Agnes Keogh, whom he married at St John's Wood Church, London, on 5 February 1863, were from this milieu. Henry's mother, Elizabeth, was a Waterford Hearn, two of whose brothers, Edward Hearn, D.D., of Warwick Street, London and Richard Hearn, D.D., buried at Tramore, were Catholic priests.[26] Agnes Keogh's mother was Catherine Lewis, an aunt of Sir George Lewis. Her father was George Keogh, a close friend of the Irish patriot and 'Liberator', Daniel O'Connell; he was, in fact, imprisoned with him.[27] Her background, therefore, contained powerful clerical and political alliances. At the time of Agnes' marriage to Molyneux, Mrs Brenane made a settlement under which she made over some thousands of acres of land, the bulk of her estate, to the newly-weds.[28]

According to Lafcadio, 'Aunty' had agonised all her widowhood about the question her husband had put to her on his deathbed; he had asked: 'Sally, you know what to do with the property?', but expired before matters could be clarified. Hearn believed 'the priests' had persuaded her that his wishes would have been to see that the property remained in the hands of Roman Catholic relations of her husband.[29] She may have been convinced that Lafcadio's and her interests would be best secured by leaving her estate in Catholic Hearn hands and she had already fallen out with the Protestant Hearns over money. The fact that the Rev. Edward Hearn featured in the marriage settlement document is as close to proof of clerical involvement as we are likely to get.[30] Mrs Brenane's age may also have been a factor: in the words of her niece, Lizzie Hardy, she '. . .was getting old and weak-minded and fell into the hands of cunning law people. . .'

Mrs Brenane had initially been suspicious of Molyneux and had resisted involvement with him for a considerable time before being won over. Henry was well-educated, speaking several languages fluently. He may have convinced her that he was worthy of better things than his position as a clerk at the Admiralty. The old lady became 'fascinated' and soon Molyneux was 'omnipotent' in the household. Then 'Auntie' told her young charge that she was going to help Molyneux for her husband's sake. She assigned herself an annuity of £400 –[31] Lafcadio thought it was £500, but was unsure of the exact amount – and went to live with the newly-weds at Redhill in Surrey where Molyneux, with his newly-acquired affluence, had taken a substantial property, Linkfield Lodge in Linkfield Lane.[32] He gave up his Admiralty post and become an importer of oriental goods, ironic in view of Lafcadio's later career!

That autumn, Patrick Lafcadio was sent off to boarding school, well away from a household where Molyneux was now in total command. He stayed at the school for four years. It is possible that Mrs Brenane maintained also a house in Dublin for the next few years: *Thoms' Directory* lists a person of the same name at 4 Sandycove Avenue, Kingstown (now Dún Laoghaire) from 1863, when she vacated the Leeson Street address, through to 1866 and at 2 Osborne Terrace in 1866/7. This would have been the kind of seaside location so much beloved of 'Auntie' but there is no other corroboration.

In his autobiographical writing, Hearn says that he was sickly as a child and was taught at home by a private tutor.[33] In addition to this and his English boarding school, most Hearn biographers have accepted that he also spent a period being educated in France. Marcel Robert, a French biographer, identified the 'Collège des Petits Precepteurs', a Catholic boarding school in Normandy, as the most likely place.[34] Lafcadio himself claimed that he went to France at sixteen and stayed there for several years. This is impossible: he was at school in England from the age of thirteen until he was seventeen. As there is no gap in his chronology after 1863 any spell in France, if it happened, must have been before that.

There is some evidence to support this, though it cannot be proved as the school records of the Normandy college have been destroyed.[35] In the *curriculum vitae* given to Waseda University near the end of his life, Hearn stated that he had been brought up – he did not say educated – in Ireland, England, Wales and 'also for some time in France'.[36] His American friend, Tunison, later recalled that he had spoken of having been at school in France. In 1890, Lizzie Hardy stated that her aunt, Mrs Brenane, was prejudiced against 'Patricio' by the Molyneux family when he was at school in France; we know, however, that he was at school in England at the time. Similarly, Lafcadio's brother believed that he had gone to a Catholic college in France, but absconded to New York in disgust.[37] In fact, his last four years before going to the United States were spent in England. Indeed, when Lafcadio corresponded with his brother in 1892, he said merely that he had spent some years in Catholic colleges without making any reference to having been in France. Hearn gave George Gould, an American friend-turned-enemy, the impression that his entire childhood was passed in an 'absurd French school',[38] yet this certainly was not true.

The excellence of Hearn's translations from French is an argument adduced by Marcel Robert in favour of his having been to school in France. He sets this against the claim by Gould, admittedly a tainted source, that Lafcadio could not speak French 'with ease or correctness'.[39] If Gould's claim were true, it would, of course, effectively disprove the contention that Hearn had been schooled in France. Gould made another claim, that Lafcadio had secured the help of a French scholar in translating Gautier's *Emaux et Camées*,[40] which may be a pointer in the right direction. The romantic aura which pervaded much early Hearn biography tended to obscure the more mundane reality that he was hard-working and highly-organised. All sources agree that his Japanese was poor yet his translations from that language are among the finest in English. This he achieved by getting other people – his wife and students mainly – to do the initial translation which he then re-wrought into masterful English. In other words, Hearn's genius as a translator lay in his command of English, not in his knowledge of other languages. His education in Ireland and England – he did, after all, have the benefit of a private tutor and an excellent school – could have given him sufficient knowledge of French for the purposes of translation – or polishing up – and correspondence without giving him that fluency in speaking the language which would have resulted from residence in the country. He did well in French at his English boarding school which, being the offshoot of a French institution, may well have had a high standard in the language.

His desire to claim a French period in his life may have had complex psychological and other causes, akin to his transplanting some of his childhood experiences out of Ireland. In his American period, he was in rebellion against the English language, hoping to model his own prose on French lines. His literary models were French. Also, a French education would help him establish himself as a Latin, a riposte to his rejection by his fair, Northern, step-mother and her golden children. It could have been part of the reconstitution of the romantic figure of Lafcadio Hearn out of the remains of the pitiful, rejected half-Irishman, Paddy Hearn. It would have done his assimilation with the Creoles of New Orleans, where the definitive change of name took place, no harm at all.

As in so many other things, Hearn's own testimony is contradictory. He lamented the 'wicked farcical waste of time' of his 'ornamental education' which had left him 'incapacitated to do anything'. It was a positive 'sorrow of sin' to have 'dissipated ten years in Latin and Greek, and stuff. . .when a knowledge of some one practical thing, and of a modern language or two, would have been of so much service'.[41] He did, of course, study French at his school. If this gripe had any basis in reality at all, he must have been lamenting a lack of real fluency in the language. Yet, if he had been educated in France, he would at least have had that fluency. His son wrote that when his father was small, '. . .he was put into a certain Roman Catholic school in France. Being of different nationality, crippled and with a queer name, 'Lafcadio Hearn', he was tormented by other boys'.[42] A possible explanation is that Hearn transposed his boarding school experience from England to France. As he sometimes pretended to be English, he could hardly admit to having been of different nationality in England. He was not crippled but he did suffer an eye disfigurement at his English school. He was not known as Lafcadio then but as Patrick, an acceptable enough name in France but identified with being Irish in England, at a time when mass Irish immigration was causing some resentment against the immigrants, even amongst the indigenous Roman Catholics.

There are other difficulties in the way of accepting that Hearn was educated in France. It never featured in his reminiscences the way the other scenes of his childhood did. It would have been unusual and somewhat brutal of Mrs Brenane to have sent the child so far away at such an early age to an institution where he would not initially even have been able to speak the language. It would have been much more in keeping with his background to have been sent first to a preparatory school in Ireland (this would correspond to the 'child-school' of his memoirs), followed by boarding school in England or Ireland.

A myth propagated by him in later years, that he had been educated for the priesthood, was repeated by a number of biographers. Thirty years later, he claimed that, following the death of his 'Episcopalian' father, he had fallen into the hands of relatives who had tried to 'make a priest' of him. They sent him to a Jesuit college where he was regarded as a fiend incarnate, and treated accordingly. He hated the Jesuits who, at this late stage in his life, were still the subject of nightmares. Later still, he would claim that the Jesuits were attempting to 'poke' him out of his Tokyo University post, on the grounds that they never ceased their pursuit of apostate former students. Yet he was, at the same time, affirming a lingering desire to be a monk, drawn by a romantic ideal of the monastery providing rest from worldly struggle.[43]

The key to this mass of contradictions lay in the interaction between his upbringing by Mrs Brenane and his experiences at St Cuthbert's College, Ushaw. Near Durham in the north of England, this boarding school where he was educated from thirteen to seventeen, was not run by the Jesuits. Fear of the dark doings of that order was a feature of the Irish Gothic literature in which Hearn was steeped, Charles Maturin's *Melmoth the Wanderer* being a classic example. The priests of Ushaw were actually of the ordinary diocesan variety. The school was what is called a 'junior seminary': its role was to feed the attached priests' seminary although it was not necessary for boys attending it to think that they had a 'vocation' for the priesthood. While Ushaw did indeed play a key role in the emergence of Roman Catholicism into the mainstream of English life in the mid-nineteenth century through its primary role of providing priests for the northern Roman Catholic dioceses of England, its secondary purpose was '. . .to provide an education for the sons of Catholic gentlemen through to University level. . .' and a small majority of the pupils in the secondary school probably had no intention of becoming priests.[44] This was actually recognised by Hearn in a letter to his brother: 'You were misinformed as to the rich aunt, or rather grandaunt, educating your brother for the priesthood. . .[though he] had the extreme misfortune to pass some years in Catholic colleges, where the educational system chiefly consists in keeping the pupils as ignorant as possible.'[45]

Molyneux probably played a crucial role in the choice of school: he had been educated at Old Hall, Ware, a similar type of Catholic educational institution to Ushaw. St Cuthbert's was, however, hundreds of miles further north, well away from Redhill, Surrey, and, as it was customary for many of the boys to remain on at the school over the holidays, Patrick Lafcadio may well have been removed almost entirely from the household by the choice of school. Indeed, his best friend at Ushaw recalled that 'he latterly never left Ushaw during vacations' which, as far as he was concerned, dealt with a query as to whether he spent his holidays with relatives in Ireland or Wales.[47]

A modern historian of Ushaw has described its exterior as 'rather grim and unprepossessing', looking a factory, and its internal life as equally cheerless:

> Little luxury could be expected in the refectory or elsewhere for that matter. Plain deal tables, scrubbed with sand, steel forks, pewter plates, tin or pewter mugs; such was its equipment. Breakfast could scarcely be called a meal. Grace was not publicly said, and few, if any sat down to eat their bread and drink their milk. . .Tea, as such, was unknown; following afternoon class, the juniors could claim a slice of bread but no more. . .
>
> Very occasionally the refectory witnessed festivity. On the Wednesday after the Epiphany the house celebrated the president's feast. In Easter Week the Divines [one of the academic levels of the seminary] enjoyed a banquet in honour of their patron St Thomas Aquinas. The Philosophers [another grade of the seminary] had their elaborate celebrations on November 25th, the feast of St Catherine of Alexandria, their patroness. . .[48]

Hearn arrived at the school on 9 September 1863. Coming from the luxury of Mrs Brenane's relaxed regime, Patrick Lafcadio must have found the spartan routine of Ushaw a distinct shock. His day, which started at 6am, was rigidly divided into periods of study, prayer and recreation. There was the traditional public school emphasis on games – battledore, trap, handball, rackets – as well as the school's own particular game, 'cat' –

which did not appeal to Patrick Lafcadio. However, although he had no interest in sport, he was so proud of his biceps that a friend christened him, 'The Man of Gigantic Muscle'.[49] It was probably at Ushaw that he developed his life-long passion for fitness and healthy bodies.

Hearn's adult writings are replete with references to the brutality of English public schools, an indication that adjustment to Ushaw was a difficult experience: 'In an English school the life is rough, very rough, and a sensitive boy is likely to suffer a great deal before he learns how to submit himself to this strange order of existence.'[50]

Years later, in Japan, Lafcadio would ask a student living at his home to desist from singing hymns loudly, as it recalled for him the unhappiness of his school days.[51] As an adult in America, he wrote to a friend that he had been crying at night, just as he used to when he returned to college after the holidays.[52] At the same time, accepting as he did that life was a struggle in which the strongest triumphed, Hearn later came to admire the practical types turned out by the English public school system: 'It is a training from childhood in self-mastery as a means to the mastery of man. . .While the prime necessity of life is intelligent fighting capacity, such training is as valuable as it is wonderful.'[53] However, he believed the system did not produce great minds and was unsuited to '. . .those gentle and sensitive natures destined to become the thinkers, the poets, the authors of their country',[54] which would obviously have included himself. Yet when, in middle age, he pondered the future of his son, he wondered if he should be sent when he was older '. . .to grim and ferocious Puritans that he may be taught the Way of the Lord?' He was then tending to the view that ecclesiastic education was founded upon the best experience of man under civilisation; things that in his youth were 'superstitious bosh', had by then become for him 'solid wisdom'.[55]

As a thirteen-year-old, the regime at Ushaw probably seemed neither bosh nor wisdom but immensely confusing. Patrick Lafcadio had not, as we have seen, been much troubled by religion in the home of his great-aunt; now, he came to an institution where the daily routine was largely defined by religious practice. Not only that but, under the influence of the Oxford Movement, a new wave of piety had gripped English

Catholicism in the decade before Lafcadio arrived at Ushaw. New styles of 'retreats' were introduced at the school, together with a 'Confraternity of the Living Rosary' and an 'Archconfraternity of the Immaculate Heart of Mary for the Conversion of Sinners'. There were public devotions in honour of 'Mary, Mother of God', and a custom was introduced of singing the *Maria Mater Gratiae* at the end of the day, along with prayers for the conversion of England to Roman Catholicism:

> Add to that Newsham's [President of Ushaw from 1837 to 1863] own musical compositions, novel in their freshness, the processions in honour of Our Lady, the statues created by Hoffmann and the paintings of Rohden, the establish-ment of the Confraternity of Help, and the interior life of the college became transformed.[56]

Under the relentless energy of Newsham and the conservative theological fervour of his vice-president, John Gillow, the atmosphere at Ushaw must have been rather heavy in the years prior to Patrick Lafcadio's arrival. However, it lightened up somewhat when Robert Tate succeeded Newsham as Patrick Lafcadio arrived in 1863. Then sixty, a huge man who enjoyed the companionship of his students, he was:

> . . .genial, sympathetic and kind to a marked degree, witty in the best heavy Victorian manner, and a sportsman who indulged his fancy for wild duck shooting, steeplechasing and hunting in the company of the gentry. . .[57]

Whether or not Tate directly influenced him, enjoyment of the companionship of his students was a trait Lafcadio would share when he became a teacher in Japan.

★ ★ ★

One particular area in which Ushaw did exert an enormous life-long influence on Hearn was through its architecture. Newsham had transformed the college physically: due to a massive building programme carried out in his presidency, the character of Ushaw changed from Georgian to Gothic. He commissioned the outstanding architect, Augustus Welby Pugin, to design a chapel, consecrated in 1848, on the lines of the chapels of New College and All Souls at Oxford.

Contemporaries were greatly impressed by what they regarded as a Gothic masterpiece. Indeed, Frederick Apthorp Paley, a

Cambridge scholar and Roman Catholic convert, described it as 'the most perfect thing conceivable', with grand services on a par with those anywhere else in England. Here Patrick Lafcadio may well have shivered at the suggestion of horror in the Gothic perfection of Pugin's masterpiece, every detail of which, down to the furnishings and decoration, the architect had supervised with loving care.

Funded by generous benefactors, Newsham continued to indulge his Gothic passion. The old chapel was gothicised as a 'public room' and it was here, with its tiers of oak benches arranged to face a rostrum under a painted hammer-beam roof that Patrick Lafcadio and his schoolmates would gather to hear the examination results read out in front of the whole school at the end of each term. Then a great Gothic library, intended to rival those of Oxford and Cambridge, was built, followed by Gothic farm buildings and a second chapel, also by Pugin. Pugin's son undertook the gothicising of the professors' dining-room and the building of a museum. Edward Pugin also designed the new Junior College, a Gothic, self-contained unit for the younger boys which opened only a few years before Patrick Lafcadio arrived at Ushaw. He was thus encased in Gothicism during his time at the school. We know that the influence of Gothic architecture, absorbed in his youth, had a life-long effect on Hearn. The process may have had its origins in the ecclesiastical architecture of Dublin but the massive ubiquity of Ushaw's Gothic must surely have made the deepest impression.[58]

Similarly, we know that his passion for reading was initially developed at Mrs Brenane's but it was probably during the Ushaw years that it developed along strongly Gothic lines. The recollections of another Ushaw boy of this era, Louis Casartelli, depict a youth of definite Gothic tendencies. Casartelli later became Bishop of Salford from 1903 to 1925 and, as a keen Orientalist, had long suspected that Lafcadio Hearn, the writer whose works on Japan were becoming increasingly popular in the late Victorian era, and the Paddy Hearn who had been his contemporary at Ushaw were one and the same.[59] Hearn's obituary in the *Manchester Guardian* of 3 November 1904 quoted the bishop's reminiscences:

> He was an eccentric, eerie sort of lad, fond of the quaint
> and the gruesome, with considerable humour and a

remarkable love of the beautiful. He was even then notable
for his power of writing really good English prose.

He was a small boy, weird-looking and untidy, a mischievous
eccentric who was continually in trouble with the authorities.
Warm and affectionate in his friendships, he impressed his
school-mates by his extraordinary abilities in English composition, which had a strong element of 'the gruesome and weird'.
Dr Casartelli remembered that he was called 'Jack' or 'Paddy' at
Ushaw – Lafcadio was quite unknown. Indeed, 'Paddy' Hearn
would never divulge what the initial 'L' in his name represented,
probably having a shrewd idea of the likely reaction of his
fellows. In the school records, his Christian name was
abbreviated to 'Pat'.

They were together for only a month: Casartelli arrived on 21
September 1867 and Hearn left on 28 October 1867.[60] Indeed, it
is possible that they never met, as Hearn may well not have
returned after the summer break in 1867 and it could have been
late October before the authorities decided that he was not
coming back; in this case, Casartelli's recollections would have
been based on secondhand reports from others. Other
reminiscences by clerical contemporaries of Hearn at Ushaw
included an anonymous Canon who wrote:

> Poor Paddy Hearn!. . .I can see his face now, beaming with
> delight at some of his many mischievous plots with which
> he disturbed the College and usually was flogged for. . .He
> was always considered 'wild as a March hare', full of
> escapades, and the terror of his masters, but always most
> kind and good-natured, and I fancy very popular with his
> school-mates. He never did harm to anybody, but he loved
> to torment the authorities. . .He laughed at his many
> whippings, wrote poetry about them and the birch, etc.,
> and was, in fact, quite irresponsible.'[61]

Achilles Daunt, who came from Kilcascan Castle in County
Cork, was his closest friend at Ushaw. He, too, remembered
Hearn's descriptive talent and love of the 'wild and ghostly' in
literature. His picturesque conversation featured heroic feats of
arms, '. . .combats with gigantic foes in deep forests, low red
moons throwing their dim light across desolate spaces, and
glinting on the armour of great champions, storms howling over
wastes and ghosts shrieking in the gale. . .' The boys regarded

him as slightly unbalanced although Daunt detected sadness beneath the gaiety of his external behaviour.[62]

Hearn may have had Achilles Daunt in mind when he wrote to an American friend 30 years later of the 'bracing tenderness [of] a college friendship'; there was nothing 'so holy' as two innocent lads '. . .living in ideals of duty and dreams of future miracles, and telling each other all their troubles, and bracing each other up'. The friendship began in a fight in which Hearn was worsted and the other became for him 'a sort of ideal'.[63] He remembered '. . .those old college friendships that. . .seem more of dreams than of reality'.[64] A story which features as fact in much previous Hearn biography was one he told to George Gould about having confessed to desiring the devil to come to him in the form of a woman so that he could yield to the temptation, much to the priest's consternation. It would be well to note, however, Lafcadio's preface to this tale: 'When I was a boy I had to go to confession, and my confessions were honest ones.' Directed as it was at the pious and humourless Gould, the story might well be ascribed to Hearn's impish sense of humour.[65]

If Hearn's account of Mrs Brenane's *laissez-faire* attitude to his religious instruction is accurate, then Ushaw was probably his first sustained contact with organised religion. The life there would have been based on a religious regime. An intelligent child whose omnivorous reading had been little supervised would naturally have reacted more critically than the most. Ushaw could well have been the beginning of Hearn's absorbing interest in – and ambiguity towards – religions of all kinds. This is of more than just biographical interest as his analysis of Japan was so fundamentally religious in nature.

It is possible that an intense early Catholic phase at the school was followed by a defiant identification with the older pagan gods. For example, a cousin who was taken to see him at Ushaw remembered being asked by him to bow to a statue of the Blessed Virgin. When, as a good Protestant, she refused, young Patrick Lafcadio became excited and begged her to tell him the reason of her refusal.[66] It would appear, therefore, that he was quite religious at some point in his Ushaw experience. There is also a hint of early religious fervour in a 'Fantastic', written when Hearn was in his 30s. He had gone to a hospital where a woman friend of his had died and he is overcome with emotion. When he is led out by a nun, he felt '. . .something unutterably strange within me. . .something in her eyes had rekindled into life something long burned out within my heart – the ashes of a Faith entombed as in a sepulchral urn. . .Yet it only lasted a moment; and the phantom flame sank back into its ashes; and I was in the sunlight again iron of purpose as Pharaoh after the death of his first-born. It was only a dead emotion, warmed to resurrection by the sunshine of a woman's eyes'.[67] The need to be 'iron of purpose' would indicate that the old emotion was strong indeed.

Perhaps a sense of rejection by the ardent Catholicism with which he was surrounded led him, in turn, to reject it. Most of the other boys would have been the products of intensely Catholic homes and Hearn, coming from a background of wealthy indifference, could never really have related to them, or they to him. This would have quickly been spotted by the college authorities. Indeed, Monsignor Joseph Corbishley, a contemporary of Patrick Lafcadio at Ushaw who was later a President of the school, told Nina Kennard that, had Hearn shown any interest in entering the priesthood, the college authorities would have discouraged him as unsuitable.[68] He remembered Paddy Hearn as a popular, imaginative prankster who 'worshipped muscle' but 'not altogether desirable' from the college's perspective, even though he was '. . .so very curious a boy, so wild in the tumult of his thoughts, that you felt he might do anything in different surroundings'.[69]

Corbishley's point about his being discouraged if he had showed any interest in the priesthood probably meant that the college authorities would have quietly discouraged the boys of particular interest to them, those with 'vocations' for the priesthood, from mingling with him. Achilles Daunt remembered him being naturally sceptical, shocking his contemporaries by questioning beliefs which they took for granted.[70] To the priests, who would have seen their first duty as protecting the 'vocations' of the future seminarians, this would have been subversive and therefore highly dangerous. Whether they rejected him, or vice-versa, or a combination of both we will never know for sure.

As might be expected in a junior seminary of that era, Latin and Greek were at the heart of an academic curriculum which aimed at providing an education in the liberal arts on a par with the best available. Patrick Lafcadio excelled in English – he was top of his class in nine out of the 12 terms which he completed – and achieved decent grades in Latin and French. His marks in arithmetic were consistently abysmal, as were his results in Greek, ironic in view of his life-long interest in ancient Greece and sturdy identification with what he saw as a cultural inheritance from the land of his birth.[71] The school was possessed of an excellent classical library and it is likely that he immersed himself in Greek culture, while finding the ancient language difficult. It is, perhaps, ironic that the source of his 'paganism' was to be found at the heart of Roman Catholicism.

In retrospect, he claimed to have been more interested in the pagan deities than the Christian God. Even so, his first notions of the pagan gods had derived from reading legends of the early Church and the lives of its saints and this, ironically, was probably the mechanism by which his allegiance was ultimately transferred from the Christian God. He imagined that those gods resembled the fairies and goblins of his nursery tales.[72] He recounted how, after graduating from such childhood classics as *The House that Jack Built*, *Babes in the Wood*, *Who Killed Cock Robin*, he went on to Bible stories and lives of the saints and martyrs. His imagination was gripped by illustrations of hideous torture and terrible deaths. Later on, Hearn read more mature works such as *Robinson Crusoe*, natural history and novels by the likes of Maria Edgeworth and Walter Scott. When the Waverley novels were still beyond him, he found 'intense delight and fear' in Scott's ballads. But the poetry which had the most profound impact was that of Milton: he read *Paradise Lost* as a child and was carried away by its tremendous imagination. The exquisite choice of strange words, such as 'cohort', 'phalanx' 'horrid' and 'ghostly', made a deep impression on him; the last two in particular remained life-long favourites. Other works, such as Lewis' *Tales of Wonder*, gave him nightmares. They seemed to correspond exactly to his own horrific dreams, the ones with goblins that had the power to do more than touch and terrify, '. . .the rearing of hideous arms and the sound of hideous laughter and the change of faces loved into forms of hate and fear'.[73] That he was provided with the work of 'Monk' Lewis, which shocked even Byron, as well as influencing Charles Maturin, is a graphic illustration of the licence he was allowed in his reading at Mrs Brenane's. If the Lewis' work was part of Cousin Jane's bequest, then she may have had an incongruously macabre streak in her otherwise religious character. Had they known of this reading, the Ushaw authorities would certainly not have approved of it.

More positively, his wide reading, particularly of beautifully illustrated art books, contributed to what he termed his 'Renaissance'. One incident he recounted involved some of the art books disappearing and being returned weeks later savagely expurgated. Previous biographers have blamed Mrs Brenane but not alone is this discordant with what we know of her character and with commonsense – placing the expensive books somewhere inaccessible would have been the obvious solution – it is not unambiguously suggested by Hearn himself. He does refer to the books being in 'our library' but says the episode happened when he '. . .was placed with all my small belongings under religious tutelage; and then, of course, my reading was subjected to severe examination'.[75] Being placed *with all his belongings* under religious tutelage clearly suggests he was at a boarding school. The fact that his reading was then subjected to severe examination indicates that previously it was not. Mrs Brenane's easy-going attitude to his religious instruction, the liberal nature of a bequest of books from a 'cousin', and the educated, literary background of the family all point to Lafcadio having been allowed very considerable latitude in his reading at the Brenane household.

The beauty of his Greek inheritance which he imbibed from books acted as an antidote to the terror he had absorbed from Christianity. For the rest of his life he would brood on the Christian faith, and immerse himself in the Bible, but he could never again accept a faith so closely allied with childish terror. He would be drawn to many religious interests and even enthusiasms but never surrender to conviction, even if religion did ultimately provide the key to Japan. By contrast, his discovery of ancient Greek culture through his reading provided him with a standard by which he could judge, and pronounce wanting, contemporary society. To him, the Greece of three or four thousand years ago was an age of 'finer humanity' when '. . .the meaning of beauty as power, of the worth of it to life and love' was properly appreciated. His Greek ancestry blended conveniently with his theory of inherited memory:

> Now I imagine something of the eternal Essence within this present shell of me must once have belonged to the world of beauty,- must have mingled freely with the best of its youth and grace and force,- must have known the world of long light limbs in the race of life, and the pride of the winner in contests, and the praise of maidens fair as daughters of the Dawn. . .All this I can believe because I could feel, while yet a boy, the divine humanity of the ancient Gods.[76]

Years of adult study later nurtured the childish growth but some of the seeds of his later philosophy, and best Japanese work, were sown in this way.

★　★　★

Before leaving Ushaw, young Patrick had the consolation of a profound inner transformation, that being wrought by his 'Renaissance', a result of his discovery of Greek beauty and the elder gods; his outlook on life now changed and the world began to glow about him:

> Glooms that had brooded over it slowly thinned away. The terror was not yet gone; but I now wanted only reason to disbelieve all that I had feared and hated. In the sunshine, in the green of the fields, in the blue of the sky, I found a gladness before unknown. Within myself new thoughts, new imaginings, dim longings for I knew not what were quickening and thrilling. I looked for beauty, and everywhere found it: in the passing faces – in attitudes and motions – in poise of plants and trees – in long white clouds – in faint-blue lines of far-off hills. At moments the simple pleasure of life would quicken to a joy so large, so deep, that it frightened me. But at other times there would come to me a new and strange sadness – a shadowy and inexplicable pain.[77]

This sounds like adolescence. His first love, at the age of fourteen, was the daughter of that very Henry Molyneux who, ironically, he believed later had ruined his life. He would meet her when on vacation from Ushaw and used to write her 'foolish' letters; he even wore a lock of her hair for a year or so. Like so much of his childhood, he embodied her in a Japanese book: 'There is one adolescent moment never to be forgotten,- the moment when a boy learns that this world contains nothing more wonderful than a certain pair of eyes.'[78]

Ushaw's most profound impact on Hearn was, however, physical rather than scholastic. When he was 16, a boy swinging on an apparatus known as the 'Giant's Stride' let go one of the ropes and its knotted end struck Hearn in the eye. An operation in Dublin failed to save the sight of the eye. According to his friend and biographer, Elizabeth Bisland, the resultant disfigurement was 'slight' but '. . .was a source of perpetual distress. He imagined that others, more particularly women, found him disgusting and repugnant because of the film that subsequently clouded the iris'.[79]

A second catastrophe struck soon after. Henry Molyneux failed in business. In November 1863, he had charged Mrs Brenane's property with the repayment of a loan from the Consolidated Bank of £7000 plus interest. A year later, an indenture charged the lands with the repayment of £11,000, plus interest. By 1866 Molyneux was bankrupt and Mrs Brenane's lands forfeit.[82] By extension, Molyneux's bankruptcy also ruined the Hearns, who were in debt to her, the security for the loan being the Westmeath property.

The ruin of young Patrick Lafcadio's world had been sealed when his father died as Mrs Brenane was taking legal action against him for the return of unpaid loans, though the youngster may have remained unaware of this. On 14 November 1865, Mrs Brenane had obtained a judgement in the Court of Queen's Bench in Ireland against Charles Bush Hearn for the sum of £639-14-4 plus £9-13-3 costs. Lands which he had at Kilbeg, part of the Correagh property, were transferred to her on foot of the judgement in February 1866.[80] Charles Hearn was at Ramptee, Madras, India, as Surgeon Major with the First Royal Regiment of Foot when these proceedings took place; he died, a ruined man, on his way home on 21 November 1866.

We can only speculate on the background to this loan – was it, for example, in any way connected with the expense of his son's education at Ushaw? Perhaps Mrs Brenane was simply a soft touch: Charles' brother, Robert Thomas, Captain and Paymaster of the 76th Regiment of Foot, had also borrowed (£1000) from 'Auntie', in January 1858. The collateral was again the Westmeath property.[81]

In October 1867, Mrs Brenane's impoverishment forced Patrick Lafcadio's withdrawal from Ushaw before he could complete his secondary education. The university education which successive generations of his family had enjoyed was then out of the question.[82] That Patrick Lafcadio was kept on at Ushaw for another year may mean that the best was done for him in difficult circumstances and his withdrawal postponed until the last possible moment. If Hearn was indeed withdrawn after only a month of the new school year in 1867, then Mrs Brenane had probably intended to allow him complete his studies but the financial catastrophe which engulfed her was such that she had no choice but to remove him.

Mrs Brenane and the Molyneuxs retired from the Surrey mansion to Tramore where they lived in numbers 42 and 46 on the Old Waterford Road until the old lady's death in 1871. She was interred in the Molyneux family plot at Tramore's Roman Catholic church.[83] Her mind had by this time deteriorated to a point where she was unaware of the humiliation of her final years.

Her niece had been anxious about the fate of 'the handsome boy Patrick' who she thought had been 'so unjustly used'.[84] Patrick Lafcadio also believed he had been unjustly used; he thought that his great-aunt had left a will which should have benefited him, but that those 'rascals', the Molyneuxs, had cheated him out of. Twenty years later he was still indignant, vowing to his brother that he would make it uncomfortable for the 'Molyneux people' some day if he could.[85] In this respect at least, Lafcadio seems to have been wrong: Mrs Brenane died intestate and it is unlikely that Molyneux inherited much with her passing. There was obviously a firm belief in the Hearn family that the Roman Catholic Church had played the leading role in Mrs Brenane's downfall and, indeed, that she had left her property to the Church. Lafcadio firmly quashed this misapprehension in correspondence with his brother: she had simply been 'the victim of a Jesuitical adventurer'[86] (although Henry Molyneux had not been educated by the Jesuits either!).

The shock and bitterness of these events lasted a lifetime. They were at their most raw when he arrived in London to stay with Catherine Delaney, a maid who had accompanied Mrs Brenane from Ireland to Redhill and who was now married to a London dock labourer. Little is known of this period of Patrick Lafcadio's life. The only source is his own highly-coloured accounts. He wrote to Achilles Daunt that he had been living in 'some evil quarter by the Thames' and had had to take refuge in the workhouse. His description of nightly horrors, '. . .of windows thrown violently open, or shattered to pieces, shrieks of agony, or cries of murder, followed by a heavy plunge in the river. . .'[87] is so lurid that one wonders if it was meant to be taken seriously.

Years later, he drew on these bitter memories when envisaging how a young Japanese samurai might have reacted to London:

> Perhaps he saw such cities as Doré saw London: sullen majesty of arched glooms, and granite deeps opening into granite deeps beyond range of vision, and mountains of masonry with seas of labour in turmoil at their base, and monumental spaces displaying the grimness of ordered power slow-gathering through centuries. Of beauty there was nothing to make appeal to him between those endless cliffs which walled out the universe and the sunset, the sky and the wind. . .
>
> He saw the harlotry and drunkenness that makes night hideous in the world's greatest city; and he marvelled at the conventional hypocrisy that pretends not to see, and at the religion that utters thanks for existing conditions, and at the ignorance that sends missionaries where they are not needed, and at the enormous charities that help disease and vice to propagate their kind.[88]

Hearn led some early biographers astray with his claims that he had gone to Mrs Brenane's chambermaid, having fled a monastery in Wales, still wearing his monk's garb. He was then supposed to have ruined a young relative of Catherine's and fled to St Giles where he lived seven to a bed and became a thief. He was caught by a missionary who got him a job as a gardener's assistant. Seven months later he had saved enough to go to America. The purpose of this particular letter, written to win the sympathy of an American lady when Hearn was in his 30s, is clearly revealed by the identification with Christ: 'And so, dear friend, the lost months of my life, like the hidden years in Christ's have been stripped of secrecy and bared to view'.[89]

The more prosaic reality may have been that arrangements were made with Catherine Delaney for Hearn to finish his secondary education at a day school in London. Nevertheless, the horror of his period there 'among the common folk' was real enough. Within a year of his disfigurement, he was cast down from being among the heirs at least to a considerable fortune and a pupil at one of England's most prestigious schools to life in London's dockland. He was also encountering industrialisation and massive urbanisation for the first time, in the worst possible circumstances. The shock of this sudden immersion in the Dickensian side of the nineteenth century stayed with Patrick Lafcadio for the rest of his days. Even towards the end of his life, he regarded London as 'the most awful city upon earth'. In middle age, Kipling's *The Light that Failed* recalled the horror of being in London without money: 'Nobody can imagine – no, not with a forty horse-power imagination – what the horror is, if he hasn't been there. And I have. . .'[90]

It is significant that the negative reaction to London on the part of the young samurai is followed by his rejection of Western society, paralleling Hearn's own development. He too:

> . . .hated its utilitarian stability; hated its conventions, its greed, its blind cruelty, its huge hypocrisy, the foulness of its want and the insolence of its wealth. Morally it was monstrous; conventionally it was brutal. . .Western superiority was not ethical. It lay in forces of the intellect developed through suffering incalculable, and used for the destruction of the weak by the strong.[91]

CHAPTER FOURTEEN

IN GHOSTLY JAPAN

UP TO THE MID-1890S, there had been the parallel development of Lafcadio Hearn's exploration of Japan and progressive rejection of the West. Then, perhaps partly as a reaction to having to live in the hated metropolis of Tokyo, he turned inward and, in conjunction with the reveries of his childhood in Ireland, that secret, tormented, magical world that he kept alive in his heart until the end, concentrated on another internal, related world – that of the supernatural.

As he explored childhood, he became, it seems, childish: Setsu said she detected a growing childishness in her husband's behaviour in his last years. When he was down, his pessimism was total; when he sang children's songs, his absorption in them was such that he seemed never to have known worry or care.[1] Hearn himself was conscious of his childishness; indeed, he told his students that to be a good father it was necessary to be able to understand the pleasures and play of a child. Many great men of literature retained 'something of the child-character'; it was '. . .the very greatest of minds that seem to be able to find supreme pleasure in little things'.[2] Yet there was also a stern side to his nature which showed itself even in his dealings with his children. To Kazuo, he was loving but severe; his son compared it to living in the shadow of a volcano.[3]

As his friendships faded, the great flow of correspondence which had been a feature of Lafcadio's adult life dried to a trickle in his last years. He continued to work '. . .steadily rather than hard. . .systematically doing just exactly so much every day, neither more nor less. . .'[4] Thus he maintained the extraordinary output of published work – roughly a volume a year. On a personal level, however, he felt his health increasingly giving way and was convinced he had not long to live. He felt 'fat, wrinkled and old' and wrote: 'I see before me the black night that knows no dawn. . .I have had warnings and each night when I retire, I feel it will be an achievement to see another sunrise.'[5] Discounting any element of self-pity, his health clearly was in decline. Ironically enough, Hearn had long been a believer in the artistic value of ill-health, that the '. . .possessor of pure horse-health never seems to have an idea of the 'half-lights'; that it was 'impossible to see the psychical under-currents of human existence without that self-separation from the purely physical part to being, which severe sickness gives – like a revelation'. People in good health imagined they could comprehend things which actually could not be understood without unpleasant experience.[6]

It may not be coincidental, therefore, that, while his health declined, Lafcadio felt he had finally achieved his desired prose style. He was, he believed, learning to master his thought completely before he put it into words, and he was now able to compose without Roget's *Thesaurus* or Skeat's *Etymology*. The Welsh poet, Edward Thomas, agreed. He described the style of the later books as '. . .a plain, lucid, unnoticeable style, a little stiff and lacking in movement and natural continuity, but for the most part leaving the reader free to listen to speeches and watch events'.[7] In Thomas's view, the contents of the later books '. . .certainly make up one of the greatest treasures ever found by a translator in an utterly foreign land. Their beauty, their splendour, tenderness or horror is not to be denied, whether readers care much or nothing for Japan'.[8] For him, Hearn's Japanese work as a whole presented '. . .a marvellously detailed picture which is yet always and everywhere alive. The personality of the writer is in his best work shown by his abnegation of personality, though this was probably due to no conscious effort. . .' He either '. . .imposed on us a personal impression of Japanese things not the less deep for its delicacy, or he has made himself a mirror in a manner unapproached by other observers of foreign countries'. He had '. . .become the things observed: he was a Japanese writer "in perfect accord with the sweet glamour of Old Japan" '.[9]

Malcolm Cowley made a similar point about this Japanese work, contrasting the effect of Hearn's translations with those of lesser writers:

> The result in their case was folklore for the laboratory, preserved in formaldehyde, whereas Hearn's version was literature. Long before coming to Japan he had shown an instinct for finding in legends the permanent archetypes of human experience – that is the secret of their power to move us – and he later proved that he knew exactly which tales to choose and which details to emphasise, in exactly the right English.[10]

Early in his stay in Tokyo, Hearn had confided to Hendrick that he wanted '. . .to do something remarkable, unique, extraordinary, audacious; and I haven't the qualifications. I want sensations – dreams – glimpses. . .'[11] He had attempted sensations and dreams but these were now put aside in favour of the staple themes of the later Tokyo period, epitomised by *In Ghostly Japan*. Completed by the end of 1898, it consisted of 14 essays whose themes tended to the arcane, with Hearn's philosophical obsessions providing a thin strand of continuity. A strong Buddhist influence – a sign that he was withdrawing from the active interpretation of Japan represented by Shinto and returning to the academic Orientalism of his American days – was evident throughout, particularly in pieces such as 'Silkworms', 'A Passional Karma', 'Footprints of the Buddha' and 'Japanese Buddhist Proverbs'.

This confirmed a suspicion in some quarters that Hearn had become a Buddhist. True, he had on occasion provided some basis for the speculation himself. He had, for example, described himself to Hendrick in November 1895 as an 'old Buddhist'.[12] But this was mere playfulness. When Guy M. Carleton sent him a copy of the *Yale University Magazine* which contained a review of his work in December 1898, he was positive in his reaction but disagreed with the statement that he had 'turned Buddhist' – the magazine's phrase – and Carleton's assertion that he had 'adopted' Buddhism. He had, he admitted, sympathy with some Buddhist doctrines and believed that the deeper teachings of Buddhism could be aligned with the 'Synthetic Philosophy' but his 'adoption' of Buddhism could go no deeper than that.[13] His poet friend, Nobushige Amenomori, took the view that Hearn had no religion; as a committed evolutionist, he simply used both Shinto and Buddhism to propagate that doctrine.[14]

Lafcadio did, however, continue to be interested in the religion of his childhood: he owned a number of Bibles and many books on Christianity. He started Kazuo reading the Old Testament, telling him that while it was unnecessary to become a Christian, everyone should be familiar with the Bible.[15] At Yaidzu, he took the Bible and made Kazuo read a few verses every morning. Kazuo had a 'strange feeling' about it. He was afraid his father would be angry but summoned up the courage to broach the subject. He asked a question about the word, 'holy'. Hearn laughed heartily and recalled having been scolded in his youth for putting such a question to Mrs Brenane.[16]

Professor Foxwell, who felt that Lafcadio was more mistaken in his attitude to the missionaries than towards anything else in Japan[17] nevertheless claimed that companionship with him induced a belief in immortality as a quiet certainty.[18]

Hearn could indeed – without disingenuousness – sympathise with individual missionaries: he wrote of the impending return to the U.S. of a Dr Davis: 'He is one of the few really estimable and impartial men among the hosts of missionaries; and I shall be rather sorry of [sic] his departure.' Yet there was not doubting the strength of his loathing of the missionary cause. He told Foxwell that missionaries should be shot on sight[19] and wrote of his love of ancient Japanese shrines and temple '. . .wherever the damned Protestant missionaries have not destroyed all ancient beauty'.[20] 'The Case of O-Dai', in the 'Studies Here and There' section of the *A Japanese Miscellany* was the tale of a Japanese lady ruined and reduced to prostitution by Christian missionaries – a kind of Christian morality tale in reverse. It was a graphic illustration of his belief in the mischief created when the religions of East and West interacted.[21]

The religion of the East and the science of the West was, however, another matter: a fragment of Buddhist lore, about a 'mountain of skulls', recounted to him by Fenollosa, was used by Hearn as a vivid illustration of the convergence of science and Buddhism – as well as the horror – favoured by Hearn. The Bodhisattva is climbing a mountain with a pilgrim who is seized by fear and trembling. He realises that the mountain is composed of skulls, '. . .with a shimmer of shed teeth strewn through the drift of it, like the shimmer of scrags of shell in the wrack of the tide'.[22] The contrast between the subtle, almost casual horror of the description here and the laboured piling on of effect in his Cincinnati work (where hideous skulls with gleaming teeth also featured) was a measure of his mastery of his craft in the meantime.

This was evident too in another chapter of *In Ghostly Japan*, 'A Passional Karma', the story of a man who caused the death of a girl who had pined away for love of him. He meets what he thinks is she. His servant witnessed the meeting and is determined to get a glimpse of her face. When he was able to do so,

> . . .an icy trembling seized him; and the hair of his head stood up.
>
> For the face was the face of a woman long dead,- and the fingers were fingers of naked bone,- and of the body below the waist there was not anything: it melted off into thinnest trailing shadow. Where the eyes of the lover deluded saw youth and grace and beauty, there appeared to the eyes of the watcher horror only, and the emptiness of death.[23]

The man was finally strangled by the ghoul, having been betrayed by his servant. Hearn ended the tale – one of his best ghost stories – by a joke at his own expense. He asks his Japanese friend who has collaborated with him on the translation of the theatrical original to take him to the graveyard where the ghosts of the story were supposedly buried. A woman cooking in a shed just inside the gate cheerfully directs them to particular graves. They bring up the characters on the inscriptions by rubbing clay on white paper laid over them. The graves turn out to be those of an innkeeper and a nun. Hearn's friend brushes aside his protests over the woman's making fun of them: he had come looking for sensation and she had done her best to oblige.[25] This story bore out a point made by Setsu, that Lafcadio's ghost stories had a humorous touch: he hated a story told only for the sake of pure horror. It also illustrated her observation that he took everything so seriously that even a ghost story seemed to him to be true. He always thought he was in the story himself: 'When he began to exclaim, "*Nanbo omoshiroi!*" (how interesting), I always observed that his face turned deadly pale, and his one eye set almost motionless.'[26]

In Ghostly Japan ended with 'At Yaidzu', a comparatively light essay in which Lafcadio shared the secret of his summer retreat with his readers. Even here he managed to preserve the ghostly character of the book by making its central theme the *Bon* or Festival of the Dead. The essay brought together themes which characterised the book as a whole: Buddhism, horror, humour, his childhood, and the sea. Overall, the book illustrated Lafcadio's statement to Amenomori that he could reach the cultivated classes abroad on the subjects of philosophy and Buddhism by flanking a paper on abstract questions with sketches or stories and the medicine was taken 'for the sake of the sugar'.[27] He did not tell Amenomori that he was using the same methods to camouflage his exploration of the darkest reaches of his own psyche.

On New Year's morning 1899, before he had travelled down to McDonald in Yokohama, a young poet whom he taught at the university had left him two presents. One was a roll of cloth to make an extraordinary and, for Lafcadio, entirely appropriate kimono. The woof of the cloth was speckled with the characters of poems. Wearing it, he would be 'literally clothed with poetry'.[28] The second gift was a manuscript collection of unfamiliar Japanese songs and ballads, with refrains from which, he told McDonald, he hoped to make a remarkable paper.[29] Hearn was struck by the 'unfamiliar emotional quality' and the unusual construction which enabled considerable effects to be achieved by reiteration and pause.

This inspired the 'Old Japanese Songs' chapter of *Shadowings*, then Hearn's current work in progress and one in which he demonstrated that his disillusionment with the East was far from complete and his command of language at its height: 'The wisdom of the East hears all things. And he that obtains it will hear the speech of insects,- as Sigurd, tasting the Dragon's Heart, heard suddenly the talking of birds.'[30] His mastery of English – and the macabre – was further demonstrated in the six 'Stories from Strange Books', the first section of the volume. The 'Fantasies' section consisted of seven fragments from his abandoned autobiographical work on sensations now worked into individual essays, some of considerable power. Writing to Elizabeth Bisland in January 1900, when the work was finished, Lafcadio described *Shadowings* as consisting of 'reveries, and sundry queer stories'.[31]

A Japanese Miscellany, the volume on which he had laboured for most of the year 1900, was dedicated to 'Mrs Elizabeth Bisland Wetmore'. He was characteristically humble in a letter to her in September 1903 about unspecified mistakes in the volume but adding that it was not a bad book in its way and hoping that she might not have reason to regret her good opinion of its author.[32] The *Miscellany* was almost a continuation of his previous work, *Shadowings*. Again there were three sections, the first two, stories and folklore/Japanese studies, being similar in both books. The third section in the *Miscellany* was called simply 'Studies Here and There'. Both volumes formed part of an even larger canvass in the sense that all Hearn's books of the Tokyo period – with the exception of *Japan: an Attempt at Interpretation* – were like individual elements of one huge work. The same themes weaved in and out – horror, folklore, previous lives, studies – of insects, Buddhist names, children's songs – autobiography, and the like.

Some of these themes – insects are possibly the best example – appear at first to the Western mind to be arcane in the extreme. Yet the reader who assimilates them will find that he has gained an considerable understanding of a unique culture. A good example of this is the chapter on dragon-flies in the *Miscellany*. After six pages of translation of poems about dragon-flies, the author says they are aesthetically slight but help in understanding the soul of 'the elder Japan'. The people who could delight in observing and writing verse about insects:

> . . .must have comprehended, better than we, the simple pleasure of existence. They could not, indeed, describe the magic of nature as our great Western poets have done; but they could feel the beauty of the world without its sorrow, and rejoice in that beauty, much after the manner of inquisitive and happy children.[33]

An even more extreme example of Hearn's method is 'Songs of Japanese Children' in the same book. At the end of a long paper – 86 pages – of seemingly interminable translations of children's songs, he reveals his true purpose: to give the reader an experience similar to passing for the first time through Japanese streets: '. . .dim surprise of another and inscrutable humanity,- another race-soul, strangely alluring, yet forever alien to your own. . .' – and he succeeds.[34]

In his book, *Lafcadio Hearn in Japan*, Yone Noguchi drew parallels between Hearn and another 'half-nocturnal' figure, Akinari Uyeda, a Japanese writer who had died early in the nineteenth century and had influenced later Japanese writers. Both were solitary figures who had endured early unhappiness and shunned society. Noguchi believed that Hearn's 'allegiance' to Uyeda was demonstrated by his translation of two of his stories from *Ugetsu Monogatari* in *A Japanese Miscellany*. These were 'Of a Promise Kept' and 'The Story of Kogi the Priest'.[35] The first had the additional attraction of having been set in Izumo. However, while 'The Story of Kogi the Priest' is one of the better 'Strange Stories', 'Of a Promise Broken' – not to be confused with 'Of a Promise Kept' – is perhaps the best for sheer spine-tingling effect. Also set in Izumo, it is the story of a young samurai who promises his dying wife that he will not remarry. In time, he is persuaded to break his promise and the dead wife comes back as a ghoul, warning the second wife to leave. Not alone does she not do so, she breaks a strict enjoinment not to tell her husband of the ghoul's visit. The husband arranges for his wife to be well guarded at night when his duties detain him at the castle but she nevertheless suffered a terrible fate:

> The head was nowhere to be seen;- and the hideous wound showed that it had not been cut off, but torn off. A trail of blood led from the chamber to an angle of the outer gallery, where the storm-doors appeared to have been riven apart. The three men followed that trail into the garden,- over reaches of grass,- over spaces of sand,- along the bank of an iris-bordered pond,- under heavy shadowings of cedar and bamboo. And suddenly, at a turn, they found themselves face to face with a nightmare-thing that chippered like a bat: the figure of the long-buried woman, erect before her tomb,- in one hand clutching a bell, in the other the dripping head. . .For a moment the three stood numbed. Then one of the men-at-arms, uttering a Buddhist invocation, drew, and struck at the shape. Instantly it crumbled down upon the soil,- an empty scattering of grave-rags, bones, and hair;- and the bell rolled clanking out of the ruin. But the fleshless right hand, though parted from the wrist, still writhed;- and its fingers still gripped at the bleeding head,- and tore, and mangled,- as the claws of the yellow crab cling fast to a fallen fruit. . .[36]

This horror mingled in Hearn's mind with a premonition of his own death, now so strong the even on the annual summer holiday to Yaidzu he insisted on continuing Kazuo's English lessons. He would say, 'learn quickly, please; time won't wait; papa's life will not wait'.[37] Kazuo also felt the strength of his father's Darwinian convictions during these holiday periods. Life was a struggle, with survival of the fittest, and this unathletic lad had to be tempered for the ordeal by attempting terrifying swimming and endurance feats.[38] In Yaidzu he gave Kazuo Charles Kingsley's *The Three Fishes* as an English lesson. He drew three pictures, one for each stanza, based on Yaidzu fishing boats. Even here, Hearn could not resist a touch of horror: the three corpses in the final picture had the faces of Kazuo, Iwao and himself.[39]

The maturity of style praised by Thomas reached it zenith in the horror stories of the later volumes. Setsu was the source of many of these. She used to help him search bookshops for books of ghost stories. She then had to assimilate the stories – she was not allowed to read them to him – giving him first the plot and then the details he asked for. Hearn, in turn, passed the stories on to his children. Kazuo remembered him telling them goblin stories in his poor Japanese, which did not stop him, however, from being so effective in the pale evening light that his son would often have to beg him to stop.[40] The stories were written with the same rapt intensity that gripped Hearn when listening to them. Amenomori once had the opportunity of watching Lafcadio at work late at night, while he was unaware that he was being observed. It was a different man to the one he knew: 'His large face was mysteriously white; his large eye gleamed. He appeared like one in touch with some unearthly presence.'[41]

Setsu's narration particularly touched Hearn's vivid imagination and he would fall under the spell of the story. For example, when she was reading the legend of 'Yurei-Daki', published in *Kotto* (1902), his face paled and his eyes became fixed to a point where Setsu felt afraid. 'Yurei-Daki' was the story of a foolish spinner who dared the wrath of a Shinto god to steal the money-box containing the contributions of his believers. O-Katsu was a bold woman and, with her child carried on her back Japanese-style, she did indeed go late at night to the shrine and snatch the box. When she returned to her companions, they went to unwrap her little boy and found her back wet: 'Ara, it is blood!' a helper screamed; the head of the child had been torn off by the vengeful deity. Lafcadio made Setsu repeat this several times: when he wrote the story, it became the most effective moment in an otherwise slight tale.[42] Lafcadio did not reveal the source in *Kotto* but he had no compunction in working household facts unvarnished into the work. His cat, Tama, ('Jewel') featured in 'Pathological', giving him an excuse to speculate on former lives of the species,[43] and his pet cricket in 'Kusa-Hibari' ['Grass-Lark']. After the tenderness of his description of this tiny creature comes a stoke of horror: Hana, the housemaid, forgot to feed him but he nevertheless bravely sang to the very end, '. . .an atrocious end, for he had eaten his own legs!'[44]

Kotto was dominated by the perennial twin themes of insects and horror. Nothing exemplifies 'the wonder which is akin to fear' that he felt towards insects than this passage from 'Gaki':

> The lips that are hands, and the horns that are eyes, and the tongues that are drills; the multiple devilish mouths that move in four ways at once; the living scissors and saws and boring-pumps and brace-bits; the exquisite elfish weapons which no human skill can copy, even in the finest watch-spring – what superstition of old ever dreamed of sights like these? Indeed, all that nightmare ever conceived of faceless horror, and that ecstasy ever imagined of phantasmal pulchritude, can appear but vapid and void by comparison with the stupefying facts of entomology. But there is something spectral, something alarming, in the very beauty of insects. . .[45]

This was the external view of insects: Lafcadio's imagination was too intense for that to satisfy him. He was inspired to imagine what it would be like to actually *be* an insect, a prospect which was not entirely theatrical for a believer in reincarnation.[46]

This was, of course, a technique that Lafcadio had worked on since his New Orleans days. There were other echoes from the past. A page-long paean of praise for Japanese women in 'A Woman's Diary'[47] showed that his ideas on this subject had not changed since his arrival in Japan and the idealisation of mother-love in 'Revery'[48] was yet another link with his infancy. Possibly the most satisfying aspect of the book was Hearn's ability to craft an arresting sentence or phrase in a seemingly casual manner, using the simplest of language. A good example is the opening of

'In a Cup of Tea':

> Have you ever attempted to mount some old tower
> stairway, spiring up through darkness, and in the heart of
> that darkness found yourself at the cobwebbed edge of
> nothing?[49]

Even in his very last days, when Hearn was feeling bitterly
disillusioned with literary work, he still managed to continue
producing an impressive output. While he prepared *Kwaidan* for
publication and polished the text of *Japan: an Attempt at
Interpretation*, he worked on yet another volume of Japanese
studies, *The Romance of the Milky Way*, essentially a continuation
of that vast amorphus work which was interrupted only by the
Attempt in these years. Three volumes of goblin poetry formed
the basis of one essay while Setsu was the source of the title story.
He was, she said, so saddened by the tale that he was moved to
tears but, whatever his emotional state, he was still capable of
writing superlative prose, as good or better than he had ever
written. 'Goblin Poetry' was a natural subject for Hearn,
combining as it did two of his enthusiasms, poetry and the
macabre. He dealt with old beliefs such as the will-o'-the-wisp
called *kitsune-bi* (fox-fire): for the purpose of deceiving men, the
goblin assumed the shape of a pretty woman. There was a
description of *Rokuro Kubi* (rotating neck), a person who could
either lengthen her neck during sleep – it would then wander off
in different directions – or a person who could detach her head
from her body – in old pictures it was usually depicted as a
woman.[50]

Kwaidan (1904), subtitled 'Stories and Studies of Strange
Things', was more devoted to the weird and bizarre than any of
Hearn's Japanese books. The horrific diet was only varied by
three 'insect-studies' and 'Hi-mawari', the flashback to his youth.
There was, however, the usual leavening of Hearnian humour,
some of it of the gallows variety. Four of the stories were made
into a successful Japanese film in the 1960s.[51] There were echoes
of the young journalist who had reported from the scaffold in the
grim humour implicit in the title of 'Diplomacy'. A samurai
averts the possibility of posthumous revenge by deflecting the
very last thoughts of a man whom he executes (in ancient Japan it
was believed that the ghost of a person killed while feeling strong
resentment could take vengeance on his killer).[52] 'Of a Mirror

and a Bell' ended with a touch of Lafcadio's puckish humour.[53]

Humour of a different kind was provided by Mrs Hearn's account of his writing of 'The Story of Mimi-Nashi-Hoïchi'.[54] This was the tale of a blind man, Hoïchi, famed for his recitations of the history of the Heiké and Genji clans and who was summoned by ghouls – ghosts of the dead warriors – to recite for them. In *Kwaidan* it is a spine-tingling tale, told with masterly skill. Hearn's absorption in the writing of it was such that when Setsu, at twilight, to test his reaction, called out 'Hoïchi, Hoïchi', he replied from within his study 'Yes, I am a blind man. Who are you?'.[55] A link with the author's lonely hours in Mrs Brenane's house in Dublin is evident in the similarity of the faceless ghost who haunted the Akasaka area of Tokyo in 'Mujina' and the apparition of 'Cousin Jane' which had terrified him then.[56]

The 'Insect-Studies' section of *Kwaidan* gave Lafcadio a chance to develop two themes which went much deeper than the ostensible subject-matter. Firstly, in 'Ants', the inevitable figure of Herbert Spencer raised his head. Hearn made his most extreme statement of allegiance: 'I most worshipfully reverence Herbert Spencer as the greatest philosopher that has yet appeared in this world. . .'[57] Observation of the social organisation of ants moved him to agree with Spencer that the value of an individual could only be in relation to society. As a result, '. . .whether the sacrifice of the individual for the sake of that society be good or evil must depend upon what the society might gain or lose through a further individuation of its members'.[58] He went on to forecast the possibility of humanity, like the ants, deciding to arrest the development of sex in its young; the majority of higher beings of the 'Coming Race' might be asexual.[59]

Those who have experienced in the twentieth century the horrors of ideologies which premised themselves on such illiberalism will recoil from these ideas but it must be remembered that Hearn did not have the horrors of Belsen or the Gulags to show him the road down which they led. The naïveté which underlay this all-embracing philosophy can be seen in Hearn's postulation of the possibility that moral notions may belong to a primitive stage of social evolution and a time might come when evil would have been atrophied out of existence and good transmuted into instinct: '. . .a state of altruism in which ethical concepts and codes will have become as useless as they would be, even now, in the societies of the higher ants.'[60] Indeed the theme of the essay, 'the awful propriety, the terrible morality, of the ant' was intended to demonstrate, not that the future must belong to Nietzsche's strong, selfish, 'blond beast', but the reverse.[61] 'Ants' revealed the possibility that contradictions lurked in Hearn's philosophy. He wrote in *Kwaidan* that 'the cosmic process seems nevertheless to affirm the worth of every human system of ethics fundamentally opposed to human egoism'.[62] This being so, Japan, where egoism had not developed to Western levels, was clearly more advanced than the West. Yet in *Japan: an Attempt at Interpretation*, written shortly afterwards, in thrall to Spencer, he argued the opposite.

In 'Mosquitos', feeling the hand of death on his shoulder, Lafcadio described in lyrical detail his wishes for his final resting place:

> I should like, when my time comes, to be laid away in some Buddhist grave-yard of the ancient kind,- so that my ghostly company should be ancient, caring nothing for the fashions and the changes of Meiji. That old cemetery behind my garden would be a suitable place. Everything there is beautiful with a beauty of exceeding and startling queerness; each tree and stone has been shaped by some old, old ideal which no longer exists in any living brain; even the shadows are not of this time and sun, but of a world forgotten, that never knew steam or electricity or magnetism or – kerosene oil! Also in the boom of the big bell there is a quaintness of tone which wakens feelings, so strangely far-away from all the nineteenth-century part of me, that the faint blind stirrings of them make me afraid,- deliciously afraid. Never do I hear that billowing peal but I become aware of a striving and a fluttering in the abyssal part of my ghost,- a sensation as of memories struggling to reach the light beyond the obscurations of a million million deaths and births. I hope to remain within hearing of that bell. . .And, considering the possibility of being doomed to the state of a *Jiki-ketsu-gaki*, I want to have my chance of being reborn in some bamboo flower-cup, or *mizutamé*, whence I might issue softly, singing by thin and pungent song, to bite some people that I know.[63]

It was a wish destined not to be fulfilled.

CHAPTER FIFTEEN

AN ATTEMPT AT
INTERPRETATION

HEARN'S FINAL years in Tokyo were dominated by two great attempts: one to interpret Japan definitively and the other to get away from it.

At the turn of the century Lafcadio suffered two blows in quick succession which reduced the final years of his life to abject, if productive, loneliness. Professor Foxwell left Tokyo University; his plain-speaking and salary demands had, it seems, moved the authorities to get rid of him.[1] Hearn continued to feel a lingering bitterness about the manner of his departure.[2] He wrote regularly to Foxwell afterwards, often expressing the hope that Foxwell could arrange for Kazuo to be educated in England. The letters of his last years were increasingly bitter; he believed that intrigues were going on to turn him out of his university post, which proved to be sound instinct rather than paranoia even if directed against the wrong people; his suspicions centred, not on the authorities, but on English colleagues whom he claimed were defaming him to the Education Department.[3]

Mitchell McDonald was the really catastrophic loss when he was ordered to service in the Philippines at this time. The reopening of relations with Elizabeth Bisland/Wetmore could, therefore, not have come at a better time. She wrote, reproaching him for his silence, and he replied in January 1900. His tone was coyly sentimental but lacking the real affection of his letters to McDonald. He replied to her charge of indifference by pointing out that he had her picture – together with that of McDonald – on his study wall, '. . .the shadow of a beautiful and wonderful person, whom I knew long ago. . .' He was anxious that she take an interest in Kazuo so that she could advise about him later on. The two younger sons were 'all Japanese' and sturdy and Lafcadio was therefore not anxious about their future; but Kazuo was '. . .altogether of another race – with brown hair and eyes of the fairy colour' and '. . .a queer little Irish accent'.[4] He continued to brood on it in correspondence with Wetmore over the next few years, at the same time touching all the old bases – that she was a fairy, capable of assuming myriad magical shapes, and so on – using the language in which he had previously expressed distrust of her to other friends, but now shaped into compliments. The practical point was to ask if she could play the 'fairy god-sister' in helping him educate Kazuo abroad and find him 'some easy situation in America'.[5]

Within the family, Lafcadio's obsession with his eldest son grew rather than diminished with the years. As he became aware of his own mortality, he felt he was involved in a desperate race against the clock to assure the boy's future. When Iwao was born in 1897 Lafcadio felt that he could be relied on '. . .to look after the ancestors and the family; Kaji won't do for a Japanese. He is much too sensitive, and, perhaps, too clever: he goes to Europe if the Gods spare me to take him there. . .' In the meantime, like Herbert Spencer, Kazuo was to be schooled at home.[6] Whereas Iwao was sent to a primary school at the age of seven, Kazuo was kept at home until he was ten. Setsu, who was embarrassed by Lafcadio's constant praise of Kazuo, suspected that he did not send the boy to school in order to see more of him. Kazuo himself noticed his father's desire to keep him by him more and more as time went on. A desk for Kazuo was set up beside his father's in the study in a corner with glass doors: Kazuo's tears sometimes stained them. One day he found Hearn wiping off tear marks and sighing, 'don't think me cruel'. When he realised that he had been discovered, he made his son write out: 'It makes papa very sorry to see them; but every little boy must cry when he begins to learn – and the glass must be washed.'[7]

An insight into Lafcadio's public standing at this time – and his determination to avoid the public's attention – was given by Osman Edwards, who was then involved in the Japan Society of London. He found that:

No man was more difficult to meet. Of the gushing American ladies who landed at Yokohama with a fixed resolve to include him among the sights to be 'done', few, if any, accomplished that object. He shrank from all society and grudged every moment away from his work. A treacherous introduction was arranged for me by one of his fellow-professors, who had the good fortune to enjoy a somewhat close intimacy, tempered by argument. The hermit was asked to lunch, and came to dinner. Had an outsider been asked to meet him, his pleasure would have been spoiled. It was necessary to pay an accidental visit to the Professor's rooms, when dinner was over, that his guest's susceptibilities might not seem to have been disregarded. Any remorse that I might have felt at indelicate intrusion was soon banished by the discovery that Hearn's long exile from Europe had caused a void, which I was fortunate to fill.[8]

A correspondence was struck up which gives a clear indication of Hearn's attitude towards two contemporary issues, the Dreyfus Affair and the Boer War. He regarded it as sinister that the Roman Catholic Church was opposed to Dreyfus and the Jews in general, strong evidence that Lafcadio was not anti-Semitic. His staunch anti-imperialism was evident in his support for the Boers, notwithstanding his admiration for Kipling, whom he regarded as having 'sinned against justice' in this case. He did, though, confess to a certain ambiguity: his father had been an officer and, when he had been a child, '. . .our house used to be peopled at times with young men in scarlet and gold. With me the love of the English army is perhaps hereditary: I could not fail to sympathize with Kipling's splendid call for help'. Still, the scenes he saw in cinema newsreels made his heart jump with sympathy for the Boers.[9]

Hearn emphasised his Irishness to Edwards; towards the end of the correspondence, he wrote of leaving Japan and perhaps going to England or the land of his ancestors: 'You know I am Irish rather than English; and I half hope to go, for a time at least, to Ireland.'[10] Hearn's Irishness was also recognised by, of all people, a British Consul, Joseph H. Longford. Longford was disappointed that Lafcadio always confined himself to the business in hand when he came to the Consulate:

One would have thought that two Irishmen, both of them Irish Nationalists in the most extreme sense of the term, both no less interested in Japan than they were in their own native country, meeting thus in a far-away land, would have developed relations of close friendship and community of thought, but all his [Longford's] efforts to break through the barrier of reserve with which Hearn surrounded himself were in vain. Hearn never came to the Consulate office except for business, never at all to the Consulate residence, never made any sign of recognition on chance meetings in the public streets, even such as common politeness required, and all attempts at friendship or even acquaintance had at last to be given up.[11]

Longford remembered a pathetic figure with '. . .an awkward shambling gait. . .shuffling through the streets of Tokyo, clinging to the shadow of the walls and steadfastly avoiding the eyes of any fellow European whom he might chance to meet. . .' though he, too, subscribed to the theory that Hearn would have been welcomed by the Western community had he not rebuffed all efforts to draw him in.[12]

He did conduct serious negotiations with the Japan Society in London about delivering a lecture there but a misunderstanding resulted in a curt termination by Hearn.[13] The theme of leaving Japan for America recurred in correspondence with Page Baker and others; he talked of being a Japanese – he was now of course a Japanese citizen – '. . .who longs unspeakably to be again among his own race and blood, among men who have the same color of soul as myself. The foreigner who believes he can understand the Japanese is stupid and foolish indeed'.[14] To Sir Edwin Arnold he described himself as having been practically isolated for years, with little chance of speaking English or French outside school. Anyone who wrote kindly of Japan needed kind friends or a position of power. He was still confident he would leave Japan 'awhile' for Kazuo's sake. Once his son was started in this new way of life he did not anticipate that he would have long to live.[15] The repair of relations with Mitchell McDonald helped somewhat to lift his spirits. They had been estranged for some time; the fault, according to Hearn, lay with neither man, though he admitted to having had suspicions of McDonald.[16] But he also wrote that when the wanderlust came upon him, he attributed it to age and the desire passed away and he settled back to enjoy his '. . .cats, dogs and insects. . .my old temples and shrines. . .'

While all this was going on with his foreign friends, he was actually having a new house built. The one he had occupied in Tomihisa-cho since his arrival in Tokyo was bordered by the Buddhist temple of Kobudera. Musing in its precincts with its magnificent old Japanese *enoki* cedars was a favourite form of relaxation of his until it was decided to cut down some of the trees to raise money for the temple. Hearn attempted to dissuade the parishioners by citing classical Japanese poems about the ghosts of ancient trees. This did not succeed so he offered to buy them but the negotiations failed and three of the cedars were felled. The resultant gap was a form of personal amputation for Hearn and triggered his desire to leave the area.[17]

Setsu proposed building a house. Lafcadio agreed but wanted it to be in Matsue or even Oki island. He must have had a retirement home in mind as he intended continuing at Tokyo University and it would obviously have been impossible to discharge his functions from either place. Setsu flatly refused.[18] Through a middleman she bought a plot with a bamboo grove in Okubo, on the outskirts of Tokyo. The site represented a form of compromise between Setsu's metropolitan preference and Lafcadio's horror of big cities. It was still relatively rural and quiet though in the spring, as the 'Quarter of the Gardener', famous for its azaleas, it attracted thousands of visitors.[19]

It was agreed between Setsu and Lafcadio that the existing home on the site would be added to. He had only two initial requests: to have a room where he could light a stove and with a west-facing desk. Otherwise he was indifferent about the whole project; Setsu and the head carpenter took charge. The property was in her name '. . .and everything was done according to her wishes, so it was quite different from father's taste', according to Kazuo.[20] Actually, like Yukio Mishima decades later, the man who denounced Westernisation was the possessor of much that was strangely at variance with the desire for pre-Meiji purity. In her visit of 1909, Nina Kennard spotted an electric lamp 'in all its electro-plated hideousness' as well as an electric bell. Hearn also planted what his family called an 'English' garden. After they had occupied it, in March 1902, Mitchell McDonald paid a visit and complimented Hearn on his new home. When he asked how much it had cost, his host replied: 'I am an adopted son. Why should I know how much my wife's house cost?' Kazuo believed that he was not being sarcastic; he had not asked and did not know.[21]

Lafcadio's contract at Tokyo University expired at the end of March 1903. Early that month, the student body became angry when word circulated that he was to leave his post because of 'personal antagonism'. According to student rumour, the Japanese Government was willing to keep him but the university authorities wanted him out.[22] All sources agree that Hearn was wonderfully popular with his students and that they were deeply upset at his departure. The exact circumstances surrounding it are not entirely clear; Hearn did want to stay but was not encouraged – to put it at its mildest – to do so. He set out his own account:

> On the 31st March, as I anticipated, I was forced out of the university – on the pretext that as a Japanese citizen I was not entitled to a 'foreign salary'. The students having made a strong protest in my favour, I was offered a reëngagement at terms so devised that it would be impossible for me to reëngage. I was also refused the money allowed to professors for a nine-month vacation after a service of six years. Yet I had served seven years.

He saw this as having been engineered by a 'politico-religious combination'[22]: the man who had so brilliantly analysed *jiujutsu* failed to see it when it was applied to himself!

The truth was that he seems to have been the victim of precisely the kind of *realpolitik* by the authorities which he had always feared in the abstract but was blinded to now because of his paranoia about the missionaries. In 1900 the Japanese Government had sent Natsume Soseki, later to be a famous novelist, to London. In the words of a modern Japanese academic:

> Of course the Japanese Government had not intended him to come to England to study literature, any more than they intended him to start formulating his own analytical theories. It was intended that he should study English, and acquire knowledge useful for the requirements of a rapidly modern [sic] Japan, hungry for knowledge of Western technology and culture. It was not his choice but that of his country.[23]

Soseki had previously been an English teacher at the Kumamoto Higher Middle School, as had Hearn, an extraordinary coincidence. To add a psychological twist to the tangled tale, Soseki, too, was later to give one of his books the title, *Kokoro*. Soseki was now appointed to replace Hearn, having just arrived back from London, where, like Hearn so many years before, he had been miserable. Soseki's misery continued when he assumed the position at Tokyo University, complaining to his wife that 'they' had chosen him to replace so estimable a figure and knowing that he lacked Lafcadio's lecturing skills.[24]

The ending of Hearn's contract was not an individual act of caprice by the authorities. In a piece which appeared in *The Literary Digest* some time previously, an anonymous traveller returned from Japan was quoted as having spotted Lafcadio in a Tokyo street. He was '. . .a tiny figure of a man in a curious mixture of Japanese and American dress. He was scarcely more than five feet tall, and his clothing hung over his shrunken figure with the grace of a blanket on a horse rack. Huge spectacles straddled his nose, and under his arm he carried half a dozen books. As the natives passed him they bowed most respectfully'. That night the hotel manager filled the traveller in on the position of the 'genius':

> He is professor of foreign literature in the university and the only foreigner left in any educational establishment in the whole empire. The university and all the noted schools ten years ago had full staffs of European and American teachers, but since the war with China the Japanese have become so chauvinistic that they have turned out all the foreign teachers from their schools, and all the foreign officers from their army. Hearn was the only American or European who survived the ax [*sic*] of reform in the university. He is, however, as much a Japanese as the Marquis Ito himself, and is so steeped in Orientalism that he has almost forgotten his English-speaking friends.[25]

It was not enough to save him.

A student recorded the events surrounding Lafcadio's departure from the university. On 2 March he went there and found the students talking agitatedly in the corridors over Hearn's 'dismissal'. On the 10th, an overflow meeting took place to discuss dissatisfaction with the action of the authorities. The chairman, a student called Mizuno, calmed the atmosphere by reminding those present of the damage which indiscretion could inflict on their careers. It was agreed to send some representatives to the director and to Hearn and to broach the issue gently. On 15 March they were told that the director was 'moved' by their enthusiasm. The next day they were told that Hearn had wept when he was approached by their representative. On the 17th there was a rumour that he had had a discussion with the director. But when they came back after the spring holiday, they found Soseki in his place. Yone Noguchi described the students as being 'wounded terribly' by this action.[26]

Hearn had been counting on an offer from Cornell but this collapsed, adding to his state of mental anguish. The previous year, Elizabeth Bisland had interested Professor Schurman, the President of Cornell, in having Lafcadio deliver a series of lectures; the blow was all the more severe now as Professor Schurman's letter of 24 December 1902 setting out the terms had promised so much. Firstly, he was very positive about what Hearn could achieve: 'I have no doubt from what I know of your writings that a course of lectures from you would broaden the horizon of our students, quicken their sympathies, and give them a new interest in Japanese society and civilization.' He offered $1,000 for twenty lectures – a few weeks' work – and suggested that Hearn would be able to increase this very considerable sum by lecturing at other universities, which he was willing to arrange. Lafcadio would have absolute freedom of choice over content and approach. Schurman even considered Kazuo's welfare in relation to the local climate.[27]

A degree of confusion existed among Hearn's early biographers about the cancellation of this offer. Bisland stated that he was about to sail for America when the blow – which she called 'breach of contract'[28] – fell; in fact it fell in March 1903 and he had not planned to leave for another few months. Kennard was under the impression that the offer was cancelled after Hearn had parted company with Tokyo University and found the excuse of a typhoid epidemic on the campus 'hardly a sufficient one';[29] she thought that reports of his poor health drifting back to Cornell might have been responsible. Professor Schurman's letter of cancellation was, however, dated 9 March 1903, before Hearn had finally parted company with Tokyo University. The logic of its contents was compelling: the typhoid epidemic had wreaked havoc on the campus and the university simply did not have the funds for the projected course of lectures.[30]

Hearn himself sympathised with Schurman's predicament.[31] He had not abandoned hope that the 'Dear Queen of the Fairies' might still find him a post in the United States which, he believed, could help him to weather the storm until political change might help him return to Japan.[32] He claimed to have material evidence that 'certain religious combinations' wanted to destroy his chances in the United States.[33] It was presumably to placate or counteract these powerful forces that, according to Bisland, he had allegedly attempted to join the Masons but found that a Japanese citizen could not be a member.[34]

Hearn had always claimed that adversity made him productive. Instead of allowing the Cornell cancellation to devastate him, he ploughed on with what were to have been the lectures there and turned them into a book considered by many to have been his finest, *Japan: an Attempt at Interpretation*. The fact of being no longer employed enabled him to concentrate his full energies on the task. Always excoriating himself for perceived inadequacies, Lafcadio wrote bitterly to Bisland that the task required training beyond his range. He pictured himself as 'blind and naked ignorance' delivering '. . .brawling judgements, unashamed, on all things, . . .I ought to keep to the study of birds and cats and insects and flowers, and queer small things,- and leave the subject of the destiny of Empires to men of brains. Unfortunately, the men of brains will not tell the truth as they see it'.[35] Lafcadio was nonetheless aware that he was breaking new ground and that the end-product would be unique. He wrote to Bisland in 1903, when he had nearly completed the draft, that it would:

> . . .form eventually a serious work upon Japan, entirely unlike anything yet written. The substantial idea of the lectures is that Japanese society represents the condition of ancient Greek society a thousand years before Christ. I am treating of religious Japan – not of artistic or economical Japan, except by way of illustration.[36]

The religion in question would be ancestor-worship, ancient and indigenous. Suited to a 'cultivated audience' only, he was confident of making a good, if 'rather queer', book.[37]

However, much of the novelty he talked of was actually old hat as far as he himself was concerned. His appreciation of the importance of Shinto to Japanese culture – the cornerstone of the book – had been formed in his first year in Japan[38] and he had differed radically over the years from most Western observers in assessing the depth of religious attachment there. In Kobe he formed the view that the seeming Japanese indifference to religion was affected and noted that the Jesuits of old, better judges than the contemporary proselytisers, had never accused the Japanese of indifference.[39] Even before he had come to Japan, he had, in an 1886 item in the New Orleans *Times-Democrat*, written of how in China there had been a reaction against Buddhism in the form of a revival of ancestor-worship.[40] As we have already seen, he had written extensively of Shinto and of parallels with ancient Greece in his earlier Japanese work.

What was new was the scale, the coherence and systematic nature of his presentation. His agnostic eye had always lit on religion. In Japan, under the influence of Spencer, he was able to study a society whose entire structure derived, he believed, from it. But whereas his ideas had always previously been scattered in bits and pieces in essays, now he set out to write a large-scale history of Japan and the nature of the forces which had shaped the people's character through analysis of its religious and social evolution.[41] Unlike previous Western historians, he was not, he said, hostile or sceptical; this was Hearn's great strength.

His weakness was that he saddled himself with Spencer's all-embracing evolutionary structure. Indeed, the work was an attempt to contain Japanese history and character within this structure. Japan, despite its wonderful civilisation, was classified as being sociologically at the stage Europe had been at hundreds of years before Christ. It had to be put on Spencer's standardised measure. Hearn did not allow that Japan's development could diverge from a single, European-based model of evolution. Still, without Spencer, Hearn might never have ventured to Japan in the first place. As he explained in *Attempt*, it was because of his interest in the 'Synthetic Philosophy' that he became interested in Buddhism which he saw as a theory of evolution.[42] One could go further and say that, by surrounding religion in a cloak of science, Spencer had made it respectable as a subject of study for Hearn. On the other hand, too much should not be made of the interest in Spencer having turned Hearn towards the Orient: as *Stray Leaves* demonstrated, his immersion in Oriental studies well predated his reading of the 'Synthetic Philosophy'.

In the *Attempt at Interpretation*, Hearn tried to trace Japanese society back to its roots: to show that the ethics of Shinto derived from the doctrine of unqualified obedience to customs originating in the family cult; that ethics, religion and government were therefore unified; and that the real rulers of the nation were the dead rather than the living, a suitably ghostly concept to appeal to Hearn.[43] Indeed, all members of the Japanese family felt themselves under 'perpetual ghostly surveillance'. In both communal and household Shinto, the underlying idea was that the welfare of the living depended on that of the dead. Neglect of the household rites would provoke the malevolence of the spirits and bring about public misfortune: the ghosts of the ancestors controlled nature and had 'fire and flood, pestilence and famine' at their disposal for vengeance. The power of the ruler was unlimited because that of the dead supported him. It stood to reason that any religion opposed to Shinto would be an attack on the whole system of society. Buddhism was accepted because it adapted to ancestor-worship and made itself an ally of social custom, but the conservatism of the ancestor-cult was exemplified by the readiness with which the two religions fell apart on the disestablishment of Buddhism in 1871. Whereas 'Shinto had no art', Buddhism had brought a 'gospel of tenderness' to Japan and gave it the arts and industries of China; it was a civilising agent. Buddhism modified and reinterpreted the old beliefs but did not attempt suppression.[44]

The greatest danger ever to threaten Japan, in Hearn's view, had been the introduction of Christianity, opposed as it was to the beliefs and traditions upon which Japanese society was founded. Filial piety in particular, the basis of everything, was downgraded by Christianity to, at best, an inferior virtue. By preaching that the supreme duty of obedience to the Pope, not the Emperor, Catholicism was attacking the 'foundations of order' and so was suppressed by the great Japanese leader, Iyéyasu, in the seventeenth century. It was probable that the Jesuits – whose attempt at conversion Hearn described as 'a crime against humanity, a labour of devastation' – had left ancestor-worship alone but the Dominicans and Franciscans scuppered this policy and hastened the ruin of the Christian missions.[45]

Japanese civilisation had reached its limit of development in the period of that later Tokugawa Shogunate, preceding the modern regime. During the Tokugawa period, a sense of beauty began to inform everything in common life but the race also 'degenerated' during this long era of peace. It was Shinto scholars who prepared the way for the end of the Shogunate, representing a '. . .reaction of native conservatism against the long tyranny of alien ideas and alien beliefs. . .', those of China. By the end of the eighteenth century, their teachings had created a strong party in favour of the official revival of Shinto, the restoration of the Emperor to supreme power and the repression of military power. The lords of Choshu, Satsuma, Tosa and Hizen saw the worth of the new ideas to their hope of ending Tokugawa domination. After Perry, when the Shogunate's inability to resist foreign aggression became manifest, its power crumbled. In 1867, the Emperor was restored to supreme military and civil power and, shortly afterwards, Buddhism was disestablished and Shinto restored as the state religion.[46]

The entire framework of society was then remodelled on European lines, with the clans dissolved, the family no longer the basic unit of society and the individual recognised by the new constitution. In thirty years, it had 'entered the circle of modern civilized powers' and the ability to do so had derived from Shinto. To fairly measure this achievement, Hearn believed that it was necessary to remember that Japan was 2,700 years 'evolutionally younger' than the contemporary Western powers at the end of the Tokugawa Shogunate. The value of religion sociologically lay in its conservatism; no essential of Shinto had been weakened by 'the long pressure of Buddhism'. The future of Japan depended on the maintenance of the '. . .new religion of loyalty, evolved, through the old, from the ancient religion of the dead. . .' into the modern sense of patriotism. It would prosper in so far as it remained faithful to its old moral ideals; up to that time, it had been wise in taking the practical things it needed from the West but rejecting its emotional and intellectual life.[47]

So far, so good, but Hearn was not clear-cut on this point. Bound as he now was by Spencer's evolutionary orthodoxy, he saw contemporary Western *laissez-faire* as the pinnacle of economic and social development. In earlier works, he had foreseen how Japan's unique culture would give it a comparative advantage in future economic competition with the West. Now he put forward the view that the capacity for industrial competition was dependent on the expansion of individualism; otherwise it would be unable to compete internationally: 'While Japan continues to think and to act by groups, even by groups of industrial companies, so long she must always continue incapable of her best.' The absence of true individual freedom would also probably make real democracy impossible. Indeed, the capacity of the Japanese for communal organisation was '. . .the strongest possible evidence of their unfitness for any modern democratic form of government'. The difference between Japan and Western democracies was the difference between '. . .compulsory and free cooperation,- the difference between the most despotic form of communism, founded upon the most ancient form of religion, and the most highly evolved form of industrial union, with unlimited right of competition'. If there was an implication here that Japan would never be able to compete fully with the Western powers, then it was at odds with most of what he had written previously and it was his earlier work which was to be vindicated by history. This underlines the pitfalls of treating the *Attempt* as a useful codification of Hearn's writings on Japan.[48]

A resolution of sorts was to say that Japan needed more freedom, but it had to be constrained by 'wisdom'. In this respect, Lafcadio had great faith in the capacity of Japanese statesmanship, in particular, to resist the 'depredations' of foreign capital.[49] He ended *Japan: an Attempt at Interpretation* by quoting with approbation Spencer's advice to the Japanese government to keep the West at arm's length.[50] He was deeply touched when a bookseller made him a present of the original of Spencer's letter to the London *Times* of 18 January 1904 containing this advice; it was, he wrote in a letter of thanks, '. . .certainly one of the most important documents ever published in relation to Japan. . .'[51]

As Lafcadio worked on *Attempt* in 1903, his attitude towards leaving Japan continued to see-saw. On 31 March, he refused a request to subscribe to a journal with a very definite statement that he was leaving the country.[52] A rather pathetic letter of 29 May 1903 to the editor of the San Francisco *Argonaut* is indicative of Lafcadio's desperation to get away. He had been encouraged by the newspaper's attitude in the past; it had apparently been positive in reply to a previous request for a position. He was now looking for something easy on the Pacific coast of the United States:

> Are there any literary possibilities in San Francisco;-
> something in the way of regular contributions, signed or
> unsigned (which I should prefer) would be very nice. My
> sight forbids anything like hard newspaper work – though I
> might attempt such with a type-writer. Could I be of use
> on *The Argonaut?*
> - I should be very thankful for a kind reply- however
> discouraging. In the meantime please allow me to request
> that this letter be considered private.[53]

As he surveyed the responses from various American institutions, he felt hope dimming. He told Bisland that the reply he had had from Johns Hopkins was not encouraging though the Lowell Institute promised better; he would be glad to speak at Leland Stanford irrespective of salary but he was convinced that any arrangement would be sabotaged by the covert power of 'certain religious bodies'.[54]

By August 1903 he was apologising to Bisland for a previous 'dismal' letter; he now felt he could 'fight it out in Japan'. He could live by his pen – he had high hopes for *Japan: An Attempt at Interpretation* in this regard – provided his health was good and there was no place in the world where the cost of living was so reasonable; in the circumstances, spending $2,000 on a return journey to the United States would make little sense.[55] He told the Japan Society in London that 1905 would the earliest he could visit England.[56] The tone of an October letter to Bisland was optimistic. He had had a charming letter from the President of Vassar and an offer from Sir William Van Horne, President of the Canadian Pacific Railroad, of a return ticket to Montreal.[57] In December 1903, the General Traffic Agent in Yokohama for the Canadian Pacific's Royal Mail Steamship Line was told by his Montreal office that Lafcadio 'contemplated a trip to Canada' and he offered to issue a return ticket to Montreal. Hearn's reply was non-committal.[58]

In October 1903, Lafcadio had announced the birth of his fourth child, Suzuko, – his third child, another son, Kiyoshi, had been born in 1899 – very simply to Bisland: 'I have a little daughter; and that anxiety is past.'[59] It is a much more battered figure which emerges from the accounts left by his family. Mrs

Hearn reminisced that when Suzuko was born he felt he would be unable to foresee her future and was 'worried over it with more sorrow than rejoicing'.[60] She recounted that he was almost unbearably lonely in the final year or two of his life. He could not bear to be parted from her, to the point of crying if she went out. He was, in effect, a child. The neighbours suspected that he had gone crazy.[61] The problem with uncritical acceptance of this account, and translation may be partly to blame, was that intellectually he was at the height of his powers and, emotionally, resolved on a course – leaving Japan – which would have meant a lengthy separation from Setsu.

His melancholy is corroborated by Kazuo. He remembered walks past a crematorium with his father who would anticipate being turned into the smoke coming out the chimney. He plodded along behind the stooped, grey figure under an understandable pall of gloom.[62] Otherwise, Kazuo believed that his father was misunderstood as a misanthrope, by foreigners at least, because he did not frequent the places which they did. His anticipation of letters from Western friends was immense, and his gratification when they were received, total.[63] He was also defended from the charge of being a misanthropic recluse in these years by Nobushige Amenomori who believed that he did not like isolation but was driven to it by city life.[64]

Towards the close of 1903, Lafcadio went for a walk on a cold winter's day. His mouth filled with blood from a burst blood vessel. He returned home in evident pain and went to bed. Dr Kizawa, the family physician, was called and diagnosed bronchial trouble. Lafcadio's health hung in the balance for a week before he rallied and began a slow recovery but it was only partial and he remained noticeably weaker than before. The muscles which had been able to swing twenty-pound dumb-bells with ease were now flabby though he could still slap his son hard, swim well at Yaidzu in the summer of 1904, and on walks he was as sure-footed as ever.[65] Dr Kizawa recommended that the proposed journey overseas be postponed indefinitely. Hearn accepted the inevitable and wrote to Bisland that he had given up the idea of taking Kazuo to the USA; he would try to make a 'nest' for him in Japan instead.[66] Setsu took advantage of the situation to press for Kazuo to receive a Japanese education. Lafcadio agreed and his son was sent to school though the home coaching was kept up.[67]

The public consciousness in Japan during the last months of Lafcadio's life was dominated by the Russo-Japanese War, which began in February 1904. Despite his anger at the Government over the Tokyo University post, Hearn was totally behind Japan. He saw the war as a necessary part of the objective process of social evolution in which the higher conditions of civilisation could only be reached by 'militancy'.[68] He interpreted this war as a struggle for existence by Japan. Russia he portrayed as capable of threatening simultaneously the civilisations of East and West and, unless checked, of absorbing Scandinavia and dominating China. Beneath a sentimental – almost pietistic – enthusiasm can be detected a delight that the war was bringing forth the finest qualities imbued by traditional, Shinto, values. He stressed the 'ascetic devotion to duty' of Commander Hirosé who died heroically in the blockade of Port Arthur and the fact that he was now 'raised. . .to the place of the Immortals'.[69] We know from domestic sources that Lafcadio himself joined wholeheartedly in the popular emotion. He would kiss the portrait of Admiral Togo with a request that he please win and sing the song of 'Hirosé Chusa', in honour of the Port Arthur hero, every day with the children.[70]

A positive spin-off of the war for Hearn was the great interest in Japan which it generated in the West. In England, Japan's ally and mentor, particularly, his books were now much more in demand.[71] This may have influenced the request of March 1904 from London University that Lafcadio deliver a course of ten lectures on the civilisation of Japan.[72] Even though the text of *Japan: an Attempt at Interpretation* was at an advanced stage of preparation and would have seemed ideal material on which to base a course of lectures, Lafcadio fussed that he would need at least eight or ten months for preparation. He suggested the summer of 1905 as the best time to aim at.

By the time he composed this reply, Lafcadio had actually secured another academic post in Japan. Waseda University in Tokyo had been founded by Count Okuma, one of the outstanding figures of the Meiji era and was – as it has remained – one of the best universities in Japan. Count Okuma offered Hearn a professorship whose 'small fees but ample leisure' put him back to a situation where he could write without being distracted by financial worries.[73] He liked Waseda very much and used to say that it was 'nothing like the governmental kind'. His experience with Tokyo University had not changed his fundamental beliefs one iota: he would still return home perspiring profusely having warned Count Okuma against foreign religious influences.[74]

The next month, June 1904, the reviews of *Kwaidan* began appearing. That in the *Atlantic Monthly* described the book as 'dainty, wistful, beautiful. . .'[75] Regarding the *hokku* in the butterfly studies, *The Athenaeum* said: 'These tiny drops of poesy have often a peculiar charm – faint, slight and evanescent, yet real, like a perfume wafted swiftly by.'[76] A very positive review by Yone Noguchi in *The Bookman* was aimed partly at refuting the notion:

> . . .that his writing is about one third Japanese and two thirds Hearn. Fortunately, his two thirds Hearn is also Japanese. At least in *Kwaidan* he is Jap [sic] through and through, in his writing and treatment. There is nothing foreign about the book. His art is nothing but the best Japanese art.[77]

In July/August 1904, Lafcadio went as usual for a seaside holiday in Yaidzu, though his stay was somewhat curtailed by the demands of his new lecturing post at Waseda. Here he rested from writing, though he did read proofs of *Japan: an Attempt at Interpretation* and devoted time to Kazuo's lessons and writing to Setsu, who had stayed at home.[78] His wretched health seemed to recover in the sea air. He claimed he was browned and had got strong again; he regained the use of his right arm which had evidently been affected by his illness,[79] but there was a pathetic reference in one letter to Setsu to 'Papa's belly. . .growing rather small'. The war was also casting its shadow: seventeen men of the village had gone to Manchuria.[80]

Nevertheless, the world as he surveyed it in September 1904 did not seem such a bad place. True, he excoriated himself as 'a dolt and a blunderer of the most amazing kind', but this was balanced by noting that he stood '. . .tolerably well in the opinion of a few estimable people, in spite of adverse tongues and pens'. Notwithstanding the vicissitudes of the past year, Lafcadio had actually made money, albeit with much economising. Circumstances may not have favoured his work on the 'rejected addresses' but he felt that in published form they would be of value. He asked Bisland not to approach any more universities on his behalf: he was now a 'burnt child' in this respect.[81]

On 19 September 1904, Lafcadio had experienced the first pangs of what was to prove a fatal illness. Setsuko found him with his hands on his chest and asked what the matter was. He replied that it was a new kind of illness, 'sickness of the heart'. He suspected that the condition was terminal and began thinking of the family's welfare after his death. The doctor was called but, after a few minutes, Hearn announced that the pain was gone and he would like a bath. Then he wanted a glass of whisky which Setsu reluctantly gave him, well watered. Looking back on this period, his family felt the omens had been bad. A few days before he died, the cherry tree in the garden blossomed out of season, regarded in Japan as a sign of ill-luck. As Kazuo prepared to set off for school on the morning of 26 September, he and his father wished each other goodnight instead of goodbye.

It was an unusually cold Monday morning. Lafcadio said, 'Oh, what bad weather! This will kill me!'[82] The family laughed. He told Setsu of a strange dream he had had the night before of a journey to a 'strange land'. They all laughed again, not realising how soon the words would become literally true. In the course of the day, he wrote a letter to his former pupil, Fujisaki, then serving with the Japanese forces in Manchuria. That evening he was in good form over supper, laughing and joking with the family. But within an hour, the chest pains of the previous week returned. Setsuko advised him to lie on his bed, which he did. A little while later he was dead. Setsu remembered that he died without any pain, with a little smile around his mouth.[83] In Kazuo's account, he expired 'regretfully resigned', with the words, '*Ah, byoki no tame*', ('Ah, on account of the sickness').[84]

CHAPTER SIXTEEN

POSTHUMOUS

> While Poe was living to reply to his enemies, the attempts
> to smirch his reputation amounted to very little, but after
> his death there was a feast of the ghouls, in which no form
> of malignity was omitted to paint him as a moral and
> physical debauchee.[1]

WHEN HEARN'S FUNERAL took place on 30 September, he
was, according to Yone Noguchi, the first foreigner ever buried
in Japan with the Buddhist rite. Only three foreigners attended.[2]
There were about 40 Japanese professors and 100 students. A
graphic account was sent to *The Critic* by Margaret Emerson,
who had gone to Japan before Hearn's death with hopes of
seeing him. She found that some of the English-speaking
community had never heard of him, the missionaries spoke of
him with horror and the business and diplomatic elements were
not personally acquainted with him. She tried Tokyo University,
to be told he had ceased lecturing there because of eye trouble.
Another English professor said he had gone home for treatment
and nobody knew where his home was. In general, the
impression she was given by the foreign community was that
he was '. . .a recluse, averse to all society, and more especially to
that of Europeans'.[3]

She was planning a letter to Lafcadio when she read of his
death in a newspaper. The paper gave details of the funeral and
she decided to attend. The procession left his home at 1.30pm:

> First came bearers of white lanterns and of wreaths and
> great pyramidal bouquets of asters and chrysanthemums;

next, men carrying long poles from which hung streamers of paper *gohei*; after them two boys in rickshaws containing birds, that were to be released on the grave, symbols of the soul released from its earthly prison. The emblems were all Buddhist, but the portable hearse, next in line, carried by six men in blue, was a beautiful object, of unpainted and unvarnished, perfectly fresh, white wood, trimmed with blue silk tassels, and with gold and silver lotus flowers at the four corners. Directly behind it, on foot, followed the chief mourners, a middle-aged Japanese man and Lafcadio Hearn's oldest son, a nice-looking boy of about fifteen. In rickshaws were his Japanese wife, all in white, the color of mourning in Japan, and his daughter.

Priests carrying the food for the dead, university professors in the Prince Albert coats and gray trousers so unbecoming to Japanese men, and a multitude of students wearing the kilted trousers (*hakama*) characteristic of the student, formed the end of the procession.[4]

The procession wound its way to the Jitoin Kobudera Temple in Ichigaya. There the funeral service began with eight priest chanting, punctuated by the tinkling of a bell. Then the Japanese chief mourner led Kazuo forward:

Together they knelt before the hearse, touching their foreheads to the floor, and placed some grains of incense upon the little brazier burning between candles. A delicate perfume of sandalwood filled the air. They again bowed to the ground and retired.

The wife next stepped forward, leading a little boy of seven in a sailor suit with brass buttons and white braid. We could see her quite plainly, a middle-aged Japanese woman with expressionless face, her hair elaborately done into stiff loops, like carved ebony, her only ornament the magnificent white brocade *obi*, reserved for weddings or funerals. She also unwrapped some grains of incense from a square of white tissue-paper and placed them on the brazier. She put the little boy's head down, and guided his hand when he took the incense.

The head priest appeared for a moment, resplendent in violet and red gauze with a stole of white and gold brocade, and a complicated twist of blue silk cords intertwined and ending in tassels thrown over his shoulder. Then Lafcadio Hearn's eldest son, accompanied by the Japanese gentleman, crossed over to our side and both bow[ed] low to the assembly, who respond[ed] by bowing to the ground. The ceremony was ended and we all slowly dispersed into the grounds.[5]

The temple was near where Hearn had lived in the Ushigome district until 1902. He had been friendly with a priest there who had later transferred to Asakusa and, as 'Archbishop Tatara', came from there to officiate at the funeral ceremony.[6] The final cremation rites took place the following day at the Zoshigaya temple.

Both Kazuo and Nina Kennard, who visited Lafcadio's grave on her 1909 trip to Japan, were deeply critical of the choice of Zoshigaya cemetery as his final resting place. To Kennard, the graveyard was not beautiful but '. . .distressingly European, with straight gravelled paths and formal plots, enclosed by a box edging and a little wicker gate'. She believed that it was a section of the cemetery allocated to foreigners.[7] Kazuo, who disliked the 'big show' made after his father's death, commented: 'So, though he is resting now in that tasteless Zoshigaya cemetery, without complaint, he must be saying, "It can't be helped", and resting in peace, in contentment.'[8]

Setsuko understood her husband's desire for an obscure old temple with quiet grounds as the place where he would like to lie in death, but claimed in her *Reminiscences* that such would have been difficult to find quickly.[9] In a 'conversation' with Yone Noguchi published in *The Japan Times* of 21 December 1904, she said that the decision to bury him at 'lonely' Zoshigaya was based on his frequent use of the place for his afternoon walks. Neither was she unaware of his preference for his children to wear kimono when he was alive; she claimed that she had intended they should wear Japanese clothes at the funeral but dressed them Western style because these clothes were easier to walk in.[10] On a practical level, the explanation simply does not hold water and she must have been aware of the symbolism of the dress. Hearn still lies in Zoshigaya cemetery where a five-foot granite shaft rises above his grave. The inscription reads simply: 'Koizumi Yakumo is buried here'.

Lafcadio's death produced a variety of effects. The Associated Press reported a general feeling of regret among the Japanese at Hearn's death.[11] To begin with, the American tributes were eulogistic. 'His death', declared the Washington *Star*, 'removes one of the most brilliant of the English stylists, and leaves a void which cannot easily be filled. For some years Mr Hearn has been devoting himself to the study of Japanese literature, and presenting to English readers versions of the folk tales, legends, and poetic prose stories which have taken high rank with the finest products of modern pens. He had caught the spirit of Japan as have few foreigners.' The New York *Post* characterised him as '. . .the accomplished, imaginative, and attractive writer who had done so much to familiarize the world with Japanese life and character'. The Chicago *Post* remarked, '. . .the Japanese and the westerner acquainted with the East alike testified to Mr Hearn's rare interpretative gift, the subtlety of his sympathy, and the effectiveness and fidelity of his expression'. The New York *Mail* believed that '. . .readers who have followed his work have not been surprised at any feature of the war with Russia. Not that he wrote of armaments or meddled with military statistics; but he entered into the thought of Japan and into a comprehension of the abilities and sympathy with the ideals of the Japanese as no outlander ever did before. The East took him to her arms and opened his eyes to the strange visions that only the Oriental can see'.[12]

A long article which appeared in the *Dayton Daily Journal* of 30 September 1904, almost certainly by his friend of former days, Tunison, was also positive for the most part but contained within it as well the harbinger of harsher future comments: '. . .in spite of his mild manners at most times and the suave elaboration of his writings, he had something of the temper of Swift and could eat his own heart for bitterness'. Tunison was positive about Lafcadio's books but claimed that he identified the theories of Spencer 'with the cyclic fantasies of orientalism'; it was open to question whether he had done harm or good to Japan 'by his advocacy of their pet superstitions'.[13]

Soon after his death, the literary magazine of Tokyo University issued a Lafcadio Hearn memorial number – an unusual honour.[14] At the other extreme, Kazuo noted that after his father's death, his photo began to appear in many publications, even in patent medicines' advertisements.[15] No doubt the widespread publicity aroused by his death occasioned the revival of interest in his essays on the part of the *Atlantic Monthly*; the issues of November 1904 and of January, April and September 1905 carried four of the seven essays which made up the posthumously-published *Romance of the Milky Way*.

Lafcadio missed, by a matter of weeks, seeing the triumphant reception accorded to *Japan: an Attempt at Interpretation*. A review in *The Academy* of 10 December 1904 declared it the most important of his works, one which could not be neglected by anyone wishing to understand the future possibilities of Japan or the meaning of its past. The *Spectator* of 14 January 1905 described it as the 'crown of his life's work' and 'the swan-song of a very striking writer' whose death was a great loss to literature. A most perceptive review was that in *The Critic* by W.E. Griffis, himself the author of a book, *The Mikado's Empire*:

> They felt that he had done his best and was degenerating. Yet here is a work which is a classic in science, a wonder of interpretation. It is the product of long years of thought, of keenest perception, or marvellous comprehension. . .His book is a re-reading of all Japanese history, a sociological appraisement of the value of Japanese civilization, and a warning against intolerant propaganda of any sort whatever. This book is destined to live, and to cause searchings of heart among those who imagine that the Japanese soul has been changed in fifty years.[16]

When *The Romance of the Milky Way* was published late in 1905 it, too, garnered some good reviews, such as that in *The Academy* of 21 December 1905. It found that the 'strange grace' of Japan was in all the works of Hearn, '. . .who loved it and was able to give it expression'.[17] However, a review in *The Athenaeum* of 31 March 1906 was more typical of a Western tendency to dismiss Hearn as superficial and unreal; his Japan was an idealisation, not to be confused with the real country of essentially prosaic people.[18]

This was, however, mild compared to the posthumous controversies which were to erupt over the next few years. Oscar Lewis, author of a 1930 work on the subject, said that after Lafcadio's death, he was the most loved and hated figure in recent literary history; no man's memory had been more savagely attacked, or defended more passionately.[19]

All the problems stemmed, directly or indirectly, from a deal done by Lafcadio's two staunchest friends. After his death, Mitchell McDonald acted as executor of his estate. He arranged the sale of the copyright of Hearn's books in the United States.[20] He agreed that Bisland should write the official biography. This was not surprising. Not alone had she introduced the two men, but she was an established author, and had already amassed a great deal of Lafcadio's correspondence.

She was confronted with problems from the outset. Professor Foxwell refused to contribute his letters from Hearn.[21] So too did Nina Kennard; there was friction between the two ladies on this point. Kennard, who claimed close connection with the Hearn family, no doubt had her own eye on the biographical possibilities. She sought to reassure readers of her 1911 biography that Hearn's widow and children would not suffer from the fact that the letters to Mrs Atkinson had not been made available to Bisland. Like Bisland, she edited out of Hearn's letters material likely to cause embarrassment, in this case to his Irish relations.[22]

Two further collections of letters caused even greater trouble, one by being given to Bisland and the other by fuelling the ambitions of a rival biographer. Dr George Gould later took savage retribution for what he saw as indiscreet use of the correspondence he had handed over to Bisland. Of more immediate concern was the controversy which had its origins in the letters which Lafcadio had written to Henry Watkin, now old and ailing and in straitened circumstances in an old folks home. He gave these to Milton Bronner, editor of *The Kentucky Post*, who edited them for publication in 1907 under the title, *Letters from the Raven*.

It was alleged in a later book that Bronner had threatened that if someone else were allowed to write Hearn's official biography, he would tell in print the story of the marriage to Mattie Foley.[23] Certainly, in a letter dated 20 July 1905, Bisland referred to a press clipping on the subject as beyond doubt the work of Bronner, who had, she said, tried to force Mrs Hearn to allow him to publish the letters '. . .and when he failed raked the slums, apparently, to find details for this disgusting story which he has been holding as a threat to blackmail Mrs Hearn's representative, Paymaster McDonald'. She claimed, in the same letter, that Bronner's attempt at blackmail had been backed up by his New York publisher which liked to '. . .use unmentionable methods of advertising. They stole *One of Cleopatra's Nights* a few years ago by legal trickery, after Worthington had plundered Lafcadio through it. He got no remuneration from either publisher. . .And yet people blame Lafcadio for being suspicious'. Bisland was bitterly critical of Watkin for lending himself to a 'hideous scandal' to get money out of letters written to him in friendship.[24]

Mattie Foley herself entered the fray under the illusion that Hearn had left a vast fortune in which she could share. She claimed that she had been separated but never divorced from him. The *Cincinnati Enquirer* printed the story in July 1906.[25] This, in turn, led to even more lurid and, in some cases, outlandish media stories. One run by the *Kansas City Journal* not only had Setsuko in the United States but even described her as a typical Japanese with 'slant eyes'.[26]

The most extraordinarily vicious attack on Hearn came from the New York *Sun* of 27 July 1906, under the heading, 'A Strange Career':

> It will surprise no one who knew Lafcadio Hearn at all well to hear that a negro woman in Cincinnati now claims recognition as his widow and seeks to obtain as such a share of the American royalties on his remarkable literary work. Hearn spent several years in the Ohio city, and it is sufficiently notorious that in his purely private and domestic relations he consorted with colored people only. Notwithstanding his extraordinary literary attainments, his profound and varied scholarship, and his brilliant and poetic intellectual equipment, Lafcadio Hearn admitted no member of his own race to genuine intimacy.

In New Orleans, Hearn was supposed to have lived with negresses – not the ordinary 'cornfield' type, but 'Congo priestesses and prophetesses', including Marie Lavaux, the 'Voodoo Queen'.

In the West Indies what he believed was African music was only, the *Sun* claimed, '. . .mere barbaric adaption of Spanish melodies'. In Japan he had '. . .formed some sort of domestic relations with a native. . .' It was, however, on his physical aspect that the newspaper surpassed itself:

> His appearance was forbidding, if not actually repulsive. Only about 5 feet tall, with one eye totally blind and the other so disabled that he had to hold papers within an inch in order to decipher them, always ill-dressed, unkempt, slovenly; with the face of a weasel and the manners of an oaf; he was nevertheless one of the most brilliant and picturesque writers of his day. . .

The paper did allow that he was '. . .a profound, versatile, and poetic thinker, one of the greatest masters of occult languages and literature the Christian world [!] has ever known'.[27] This attack provoked letters of defence from George Gould to *The New York Times*, and Ellwood Hendrick and Richard Barry to the *Sun*. Page Baker took up the cudgels in the New Orleans *Times-Democrat*.[28]

The New York Times republished Baker's article and then printed Gould's letter, dated 14 August 1906. Gould stated bluntly that the *Sun*'s allegations were untrue, a strange perversion of justice. Gould, at this point, saw himself as a valued collaborator in the preparation of Bisland's biography, a labour of love by his American friends to raise funds for Kazuo's education.[29]

In life, Bisland had seen Lafcadio as a child-genius, '. . .always the prey of the vile in consequence'. After his death, she was appalled by the behaviour of his friends and found the '. . .revelations of cupidity, jealousy, and coarseness. . .from some whom he loved and trusted. . .too amazing'.[30] Bisland did not specify who she had in mind, but as this letter predated the *Sun* controversy, she may have been referring to the determination of such former friends as Krehbiel and Tunison to get her to expose the less attractive side of her subject. To Krehbiel, Hearn was a 'little beast'; he was disgusted by Bisland's failure to be shocked at his story of Hearn being found in a brothel with a prostitute in the middle of the floor and Lafcadio was walking around her, '. . .his one eye six inches from her, admiring her fine lines'. Bisland laughed and said it proved that Hearn's interest in negro women was purely aesthetic.[31]

In his *Afro-American Folksongs*, published in 1914, Krehbiel revealed a more balanced attitude towards his dead friend. While dismissive of Hearn's musical abilities, he reminisced about their collaboration in trying to unearth African survivals in American folk music. By this time, the inspiration which negro music had provided for Dvorak's *From the New World* symphony had given respectability to the genre. Krehbiel drew heavily on *Two Years in the French West Indies* – a 'peculiarly fascinating book' – as a source of material on Creole music but stated that, as a 'sobersided student of folk music who believed in scientific methods' he had reacted in lukewarm fashion to his 'fantastical friend's' suggestion that he investigate possible physiological differences in the vocal cords of negroes and whites, which he attributed to Lafcadio's 'riotous' imagination.[31a]

Adverse speculation about Hearn's life-style in the United States has continued into our own era. A 1961 biography of Rudolph Matas claimed that Lafcadio was never at ease with cultured women: 'Only in the presence of such social inferiors as the crib-house prostitutes was the burden eased.' Hearn was supposed to have occasionally vanished from sight '. . .for a wild fling among negro brothels', which Matas tried to prevent by showing him the effects of venereal disease. No source is identified but Matas had indeed warned Hearn about the dangers of venereal disease.[32]

Whether she was intimidated by their mass or impressed by their quality, Bisland decided that her biography would consist mainly of Hearn's letters, with only a short biographical introduction. Had she given the letters in their entirety, or even owned up to how she was editing them, she might have stayed within the bounds of scholarship. Unfortunately, she surreptitiously omitted large chunks of some letters and altered others. In one letter to Gould she silently omitted three long paragraphs at the beginning and changed the affectionate 'Hearney boy' signature to a neutral 'Hearn'.[33] In another, to Ellwood Hendrick, she again left out the first paragraph and altered a reference to herself.[34] To her credit, Bisland did not deny that editing had taken place: she defended it on the grounds that she was excluding anything not relevant to Hearn's artistic development.[35] She donated the profits to Lafcadio's widow and children and the book appears to have sold well.

To one commentator, that was enough to excuse the defects in her work, but not all reviewers were so charitable. *The New York Times* did Bisland the favour of devoting the entire front page of its literary section on 1 December 1906 to a review of the book. However, the reviewer, James Huneker, was not well disposed towards Hearn. He put forward the view, later expounded by Gould, that Lafcadio's defective eyesight conditioned his life and art. The review presaged Gould in other ways. Huneker stressed the influence of the French Romantic 'sentimental sensualists' and Poe; Hearn was accused of lacking '. . .apprehension of the gravity of Occidental ethical teaching'. There was an echo of the controversy of a few months earlier as well as an anticipation of Gould's later book in a passage which attributed Hearn's enthusiasm for Spencer to the need of '. . .his feminine fluidity to lean on a strong, positive brain. . .' A '. . .hater of social conventions, despiser of Christianity, a proselyte to a dozen creeds, from the black magic of Voodooism to Japanese Shintoism. . .', Lafcadio was supposed never to have quite shaken off the influence of 'his Christian ancestry': his character was that of '. . .a Christian of Greek and Roman Catholic training, a half Greek, half Celt, whole gypsy, masquerading as an Oriental'.

The Hearn with which Huneker concerned himself was the young man of Cincinnati, the author who tried to dazzle by translating the approach of the French Romantics into English literature. It was not the mature figure of the Japanese period. It is possible to claim that the results of Hearn's use of folklore were meagre only by ignoring his Japanese work. And Japan – to Huneker, 'delicious, malodorous' – does indeed attract little attention in the review, except for the spurious claim that he had '. . .warned us of Japan, the new Japan – though not in a friendly way; he would have been glad to see Western civilization submerged by the yellow race'.[36] Other reviewers did not adopt Huneker's magisterial tone, but many concurred that Hearn's was a partial achievement.[37]

While the critics divided on the merits of Bisland's biography – and its subject – George Gould's reaction was one of unalloyed dismay. He had given his collection of Hearn's letters in the belief that his position would be protected, that he would be the beneficiary of the lack of scruple which Bisland had applied to the selection and alteration of material concerning herself. Gould had hoped to figure as one of the devoted band of admirers who were working on behalf of the dead Hearn, whose works enthralled him in spite of all that had passed between them. Gould had much to gain from such a scenario and, correspondingly, a great deal to lose from the publication of the damaging material in Bisland's work. He was making his mark as an author and developing contacts in the world of literature. Laura Stedman, for example, daughter of Edmund Clarence Stedman, the New York stockbroker and literary figure, compiled the bibliography for Gould's 1908 book on Hearn and collaborated with him in the production of his most important work, the *Life and Letters of Edmund Stedman*, published in 1910. They were married in 1917.

It is unlikely that Gould would have known the contents of Bisland's book when he wrote an article, 'Lafcadio Hearn, a study of his personality and art', for the October/November 1906 issue of *The Fortnightly Review*. Hearn was portrayed as an 'affectionate and sweet-natured man', whose memory was being blackened '. . .by a lot of atrocious lies, and insinuations more vile than lies'. Poor Gould obligingly quoted chunks of savage irony from Hearn's letters and explained, uncomprehendingly, that these represented the success of his efforts to awaken the writer's 'spiritual sense'. His deeper purpose, however, was to apply Maxime du Camp's theory of literary myopia to Hearn. Intellect was supposedly the product of vision. Gould, however, was confused about the application of this theory: Hearn had lacked good vision but was yet a true poet. A resolution of sorts was to dub him 'the poet of myopia', for whom the world of reality had to be '. . .transported by the magic carpet to the door of his imagination and fancy'.[38]

The ambiguities and contradictions, combined with flashes of insight, which marked the article, paled by comparison with *Concerning Lafcadio Hearn*, the book Gould published a year-and-a-half later, to counter Bisland's 'manipulated biography'.[39] Hearn's friends found out about its contents and made a last-ditch effort to avert publication. The Cincinnati *Enquirer* of 11 May 1908, in a sensational article, claimed that, as the book was going to press, Hearn's widow was threatening a libel suit if the book were not withdrawn. Gould's reaction was, supposedly, that if pressured, he would publish a second, even more damaging, volume. New York friends of Hearn had reportedly gone to Philadelphia the previous day demanding withdrawal of the book. Gould was said to have left the conference in high dudgeon.[40] The New York *World* also reported threats of libel to get the publishers to withdraw *Concerning Lafcadio Hearn*. It published a letter from Milton Bronner claiming that Gould may have been deceived by those pretending to be friends of Hearn.[41]

Publication of the book went ahead. This prompted Ellwood Hendrick to write a letter of rebuttal on various points to *The New York Times* of 14 May 1908.[42] Gould hit back with a highly effective letter to the same paper two days later. He quoted a damaging extract from a letter attributed to McDonald which allowed that Hearn had suffered from hallucinations of persecution and promised that nothing detrimental would appear in Bisland's book without giving Gould an opportunity to refute it. Gould subsequently acknowledged that the letter had been written, not by McDonald, but by Ferris Greenslet of Houghton, Mifflin. He attributed the error to *The New York Times* but it had by then served its purpose.[43]

Gould was also able to quote a poisoned paragraph from a letter Page Baker had written to him following the publication of *Concerning Lafcadio Hearn*: 'You have a very profound knowledge of Hearn's character, or shall I say lack of character, and the limitations of his art.' He also drew on an 'editorial' review of his book by Marion Baker in the *Times-Democrat*:

> Dr. Gould was shocked, as many have been, by the revelation of Hearn's utter disloyalty to friends and those who had been helpful to him. . .Dr. Gould remarks that Hearn never forgave him for inducing him to go to Japan. Doubtless the erratic, unreasonable being did bear a grudge against a man who persuaded him to seek a country where, through marriage – here as elsewhere he was 'always the slave of circumstances' – he found himself enmeshed by serious domestic duties from which he could not break loose. We learn, through his *Life and Letters*, that his marriage was the suggestion of a Japanese friend (thus we see him again, as Dr. Gould says, 'the mirror of the friend of the instant)'.[44]

This use of his marriage as a weapon of indictment may have represented the nadir of the depths plumbed by Hearn's former friend; in terms of the points-scoring contest being conducted, it was probably effective. For good measure, Gould threw in the full text of the notorious *Sun* editorial of two years earlier. Shrewdly, he added some quotes from his own letter of protest, no doubt as a defence against appearing to change tack in the meantime. But he was probably sincere when he added that he wished Hendrick were welcoming him as a helper, as he had done previously.

Gould's decline from associate of the Bisland/McDonald/Hendrick circle to outcast may have been occasioned by what was regarded as sharp practice over the library or the revelation in the letters of the extent of Hearn's contempt for him, or a combination of both. Whatever the cause, it was to prove costly to Hearn's reputation. To the objective reader of the correspondence between Hendrick and Gould in *The New York Times*, the doctor must have seemed to have acquitted himself extremely well.

The dispassionate tone employed so successfully by Gould in the newspaper correspondence (he ended with a plea for more 'good will' between Hendrick and himself) was not evident in his book, *Concerning Lafcadio Hearn*. Here was the passionate desire of a proud man publicly humbled to retrieve his position. Now that the smoke of battle has cleared, it is the ambiguity of the author towards a subject for whom he felt great affection and equally great frustration which comes across most strongly. Which is not to say that Gould missed the point entirely. For example, he was capable of acutely summarising Hearn's achievement: 'His amazing merit is that while without the great qualities which make the greatest writers, he wrought such miracles of winning grace and persuading beauty.'[45]

Elsewhere, however, Gould's confused attitude towards his subject reached the point of absurdity. There was the assertion that Lafcadio:

> . . .had no mind, or character, to be possessed of loyalty or disloyalty. . .of all men who have ever lived, Hearn, mentally and spiritually, was most perfectly an echo. . .almost his sole merit, and his unique skill lay in the strange faculty of coloring the echo with the hues and tints of heavenly rainbows and unearthly sunsets, all gleaming with a ghostly light that never was on sea or shore.[46]

Pathetically, this was an echo of Hearn himself. Kazuo recalled his father often saying that his work was only an echo. Even more striking is a passage in a letter written in 1890:

> What they admired, I do not know, for I have no originality. I am but an echo of other people's stories and experiences, but if I can color this echo with the iridescence of the soap bubble. . .I shall be satisfied.

He went on to say that he had 'no character' and was a 'tainted, defiled soul, so repulsive in appearance. . .' In Gould's hands, this would become deadly ammunition.[47]

Not that Gould liked the colouring of the echo; developing again his theory of myopia and marrying it to his distaste for

Lafcadio's early literary models, he found his work 'altogether too sexually and sensually charged'. Hearn was, however, saved from the fate of falling into the 'quagmire' with Flaubert, Zola, Wilde and Shaw by his poverty and the fact that he was at least partly Anglo-Saxon, so that he 'shrank from perfection in the method'.[48] Quite what influence Shaw had exercised on Hearn is not clear; there is no evidence that he had read him. Naming Zola as a mentor for Lafcadio was unfortunate considering that he had come to regard the Frenchman as '. . .the idealist of the Horrible, the Foul, the Brutal, the Abominable. . .' and doubted that '. . .anything but evil can be the general outcome of such studies of human nature'.[49]

Gould, the stern moralist, recounted with unintentional comedy his efforts to give Hearn a 'soul'. His pupil had, he imagined, 'acknowledged the vision' but slipped from its clutches to fall under the sway of 'the Oriental and semi-barbarous'.[50] This pathetic creature was totally devoid of 'character' (in Gould's view the effort of the individual to overcome 'circumstance') and had lived a life of '. . .physical and mental anguish, denied desire, crushed yearnings, and unguided waywardness'.[51] Gould's shrewd objective in all this was to show that there was no excuse for a biography of him.[52] He poured scorn on Lafcadio's command of French, though at another point he referred to his 'magnificent' translations from that language.[53] Similarly, his deficiency in Japanese was supposed to have grievously limited his work as an interpreter of Japan though it was also conceded that he had produced 'magnificent works' there, 'one of our most profound literary treasures'. Not bad for a man who had 'created or invented nothing'![54]

Concerning Lafcadio Hearn divided the critics. The New York *Sun*, not surprisingly, saw it as a vindication of their comments two years earlier which they assured their readers had been made '. . .with a view to emphasising his undoubted literary achievements'! It paid tribute to the 'profound and passionate genius' who had produced '*Cheeta*' (*sic*).[55] There was an echo of the *Sun*'s 1906 line in an editorial in a Dayton newspaper, probably by Tunison: 'Misshapen, almost blind, weak morally and repulsive in many ways, Hearn had the soul of a poet and wrote like an angel.' The reviewer was positive towards Gould's book, although it was Tunison who emerged as the real hero.[56] The *Times-Democrat* of New Orleans was even warmer towards *Concerning Lafcadio Hearn*, describing it as a 'masterly work' and accepting unquestioningly the theory of myopia and Gould's allegations of 'utter disloyalty'. The Bakers were other friends who apparently did not like the mirror held up to them by Bisland's *Life and Letters*. Hearn was disparaged as 'erratic, unreasonable' and 'this morbid offspring of mongrel races'.[57]

There was a good deal of other media support for Gould but equally there was a range of negative opinions ranging from scepticism to hostility. The *Sun* was now happy to provide a platform to Gould's opponents, such as Yone Noguchi, who wrote from Keio Gijiku University in Tokyo to lament that Gould had made 'such an awful exposure of himself through Hearn'.[58] It also printed a letter from a New York doctor pouring scorn on Gould's myopic analysis of Hearn's literary output.[59] A review of *Concerning Lafcadio Hearn* in the *Montgomery County Reporter* of Dayton, Ohio, by a reporter who had known Hearn, also dismissed the eyesight explanation of Hearn's work; the author remembered having:

> . . .seen him, time after time, walk to a piece of furniture, pass his hand around it, satisfy himself where the shadow was and where it was not, and then walk off perfectly content. There might have been a dozen reporters in that room, but the one who would have attempted to fool Hearn about what Hearn himself had tested would have presented a very sorry spectacle afterwards.[60]

Gould may have relied on his revelations so shocking contemporary public opinion that he would enjoy unquestioning support. Instead, he found himself subjected to disbelief and ridicule. The reviewer in the *Chicago Herald*, for example, concluded that Hearn's great sin was having too much originality to let himself be forced into Gould's mould of thought.[61] Another Chicago paper concluded that Hearn's temperament may have been defective but it had produced beautiful art: 'Because the pianist maltreats his wife it doesn't follow he maltreats the piano.'[62] Gould fared even worse elsewhere. The New Orleans *Daily Picayune* found him contradictory and trite: 'As an example of inconsistency and the most astounding self-deception as to motive, we know of nothing to touch this book.'[63]

Nina Kennard, who announced her arrival in the field of Hearn studies with an article in the January 1906 number of *The Nineteenth Century and After*, was altogether a more objective figure. In the spring of 1909, she accompanied Hearn's half-sister, Mrs Atkinson, and her daughter to Japan to see for themselves the circumstances of Lafcadio's family and to find out if his wishes about Kazuo being educated abroad could be put into effect.[64] They were received with politeness and shown impeccable hospitality but the shutters went up when the subject of Kazuo's education was raised. He was, they were told, a Japanese who must conform to the dictates of his authorities or renounce his citizenship.[65]

Kennard was fascinated by what she saw as the Irish inheritance of Lafcadio's children: they all had Irish eyes and an Irish smile.[66] Kazuo had a dual personality. Sometimes he seemed not to be Japanese at all, rather an Irishman and a Hearn, resembling his cousin, Carleton Atkinson, with the '. . .same gentle manner, soft voice, and the near-sighted eyes, obliging the wearing of strong glasses'. Then a Japanese expression would fall over his face like a curtain and he would revert to being a Japanese again.[67]

On 19 September 1904, when he had had his first heart attack, Lafcadio has written a letter to Professor Ume, a former colleague at Tokyo University, asking him to care for his family after his death. When he recovered, he destroyed the letter. According to Setsu, her husband did not leave 'any will to speak of', a curious phrase which may have meant that he expressed his wishes, perhaps in written, but not legally binding, form.[68] Maybe there was another letter to Professor Ume. In 1909, Kennard went to see him but he refused to discuss the question.[69] Professor Ume had played a key role in settling affairs after Lafcadio's death. Most of Hearn's copyrights were disposed of on the basis of a proposal of his. There was apparently enough income for the family to live in fairly easy circumstances.[70] Mitchell McDonald seems to have handled the ongoing business affairs of the estate. He may well have been advising Setsu in 1912 when Harper made contact, putting in train the arrangements for the 'extra sale' of three of Lafcadio's works, *Youma*, *Chita*, and *Two Years in the French West Indies*.[71]

Ten years later Harper and Houghton Mifflin published a uniform edition of Hearn's work.[72]

After Hearn's death, his Tokyo house was divided into two parts, with Captain Fujisaki, his former Izumo student, occupying the front part. Yone Noguchi compared his role to that of the guardian god, Niwo, at a Buddhist temple. Hearn's family had the rest of the house. Noguchi left a good description of how Hearn's house was preserved. His writing table remained in the study and the books on the shelves; the household shrine burned there. His children still bade him goodnight, his favourite incense still burned and his family still wore the kimono patterns he had liked.[73]

Noguchi's account was dated August 1909, just a few months after Nina Kennard's visit to the Koizumi household. She had noted that the glass windows and American stove which Lafcadio had installed had been removed after his death because his family believed that they were unhealthy. Her bright eye spotted that his study still retained an electric lamp and bell, appliances which were part of the Western intrusion into Japan he had so regretted. Otherwise, the things he had collected, plus photos of Bisland and McDonald, had been stored in a warehouse.[74]

★ ★ ★

Had Lafcadio lived, he would probably have been pleased at the development of his children. Kazuo's education at Waseda University was financed by McDonald and Bisland[74]; he appeared in a contemporary record in the 1920s as 'an excellent gentlemanly fellow', looking European, but speaking good Japanese. Iwao, the second son, adopted the name Inagaki, 'entering the house of his mother's [adopted] parents'. He was a tall, strong, handsome man with a high nose but otherwise entirely Japanese in appearance; he was then studying electrical engineering at Kyoto University. A promising scholar, he had been a champion baseball player in high school. Kiyoshi, the third son, studied Western painting. Suzuko, the daughter, was at home with her mother in the early 1920s.[76]

Mitchell McDonald was killed at his own hotel by the great Kanto earthquake of 1923, as were most of the guests and staff. His body was taken to a US warship anchored at Yokohama and later buried at the American cemetery there.[77] After his death,

Hearn's family entrusted the business of relations with publishers to Bisland and Ellwood Hendrick.[78] Wanting to avoid 'temptation', Hendrick had given his collection of correspondence with Hearn to New York institutions. Later, after the 1923 earthquake, he wished he still had the letters to sell for the benefit of Hearn's family which had been left 'somewhat embarrassed' by the death of McDonald and obligations towards homeless neighbours, though they were not in dire need.[79]

In 1924, Hearn's library was sold to the Toyama High School. Mrs Hearn wanted it safe in a Tokyo university in the aftermath of the earthquake, but there was a haggling over costs. Then the Director of the Toyama school, a brother of a former pupil of Hearn's, made an offer which was accepted. The purchase was made on behalf of the school by a Mrs Haruko Baba, for which she was awarded the Dark Blue Ribbon Decoration by the Government.[80]

The institutionalisation of a man whose relationship with institutions had always been uneasy continued apace. In 1929, the twenty-fifth anniversary of his death, a commemorative ceremony was held at his grave in Tokyo. Representatives of the Government, the leading educational institutions, and the foreign embassies took part in a simple ceremony conducted by a Buddhist priest.[81] A few years later, the 'Lafcadio Hearn Memorial Committee' set about raising 5000 yen to build a memorial museum at Matsue. The city contributed a site near where Hearn had lived. The museum was for housing manuscripts and other memorabilia. The Committee's Executive Council included S. Ichikawa, Professor of English at Tokyo Imperial University and author of *Some New Letters and Writings of Lafcadio Hearn*, and former Hearn pupils, Ochiai, now Professor of English at the Peers' School and Otani, Professor of English at Hiroshima College.[82]

The establishment of the museum and library were reflective of a growth of appreciation of Hearn in his adopted home. As the Japanese journalist and author, K.K. Kawakami, put it in 1926:

> . . .in Japan admiration for this romantic genius as a man of letters and as a devoted, inspiring teacher seems to have become, with the passage of the years, more and more profound. While he lived, few Japanese, not even those who were admitted to the intimacy of his singularly

secluded life, realised that here was a master whose writings were destined to secure a permanent place in English literature. Today all Japanese are eager to honor the memory of the man who did more than any other writer to interpret to the Occident the beautiful, if not the best, side of their spiritual life. They are as proud that their's was the country which inspired Hearn's exquisite lines as they regret that the treatment which he received in their midst was not generous – certainly far from commensurate with his abilities and his service.[83]

With the rise of Japanese militarism and the coming of the Second World War, Hearn became something of a political football. He was blamed on one side for misleading the West with a generally 'soft' interpretation of Japan, one which portrayed the Japanese as 'cute dolls in picturesque settings'.[84] There were others, such as Warren W. Clary, writing in 1943, who bemoaned the fact that Hearn's writings, which could have enabled the US to understand Japan before Pearl Harbor, had been generally neglected. He rejected the notion that Hearn had seen only a fairyland in Japan; on the contrary, his writings contained '. . .a complete warning of what would result from the modernization of Japan. . .The trouble was that political leaders and others who might have profited from these warnings never read them'.[85] The fifteenth edition of the *Encyclopaedia Britannica* claimed that Lafcadio had '. . .deplored the rise of Japanese militarism and foresaw the struggle between Japan and the West'.[86] Lafcadio might have smiled wryly had he been able to witness the struggle for his reputation. Perhaps the tribute paid by Yone Noguchi in 1910 would have moved him most:

> We Japanese have been regenerated by his sudden magic, and baptised afresh under his transcendental rapture; in fact, the old romances which we had forgotten ages ago were brought again to quiver in the air, and the ancient beauty which we buried under the dust rose again with a strange yet new splendor. He made us shake the old robe of bias which we wore without knowing it, and gave us a sharp sensation of revival.[87]

LIST OF ABBREVIATIONS USED IN THE REFERENCES

Attempt   *Japan: an Attempt at Interpretation*, Lafcadio Hearn, The Macmillan Co., New York, 1904, Reprinted by Charles E. Tuttle Company, Inc. Rutland, Vermont and Tokyo, 1956

BB+OS   *Barbarous Barbers and Other Stories by Lafcadio Hearn*, Ichiro Nishizaki (ed), Hokuseido Press, Tokyo, 1939

Bib/PDIP   *Lafcadio Hearn, A Bibliography of his Writings*, PD and Ione Perkins, Houghton Mifflin Company, Boston and New York, 1934

Bisland   The brief biography by Elizabeth Bisland, pp 1-150, in LL+EB1

Chita   *Chita: A Memory of Last Island*, Lafcadio Hearn, Harper & Brothers, New York, 1898; reprinted by AMS Press, New York, 1969

CLH   *Concerning Lafcadio Hearn*, George M Gould, MD, with a bibliography by Laura Stedman, George W Jacobs and Company, Philadelphia, 1908

Col   Rare Books and Manuscript Library, Columbia University, New York

Cornell   Department of Rare Books, Cornell University Library, Cornell University, Ithaca, New York

E+R   *Exotics and Retrospectives*, Lafcadio Hearn, Little, Brown and Co., Boston, 1898, Republished by Charles E. Tuttle Company, Inc. of Rutland, Vermont & Tokyo, Japan, 1971

East   *Out of the East*, Lafcadio Hearn, Houghton Mifflin Company, Boston 1897, Reprinted by Charles E. Tuttle Company Inc. Rutland, Vermont, and Tokyo, 1972

Echo   *Re-Echo*, Kazuo Koizumi, The Caxton Printers, Caldwell, Idaho, 1957

ES   *Lafcadio Hearn*, Elizabeth Stevenson, The Macmillan Company, New York, 1961

F/I   *Father and I, Memories of Lafcadio Hearn*, Kazuo Koizumi, Houghton Mifflin Company, Boston and New York, 1935

Fantastics   *Fantastics and Other Fancies*, Charles Woodward Hutson (ed), Houghton Mifflin Company, Boston, 1914, Reprinted by Arno Press, 1976

Foxwell   'Reminiscences of Lafcadio Hearn', Professor Ernest Foxwell, *Japan Society Transactions and Procedures*, London, 1908, Session 17, Vol 8, 68-94

Frost/TJ   Two Unpublished Lafcadio Hearn Letters, OJ Frost (ed), *Today's Japan*, Vol 5, 1960

Fugii   'Mrs Hearn's Daily Life', S Fugii, *The Japan Magazine*, Vol II, No 8, Jan 1921

Ghostly   *In Ghostly Japan*, Lafcadio Hearn, Little, Brown, and Co, Boston, 1899;

reprinted by Charles E Tuttle Company, Inc, Rutland, Vermont, and Tokyo, 1971

Gleanings *Gleanings in Buddha Fields*, Lafcadio Hearn, Houghton Mifflin Company, Boston 1897, Reprinted by Charles E. Tuttle Company, Inc. Rutland, Vermont, and Tokyo, 1971

Glimpses *Glimpses of Unfamiliar Japan*, Lafcadio Hearn, Houghton Mifflin Company, Boston, 1894; reprinted by Charles E Tuttle Company, Inc, Rutland, Vermont, and Tokyo, 1976

GO,D Genealogical Office, Dublin

H/Ya 'Hearn at Yaidzu', included in LHIJ

H+HB *Hearn and his biographers, The record of a literary controversy*, Oscar Lewis, 1930

HM&Co Houghton Mifflin Company

HUC *A History of Ushaw College*, David Milburn, Ushaw College, Durham, 1964

Hul The Houghton Library, Harvard University, Cambridge, Massachusetts

Hunt The Huntington Library, San Marino, California

JLH1 *Japanese Letters* included in LL+EB3

JLH2 *The Japanese Letters of Lafcadio Hearn*, Elizabeth Bisland Wetmore, Houghton Mifflin Company, The Riverside Press Cambridge, Boston and New York, 1910

Kneeland 'Lafcadio Hearn's Brother', Henry Tracy Kneeland, *Atlantic Monthly*, CXXXI, (Jan 1923)

Kokoro *Kokoro*, Lafcadio Hearn, Houghton Mifflin Company, Boston 1896, Reprinted by Charles E. Tuttle Company, Inc. Rutland, Vermont, and Tokyo, 1972

Kotto *Kotto*, Lafcadio Hearn, Macmillan Co, New York, 1902; reprinted by Charles E Tuttle Company, Inc, Rutland, Vermont, and Tokyo, 1972

Kwaidan *Kwaidan*, Lafcadio Hearn, Houghton Mifflin Company, Boston 1904, Reprinted by Charles E. Tuttle Company, Inc. Rutland, Vermont, and Tokyo, 1971

LBHC *Letters from Basil Hall Chamberlain to Lafcadio Hearn*, compiled by Kazuo Koizumi, Hokuseido Press, Tokyo, 1936

Letter 'A Letter from Japan', Lafcadio Hearn, *Atlantic Monthly*, November 1904, Vol 94, No 565, 625-633

LFR *Letters from the Raven. Letters from Lafcadio Hearn to Henry Watkin*, Milton Bronner (ed), Brentano's, New York, 1907

LH/Man *Lafcadio Hearn, The Man*, Nobushige Amenomori, Atlantic Monthly, September 1905, Vol 96, No 3

LH Lafcadio Hearn

LH+EH 'Lafcadio Hearn', Ellwood Hendrick, *Bulletin of the New York Public Library*, December 1929

LHIJ *Lafcadio Hearn in Japan, With Mrs Hearn's Reminiscences*, Yone Nochuchi, Elkin Matthews, London, and Kelly and Walsh, Yokohama, 1910, reprinted by Folcroft Library Editions, 1978

LHSPA 'Lafcadio Hearn, A study of his personality and art', by George M Gould, *Putnam's Monthly*, (new series) Vol 1, 97-107 and 155-6, Oct/Nov 1906, New

York, 97–166

Lilly   The Lilly Library, Indiana University, Bloomington, Indiana

LL+EB   *The Life and Letters of Lafcadio Hearn*, Elizabeth Bisland (ed). The editions used are Vols XIII, XIV, and XV of the Koizumi Edition of the Writings of Lafcadio Hearn, in Sixteen Volumes, Houghton Mifflin Company, The Riverside Press, Cambridge, Boston and New York, 1923. The abbreviations for each volume are respectively, LL+EB1; LL+EB2; and, LL+EB3

LOM   *Letters of Ozias Midwinter*, included in LFR

LPM   'Letters of a Poet to a Musician. Lafcadio Hearn to Henry E. Krehbiel', *The Critic*, Vol 48–9, Jan–Sept 1906, 309–18

LTL   *Letters to a Lady*, included in LFR

MHR   'Reminiscences of Lafcadio Hearn', by Mrs Hearn, translated by Paul Kiyoshi Hisada and Frederick Johnson, *Atlantic Monthly*, Boston, 1918, Vol 122, 342–351

Mid   Special Collections, Middlebury College, Vermont

Milky   *The Romance of the Milky Way*, Lafcadio Hearn, Houghton Mifflin Company, Boston 1904, Reprinted by Charles E. Tuttle Company, Inc. Rutland, Vermont, and Tokyo, 1974

Mis/Mor   *'Miscellanies' by Lafcadio Hearn*, Albert Mordell (ed), London, Heinmann Ltd., 1924

Misc   *A Japanese Miscellany*, Lafcadio Hearn, Little, Brown, and Co., Boston 1901, Reprinted by Charles E. Tuttle Company, Inc. Rutland, Vermont, and Tokyo, 1967

MLBHC   *More Letters from Basil Hall Chamberlain to Lafcadio Hearn*, compiled by Kazuo Koizumi, Hokuseido Press, Tokyo, 1937

Mor   The Pierpont Morgan Library, New York. Its collection of Hearn material includes contemporary press clippings

New/Matas   'Newly Discovered Letters from Lafcadio Hearn to Dr Rudolph Matas', Ichiro Nishizaki (ed), *Ochanomizu University Studies*, March 1956

NK   *Lafcadio Hearn*, Nina H. Kennard, 1912, reprinted by the Kennikat Press, Inc./ Port Washington, N.Y., 1967

NLHL   'New Lafcadio Hearn Letters', Sanki Ichikawa (ed), *The Living Age*, 24/7/ 1926, Vol 330, no 4281, 366–72

NYPL   New York Public Library

NYPL Berg   Berg Collection, New York Public Library

Pagan   *Letters to a Pagan*, Robert Bruna Powers, (publisher and author of the Introduction), Detroit, 1933 (The letters of Lafcadio Hearn to Countess Annetta Halliday Antona)

Poetry   *On Poetry*, Lafcadio Hearn, R Tanabe, T Ochiai, and I Nishizaki (ed), Hokuseido Press, Tokyo, Third Revised Edition, 1941

Poets   *On Poets*, Lafcadio Hearn, R Tanabe, T Ochiai, and I Nishizaki (ed), Hokuseido Press, Tokyo, Third Revised Edition, 1941

Selected   *The Selected Writings of Lafcadio Hearn*, Malcolm Cowley (ed), The Citadel Press, New York, 1949,

Shadowings   *Shadowings*, Lafcadio Hearn, Little, Brown, and Co., Boston 1900, Reprinted by Charles E. Tuttle Company, Inc. Rutland, Vermont, and Tokyo, 1971

SNLW   *Some New Letters and Writings of Lafcadio Hearn*, collected and edited by Sanki Ichikawa, Tokyo, Kenkyusha Publishers, 1925

SW   *Lafcadio Hearn, Selected Writings 1872-1877*, Wm. S. Johnson (ed), Woodruff Publications, Indianapolis, 1979

Tex   Harry Ransom Humanities Research Centre, The University of Texas, Austin, Texas

Thomas   *Lafcadio Hearn*, Edward Thomas, Houghton Mifflin Company, Boston, 1912

Tinker   *Lafcadio Hearn's American Days*, Edward L Tinker, Dodd, Mead and Company, Inc., New York, 1924

TLS   Typescript letter

Tul   Howard-Tilton Memorial Library, Tulane University, New Orleans, Louisiana

TYFWI   *Two Years in the French West Indies*, Lafcadio Hearn, Harper & Brothers, New York and London, 1890, republished by Literature House, N.J., 1970

Vir   University of Virginia Library, Charlottesville, Virginia. Its collection of Hearn material includes contemporary press clippings

VMW   *Lafcadio Hearn*, Vera McWilliams, Houghton Mifflin Company, Boston, 1946, reprinted Cooper Square Publishers, Inc., New York, 1970

W+M   The Earl Gregg Swem Library, The College of William and Mary, Williamsburg, Virginia

Youma   *Youma, The Story of a West Indian Slave*, Lafcadio Hearn, Harper & Brothers, New York, 1890; reprinted by AMS Press, New York, 1969

Young   *Young Hearn*, OW Frost, Hokuseido Press, Tokyo, 1958

REFERENCES

LETTERS

All letters are by Lafcadio Hearn unless otherwise stated. The amount of information available about the letters varies widely – in some cases letters are not dated, have no address, or even addressee. I have, in most cases, given the maximum information available, in the following order: addressee, date, place from which it was written. In dating, the day comes first, followed by the month, followed by the year. In some cases, where I was reasonably sure that I could deduce the information with a fair degree of accuracy, but where it was not clear on the manuscript, I entered it in square brackets. Where institutions have provided their own reference numbers for material in their collections, it has been added in brackets at the end of the reference.

CHAPTER 1

1   'A Ghost', Lafcadio Hearn, *Harper's Magazine* Vol 80, December 1889, 116-119
2   See, for example, *Lafcadio Hearn and the Vision of Japan*, Carl Dawson, The Johns Hopkins University Press, Baltimore and London, 1992, 7

CHAPTER 2

1   Vir MSS by LH
2   Pagan 74,5
3   Vir MSS fragment by LH, 'Memories'
4   Vir MSS fragment by LH, 'Intuition'
5   Bisland 36-40; Bisland quoted the fragment, 'Intuition', the manuscript of which is in the University of Virginia collection, but, like so much else in her book, the transcription is less than perfect
6   NK 47-8
7   CLH 15
8   Article in *The Journalist* (New York), by Jesse H. Webb, 27/2/1892
9   'Lafcadio Hearn's First Embroglio with his Slanderers. Lafcadio Hearn. His Life in Cincinnati Described By a Loving Friend – Some Corrections', letter from H Watkin, *The Tribune*, Cincinnati, 19 Jan 1895
10   NK 83-4
11   JLH2, 385, to Basil Hall Chamberlain, 22/9/1894
12   'A Discovery of Early Hearn Essays', Albert Mordell, *Today's Japan*, Vol 4, No 1, Jan 1959
13   Mor Press Clippings, obituary of LH in unidentified Cincinnati newspaper,

September 1904; obituary of LH, probably by his friend, Tunison, in the *Dayton Daily Journal*, 30/9/1904 (MA 2534-5); and Bisland 45

14 Quoted in ES 37

15 SW 212-219, bibliography by OW Frost

16 *Occidental Gleanings: Sketches and Essays Now First Collected*, 2 vols, Albert Mordell (ed), Dodd, Mead, & Co, Inc, 1925; and Heinmann, London, 1925 (edition used by author), 24-35

17 Mis/Mor Vol 1, Introduction XXIX

18 BB+OS 1-9

19 'Occult Science', Cincinnati , *11/1/1874*

20 Article in *The Journalist*, Jesse H Webb, op cit

21 Mor Press Clippings, *The Post*, 17/10/1907, review of *Letters from the Raven* (MA 2534-5)

22 Mor Press Clippings, *The Literary Digest*, no date (MA 2534-5)

23 Bisland 48-9

24 The text is reproduced in Selected 233-7

25 'Golgotha', Cincinnati , *29/11/1874*

26 'Shall We Burn or Bury?' Cincinnati , *3/1874*

27 'The Dance of Death', Cincinnati , *3/5/1874*

28 'Les Chiffonniers', Cincinnati , *26/7/1874*

29 SW 152-61; Poets 777; 815, and Ken 92

30 'Protestant Magic: W.B. Yeats and the Spell of Irish History', R.F. Foster, Chatterton Lecture on Poetry, *Proceedings of the British Academy*, LXXV, 1989, 243-266

31 'A Discovery of Early Hearn Essays', Albert Mordell, op cit

32 'Celts, Carthaginians and constitutions: Anglo-Irish literary relations 1780-1820', Norman Vance, University of Sussex, *Irish Historical Studies*, March 1981

33 Poets 116

34 Poetry 253-55

35 Poetry 145

35a MSS Hearn letter to W.B. Yeats 22/6/1901, Tokyo, photocopy provided by Dr John Kelly of St John's College, Oxford; I am indebted to Dr Kelly (through the medium of Professor Roy Foster) for bringing to my attention these contacts between Hearn and W.B. Yeats, never before alluded to in print, to the best of my knowledge

35b *Confessions of an Un-Common Attorney*, Richard Hine, 1945 (information also provided by Dr Kelly)

36 Poetry 257

37 Poetry 2

38 Poetry 267

39 *Ye Giglampz*, Vol 1, No 2, 28/6/1874

40 Poetry 13

41 LPM 311, autumn 1878

42 *Stephen Hero*, James Joyce, Jonathan Cape, 245

42a MSS Hearn letter to W.B. Yeats, 22/6/1901, Tokyo, photocopy provided by Dr John Kelly of St John's College, Oxford

43 Poetry 58

44 Poetry 66

45 'Levee Life', Cincinnati *Commercial*, 17/3/1876

45a *Afro-American Folksongs*, Henry Edward Krehbiel, G. Schirmer, New York and London, 1914, 38 and 134-5

46 See, for example, 'Dolly: An Idyll of the Levee', Cincinnati *Commercial*, 27/8/1876

47 'Levee Life', Cincinnati *Commercial*, 17/3/1876

48 Obituary of LH, *Dayton Daily Journal*, 30/9/1904, op cit
49 Introduction by Elizabeth Bisland to *The Temptation of St Anthony*, Lafcadio Hearn, London, Grant Richards, 1911
50 CLH 42
51 The story of the editorial wrangling on *Ye Giglampz* between Farny and himself was spelled out in detail by LH in 'Ye Giglampz', Cincinnati , *4/10/1874*
52 *Ye Giglampz*, Vol 1, No 1, 28/6/1874; see also the book, *Ye Giglampz*, Crossroad Books, Cincinnati, 1983. Introduction, history and notes by Jon C. Hughes, Yeatman Anderson III and James R. Hunt
53 *Ye Giglampz* Vol 1, No 1, 28/6/1874
54 'Ye Giglampz', Cincinnati , *4/10/1874*
55 Also quoted in CLH 43-47
56 Article in *The Journalist* by Jesse H. Webb, op cit 55
57 Mor Press Clippings, Unidentified New York newspaper, 11/6/1908, review of books on LH by H.S. Fuller (MA 2534-5)
58 Letter by Watkin to the Cincinnati *Tribune*, 19/1/1895, op cit
59 BB+OS 10-20
60 Frost/TJ
61 See, for example, H+HB 45; and Pagan 34
62 'Some Strange Experiences', Cincinnati *Commercial*, 24/10/1875
63 Frost/TJ
64 Frost/TJ
65 CLH 49
66 Mor, MSS letter LH to Mrs Freeman, no date, Cincinnati (MA 2534-5-15)
67 Frost/TJ
68 NYPL Berg, *Cincinnati Times Star*, review of NK by Merrick Whitcomb, 15/3/[1913?]
69 Frost/TJ
70 NYPL Berg, MSS letter to Ellwood Hendrick, 21/1/1895, Kobe
71 Pagan 34
72 *The Item*, 12/12/1880
73 JLH2, 231, to Basil Hall Chamberlain, 22/1/1874
74 LFR 81-3, 24/11/1882
75 LL+EB2, 204-5, to Ellwood Hendrick, Nov 1892
76 Tinker 36
77 LL+EB2, 137-8, to Basil Hall Chamberlain, 1891, Matsue
78 Mor, MSS Hearn letter to Mrs Freeman (MA 2534-5:4)
79 Mor, MSS letter Mrs Freeman to Lafcadio Hearn (MA 2534-5:69) and MSS letter Watkin to Mrs Freeman (MA 2534-5:11)
80 Quoted in CLH 51
81 Mor, MSS letter Mrs Freeman to Lafcadio Hearn, 9/5/[1876] (MA 2534-5:51)
82 Mor, MSS letter Mrs Freeman to Lafcadio Hearn, 9/6/[1876] (MA 2534-5:34)
83 Mor, 2 MSS letters Watkin to Mrs Freeman, no date, no address (MA 2534-5:11 and MA 2534-5:18)
84 Mor, MSS letter Mrs Freeman to Watkin, 25/10/[1876] (MA 2534-5:57)
85 Mor, MSS Hearn letter to [Watkin], 1/11/[1876], (MA 2534-5:62) and MSS Hearn letter to Mrs Freeman, no date, no address (MA 2534-5:19)
86 Mor, MSS letter Mrs Freeman [to Watkin], 24/11/1876 (MA 2534-5:67); and MSS letter Mrs Freeman [to Watkin], no date, no address, (MA 2534-5:68)
87 LFR
88 Pagan 68-74 Considerable doubt has been cast on the authenticity of Hearn's authorship of some, at least, of these letters (see ' "Letters to a Pagan" Not by Hearn',

Albert Mordell, *Today's Japan*, Vol 5, No 1, 89–98). A few quotations have been used in this book, but only to illustrate points which are in line with other evidence
89   Pagan 96
90   Pagan 92
91   Pagan 93-4
92   Pagan 91, 79-84
93   Bisland 50
94   NK 99
95   LPM 310
96   ES 54
97   Young 120
98   'Pariah People', Cincinnati *Commercial*, 22/8/1875
99   'Balm of Gilead', Cincinnati *Commercial*, 3/10/1875
100 'Haceldama', Cincinnati *Commercial*, 5/9/1875
101 'Gibbeted', Cincinnati *Commercial*, 26/8/1876
102 'Lafcadio Hearn. Some Personal Recollections of Cincinnati Associations', HS Fuller, *School* (New York), 11/6/1908
103 'Gibbeted', op cit
104 Bisland 60-1
105 Letter from Watkin to the Cincinnati *Tribune*, 19/1/1895, op cit
105a 'Lafcadio Hearn in New Orleans: 1. On the Item', John S. Kendall, *Double Dealer*, Vol 111, No 17, May 1922, 234–42
106 LFR 46
107 LL+EB2, 22, to Gould, 1887, New Orleans
108 Mor MSS letter to Mrs Freeman

CHAPTER 3

1   LFR 81-3
2   'The Scenes of Cable's Romances', Lafcadio Hearn, *Century Magazine*, Nov 1883
3   LFR 64
4   LL+EB1, 162-3
4a   Quoted in 'Lafcadio Hearn in New Orleans: 1. On the Item', John S. Kendall, *Double Dealer*, Vol 111, No 17, May 1922, 234–42
5   LL+EB1, 160-1
6   LL+EB1, 155, to Krehbiel, 1877
7   Frost/TJ
8   'Notes on Forrest's Funeral', Lafcadio Hearn, Cincinnati *Commercial*, 6/11/1877
9   'A Romance of Bitterness', Lafcadio Hearn, Cincinnati *Commercial*, 18/2/1878
10   JLH1, 457, to Basil Hall Chamberlain, 7/7/1893
11   'The City of the South', Lafcadio Hearn, Cincinnati *Commercial*, 10/12/1877
12   LL+EB1, 155, to Krehbiel, 1877, New Orleans
13   LOM 185
14   LFR 47-8, Feb 1878
15   LL+EB1, 157, to Krehbiel, 1877, New Orleans
16   'Lafcadio Hearn's Cartoons' in *Creole Sketches*, Ethel Hudson, New York, 1904, XVII-XXV
17   Creole Sketches, op cit, XIX-XX
18   LL+EB1, 164-5, to Krehbiel, 1878, New Orleans
19   Creole Sketches, op cit, XIX-XX
20   *The Item*, 25/6/1878 and 9/7/1878
21   *The Item* 17/2/1880, 16/9/1880, and 18/11/1880
22   *The Item* 5/6/1881

23 'That Parlour', Lafcadio Hearn, *The Item*, 28/9/1881
24 LOM 159
25 LL+EB1, 195, to Krehbiel, 1879, New Orleans
26 Hul MSS letter to Marion Baker, envelope addressed to Marion Baker as Literary Editor of the *Times-Democrat*, 9/9/1884, Grande Isle
27 JLH1, 400, to Basil Hall Chamberlain, 17/4/1894
28 NYPL Berg, MSS letter to WD O'Connor, 7/3/1884, New Orleans
29 LL+EB2, 314-5, to Basil Hall Chamberlain, Feb 1895, Kobe
30 'Recollections of Lafcadio Hearn' by Benjamin Forman, in *The Stylus*, Houston, Texas, March 1917, and New/Matas 90
31 Bisland 65-7
32 *Times-Democrat* 6/6/1880
33 *Times-Democrat* 25/11/1885
34 *Times-Democrat* 6/4/1884
35 *Times-Democrat* 12/4/1886
36 'His Heart is Old', Lafcadio Hearn, *Times-Democrat*, 7/5/1882
37 *Times-Democrat* 13/9/1885
38 Quoted in Tinker 243-8
39 *Times-Democrat* 29/3/1885
40 'The Dawn of the Carnival', Lafcadio Hearn, *The Item*, 2/2/1880
41 'The Heart is Old', Lafcadio Hearn, *Times-Democrat*, 7/5/1882
42 NYPL MSS letter by unspecified author to CE Miller, 17/12/1886
43 LPM 313, to Krehbiel, Feb/Mar 1881
44 LL+EB1, 206-9, 1880, New Orleans
45 LH+EH
46 NYPL Berg, to Ellwood Hendrick, 21/1/1895, Kobe
47 Quoted in Tinker 175
48 LL+EB2, 13-14, to Elizabeth Bisland, 7 and 14/4/1887
49 LL+EB2, 13-14, to Elizabeth Bisland, 7 and 14/4/1887
50 Fantastics 15-17
51 Col MSS letter to Gould, 1887, New Orleans
52 Fantastics 18-21
53 Quoted in Young 196
54 NK 149 and Tinker 256
55 Hul MSS letter to Mrs Baker, 21/8/1886, New Orleans
56 Tinker 359-64
57 LH+EH
58 Bisland 72-4; 'Recollections of Lafcadio Hearn, Benjamin Forman', op cit; and New/Matas 90
59 Bisland 72-4
60 Tinker 241-2
61 'Lafcadio Hearn and Denny Corcoran', Lucille Rutland, *Double Dealer*, Feb 1922; and Tinker 200
62 Catalogue of the Lafcadio Hearn Collection of the Howard-Tilton Memorial Library, Tulane University, New Orleans
63 Tinker 214, 216
64 'Lafcadio Hearn and Denny Corcoran', Lucille Rutland, op cit

CHAPTER 4

1 Bib/PDIP 1
2 Hul MSS letter to HM&Co, New Orleans, received 27/5/1885
3 LL+EB1, 243, to Rev Wayland Ball, 1882, New Orleans

4   LL+EB1, 262, to WD O'Connor, March 1883, New Orleans
5   LL+EB2, 69, to Gould, April 1889, St Pierre, Martinique
6   LL+EB1, 237, to Jerome A Hart, New Orleans
7   'One of Cleopatra's Nights' is available to the modern reader in paperback in *The Dedalus Book of Femmes Fatales*, edited by Brian Stableford, Dedalus, Cambs, England, 1992, 33-70
8   The review is quoted in Bisland 75-6
9   Thomas 43-4
10 Mor MSS Hearn letter to Emil Gullman, 15/11/1900, Tokyo (MA 2532)
11 *Walt Whitman, A Life*, Justin Kaplan, New York, 1980, 255-6
12 LL+EB3, 68, to Mitchell McDonald, Feb 1899, Tokyo
13 NYPL MSS Hearn letter to WD O'Connor, 9/8/1883
14 NYPL MSS Hearn letter to WD O'Connor, 5/2/1884, New Orleans
15 See, for example, NYPL MSS Hearn letter to WD O'Connor, 7/3/1884, New Orleans
16 LL+EB1, 232, to Krehbiel, 1882, New Orleans
17 LL+EB1, 318, to Krehbiel, May 1884, New Orleans
18 LL+EB1, 255-6, to Rev Ball, 1883, New Orleans
19 LL+EB1, 370-1, to Krehbiel, 1886, New Orleans
20 LHSPA 162
21 LL+EB1, 376, to Krehbiel, 1886, New Orleans
22 LL+EB1, 287, to Krehbiel, Dec 1883, New Orleans
23 Fantastics 13-14
24 Fantastics 180-1
25 'Les Coulisses', Lafcadio Hearn, *The Item*, 6/12/1879
26 'Spring Phantoms', Lafcadio Hearn, *The Item*, 21/4/1881
27 LL+EB1, 216-7, to Krehbiel, 1881, New Orleans
28 LL+EB1, 211, to Krehbiel, 1880, New Orleans
29 LL+EB1, 217, to Krehbiel, New Orleans
30 LL+EB1, 240, Quoted by LH in letter to Jerome A Hart, Jan 1883
31 Hunt MSS Hearn letter to Krehbiel, 18/9/1883
32 Hul MSS Hearn letter to HM&Co, received 3/1/1883, New Orleans
33 Hunt MSS Hearn letter to Krehbiel, 18/9/1883, New Orleans
34 NYPL Berg MSS Hearn letter to WD O'Connor, 7/3/1884
35 Hunt MSS Hearn letter to Krehbiel, no date, no address
36 Mor, MSS Hearn letter to Howard Malcolm Ticknor, 25/6/1884 (MA 2533)
37 LL+EB1, 271, to Krehbiel, Sept 1883, New Orleans
38 Hunt MSS Hearn letter to Krehbiel, no date, no address
39 LL+EB1, 318, to Krehbiel, May 1884, New Orleans
40 LL+EB1, 314-5, to Krehbiel, March 1884, New Orleans
41 Mor letter from James R Osgood & Co to Lafcadio Hearn, 2/12/1884 (MA 2533)
42 Mor, secretarial copy of a letter from RH Stoddard to Lafcadio Hearn, Mattapoisett, Mass, 22/2/1885
43 LFR 69
44 *The Item* 17/4/1880
45 'A Kiss Fantastical', Lafcadio Hearn, *The Item*, 8/6/1881
46 'The Tale of a Fan', Lafcadio Hearn, *The Item*, 1/7/1881
47 Hul MSS Hearn letter to HM&Co, received 19/5/1886, New Orleans
48 LL+EB2, 31, to Krehbiel, 1887, New Orleans
49 LL+EB3, 100, to Mitchell McDonald, March 1898, Tokyo
50 LTL 133, 1876
51 LPM 310, 1878

52   LL+EB1, 285, to Krehbiel, 1883, New Orleans
53   'The East at New Orleans', Lafcadio Hearn, *Harper's Weekly*, 31/5/1885
54   LOM 196, 31/1/1885
55   LL+EB2, 29-32, to Krehbiel, 1887, New Orleans
56   'Metempsychosis', Lafcadio Hearn, *The Item*, 7/9/1880
57   LL+EB1, 285-6, to O'Connor, 1883, New Orleans
58   *Times-Democrat*, December 1886
59   LL+EB1, 305-6, to Krehbiel, March 1884, New Orleans
60   NYPL MSS Hearn letter to O'Connor, 25/4/1886, New Orleans
61   LL+EB1, 371, to Krehbiel, 1886, New Orleans
62   LL+EB2, 15, to Elizabeth Bisland, 7+14/4/1887
63   W+M 2 MSS Hearn letter to Coleman, 1887 and 4/3/1887
64   W+M MSS Hearn letter to Coleman, 1886/7, New Orleans
65   'The Recent Movement in Southern Literature', Charles W Coleman, *Harper's Magazine*, Vol 74, No 444, May 1887, 837-55
66   W+M MSS Hearn letter to Coleman, [1886(?)], New Orleans
67   LL+EB1, 188-9, to Krehbiel, 1879, New Orleans
68   LL+EB1, 346, to O'Connor, July 1885, New Orleans
69   LFR 67
70   LL+EB1, 210, to Krehbiel, 1880, New Orleans
71   LL+EB1, 328, to Krehbiel, Oct 1884, New Orleans
72   NYPL MSS Hearn letter to F Page Wood, 1884, Grande Isle
73   'Recollections of Lafcadio Hearn', Forman, op cit
74   'Lafcadio Hearn and Denny Corcoran', Lucile Rutland, op cit
75   Hul MSS Hearn letters to Mrs Courtney, 5/8/1886 and 29/7/1886
76   Hul MSS Hearn letter to Marion Baker, no date, Grande Isle, and Hul series to Mrs Courtney
77   See, for example, 'The Jew Upon the Stage', Lafcadio Hearn, *Times-Democrat*, 18/4/1886; 'Note on a Hebrew Funeral', Lafcadio Hearn, *Times-Democrat*, 16/10/1884; 'A Jew', Lafcadio Hearn, *The Item*, 29/6/1881; 'A Peep Between the Leaves of the Talmud', Lafcadio Hearn, *Times-Democrat*, 9/7/1882; 'Government Policy and the Jews', Lafcadio Hearn, *The Item*, 30/8/1881; 'Jewish Emigrants for Louisiana', Lafcadio Hearn, *The Item*, 20/9/1881; 'The Hebrews of Cincinnati', Lafcadio Hearn,Cincinnati , 9/11/1873; 'The Hebrew College', Lafcadio Hearn, Cincinnati Commercial, 19/9/1875; 'China and the Western World', Lafcadio Hearn, *Atlantic Monthly*, April 1896
78   NYPL Berg MSS Hearn letter to WD O'Connor, 8/3/1885, New Orleans; also in LL+EB1, 285, but dated 1883
79   NYPL Berg MSS Hearn letter to WD O'Connor, 13/7/1885, New Orleans
80   W+M MSS Hearn letter to Coleman, 3/5/1887, New Orleans
81   LL+EB2, 51-2, to Gould, June 1888, Grande Isle
82   Bisland 77-8
83   Bisland 91
84   W+M MSS Hearn letter to Coleman, [1886/7(?)], New Orleans
85   Col MSS Hearn letter to Joseph Harper, April [1890], Yokohama
86   W+M MSS Hearn letter to Coleman, 4/3/1887, New Orleans
87   W+M MSS Hearn letter to Coleman, 27/6/1887, New York
88   'New Letters from the French West Indies', Ichiro Nishizaki, reprinted from *Ochanomizu University Studies in Arts and Culture*, Vol 12, Tokyo, June 1959
89   Hul incomplete MSS Hearn letter, no addressee [Mrs Courtney?], no date, no address
90   LPM 315
91   Tinker 273

92   NYPL MSS Hearn letter to Elizabeth Bisland, 1887, New York

CHAPTER 5

1   W+M MSS Hearn letter to Coleman, New York, c/o Krehbiel, 27/6/1887
2   LL+EB2, to Gould, Grande Anse, Martinique, June 1888
3   TYFWI 5-6
4   TYFWI 15
5   TYFWI 19
6   TYFWI 20
7   TYFWI 56
8   TYFWI 57
9   TYFWI 86-7
10   NYPL, Berg, MSS Hearn letter to Elizabeth Bisland, Georgetown, Demerara, 16/7/1887
11   Quoted in CLH, 94-5
12   NYPL Berg, MSS Hearn letter to Captain Hubbard, 11/10/1887, off Martinique
13   Hunt MSS Hearn letter to Annie Alden, St Pierre, Martinique, no date
14   TYFWI 5
15   Hunt MSS Hearn letter to Annie Alden, no date, no address
16   Hunt MSS Hearn letter to Annie Alden, no date, no address
17   Hunt MSS Hearn letter to Alden, no date, no address
18   Hunt MSS Hearn letter to Annie Alden, no date, St Pierre, Martinique,
19   Hunt MSS Hearn letter to Annie Alden, no date, St Pierre, Martinique
20   TYFWI 422,3
21   Hunt MSS Hearn letter to Alden, 8/2/1888, St Pierre, Martinique
22   Hunt MSS Hearn letter to Alden, no date, no address
23   Hunt MSS Hearn letter to Alden, 8/2/1888, St Pierre, Martinique
24   Ibid
25   Hunt MSS Hearn letter to Alden, 26/5/1888, St Pierre, Martinique
26   Quoted in CLH, LH to Matas, 30/7/[1888] (the letter is incorrectly dated 1887 by Gould), St Pierre, Martinique
27   LL+EB2, 52, to Gould, June 1888, Grand Anse, Martinique
28   Col, contract for TYFWI, 9/10/1889, New York; and Bib/PDIP
29   Hunt MSS Hearn letter to Alden, 17/7/1888, St Pierre, Martinique
30   Hunt MSS Hearn letter to Alden, 8/8/1888, St Pierre, Martinique
31   Hunt MSS Hearn letter to Alden, 5/9/1888, St Pierre, Martinique
32   Hunt MSS Hearn letter to Alden, 1888, West Indies
33   LL+EB2, 59, to Gould, St Pierre, Martinique
34   Hunt MSS Hearn letter to Alden, no date, no address
35   Hunt MSS Hearn letter to Alden, West Indies, [1888?]
36   TYFWI 218-9
37   TYFWI 83
38   TYFWI 97-8
39   EG, TYFWI 104, 248-9, 253
40   TYFWI 49
41   TYFWI 409-410
42   TYFWI 177
43   TYFWI 157
44   TYFWI 182
45   TYFWI 367-8
46   TYFWI 266
47   TYFWI 257

48   TYFWI 256
49   TYFWI 343-4
50   TYFWI 184-201
51   TYFWI 369
52   TYFWI 316, 358
53   TYFWI 103
54   TYFWI 180
55   TYFWI 193
56   *The New York Times*, 1/9/1890, quoted in CLH 231
57   Quoted in contemporary publicity material issued by Harper & Brothers, New York
58   Quoted in contemporary publicity material issued by Harper & Brothers, New York
59   Thomas 53-55
60   LL+EB3, to Mitchell McDonald, Jan 1898, Tokyo
61   Col contract for *Youma*, 24/2/1890, New York
62   Youma 130-1
63   Chita 142-3
64   TYFWI 431-4
65   TYFWI 415-6
66   LL+EB2, 17-18 to Gould, April 1887, New Orleans
67   *Times-Democrat* 8/5/1887, reference by LH was to a paper contributed by Gould and a Dr L Webster to the *American Journal of Ophthalmology*
68   LL+EB2, 20-1, to Gould, 1887, New Orleans
69   LL+EB2, 22, to Gould, New Orleans
70   LL+EB2, 20, to Gould, 1887, New Orleans
71   Hunt MSS Hearn letter to Alden, no date, no address
72   LL+EB2, 53, to Gould, August 1888, St Pierre, Martinique
73   LL+EB2, 54-5, 62, to Gould, August 1888, St Pierre, Martinique
74   LL+EB2, 56
75   LL+EB1, 161, to Basil Hall Chamberlain, August 1891, Matsue
76   Col MSS Hearn letter to Gould, 1887, New Orleans
77   LL+EB2, 69, to Gould, April 1889, St Pierre, Martinique
78   *The New York Times*, 14/5/1908, letter from Ellwood Hendrick.
79   *The New York Times*, 16/5/1908, letter from Gould, allegedly quoting from a letter to him from Redway
80   LHSPA
81   LL+EB2, 75-6
82   Hunt MSS Hearn letter to Alden, no date, Philadelphia
83   Hunt MSS Hearn letter to Alden 25/6/1889, Philadelphia
84   Hunt MSS Hearn letter to Alden, no date, Philadelphia
85   Hunt MSS Hearn letter to Alden, no date, Philadelphia
86   Hunt MSS Hearn letter to Alden, 3/7/1889, Philadelphia
87   Hunt MSS Hearn letter to Alden, no date, Philadelphia
88   LHSPA 163
89   Col, Fragment, Probably to Gould, no date, no address
90   Hunt MSS Hearn letter to Alden, no date, no address [probably Philadelphia]
91   LL+EB2, 84-5, to Gould
92   LL+EB2, 94-5, 1889, to Gould
93   Quoted in CLH 24; also in LL+EB2, 94-5
94   LL+EB2, 91-3, 1889, to Gould
95   *The New York Times*, 14/5/1908, letter from Elwood Hendrick

96   *The New York Times*, 16/5/1908, letter from Gould
97   ibid
98   LHSPA
99   LHSPA
100 Col 2 MSS Hearn letters to Gould, 21/10/1889 and Oct/Nov 1889, US Hotel, New York
101 Col MSS Hearn letter to Mrs Harriet F Gould, Nov 1889, New York
102 Col MSS Hearn letter to Gould, no date, no address
103 Col MSS Hearn letter to Gould, Nov 1889 (not dated by LH), New York
104 Col MSS Hearn letter to Gould, 1889, [New York (?)]
105 LH+EH
106 Col MSS Hearn letter to Gould, 1889, US Hotel, New York
107 ibid
108 Col MSS Hearn letter to Gould, Oct/Nov 1889, New York
109 Hunt MSS Hearn letter to Alden, no date, Philadelphia
110 Quoted in CLH 226
111 Col MSS Hearn letter to Gould, 1889
112 Previous 3 paras based on LH+EH
113 NYPL MSS Hearn letter to the Editors of *Century* Magazine
114 LL+EB3, 79, to Mitchell McDonald, Jan 1889, Tokyo
115 Fales, MSS Hearn letter to Harper & Bros, 7/1/1890
116 Col, Contract for *Youma*, 24/2/1890
117 See, for example, review in *The New York Times*, 1/9/1890 and reviews in the New York *Herald*, Boston *Beacon*, The *Sun* (New York), and the Chicago *News*, quoted in contemporary Harper & Brothers, New York, publicity material
118 LL+EB2, 79, to Elizabeth Bisland, Philadelphia 1889
119 NYPL, MSS Hearn letter to Elizabeth Bisland, no date, Philadelphia
120 Ibid
121 *The New York Times*, 16/5/1908, letter from Gould
122 NYPL MSS Hearn letter to Elizabeth Bisland, 1889; see also LL+EB2, 96
123 Col MSS Hearn letter to Gould, no date, New York
124 Col MSS Hearn letter to Gould, Nov 1889, New York
125 LL+EB2, 101, to [Elizabeth Bisland], 7/8 March 1990
126 VMW 267
127 Mor, MSS Hearn letter to Mrs Rollins, 17/12/1895, Kobe (MA 2533)
128 ES 198
129 Pagan 89
130 H+HB 8

CHAPTER 6

1   LFR 94
2   Glimpses 7
3   Glimpses 1
4   JLH2, 311, to Basil Hall Chamberlain, 16/5/1894
5   Glimpses 1
6   JLH2, 3-4, to Basil Hall Chamberlain, 4/4/1890, Yokohama
7   Glimpses 10
8   Glimpses 28
9   Vir MSS Hearn letter to Ernest Fenollosa, no date, no address
10 H+HB 10-11
11 LL+EB2, 103
12 Glimpses 15

13   East 314
14   Glimpses 10
15   H+HB 10, to Tunison, Yokohama
16   Glimpses 20
17   JLH2, 313, to Basil Hall Chamberlain, no date but in mid 1894 sequence
18   Glimpses 2
19   East 325
20   *Kimono*, John Paris (Frank Ashton-Gwatkin), Penguin, 1947 edition, 32-3 and 97-8,
21   Pagan 85
22   LL+EB2, 104
23   H+HB 9-10
24   Attempt 481-6
25   Pagan 84-5
26   LL+EB2, 102-3. That opinion never changed.
27   Glimpses 2-3
28   Glimpses 21-2
29   Glimpses 11
30   Glimpses 7-8
31   Glimpses 8
32   JLH2, 6, to Basil Hall Chamberlain, 9/4/1890, Tokyo
33   'A Japanese Miscellany, My Shortlived Connection with Hearn', in *Stray Leaves and Sketches*, Edward B Clarke, Kenkyusha, Tokyo, 1936, 1-14
34   NYPL Berg, MSS Hearn letter to EH
35   JLH2, 5, to Basil Hall Chamberlain, 6/4/1890, Yokohama
36   Tex MSS Hearn letter to Patten, 19/2/1887, New Orleans
37   Tex MSS Hearn letter to Patten, no date, no address
38   Tex MSS Hearn letter to Patten, no date, no address
39   Tex MSS letter H Alden to Patten, 21/12/1889, New York
40   Tex MSS Hearn letter to Patten, 3/2/1890, New York
41   VMW 261
42   Tex MSS Hearn letter to Patten, no date, no address
43   Tex MSS Hearn letter to Alden, 12/2/1890, New York
44   VMW 257
45   Vir MSS Autobiographical Notes written in Japan by Lafcadio Hearn, no date, no address
46   Tex MSS Hearn letter to Patten, no date, no address
47   H+HB 9
48   Col MSS Hearn letter to Henry Harper, April (?) 1890, Yohohama
49   Mor, Harper Collection, MSS Hearn letter to Harper & Bros, no date, no address (MA 1950)
50   Mor, Harper Collection, MSS Hearn letter to Messrs Harper & Bros, Publishers, 5/5/1890, Yohohama (MA 1950)
51   Tex 2 MSS letters Weldon to Patten, 7/5/1890 and 9/5/1890, Yokohama
52   The Library of Congress, Washington, DC, letterbook copy of a letter Alden to Lafcadio Hearn, 3/6/1890, New York
53   VMW 273
54   Hunt MSS Hearn letter to Harper & Bros
55   Mor, Harper Collection, Harper's memo of sales, 5/3/1890 -19/9/1890 (MA 1950)
56   NYPL MSS letter JS Alden to HM Alden, 4/7/1890, NY
57   NYPL MSS letter Gould to Alden, 30/3/1890, Philadelphia

57a Col MSS Hearn letter to Alden, no date, no address
58   Col MSS Hearn letter to Gould, 30/4/1890
59   Col MSS Hearn letter to Gould, no date, no address
60   Col MSS Hearn letter to Gould, no date, no address
61   *The New York Times*, 16/5/1908, letter from Gould
62   Col MSS Hearn letter to Gould, no date, no address
63   *The New York Times*, 14/5/1908, letter from Ellwood Hendrick
64   *The New York Times*, 16/5/1908, letter from Gould
65   Letter of April 1893, Gould to Hearn, quoted in Hendrick's letter to *The New York Times*, 14/5/1890
66   JLH2, 3, to Basil Hall Chamberlain, 4/4/1890, Yokohama
67   JLH2, 4, to Basil Hall Chamberlain, 4/4/1890, Yokohama
68   *An Ape of the Gods. The Art and Thought of Lafcadio Hearn*, Beong-cheon Yu, Wayne State University Press, Detroit, 1964, appendix, 292

CHAPTER 7

1   Pagan 89-90, December 1890, Matsue
2   Glimpses 162-3
3   Glimpses 447-8
4   Glimpses 462-3
5   JLH2, 344, to Basil Hall Chamberlain, 15/7/1894, Yokohama
6   LL+EB1, 114
7   LL+EB2, 116-7, to Basil Hall Chamberlain, Nov 1890
8   LHIJ 74-5, 'Mrs Hearn's Reminiscences'
9   Mor MSS Hearn letter to Mrs Rollins, 5/12/1890, Matsue (MA 2533)
10   Tex MSS Hearn letter to Basil Hall Chamberlain, 26/12/1893
11   NK 359
12   LHIJ 32
13   LH+EH
14   F/I 165
15   NLHL 372
16   LL+EB1, 116-7
17   NK 278
18   F/I 133
19   Foxwell 87
20   LHIJ Preface VI
21   LL+EB2, 146
22   Glimpses 383
23   LL+EB2, 148
24   LL+EB2, 124-5, to Basil Hall Chamberlain, Jan 1891, Matsue
25   LL+EB2, 125-6, to Basil Hall Chamberlain, Jan 1891, Matsue
26   LL+EB2, 142-3, to Basil Hall Chamberlain, August 1891, Matsue
27   Pagan, 95, no date, Matsue
28   LL+EB2, 163-5, to Hendrick, August 1891, Matsue
29   Pagan 88-92
30   LL+EB2, 133-4, to Basil Hall Chamberlain, June 1891, Matsue
31   Glimpses 668-74
32   Mor to Mrs Rollins, 5/12/1890, Matsue (MA 2533)
33   Glimpses 575-6
34   Glimpses 620
35   Glimpses 657-9
36   Glimpses 683

37 Glimpses 676
38 Glimpses 471
39 Glimpses 121-8
40 LL+EB2, 109-110, to Basil Hall Chamberlain, Sept 1890, Matsue
41 Glimpses 208-9
42 Glimpses 627-8
43 Glimpses 650
44 JLH1, 363-5, to Basil Hall Chamberlain, 23/1/1893
45 JLH1, 381, to Basil Hall Chamberlain, 6/2/1893
46 Hul MSS Hearn letter to Scudder, 11/8/1891, Matsue
47 Mid MSS Hearn letter to Scudder, received 3/9/1891
48 Mid MSS Hearn letter to Scudder, 24/9/1891, Matsue
49 Mid MSS Hearn letter to Scudder, 5/8/[1893?]
50 Mid MSS Hearn letter to Scudder, 14/11/1891, Kumamoto
51 LBHC 120-1
52 LBHC 135
52a 'On the Manners and Customs of the Loochooans', Basil Hall Chamberlain,
Transactions of the Asiatic Society of Japan, Vol XXI, 1893
53 LL+EB2, 111, to Basil Hall Chamberlain, Sept 1890
54 LL+EB2, 115, to Basil Hall Chamberlain, Nov 1890
55 *Things Japanese*, Basil Hall Chamberlain, Fifth Revised Edition, London, J
Murray; Yokohama, Kelly and Walsh, Ltd, 1905; reprinted in paperback as *Japanese
Things*, by Charles E Tuttle, Co., Rutland, Vermont and Tokyo, 1971, 339
56 *A Handbook for Travellers in Japan*, Third Edition, Basil Hall Chamberlain and WB
Mason, John Murray, London and Kelly and Walsh, Ltd, Yokohama, 1891
57 MLBHC 30
58 Hul MSS Hearn letter to Page Baker, 19/10/1891
59 Glimpses 685
60 Glimpses 686-7
61 LHIJ 122-4

CHAPTER 8

1   LL+EB2, 174-5, to Otani, Nov 1891, Kumamoto
2   Hul MSS Hearn letter to Scudder, 18/12/1891
3   LL+EB2, 205-6, to Ellwood Hendrick, Nov 1892
4   East 157-242
5   LL+EB2, 186-7, to Ellwood Hendrick, Jan 1892, Kumamoto
6   F/I 22
7   LL+EB2, 178, to Nishida, Dec 1891, Kumamoto
8   JLH1, 360-1, to Basil Hall Chamberlain, 19/1/1893
9   JLH1, 367-8, to Basil Hall Chamberlain, 4/2/1893
10 LL+EB2, 212, to Nishida, Jan 1893, Kumamoto
11 LHIJ 63-4
12 LHIJ 24
13 JLH2, 261, to Basil Hall Chamberlain, 4/3/1894
14 Glimpses 575
15 Glimpses 618
16 Col MSS Hearn letter to Basil Hall Chamberlain, 28/1/1893
17 JLH1, 356, to Basil Hall Chamberlain, 17/1/1893
18 JLH1, 464, to Basil Hall Chamberlain, 16/7/1893
19 JLH1, 345, to Basil Hall Chamberlain, 12/12/1892, Kumamoto
20 JLH1, 348, to Basil Hall Chamberlain, 21/12/1892, Kumamoto

21 SNLW 61
22 JLH1, 358-9, to Basil Hall Chamberlain, 17/1/1893
23 JLH2, 433-4, to Mason, 1/11/1892
24 JLH1, 411-2, to Basil Hall Chamberlain, 19/4/1893
25 Col MSS Hearn letter to Basil Hall Chamberlain, 5/2/1893
26 Col MSS Hearn letter to Basil Hall Chamberlain, 23/1/1893
27 'Lafcadio Hearn in his Lecture Room', LHIJ, 125-145
28 *The New York Times*, 14/5/1908, letter from Ellwood Hendrick
29 JLH1,453, to Basil Hall Chamberlain, 27/6/1893
30 LL+EB2, 224, to Ellwood Hendrick, April 1893, Kumamoto
31 Col MSS Hearn letter to Basil Hall Chamberlain, 9/6/1893
32 LL+EB2, 225, to Ellwood Hendrick, April 1893, Kumamoto
33 Col MSS Hearn letter to Basil Hall Chamberlain, 4/2/1893
34 LBHC 16
35 MLBHC 67-9
36 JLH1, 430, to Basil Hall Chamberlain, 5/5/1893
37 The story of LH's relationship with his brother is told in 'Lafcadio Hearn's Brother', by Henry Tracy Kneeland, *Atlantic Monthly*, CXXX, Jan 1923. Unfortunately, the letters between the two have been poorly transcribed by Kneeland; the quotations used are on the basis of the manuscript originals in the Houghton Library, Harvard (HUL)
38 Hul MSS Hearn letter to James D Hearn, Philadelphia
39 Hul MSS Hearn letter to James D Hearn, New York
40 Hul MSS Hearn letter to James D Hearn, 16/1/1890, New York
41 ibid
42 NK 101
43 Hul MSS Hearn letter to James D Hearn
44 Hul MSS Hearn letter to James Hearn, 28/2/1892, Kumamoto
45 ibid
46 F/I 143
47 NK 232
48 *A History of Modern Japan*, Richard Storry, London, 1960, 70
49 NK 234
50 NK 235
51 JLH1, 421, to Basil Hall Chamberlain, 12/5/1893
52 Mid MSS Hearn letter to Scudder, 12/8/1893, Kumamoto
53 East 20-1
54 JLH2, 360-1, to Basil Hall Chamberlain, 24/7/1894
55 JLH2, 349-50, to Basil Hall Chamberlain, 20/7/1894, Tokyo
56 LL+EB2, 258-9, to Ellwood Hendrick, Nov 1893, Kumamoto
57 LL+EB2, 266-8, to Nishida, Nov 1893
58 SNLW 101-2
59 LL+EB2, 175-6, to Otani, Nov 1891, Kumamoto
60 East 71-2
61 Tex MSS Hearn letter to Ochiai, 27/3/1894, Kumamoto
62 NYPL MSS Hearn letter to WD O'Connor
63 JLH1, 400, to Basil Hall Chamberlain, 17/4/1893
64 JLH1, 448, to Basil Hall Chamberlain, 19/6/1893
65 LL+EB2, 228, to Ellwood Hendrick, April 1893, Kumamoto
66 MLBHC 163
67 JLH2, 259, to Basil Hall Chamberlain, 25/2/1894
68 East 188-193

69   East 202
70   East 208-9
71   East 325-6
72   East 148
73   Mid MSS Hearn letter to Scudder, 14/11/1893
74   NK 285
75   Mid MSS Hearn letter to Scudder, 14/11/1893
76   JLH2, 373, to Basil Hall Chamberlain
77   East 333-4
78   JLH2, 341, to Basil Hall Chamberlain, 15/7/1894, Yokohama
79   JLH2, 346, to Basil Hall Chamberlain, 20/7/1894, Tokyo
80 JLH2, 356-7, to Basil Hall Chamberlain, 22/7/1894
81   MLBHC 137
82   JLH2, 342, to Basil Hall Chamberlain, 17/7/1894, Tokyo
83   JLH2, 299, to Basil Hall Chamberlain, 7/4/1894
84   JLH2, 327-8, to Basil Hall Chamberlain
85   JLH2, 309-10, to Basil Hall Chamberlain, 16/5/1894
86   JLH1, 417, to Basil Hall Chamberlain, 2/5/1893
87   JLH2, 227, to Basil Hall Chamberlain
88   LL+EB2,236, to Ellwood Hendrick, July 1893, Kumamoto
89   SNLW 102
90   Lilly MSS Hearn letter to Basil Hall Chamberlain, 8/6/1894, Kumamoto
91   ibid
92   Col MSS Hearn letter to Basil Hall Chamberlain, 10/6/1894
93   NLHL 369
94   NLHL 368
95   SNLW 152
96   NLHL 368-9
97   SNLW 136-7
98   LL+EB2, 190, to Ellwood Hendrick, April 1892, Kumamoto
99   JLH2, 368, to Basil Hall Chamberlain, 12/8/1894
100 JLH2, 379, to Basil Hall Chamberlain, 11/9/1894
101 LL+EB2, 285-6, to Page Baker, 1894, Kumamoto
102 LFR 100

CHAPTER 9

1   NK 270
2   JLH2, 395, to Basil Hall Chamberlain, received 14/10/1894
3   NK 195
4   LL+EB2, 295-6, to Ellwood Hendrick, Sept 1894, Matsue
5   Editorials from the Kobe Chronicle, Makato Sangu (ed), Tokyo, 1960, 27-8
6   LL+EB2, 295-6, to Ellwood Hendrick, Sept 1894, Matsue
7   A Concise History of East Asia, CP FitzGerald, Pelican, London, 1974, 220
8   LL+EB2, 312, to Basil Hall Chamberlain, Jan 1895, Kobe
9   LBHC 112-4, Basil Hall Chamberlain to Lafcadio Hearn, 8/9/1894, Miyanoshita
10   JLH2, 391, to Basil Hall Chamberlain, 9/10/1894
11   JLH2, 391-4, to Basil Hall Chamberlain, received 14/10/1894, Kobe
12   Atlantic Monthly, June 1895, Vol 75,6, 830-35
13   Mid MSS Hearn letter to Scudder, no date, no address
14   LL+EB2, 336-7, to Basil Hall Chamberlain, March 1895, Kobe
15   LL+EB2, 360, to Basil Hall Chamberlain, April 1895
16   LL+EB2, 379, to Page Baker, July 1895, Kobe

17 NK 277
18 SNLW 132-3
19 Hul MSS Hearn letter to Page Baker, 20/4/1895, Kobe
20 Mid MSS Hearn letter to Scudder, 1/8/1895, Kobe
21 NK 279 + F/I 164
22 LBHC 118, 9/2 1895, Atami
23 LL+EB2, 314, to Basil Hall Chamberlain, Feb 1895, Kobe
24 NLHL 369
25 Mid MSS Hearn letter to Scudder, 7/7/1895
26 Mid MSS Hearn letter to Scudder, 28/8/1895, Kobe
27 Mid MSS Hearn letter to Scudder, 5/2/1895, Kobe
28 See the reviews of *Out of the East* in *The Academy* and *The Spectator*, quoted in CLH 280 and 282, and the New York *Daily Tribune* of 31/3/1895, as well as LH himself on the subject in LL+EB2, 370, to Basil Hall Chamberlain, May 1895, Kobe
29 Kokoro 65
30 Kokoro 8-40
31 Kokoro 54-5
32 Kokoro 145
33 Kokoro 138
34 Kokoro 189
35 Kokoro 226
36 Kokoro 150
37 Gleanings 97-123
38 LL+EB3, 61-2, to Nishida, 1897, Tokyo
39 Gleanings 146-7
40 Gleanings 152
41 Gleanings 5-6
42 NYPL Berg MSS Hearn letter to Ellwood Hendrick, 12/11/1895, Kobe
43 LH+EH
44 Hul MSS Hearn letter to Page Baker, 6/7/1895, Kobe
45 MLBHC 208
46 NYPL Berg, to Ellwood Hendrick, no date, no address; probably early 1896, from Kobe
47 LL+EB2, 385, to Ellwood Hendrick, Sept 1895, Kobe
48 MLBHC 174-5
49 MLBHC 183-5, letter from Toyoma to Lafcadio Hearn, 13/12/1895
50 Glimpses 237-41
51 NK 290-1

CHAPTER 10

1   LL+EB3, 13, 41-2, to Ellwood Hendrick, Jan and Oct 1896, Tokyo
2   Pagan 111
3   Quoted in Bisland 52-3
4   NK 144-5
5   Foxwell 88
6   LL+EB3, 117, to Fenollosa, May 1898, Tokyo
7   NK 142
8   Foxwell 86-7
9   LL+EB3, 94-5, to Mitchell McDonald, Feb 1898, Tokyo
10 LL+EB3, 134, to Ellwood Hendrick, 1898, Tokyo
11 Col MSS document signed by LH at Yokohama 12/3/1898, Power of Attorney to McDonald

12   Foxwell 85
12a Quoted in *Fenellosa: The Far East and American Culture*, Lawrence W Chisolm, Yale
University Press, New Haven and London, 1965
13   LL+EB3, 116, to Ernest Fenollosa, May 1898, Tokyo
14   LL+EB3, 148, to Ernest Fenollosa, Dec 1898, Tokyo
15   Poets V-VI
16   Foxwell 84
17   LL+EB3, 42-3, to Ellwood Hendrick, Oct 1896, Tokyo
18   NLHL 370
19   LHIJ 107-8
20   LL+EB3, 39, to Ellwood Hendrick, Oct 1896
21   Pagan 107
22   F/I 55-9
23   JLH2, 354-5, to Basil Hall Chamberlain, 21/7/1894, Tokyo
24   Foxwell 74
25   Mor MSS Hearn letter to JB Stetson Co Philadelphia, 1/1/1897 (MA 2532)
26   LL+EB3, 64-8, to Ellwood Hendrick, August 1897, Tokyo
27   NYPL Berg, MSS Hearn letter to Ellwood Hendrick, 29/7/1897
28   F/I 90
29   LHIJ 81-3
30   LHIJ 67
31   LHIJ 89-90
32   E+R 3-39
33   TYFWI 293

CHAPTER 11

1   LL+EB2, 343, to Basil Hall Chamberlain, April 1895, Kobe
2   JLH2, 370-1, to Basil Hall Chamberlain, 21/8/1894
3   LL+EB3, 247, to Elizabeth Bisland, Dec 1903, Tokyo
4   Poets 152
5   LL+EB3, 132-3, to Ellwood Hendrick, 1898, Tokyo
6   NK 45
7   Kneeland
8   PRO London, *Army List*, 1843
9   PRO London, WO 76/105, *Succession of Surgeons and Assistant Surgeons in the
Notts and Derby Regiment*
10   Kneeland
11   NK 20-1
11a *Lafcadio Hearn (Koizumi Yakumo): His Life, Work and Irish Background*, Sean G Ronan
and Toki Koizumi, Ireland-Japan Association, 1991
12   Public Record Office, London, WO 25/3240 f 820, Marriage report of Charles
Bush Hearn, received at the War Office, London, on 6/9/1852
13   *Army List*, 1858/9
14   PRO London, WO 25/3240 f 821, covering letter with his marriage report from
Charles Bush Hearn to the War Office, London, from Grenada, received 6/9/1852
15   PRO London WO 25/746 f 71
16   NK 240
17   MLBHC 205-7, Letter from Lizzie Hardy to Lilla Hearn, 1890
18   LL+EB1, 269-70, to John Albee, 1883, New Orleans
19   Kneeland; Hul MSS Hearn letter to James D Hearn, New York
20   Kneeland; Hul MSS Hearn letter to James D Hearn, New York
21   Vir Press Cuttings, reproduction in unidentified US newspaper of 1909 article in

the *Manchester Guardian* contains useful information on family background

22   NK 14

23   *A Genealogical and Heraldic History of the Colonial Gentry*, Sir Bernard Burke, Vol 27, 6; Burke seems to have combined the knowledge that Hearn or Heron was a common surname in England with the first appearance of Archdeacon Daniel Hearn in official Irish records to decide that he had settled in Ireland about 1713

24   *Alumni Dublinensis*, George Burtchaell, Thomas Ulick Sadlier (ed), Dublin, 1935

25   *Watson's Almanac*, 1826, Dublin, gives the date of the Duke of Dorset's arrival in Ireland as 26/9/1735

26   GO,D *Registered Pedigrees*, Vol 27, 6

27   *Fasti Ecclesiae Hibernicae*, Henry Cotton, Dublin, MDCCCXLV, 125; and GO,D, letter from Rev Canon Swanzy, 9/2/1928

27a Letter to the author from David Woodworth, The GPA-Bolton Library, The Deanery, Cashel, 7 June 1988

28   *A History of the City of Dublin*, JT Gilbert, Dublin, 1861, Vol III, 295

29   Registry of Deeds, Dublin, *Abstract of Wills*, Vol II, 1746-85, P Beryl Eustace (ed), Dublin, Stationary Office, 1954, 170, 241, 113854

30   *Genealogical and Heraldic History*, Burke, op cit, 106-7

31   Genealogical Office, Dublin, *Grants and Confirmations of Arms*, MS 110, 1880-97

32   *King's Inns Admission Papers*, E Keane, P Beryl Phair, T Sadlier (ed), PRO, Dublin, 1982 ·

33   *Alumni Dublinensis*, George Burtchaell, Thomas Ulick Sadlier (ed), Dublin, 1935

34   PRO London, WO 25/746 f 71, *Statement of Service of Major Daniel James Hearn*, 25/9/1809

35   GO,D, Donovan, 384, and Land Registry, Dublin, 640-470402

36   *The Parliamentary Gazetteer of Ireland*, 1844-5, Dublin, 1845, 63

37   Land Registry, Dublin, 1860-20-266 and 1860-27-125

38   *A Topographical Dictionary of Ireland*, Samuel Lewis, 1837, 55-6

39   *Tithe Applotment Book*, 1832

40   'Lafcadio Hearn', Nina Kennard, *The Nineteenth Century and After*, Vol 59, Jan 1906, 135-50

41   *Topographical Dictionary of Ireland*, Lewis, op cit, 55-6

42   NK 24

43   *Tithe Applotment Book*, 2/6/1827, Parish of Ardnurcher

44   Land Registry, Dublin, 1860-20-266

45   *Tithe Applotment Book*, 2/6/1827, Parish of Ardnurcher

46   *Thom's Directory*, Dublin, 1848

46a 'British art students in Paris 1814-1890; demand and supply', Edward Morris and Amanda McKay, *Apollo*, February 1992; see also *A Free Spirit: Irish Art 1860-1960*, Kenneth McConkey, Antique Collectors' Club in Association with Pym's Gallery, London 1990

46b 'Jean Paul Laurens' by Richard Hearn in *Toilers in Art*, Henry C Ewart (ed), Isbister & Company, London, 1891, 124

47   NK 175-6 and 35

48   Kennard, *The Nineteenth Century and After*, op cit

49   'Lafcadio Hearn and his relations in Dublin', Lilo Stephens, *Eigo seinen, The Rising Generation*, 1/5/1973, Vol CXLX, No 2, 38-9

50   *Thom's Directory*, Dublin, 1851, 802-3, and *Thom's Directory*, 1854 - these directories show that a Thomas Alexander, M.D., was living in the house both during and after the Hearns' sojourn there; hence the deduction that he was no relation

51   Quoted in NK 25

52   MLBHC, 205-7, letter from Lizzie Hardy to Lilla Hearn

53 NK 26. Kennard uses the plural even though Rosa only had Patrick Lafcadio with her in Ireland
54 NK 30
55 NK 25
56 NK 30
57 *The Parliamentary Gazetteer of Ireland, 1844-5*, op cit, 792 and *Topographical Dictionary*, Lewis, op cit, 385
58 Land Registry, Dublin, 1846-6-23
59 Lilo Stephens, op cit
60 NK 28-9
61 *Thom's Directories*, 1848-51, and *Pettigrew and Oulton's Almanac and Dublin Directory 1850*
62 *Thom's Directories*, Dublin 1851-68
63 *Thom's Directory* 1855, 1095
64 Vir MSS Autobiographical notes made by LH in Japan, no date, no address
65 JLH2, 212-3, to Basil Hall Chamberlain, 14/12/1893
65a 'Toy-Time', Lafcadio Hearn, *The Double Dealer*, Vol III, No 13, Jan 1922, 8
66 Vir MSS Autobiographical notes made by LH in Japan, no date, no address
67 Lilo Stephens, op cit
68 Quoted in NK 31-2
69 Lilo Stephens, op cit
70 Grant Books, Dublin, 1800-58. *Appendix to the Thirteenth Report of the Deputy Keeper of the State Papers in Ireland* (1899) Marriage affidavit 482
71 Vir Press Cuttings, *Manchester Guardian* article, op cit
72 Lilo Stephens, op cit
73 Young, 32-3
74 MLBHC 205-7, letter from Lizzie Hardy to Lilla Hearn, op cit, and Kneeland op cit
75 E+R 293-9
76 'The Gipsy's Story', *The Item*, 18/8/1881
77 Kotto 210
78 NK 27
79 Hul MSS letter to James D Hearn, 19/1/1890, NY
80 Mor MSS Hearn letter to Mrs Freeman, no date, no address, (MA 2534-5:6)
81 MLBHC 205-7, Letter from Lizzie Hardy to Lilla Hearn, op cit
82 Bisland 8
83 Vir MSS Autobiographical notes, no date, no address
84 Quoted in NK 35
85 NK 231
86 Genealogical Office, Dublin, Donovan, 384 h 123
87 Land Registry, Dublin, 1860-20-266
88 Registry of Deeds, Dublin, 1866-4-141
89 Hul MSS Hearn letter to James D Hearn, 16/1/1890, NY
90 Bisland 11
91 NK 16-7
92 Pagan 58-9
93 Quoted in NK 19
94 MLBHC 201
95 'Hereditary Memories', *The Item*, 22/7/1880
96 NK 244, letter to Mrs Atkinson
97 'Among the Spirits', Cincinnati , *21/1/1874*

CHAPTER 12

1   LL+EB3 66
2   E+R 157-8
3   E+R 171,2
4   MID MSS Hearn letter to Scudder, Tokyo, 28/12/94
5   NYPL Berg, MSS Hearn letter to Ellwood Hendrick, Tokyo, 29/4/97
6   E+R 275-6
7   E+R 288-9
8   Shadowings 222
9   Shadowings 213-222
10 Shadowings 222
11 'Nightmare Touch', Shadowings, 238-41
11a Chita 156-62
12 'Nightmare Touch', Shadowings 235-246
13 Mis/Mor XXIX-XXX
14 'Vespertina Cognito', E+R, 280-7
15 'By the Japanese Sea', Glimpses, 523-4
16 E+R 293-9
17 'The Gipsy Story', *The Item*, 18/8/1881
18 Kotto 210
19 NK 27
20 HUL MSS Hearn letter to James D. Hearn, New York, 19/1/1890 (Also incorrectly transcribed in Kneeland)
21 Pagan 58-9
22 LTL 135-7, 1876

CHAPTER 13

1   Poets 462
2   *A Topographical Dictionary of Ireland*, Lewis, op cit, 462
3   LL+EB1, 159
4   NK 39
5   NK 34
6   *Thom's Dublin Directory*, Dublin, 1860
7   *Topographical Dictionary*, Lewis, op cit, 392
8   *Griffith's Valuation*, Ordnance Survey, Dublin, 120
9   *The Parliamentary Gazetteer of Ireland*, op cit, 483-5
10 NYPL Berg, to Ellwood Hendrick, Kobe, 29/8/1895
11 Quoted in NK 41, LH to Mrs Atkinson, probably Nov 1891
12 F/I 97
13 *Topographical Dictionary*, Lewis, op cit, 392
14 Kwaidan 167-8
15 NK 43
16 NK 32
17 Bisland 30
18 Quoted in NK 42, LH to Mrs Atkinson
19 LHIJ, 'Mrs Hearn's Reminiscences', 52-55
20 VIR LH's MSS Autobiography
21 Bisland 30
22 VIR LH's MSS Autobiography
23 Quoted in Bisland 25
24 GO,D 815 (20) Draft pedigrees, abstracts of deeds of family Molyneux

(watchmakers) and Tramore Co Waterford and Hearns of Waterford. Typed document of 31/1/1927 signed by Henry Kenny

25   Ordnance Survey Map of Dublin, 1864
26   GO,D 815 (20)
27   Ibid
28   Registry of Deeds, Dublin, 1864-35-179
29   NK 47
30   Registry of Deeds, Dublin, 1864-35-179; a memorial registered on 17/11/1864 recites an indenture of 3/2/1863 'purporting' to be a settlement on the marriage of Molyneux and Agnes Keogh; the Rev Edward Hearn was '5th part' in the 1863 indenture
31   Ibid
32   Ibid; the memorial lists Henry Hearn Molyneux as having addresses at Linkfield Lane, Surrey, and No 8, Copthall Court, London
33   VIR LH's MSS Autobiography
34   *Lafcadio Hearn*, Marcel Robert, Hokuseido Press, Tokyo, 1950, 54
35   Young 55
36   *Ape of the Gods*, op cit, 292, Appendix
37   Kneeland
38   LHSPA 157
39   CLH 18
40   CLH 18
41   LFR 108
42   F/I 149
43   JLH1, 369-70, to Basil Hall Chamberlain, 4/2/1893
44   HUC 139
45   Kneeland
46   HUC contains useful information on Old Hall, Ware and its relationship with Ushaw
47   NK 65
48   HUC 136
49   NK 63-4
50   Poets 574
51   F/I 62
52   LFR 38
53   JLH2, 149-50, to Basil Hall Chamberlain, 16/8/1893
54   Poets 447
55   Bisland 31
56   HUC 175-6
57   HUC 267
58   HUC 215-229
59   *The Ushaw Magazine*, December 1904
60   Ushaw school records
61   NK 60-1
62   NK 63-4
63   LL+EB2, 308, to Ellwood Hendrick, Kobe, Jan 1895
64   LL+EB3, 105, to Mitchell McDonald, Tokyo, March 1898
65   LHSPA 105
66   Bisland 30
67   *Times-Democrat*, 21/5/1882
68   NK 57
69   NK 61-2

70   NK 63
71   Ushaw school records
72   'Idolatry' by Lafcadio Hearn, quoted in Bisland 23
73   Vir MSS LH autobiographical fragment
74   NK 54-5
75   Bisland 26
76   Vir MSS LH Autobiographical fragment
77   Bisland 28
78   Shadowings 265
79   Bisland 31
80   Registry of Deeds, Dublin, 1866-4-141
81   Registry of Deeds, Dublin, 1864-35-179
82   Registry of Deeds, Dublin, 1866-4-141
83   'Lafcadio Hearn' by Taro Matsuo, *The Hosei University Economic Review*, Vol LI, No 1, 1983
84   MLBHC 205-7, Letter from Lizzie Hardy (a niece of Mrs Brenane) to Lilla Hearn (LH's half-sister)
85   Kneeland
86   Ibid
87   Bisland 33
88   Kokoro 198-201
89   Pagan 68-75
90   JLH2, 434-5, to Mason
91   Kokoro 204-5

CHAPTER 14

1   LHIJ 57-8
2   Poets 498-9
3   F/I 177
4   LL+EB3, 204
5   Pagan 107-8
6   LL+EB2, 135-6
7   Thomas 79
8   Thomas 77-8
9   Thomas 92
10   Selected, Introduction, 15
11   NYPL Berg, to Ellwood Hendrick, 2/2/1897
12   NYPL Berg, to Ellwood Hendrick, Kobe, 12/11/1895
13   Yale MSS Hearn letter to Guy M Carleton, Tokyo, 19/12/1898
14   LH/Man 521
15   F/I 157
16   F/I 159-60
17   Foxwell 72
18   Foxwell 92
19   Foxwell 72
20   Pagan 109-11
21   Misc 231-40
22   Ghostly 5
23   Ghostly 87-8
24   Ghostly 113
25   LHIJ 55-6
26   LHIJ 58

27 LH/Man 523
28 Shadowings 158
29 LL+EB3, 160-1, to Mitchell McDonald, Jan 1899, Tokyo
30 Shadowings 101
31 LL+EB3, 197, to Elizabeth Bisland, Jan 1900, Tokyo
32 NYPL MSS Hearn letter to Elizabeth Bisland, Sept 1903, Tokyo
33 Misc 112-3
34 Misc 221-2
35 LHIJ 1-18
36 Misc 29
37 Echo 143
38 F/I 98
39 Echo 40-3
40 F/I 75
41 LH/Man 524
42 MHR 347
43 Kotto 217-224
44 Kotto 240-1
45 Kotto 195
46 Kotto 196-9
47 Kotto 124-5
48 Kotto 210
49 Kotto 11
50 Milky 56-70
51 For information on the film, *Kwaidan*, see *Horror, A Connoisseur's Guide to Literature and Film*, Leonard Wolf, Facts on File, New York/Oxford, 1989, 129-131
52 Kwaidan 43-49
53 Kwaidan 51-61
54 Kwaidan 1-20
55 Bisland 141
56 I am indebted to Elizabeth Stevenson for this insight, ES 299
57 Kwaidan 237
58 Kwaidan 221
59 Kwaidan 238
60 Kwaidan 233-4
61 NYPL MSS Hearn letter to Elizabeth Bisland, Sept 1904, Tokyo
62 Kwaidan 240
63 Kwaidan 211-2

CHAPTER 15

1 Mor MSS Hearn letter to Gullman, 11/11/1899 (MA 2532)
2 Mor MSS Hearn letter to Gullman, 3/3/1900 (MA 2532)
3 Foxwell 90
4 LL+EB3, 195-8, Jan 1900, Tokyo
5 LL+EB3, 212-6, to Elizabeth Bisland, July and August 1902, Tokyo and Yaidzu
6 NYPL Berg, to Ellwood Hendrick, 15/4/1897
7 F/I 144-5
8 'Some Unpublished Letters of Lafcadio Hearn', by Osman Edwards, *Transactions of the Japan Society of London*, Vol XVI, 16-35
9 Ibid
10 Ibid
11 Ibid

12 Ibid
13 Vir MSS Hearn letter to Albert Brice, Assistant Secretary of the Japan Society, London, 23/12/1901
14 Pagan 109-11, 1901, Tokyo
15 Iowa University MSS Hearn letter to Sir Edwin Arnold, 26/1/1903
16 NYPL MSS Hearn letter to Elizabeth Bisland, 15/3/1903
17 MHR 345
18 F/I 187-8
19 Letter 627
20 F/I 193
21 F/I 195
22 'Hearn Sen-Sei, Memories of Lafcadio Hearn' by Mock Joya, *The Bookman*, Vol 39, 1914
23 LL+EB3, 232-3, to Elizabeth Bisland, 1903, Tokyo
24 'Natsume Soseki and Lafcadio Hearn: Similarities and Differences', by Masayuki Ikeda, paper given at the Soseki Conference, University of London, 17/7/1987 and published in a book of essays, mainly in Japanese, *A Comparative Cultural Approach to Images of Japan*, 1989, ISBN 4-7923-7039-6
25 Mor press cuttings, *The Literary Digest*, No date on copy (MA2534-5)
26 LHIJ 128-45
27 Cornell TLS, Schurman to Lafcadio Hearn, 24/12/1902
28 Bisland 144
29 NK 347
30 Cornell TLS, Schurman to Lafcadio Hearn, 9/3/1903
31 LL+EB3, 235, to Elizabeth Bisland, July 1903, Tokyo
32 NYPL MSS Hearn letter to Elizabeth Bisland, 1903, Tokyo
33 NYPL MSS Hearn letter to Elizabeth Bisland, 15/3/1903
34 LL+EB3, 241, to Elizabeth Bisland, 1903, Tokyo
35 NYPL MSS Hearn letter to Elizabeth Bisland, Sept 1904, Tokyo
36 LL+EB3, 245, to Elizabeth Bisland, 1903, Tokyo
37 LL+EB3, 240, to Elizabeth Bisland, 1903, Tokyo
38 See, for example, LL+EB2, 127-9, to Basil Hall Chamberlain, April 1891, Matsue
39 LL+EB2, 389, to Basil Hall Chamberlain, Sept 1895
40 *Times-Democrat* 26/12/1886
41 Attempt 457
42 Attempt 210
43 Attempt 32
44 Attempt 188-90
45 Attempt 303, 319-20, 328, 337-8
46 Attempt 343, 357,359, 368-9, 372-3
47 Attempt 47, 376, 387, 379-80, 301-2, 442
48 Attempt 454, 450, 254-5
49 Attempt 455-6
50 Attempt 481-3
51 Fales Library, New York University, Division of Special Collections, MSS Hearn letter to L Wilson, Messrs Kelly and Walsh, Booksellers
52 Hul MSS letter, no addressee, 31/3/1903, Tokyo
53 Vir MSS Hearn letter to Editor of San Francisco *Argonaut*, 29/5/1903
54 LL+EB3, 236, to Elizabeth Bisland, 1903, Tokyo
55 LL+EB3, 243-4, to Elizabeth Bisland, Aug 1903
56 Vir MSS Hearn letter to Albert Brice, Assistant Secretary, The Japan Society, London, 5/9/1903

57 LL+EB3, 246, to Elizabeth Bisland, Oct 1903, Tokyo
58 Vir TLS Canadian Pacific Royal Mail Steamship Line, to LH from Payne, 2/12/ 1903
59 LL+EB3, 246, to Elizabeth Bisland, Tokyo
60 MHR 350
61 LHIJ 57- 61
62 F/I 174
64 LH/Man 515-6
65 F/I 183
66 LL+EB3, 230, to Elizabeth Bisland, Jan 1903, Tokyo
67 F/I 146-7
68 LL+EB3, 250-1, to Ernest Crosby, August 1904, Tokyo
69 Letter
70 LHIJ 56-7
71 Foxwell 90
72 Vir TLS to LH from PJ Hartog, Registrar, University of London, 26/4/1904
73 NYPL MSS Hearn letter to Elizabeth Bisland, Sept 1904, Tokyo
74 F/I 199
75 *Atlantic Monthly*, Vol 93, June 1904, 857
76 *The Athenaeum*, No 4012, 17/9/1904, 373-4
77 Vir Press Cuttings, *The Bookman*, no date
78 F/I 91
79 NYPL MSS Hearn letter to Elizabeth Bisland, Sept 1904, Tokyo
80 LHIJ 443
81 NYPL MSS Hearn letter to Elizabeth Bisland, Sept 1904, Tokyo
82 F/I 204
83 'The Last Days of Lafcadio Hearn', by Mrs Hearn, translated by Paul Kiyoshi Hisada, *Atlantic Monthly*, Boston, 1917, Vol 119, 349-51
84 F/I 207

CHAPTER 16

1   SW 152
2   *Dealer and Stationer*, 19/12/1904
3   'Lafcadio Hearn's Funeral' by Margaret Emerson, *The Critic*, Jan 1905
4   Ibid
5   Ibid
6   F/I 126
7   NK 382
8   F/I 181
9   MHR 351
10 *The Japan Times*, 21/12/1904
11 Mor Press Clippings, Associated Press cablegram, dated 28/9/1904, Yokohama, carried in unidentified newspaper (MA 2534-5)
12 Vir Press Clippings, *Riverside Bulletin*, November 1904
13 *The Dayton Daily Journal* 30/9/1904
14 LHIJ 128
15 F/I 3
16 *The Critic*, Vol 46, Feb 1905, 185
17 *The Academy*, Vol 69, 21/12/1905, 1257-8
18 *The Athenaeum*, No 4092, 31/3/1906, 388-9
19 H+HB, Preface
20 H+HB 27

21 Foxwell 90

22 NK 135

23 H+HB 27

24 H+HB, between pages 72 and 73, Facsimile of letter from Bisland to a Mr Hill, 20/7/1905

25 H+HB 45-7

26 Mor Press Clippings, *Kansas City Journal*, 27 Oct [1906?] (MA 2534-5)

27 The *Sun*, (New York) 27/7/1906

28 The *Sun*, (New York) 2/8/1906

29 *The New York Times*, 14/8/1906, reprinted in the New Orleans *Times-Democrat*, 20/8/1906

30 H+HB, 72- 73, Facsimile of Hill letter op cit

31 H+HB 81-2

31a *Afro-American Folksongs*, Krehbiel, op cit, 39

32 *Discoveries; Essays on Lafcadio Hearn*, Albert Mordell, Orient/West Incorporated, Tokyo, 1964, 174-5

33 LL+EB2, 94-5, to Gould, 1889; CLH 23-4

34 LL+EB2, 304-7; and NYPL Berg, to Ellwood Hendrick, 14/1/1895

35 LL+EB1, Preface, VI-VII

36 *The New York Times*, 1/12/1906

37 See, for example, the reviews of Bisland in *The North Atlantic Review*, Vol 187, 15/2/1907, 417-21; *Atlantic Monthly*, Vol 99, Feb 1907, 261-72; *The Academy*, Vol 72, 26/1/1907, 88-9

38 LHSPA

39 New York *Herald*, 17/3/1930, letter from Laura Stedman Gould

40 Cincinnati , *11/5/1908*

41 New York *World*, 12/5/1908

42 *The New York Times* 14/5/1908, letter from Hendrick

43 Philadelphia *Public Ledger* 19/5/1908

44 *The New York Times*, 16/5/1908; quotation is from The New Orleans *Times-Democrat* of 3/5/1908

45 CLH 184

46 CLH 7

47 Pagan 88, December 1890, Matsue

48 CLH 167-8

49 JLH2, 156, to Basil Hall Chamberlain, 1/9/1893

50 CLH 97

51 CLH 169

52 CLH 3

53 CLH 69

54 CLH 18, 99, 101, 6

55 The *Sun*, (New York), 14/6/1908

56 Vir press clippings, review of CLH in unidentified Dayton newspaper

57 *Times-Democrat*, 3/5/1908

58 The *Sun* (New York) 2/7/1908

59 The *Sun* (New York) 6/7/1980

60 Vir Press Clippings, *Montgomery County Reporter*, Dayton, Ohio, no date

61 Chicago *Herald*, 23/5/1908

62 Chicago *Evening Post*, 30/5/1908

63 Vir Press Clippings, The *Daily Picayune*, no date

64 NK 271

65 NK 341

66   NK 381
67   NK 360
68   'A Conversation with Mrs Hearn' by Yone Noguchi, *The Japan Times*, 21/12/1904
69   NK 374-5
70   Fugii 430
71   Col MSS letter from Harper to Mrs Hearn, 17/9/1912 and 25/11/1912
72   Col Memo of Agreement between Harper and Houghton Mifflin, 8/2/1922
73   LHIJ 36
74   NK 366-8
75   F/I 12
76   'Mrs Hearn's Daily Life', by S Fukii, *The Japan Magazine*, Vol 11, No 8, Jan 1921, 429-30
77   Hul MSS letter Mrs Hearn to Ferris Greenslet, HM&Co, 20/10/1924
78   Hul Kazuo Koizumi to Greenslet, HM&Co, 5/2/1924
79   Hul MSS letter from Hendrick to Ferris Greenslet, HM&Co, 28/12/1923, New York
80   NYPL Berg, Catalogue of the LH Library at the Toyama High School, 1927 edition
81   Cincinnati , *Sunday Magazine*, article by James Hoeck, *7/4/1929*
82   Hul TLS document issued by the LH Memorial Committee
83   'Lafcadio Hearn - Lover or Hater of Japan', KK Kawakami, *Japan* (magazine), San Francisco, 1926, Vol 15, 13-14, 44
84   'Lafcadio Hearn after New Orleans', by Warren C Odgen, *Dixie* Magazine, 29/7/1962
85   'Japan: The Warnings and Prophecies of Lafcadio Hearn', by William W Clary, *Claremont Oriental Studies*, No 5, April 1943
86   The New *Enclopaedia Britannica*
87   LHIJ 17

BIBLIOGRAPHY

INSTITUTIONS HOLDING PRIMARY SOURCE MATERIAL

IRELAND

Public Record Office, Dublin
The *Tithe Composition Applotment Books* for Ireland (except Northern Ireland, where the Hearn family also held land; a microfilm copy of the Northern books is available in the National Library, Dublin) are in the PRO, Dublin. This land survey, carried out following an Act of Parliament of 1823 in the context of tithes to be paid the then-Established Church of Ireland, is a primary source of information on the Hearn property in Co Westmeath in the nineteenth century. The PRO also holds copies of the Reports of the Deputy Keeper of the Public Records and Keeper of the State Papers of Ireland, the source for Irish wills of the last 300 years, as well as the wills themselves, another primary source on the Hearn family, and *Griffith's Poor Law Valuation*.

Trinity College, Dublin
The *Dublin University Calenders* for the 1830s contain information on Charles Bush Hearn.

Valuation Office, Dublin
The records at the Valuation Office give details of the occupants of Dublin houses.

Registry of Deeds, Dublin
Documents found at the Registry throw a radical new light on the Hearn family background by revealing a chain of events which led from Lafcadio's father being in debt to Mrs Brenane, Lafcadio's great-aunt and effective parent figure, to his ruin as she pursued him through the courts in the face of her own bankruptcy.

Land Registry, Dublin
Documents found here also provide a new insight into the Hearn family history, this time by showing the family lands in Co Westmeath were gained by marriage by Lafcadio's grandfather, rather than the romantic notion which has hitherto been accepted, that they were a reward to a distant ancestor by a Lord Lieutenant of Ireland.

Genealogical Office, Dublin
Documents at the Office contain a good deal of genealogical material, not just on the Hearns (including the family's armorial bearings) but also on the Molyneux connection.

National Library, Dublin
D 8345-8419 contains 75 deeds relating to Hearn family property, mainly in the nineteenth century.

BRITAIN

Public Record Office, London

The War Office papers contain useful material on the members of the Hearn family who served in the British Army, particularly Lafcadio's father, Charles Bush Hearn, and his grandfather, Daniel James Hearn. Some of this important primary material, such as WO 25/746 f 71, *Statement of Service of Major Daniel James Hearn*, 29/9/1809, has not, so far as I am aware, been used by any previous Hearn scholar. The PRO also contains useful secondary material such as the *Army Lists* for the periods of service of the members of the Hearn family.

Ushaw College, Durham

Hearn's school records are held at Ushaw, as is an interesting collection of 1860s photographs of the school.

UNITED STATES

The following institutions in the United States have collections of Hearn material ranging from a single item to extensive quantities, not only of manuscripts, but also of other relevant material, such as contemporary press cuttings. This material, together with his own writings, has formed the backbone of my reappraisal of Hearn. Unfortunately, I had left Japan before I began researching this book and therefore did not have the opportunity to sample the collections there but the fact remains that the vast bulk of original Hearn correspondence is held in the United States.

Department of Rare Books
and Special Collections
The University of Rochester Library
Rochester
New York

Department of Rare Books
and Special Collections
The Public Library of Cincinnati
and Hamilton County
800 Vine Street
Library Square
Cincinnati
Ohio

Department of Rare Books and Manuscripts
Boston Public Library
Boston
Massachusetts

Department of Rare Books
Cornell University Library
Cornell University
Ithaca
New York

Division of Special Collections
Fales Library
New York University
New York

Literary Manuscripts Department
The Huntington Library
1151 Oxford Road
San Marino
California

Manuscript Department
The Houghton Library
Harvard University
Cambridge
Massachusetts

Manuscripts Department
University of Virginia Library
Charlottesville
Virginia

The University Libraries
The University of Iowa
Iowa City
Iowa

Manuscripts Department
The Earl Gregg Swem Library
The College of William and Mary
Williamsburg
Virginia

Dawes Memorial Library
Marietta College
Marietta
Ohio

Rare Books Room
University of Illinois Library
Urbana
Illinois

Howard-Tilton Memorial Library
University Libraries
Tulane University
New Orleans
Louisiana

Lafcadio Hearn Papers
Edmund C Stedman Papers
Harper Brothers Records
Rare Books and Manuscript Library
Butler Library
Columbia University
New York
Harry Ransom Humanities Research Centre
The University of Texas at Austin
Austin
Texas
Abernethy Library
Middlebury College
Starr Library
Middlebury College
Middlebury
Vermont
Special Collections
Harold B Lee Library
Brigham Young University
Provo
Utah
Special Collections/The John Hay Library
Brown University Library
Providence
Rhode Island
The Historical Society of Pennsylvania
1300 Locust Street
Philadelphia
Pa.
Henry W and Albert A Berg Collection
The New York Public Library
Astor, Lenox and Tilden Foundations
Lafcadio Hearn. Personal Miscellaneous Papers
Rare Books and Manuscripts Division
The New York Public Library
Astor, Lenox and Tilden Foundations
The Research Libraries
New York Public Library
New York
New York

Harper Collection
Hearn-Freeman-Watkin Collection
The Pierpont Morgan Library
New York
New York
The Lilly Library
Indiana University
Bloomington
Indiana
The Beinecke Rare Book
   and Manuscript Library
Yale University
New Haven
Connecticut
The Estelle Doheny Collection
The Edward Laurence Doheny
   Memorial Library
St John's Seminary
Camarillo
California
The Newberry Library
Chicago
Illinois
Manuscript Division
The Library of Congress
Washington
D.C.
Troy H. Middleton Library
Louisiana State University
Baton Rouge
Louisiana

ARTICLES BY LAFCADIO HEARN

Hearn wrote regularly for the following newspapers in his journalistic career: the Cincinnati *Enquirer* 1872-5; *Ye Giglampz* June-August 1874; Cincinnati *Commercial* 1875-77; New Orleans *Item* 1878-81; New Orleans *Democrat* 1880-81; New Orleans *Times-Democrat* 1881-87; and, the Kobe *Chronicle* 1894-95. Much of this material is available to the modern reader in various books listed in this bibliography. It would, in any case, be impractical to attempt to list this great mass of material. It may, however, be useful to list the articles which appeared in major periodicals from 1882 onwards but were not incorporated in books by Hearn himself, not all of which are available in compilations:

'A Story of Pompeii', Theophile Gautier, translated by Lafcadio Hearn, The *Argonaut*, San Francisco, 17 and 24/6/1882

'The Little Dauphin's Death', Alphonse Daudet, translated by Lafcadio Hearn, The *Argonaut*, San Francisco, 16/9/1882

'New Orleans in Carnival Garb', Lafcadio Hearn, *Harper's Weekly*, 24/2/1883

'The New Cotton Exchange in New Orleans', Lafcadio Hearn, *Harper's Weekly*, 17/3/1883

'Saint Malo', Lafcadio Hearn, *Harper's Weekly*, 31/3/1883

'The Scenes of Cable's Romances', Lafcadio Hearn, *Century Magazine*, November 1883

'Quaint New Orleans and its Habitants', Lafcadio Hearn, *Harper's Weekly*, 6/12/1884

'The New Orleans Exposition', Lafcadio Hearn, *Harper's Weekly*, 3 and 31/1/1885

'The Creole Patois', Lafcadio Hearn, *Harper's Weekly*, 10 and 17/1/1885

'The East at New Orleans', Lafcadio Hearn, *Harper's Weekly*, 7/3/1885

'Mexico at New Orleans', Lafcadio Hearn, *Harper's Weekly*, 14/3/1885

'The New Orleans Exposition. Some Oriental Curiosities', Lafcadio Hearn, *Harper's Bazaar*, 28/3/1885

'The New Orleans Exposition. Notes of a Curiosity Hunter', Lafcadio Hearn, *Harper's Bazaar*, 4/4/1885

'The Government Exhibit at New Orleans', Lafcadio Hearn, *Harper's Weekly*, 11/4/1885

'The Last of the Voudoos', Lafcadio Hearn, *Harper's Weekly*, 7/11/1885

'The Last of the New Orleans Fencing Masters', Lafcadio Hearn, *Southern Bivouac*, November 1886 and *Double Dealer*, January 1921

'New Orleans Superstitions', Lafcadio Hearn, *Harper's Weekly*, 25/12/1886

'Rabyah's Last Ride. A Tradition of Pre-Islamic Arabia', Lafcadio Hearn, *Harper's Bazaar*, 2/4/1887

'A Ghost', Lafcadio Hearn, *Harper's Magazine*, December 1889

'Karma', Lafcadio Hearn, *Lippincott's Magazine*, May 1890

'A Study of Half-Breed Races in the West Indies', Lafcadio Hearn, *Cosmopolitan*, June 1890

'West Indian Society of Many Colorings, Lafcadio Hearn, *Cosmopolitan*, July 1890

'A Winter's Journey to Japan', Lafcadio Hearn, *Harper's Monthly*, November 1890

'From My Japanese Diary', Lafcadio Hearn, *Atlantic Monthly*, November 1894

'China and the Western World', Lafcadio Hearn, *Atlantic Monthly*, April 1896

'The Ballad of Shun Toku Maru', Lafcadio Hearn, *The Chrysanthemum*, San Francisco, 1897, Vol 2, No 1, 6-8

'Notes on a Trip to Izumo', Lafcadio Hearn, *Atlantic Monthly*, May 1897

'Lafcadio Hearn', Lafcadio Hearn, *Harper's Weekly*, 15/10/1904

'The Nun Ryonen', Lafcadio Hearn, *Transactions of the Japan Society*, London, 1905, Vol VI, Part III, 373-388

'Three Popular Ballads', Lafcadio Hearn, *Transactions of the Asiatic Society of Japan*, Vol XXII, 1894

'Two Memories of a Childhood', Lafcadio Hearn, *Atlantic Monthly*, October 1906

BOOKS BY LAFCADIO HEARN

THESE ARE THE WORKS WHICH HEARN WROTE AS BOOKS FOR PUBLICATION IN HIS LIFETIME:

A Japanese Miscellany, Lafcadio Hearn, Little Brown and Company, Boston, 1901; Reprinted by Charles E. Tuttle Company, Inc. Rutland, Vermont, and Tokyo, 1967

Chin Chin Kobakama, Rendered into English by Lafcadio Hearn, T. Hasegawa, Tokyo, 1903

Chita: A Memory of Last Island, Lafcadio Hearn, Harper and Brothers, New York, 1889

Clarimond, Theophile Gautier, Translated by Lafcadio Hearn, Brentano's, New York, 1899

Exotics and Retrospectives, Lafcadio Hearn, Little, Brown and Co., Boston, 1898, Republished by Charles E. Tuttle Company, Inc. of Rutland, Vermont & Tokyo, Japan, 1971

Gleanings in Buddha Fields, Lafcadio Hearn, Houghton Mifflin Company, Boston 1897, Reprinted by Charles E. Tuttle Company, Inc. Rutland, Vermont, and Tokyo, 1971

Glimpses of Unfamiliar Japan, Lafcadio Hearn, Houghton Mifflin Company, Boston, 1894; Reprinted by Charles E. Tuttle Company, Inc. Rutland, Vermont, and Tokyo, 1976

Gombo Zhebes. Little Dictionary of Creole Proverbs, Selected from Six Creole Dialects. Translated into French and into English, with Notes, Complete Index to Subjects and Some Brief Remarks upon the Creole Idioms of Louisiana, Lafcadio Hearn, Will H Coleman, New York, 1885

In Ghostly Japan, Lafcadio Hearn, Little Brown and Company, Boston, 1899, Reprinted by Charles E. Tuttle Company, Inc. Rutland, Vermont, and Tokyo, 1971

Japan: an Attempt at Interpretation, Lafcadio Hearn, The Macmillan Co., New York, 1904, Reprinted by Charles E. Tuttle Company, Inc. Rutland, Vermont and Tokyo, 1956

Kokoro, Lafcadio Hearn, Houghton Mifflin Company, Boston 1896, Reprinted by Charles E. Tuttle Company, Inc. Rutland, Vermont, and Tokyo, 1972

Kotto: Being Japanese Curios, With Sundry Cobwebs, Lafcadio Hearn, The Macmillan Company, New York, 1902; Reprinted by Charles E. Tuttle Company, Inc. Rutland, Vermont, and Tokyo, 1971

Kwaidan: Stories and Studies of Strange Things, Lafcadio Hearn, Houghton Mifflin Company, Boston, 1904; Reprinted by Charles E. Tuttle Company, Inc. Rutland, Vermont, and Tokyo, 1971

La Cuisine Creole: A Collection of Culinary Receipts from Leading Chefs and Noted Creole Housewives, Who Have Made New Orleans Famous for its Cuisine, Lafcadio Hearn, Will H. Coleman, New York, 1885; reprinted as *Lafcadio Hearn's Creole Cook Book*, with the addition of a collection of drawings and writings by Lafcadio Hearn during his sojourn in New Orleans from 1877 to 1887, Pelican Publishing House, New Orleans, 1967

One of Cleopatra's Nights, and Other Fantastic Romances, Theophile Gautier, Translated by Lafcadio Hearn, R Worthington, New York, 1882

Out of the East, Lafcadio Hearn, Houghton Mifflin Company, Boston 1897, Reprinted by Charles E. Tuttle Company, Inc. Rutland, Vermont, and Tokyo, 1972

Shadowings, Lafcadio Hearn, Little, Brown, and Co., Boston 1900, Reprinted by

Charles E. Tuttle Company, Inc. Rutland, Vermont, and Tokyo, 1971

Some Chinese Ghosts, Lafcadio Hearn, Roberts Brothers, Boston, 1887

Stray Leaves from Stray Literature, Lafcadio Hearn, J.R. Osgood and Co, Boston, 1884; reprinted by Folcroft Library Editions, 1974

The Goblin Spider, Rendered into English by Lafcadio Hearn, T. Hasagawa, Tokyo, 1899

The Temptation of St Anthony, Gustave Flaubert, Translated by Lafcadio Hearn, The Alice Harriman Company, New York and Seattle, 1910

The Romance of the Milky Way, Lafcadio Hearn, Houghton Mifflin Company, Boston 1904, Reprinted by Charles E. Tuttle Company, Inc. Rutland, Vermont, and Tokyo, 1974

The Old Woman Who Lost Her Dumpling, Rendered into English by Lafcadio Hearn, T. Hasegawa, Tokyo, 1902

The Crime of Sylvestre Bonnard. Member of the Institute, Anatole France, Translated by Lafcadio Hearn, Harper and Brothers, New York, 1890

The Boy Who Drew Cats, Rendered into English by Lafcadio Hearn, T. Hasegawa, Tokyo, 1898

The Fountain of Youth, Rendered into English by Lafcadio Hearn, T. Hasegawa, Tokyo, 1930 (third printing)

Two Years in the French West Indies, Lafcadio Hearn, Harper & Brothers, New York and London, 1890; republished by Literature House, N.J., 1970

Youma, The Story of a West Indian Slave, Lafcadio Hearn, Harper & Brothers, New York, 1890; reprinted by AMS Press Inc, New York, 1969

ARTICLES

'A Celtic-Greek Poet', (contains a letter from Lafcadio Hearn to Jerome A. Hart of 29/5/1903), *Argonaut*, San Francisco, 29/12/1906

'A Note on Lafcadio Hearn's Brother: with Text of Letter from Japan', R.M. Lawless, *American Literature*, Vol 10, March 1939, 80-3

'A Discovery of Early Hearn Essays', Albert Mordell, *Today's Japan*, Vol 4, No 1, Jan 1959

'A Japanese Miscellany: My Short Lived Connection with Hearn', Edward B Clarke, in *Stray Leaves. Essays and Sketches*, (pp 1-14), Kenkyusha, Tokyo, 1936

'A New Study of Lafcadio Hearn', *Times-Democrat*, New Orleans, (review of George Gould's *Concerning Lafcadio Hearn*), 3 May 1908

'A Letter from Japan', Lafcadio Hearn, *Atlantic Monthly*, November 1904, Vol 94, No 565, 625-633

'A Letter from Lafcadio Hearn', *Studies in English Literature*, 11, 1, January 1931

'American Days of Lafcadio Hearn', Hugh Harting, *Landmark*, London, Vol 9, 1927, 113-6

Article in *The Journalist* (New York), Jesse H. Webb, 27/2/1892

'British art students in Paris 1814-1890; demand and supply', Edward Morris and Amanda McKay, *Apollo*, February 1992

'Celts, Carthaginians and constitutions: Anglo-Irish literary relations 1780-1820',

Norman Vance, *Irish Historical Studies*, Vol XXII, No 87, March 1981

'Civilized Nomad', Harry T. Levin, *New Republic*, Vol 114, 22 April 1946, 588-9

'Days with Lafcadio Hearn', Mock Joya, *Lippincott's Magazine*, Vol XCV, No 567, March 1915, 85-91

'East Irish', Michael Diskin, *The Irish Times*, 3 May 1988

'Hearn-Gould Controversy, Threat of a Lawsuit to Determine Title to a Collection of Books Sent to Philadelphia by Hearn', *Public Ledger*, 19 May 1906

'Hearn and Japanese Thought', Mitake Katsube, *Today's Japan*, Vol 4, No 1, Jan 1959

'Hearn Sen-Sei: Memories of Lafcadio Hearn', Mock Joya, *Bookman*, Vol XXXIX, No 2, April 1914, 172-8

'Hearn and Chamberlain', Sanki Ichikawa, *Studies in English Literature*, 16, October 1939, 621-2

'Hearn Fight With His Worse Self', (Review of George Gould's *Concerning Lafcadio Hearn*), *The Literary Digest*, 2 May 1908

'Hearn's Cartoons', Colonel John W Fairfax, in *Creole Sketches*, Ethel Hudson, Houghton Mifflin Company, Boston and New York, 1924

'Hearn's Friends Fight Attacks by Author', *Cincinnati Post*, 19 May 1908

'Hearn's Japanese Friends', *The New York Times*, 2 July 1911

'Japan: The Warning and Prophecies of Lafcadio Hearn', William W. Clary, *Claremont Oriental Studies*, No 5, April 1943

'Japanese Sources of Lafcadio Hearn', G.R. Bedinger, *The Independent*, 73, 21 November 1912

'Lafcadio Hearn in New Orleans, I, On the Item', John S Kendall, *Double Dealer*, Vol III, No 17, May 1922, 234-42

'Lafcadio Hearn in New Orleans, II, On the Times-Democrat', John S. Kendall, *Double Dealer*, Vol III, No 18, June 1922, 313-23

'Lafcadio Hearn', Ferris Greenslet, *Atlantic Monthly*, Vol 99, Feb 1907, 261-72

'Lafcadio Hearn - Lover or Hater of Japan: Concerning Some Newly Discovered Letters', K.K. Kawakami, *Japan* (magazine), San Francisco, 1926, Vol 15, 13-14, 44

'Lafcadio Hearn', Ellwood Hendrick, *Bulletin of the New York Public Library*, December 1929

'Lafcadio Hearn and Denny Corcoran', Lucile Rutland, *Double Dealer*, 3, 14, February 1922

'Lafcadio Hearn and Modern French Literature', Osman Edwards, *Albany Review*, November 1907

'Lafcadio Hearn', Ellwood Hendrick, *The Nation*, Vol 116, 11 April 1923, 432-3

'Lafcadio Hearn Traduced, He Says, Writer's Letters Brought Forth to Defend His Memory from Dr. G. M. Gould's Book. A "Philadelphia Doctor", Story of Their Acquaintance, Hearn's Loan and Pledged Library, Now Told for the First Time', letter from Ellwood Hendrick, *The New York Times*, 14 may 1908

'Lafcadio Hearn: A Dreamer', Yone Noguchi, *Current Literature*, Vol XXXVIII, No 6, June 1905, 521-3

'Lafcadio Hearn', Robert Young, *Living Age*, Vol 252, 23 March 1907, 760

'Lafcadio Hearn on the Decadent School', *Craftsman*, Vol 13, Oct/Nov 1907

'Lafcadio Hearn', Joseph Tunison, *Book Buyer*, Vol XIII, No 4, May 1896, 209-11

'Lafcadio Hearn's Funeral', Margaret Emerson, *The Critic*, Vol 46, Jan 1905

'Lafcadio Hearn: the Author of Kokoro', John A. Cockerill, *Current Literature*, Vol

XIX, No 6, June 1896

'Lafcadio Hearn, A study of his personality and art', by George M. Gould, *Putnam's Monthly*, Vol 1, (new series), New York, 1906, 97-107; 156-166

'Lafcadio Hearn', George Gould, *Biographical Clinics*, IV, Blakiston Company, Philadelphia, 1906, 209-37

'Lafcadio Hearn, The Man', Nobushige Amenomori, *Atlantic Monthly*, September 1905, Vol 96, No 3,

'Lafcadio Hearn's Brother', Henry Tracy Kneeland, *Atlantic Monthly*, CXXXI, (Jan 1923)

'Lafcadio Hearn (1850-1904) - His Irish Background and Appreciation of Japanese Culture', Taro Matsuo, *The Hosei University Economic Review*, Vol LI, No 1, 1983

'Lafcadio Hearn', Percy H. Boynton, *Virginia Quarterly Review*, Vol 3, 1927, 418-424

'Lafcadio Hearn. Some Personal Recollections of His Cincinnati Associations', H.S. Fuller, *School*, New York, 11 June 1908

'Lafcadio Hearn's First Embroglio with his Slanderers. Lafcadio Hearn. His Life in Cincinnati Described By a Loving Friend - Some Corrections', letter from H. Watkin, *The Tribune*, Cincinnati, 19 Jan 1895

'Lafcadio Hearn and His Friends', letter from Laura Stedman Gould, New York *Tribune*, 17 Aug 1930

'Lafcadio Hearn and his relations in Dublin', Lilo Stephens, *Eigo seinen, The Rising Generation*, Vol CXLX, No 2, 1/5/1973

'Lafcadio Hearn: A French Estimate', Michael Monahan, *Forum*, Vol XLIX, March 1913, 356-66

'Lafcadio Hearn, Journalist and Writer on Japan', D.H. Langton, *Manchester Quarterly*, No CXXI, Jan 1912, 1-28

'Lafcadio Hearn - Cincinnati's Stepchild', Walter R. Keagy, *The Quarterly Bulletin*, Historical and Philosophical Society of Ohio, April 1950, Cincinnati, 1950, 113-127

'Lafcadio Hearn's "Kwaidan"', *The Bookman*, Vol XX, No 2, Oct 1904, 159-60

'Lafcadio Hearn', *Riverside Bulletin*, Houghton Mifflin Company, Boston, 1904

'Lafcadio Hearn's Love for the Horrible', Richard Le Galliene, *The Literary Digest International Book Review*, Mar 1926

'Lafcadio Hearn's Farewell Cherry-Blossom', *The Literary Digest*, 5 February 1910

'Lafcadio Hearn, Restaurateur...', *The New York Times*, 3 Aug 1924

'Lafcadio Hearn', [Joseph S. Tunison?], *The Dayton Daily Journal*, 30 Sept 1904

'Lafcadio Hearn', Paul Elmer More, *Atlantic Monthly*, 41, February 1903, 204-211

'Lafcadio Hearn after New Orleans', Warren C. Ogden, *Dixie* (Magazine), 29 July 1962

'Lafcadio Hearn', The *Sun*, New York, 14 June 1908

'Lafcadio Hearn, A Sympathetic Japanese Defence of Him and Criticism of His Biographer', letter from Yone Noguchi (in response to George Gould's *Concerning Lafcadio Hearn*), The *Sun*, New York, 2 July 1908

'Letters of a Poet to a Musician. Lafcadio Hearn to Henry E. Krehbiel', *The Critic*, Vol 48-9, Jan-Sept 1906, 309-18

'Letters of Lafcadio Hearn to His Brother', E.C. Beck, *The English Journal*, Vol 20, 1913, 287-92

' "Letters to a Pagan" not by Hearn', Albert Mordell, *Today's Japan*, Vol 5, No 1, 89-98

'Menace With Damages Suit, For $250,000 Is Dr Gould, the Critic of Hearn, By His Japanese Wife and the Children, Whose Legitimacy Is Put in Doubt By Book. Making Analysis of Genius of the Writer. Alienist Threatened to Extend Publication. Savants of Royal Tokyo University Have Taken Matter Up, But Alienist is Obdurate', Cincinnati *Enquirer*, 11 May 1908

"Milton Brenner [*sic*] Thinks Dr Gould Has Been Deceived', (letter from Milton Bronner), The New York *City World*, 12 May 1908

'Mrs Hearn's Daily Life', S. Fugii, *The Japan Magazine*, Vol II, No 8, Jan 1921

'My Recollections of Lafcadio Hearn', Rudolph Matas, *The Tulanian*, 14, April 1941, 6-10

'My Teacher, Lafcadio Hearn', Motoi Kurihara, *Today's Japan*, Vol 4, No 1, Jan 1959

'New Light on Lafcadio Hearn', Hakucho Masamune, *Contemporary Japan*, Vol 2, 1933, 270-80; and in *Sketches of Men and Life*, Ippei Fukuda, Kenkyusha, Tokyo, 1933

'New Lafcadio Hearn Letters', Sanki Ichikawa (ed), *The Living Age*, Vol 330, no 4281, 24/7/1926, 366-72

'New Letters from the French West Indies', Ichiro Nishizaki, reprinted from *Ochanomizu University Studies in Art and Culture*, Tokyo, Vol 12, June 1959

'Newly Discovered Letters from Lafcadio Hearn to Dr Rudolph Matas', Ichiro Nishizaki (ed), *Ochanomizu University Studies*, March 1956

'On the Manners and Customs of the Loochooans', Basil Hall Chamberlain, *Transactions of the Asiatic Society of Japan*, Vol XXI, 1893

'Protestant Magic: W.B. Yeats and the Spell of Irish History', R.F. Foster, Chatterton Lecture on Poetry, *Proceedings Of The British Academy*, LXXV, 1989, 243-66

'Quarrel Over Hearn' (review of George Gould's *Concerning Lafcadio Hearn*), *The Dayton Daily News*, 3 June 1908

'Recent Books on Japan', (Joint Review of Hearn's *Glimpses of Unfamiliar Japan* and *Out of the East*), [Ernest Fenollosa?], *Atlantic Monthly*, Vol 75-6, June 1895, 830-5

'Recollections of Lafcadio Hearn', Benjamin Forman, *The Stylus*, Austin, Texas, March 1912

'Reminiscences of Lafcadio Hearn', Professor Ernest Foxwell, *Japan Society Transactions and Procedures*, Session 17, Vol 8, London, 1908, 68-94

'Reminiscences of Lafcadio Hearn', by Setsuko Koizumi (Mrs Hearn), translated by Paul Kiyoshi Hisada and Frederick Johnson, *Atlantic Monthly*, Boston, 1918, Vol 122, 342-351

'Some New Materials and Investigation concerning Lafcadio Hearn's Matsue Days', Yasuyuki Kajitani, *Journal of Shimane University*, 10, 11, 1961

'Some Martinique Letters of Lafcadio Hearn', with an introduction by Elizabeth Bisland, *Harper's Magazine*, 142, March 1921

'Some Unpublished Letters of Lafcadio Hearn', Osman Edwards (ed), reprinted from *The Transactions of the Japan Society of London*, Vol XVI, 16-35

'Stranger Than Fiction', Lafcadio Hearn, *Atlantic Monthly*, Vol 95, 1905, 494-496

'The Last Days of Lafcadio Hearn', by Mrs Hearn, translated by Paul Kiyoshi Hisada, *Atlantic Monthly*, Boston, 1917, Vol 119, 349-51

'The Recent Movement in Southern Literature', Charles W. Coleman, *Harper's Magazine*, Vol 74, No 444, May 1887, 837-55

'The Achievement of Lafcadio Hearn', Allen E. Tuttle, *The Dublin Magazine*, April-June 1956

'The Loose Foot of Lafcadio Hearn', Roger McHugh, *The Irish Times*, 24/4/1981

'The Birth of Lafcadio Hearn', Orcutt William Frost, *American Literature*, Vol XXIV, No 3, Nov 1952, 372-7

'The Japanese Herun', Christian Mildred, *Newcomb Alumnae News*, 12, Spring 1945

'Tinker Tells of Hearn as a Restaurateur', Edward Larocque Tinker, New Orleans *Item Magazine*, 24 August 1924

'Two Unpublished Lafcadio Hearn Letters', O.J. Frost (ed), *Today's Japan*, Vol 5, 1960

BOOKS

Appendix to the Thirtieth Report of the Deputy Keeper of the Public Records and Keeper of the State Papers of Ireland. An index of the Act or Grant Books and Original Wills of the Diocese of Dublin from 1800 to 1858, HM Stationary Office, Dublin, 1899

A Census of Ireland c. 1659, Seamus Pender (ed), Stationary Office, Dublin, 1939

A Comparative Cultural Approach to Images of Japan, 1989, ISBN 4-7923-7039-6

A Concise History of East Asia, C.P. Fitzgerald, Pelican, London, 1974

A Free Spirit: Irish Art 1860-1960, Kenneth McConkey, Antique Collectors' Club in association with Pym's Gallery, London, 1990

A Handbook for Travellers in Japan, Basil Hall Chamberlain and W.B. Mason, John Murray, London and Kelly and Walsh, Ltd, Yokohama, Third Edition, 1891

A Genealogical and Heraldic History of the Colonial Gentry, Sir Bernard Burke, London, 1891

A History of the City of Dublin, J.T. Gilbert, Dublin, 1861

A History of Modern Japan, Richard Storry, London, 1960

A General Catalogue of Hearn Collections in Japan and Overseas, compiled by Kenji Zenimoto, The Hearn Society, Matsue, 1991

A Topographical Dictionary of Ireland, Samuel Lewis, 1837

A History of Ushaw College, David Milburn, Ushaw College, Durham, 1964

Abstract of Wills, Vol 11, 1746-85, Registry of Deeds, Dublin, P. Beryl Eustace (ed), Dublin, Stationery Office, 1954

Afro-American Folk Songs, Henry E. Krehbiel, G. Shirmer, New York, 1914

Alumni Dublinenses, George Dames Burtchaell, Thomas Ulick Sadleir (ed), Dublin 1935

An Ape of the Gods. The Art and Thought of Lafcadio Hearn, Beong-cheon Yu, Wayne State University Press, Detroit, 1964

An American Miscellany, Lafcadio Hearn, Article and stories now first collected by Albert Mordell, Dodd, Mead and Company, New York, 1924

Articles On Literature and Other Writings from the Cincinnati Enquirer, Lafcadio Hearn, AMS Press, New York, 1975

Barbarous Barbers and Other Stories by Lafcadio Hearn, Ichiro Nishizaki (ed), Hokuseido Press, Tokyo, 1939

Bibliography of American Literature, Jacob Blanck, Vol IV, Yale University Press, New Haven and London, 1963

Biographical Succession List of Kilmore, J.B. Leslie, RCB Library, Dublin, Ms. 61/2/11

Blue Ghost. A Study of Lafcadio Hearn, Jean Temple, J. Cape, H. Smith, New York,

1931

Catalogue of the Lafcadio Hearn Library in the Toyama High School, Toyama, Japan, 1927, Toyama, 1927

Catalogue of First and Other Editions of Mark Twain, Samuel Langhorne Clemens, and of Lafcadio Hearn, American Art Association, New York, 1914

Catalogue of the Lafcadio Hearn Collection at the Embassy of Ireland, Tokyo, Embassy of Ireland, Tokyo, 1988

Children of the Levee, O.W. Frost (ed), introduction by John Ball, University of Kentucky Press, Lexington, 1957

Concerning Lafcadio Hearn, George M. Gould, MD, with a bibliography by Laura Stedman, George W. Jacobs & Company, Philadelphia, 1908

Concise Directory of Irish Biography, J.S. Crone (ed), Dublin 1928, 2nd Edition, 1937

Confessions of an Un-Common Attorney, Richard Hine, 1945

Creole Sketches, Ethel Hudson, New York, 1904

Descriptive Catalogue of Hearniana in the Hearn Library of the Toyama University, Toyama University Library, Toyama, 1959

Discoveries: Essays on Lafcadio Hearn, Orient/West Inc, Tokyo, 1964

Editorials from the Kobe Chronicle, Makoto Sangu (ed), Hokuseido Press, Tokyo, 1960

Editorials, Lafcadio Hearn, Charles Woodward Hutson (ed), Houghton Mifflin Company, Boston and New York, 1926

Edward Thomas, A Portrait, R. George Thomas, Clarendon Press, 1985, Oxford University Press, Oxford, 1987

Edward Thomas, W. Cooke, Faber and Faber, London, 1970

Fantastics and Other Fancies, Lafcadio Hearn, Charles Woodward Hutson (ed), Houghton Mifflin Company, Boston and New York, 1914; reprinted by Arno Press Inc, 1976

Fasti Ecclesiae Hibernicae, Henry Cotton, Dublin, MDCCCXLV

Father and I, Memories of Lafcadio Hearn, Kazuo Koizumi, Houghton Mifflin Company, Boston and New York, 1935

Fenellosa: The Far East and American Culture, Lawrence W. Chisolm, Yale University Press, New Haven and London, 1965

Grant Books Dublin, 1800-58, Appendix to the Thirteenth Report of the Deputy Keeper of the State Papers in Ireland, HM Stationary Office, Dublin, 1899

Griffith's Poor Law Valuation, Public Record Office, Dublin

Handbook on Irish Genealogy, (Sixth Edition), revised and edited by Donald F. Begley, Irish Genealogical Office, Heraldic Artists Ltd, Dublin, 1984

Hearn and his biographers, The record of a literary controversy, Oscar Lewis, The Westgate Press, San Francisco, 1930

Historical Sketch Book and Guide to New Orleans and Environs, Edited and Compiled by several leading writers of the New Orleans press [including Lafcadio Hearn], Will H. Coleman, New York, 1885

Horror, A Connoisseur's Guide to Literature and Film, Leonard Wolf, Facts on File, New York/Oxford, 1989

I Remember, Henry Harper, Harper and Brother, New York, 1934

Irish Families, Edward Mac Lysaght, Dublin, 1978

Japanese Goblin Poetry, Rendered into English by Lafcadio Hearn, and illustrated by his own drawings, compiled by Kazuo Koizumi, Oyama, Tokyo, 1934

Japanese Lyrics, Translated by Lafcadio Hearn, Constable and Co, London; Houghton Mifflin Company, Boston and New York, 1915; reprinted by Folcroft Library Editions, 1971

Kimono, John Paris, Penguin, London, 1947

Karma, Lafcadio Hearn, Boni and Liveright, New York, 1918

King's Inns Admission Papers, E. Keane, P. Beryl Phair, and T. Saldier (ed), PRO, Dublin, 1982

La Nouvell Atala ou La Fille de l'Esprit Legende Indienne, par Chahta-Ima, Adrien Rouquette, (Hearn review PP 126-9), Imprimerie du Propagatetr [sic] Catholique, New Orleans, 1879

Lafcadio Hearn and the Vision of Japan, Carl Dawson, The Johns Hopkins University Press, Baltimore & London, 1992

Lafcadio Hearn - Editorials, Charles Woodward Hutson (ed), Houghton Mifflin Company, 1926

Lafcadio Hearn, Edward Thomas, Houghton Mifflin Company, Boston, 1912

Lafcadio Hearn (Koizumi Yakumo), His Life, Work and Irish Background, Sean G. Ronan and Toki Koizumi, Ireland Japan Association, 1991

Lafcadio Hearn, Nina H. Kennard, 1912, reprinted by the Kennikat Press, Inc./Port Washington, N.Y., 1967

Lafcadio Hearn, Elizabeth Stevenson, The Macmillan Company, New York, 1961

Lafcdio Hearn: Japan's Great Interpreter. A New Anthology of His Writings, 1894-1904, Louis Allen & Jean Wilson (eds), The Japan Library Ltd., Folkestone, Kent, 1992

Lafcadio Hearn in Japan, With Mrs Hearn's Reminiscences, Yone Nochuchi, Elkin Matthews, London, and Kelly and Walsh, Yokohama, 1910, reprinted by Folcroft Library Editions, 1978

Lafcadio Hearn's Japanese Wife. Her Memoirs and Her Early Life, Yoji Hasegawa, Micro Printing Co., Tokyo, 1988

Lafcadio Hearn: A Bibliography of His Writings, P.D. and Ione Perkins, Houghton Mifflin Company, Boston, 1934

Lafcadio Hearn, Selected Writings 1872-1877, Wm. S. Johnson (ed), Woodruff Publications, Indianapolis, 1979

Lafcadio Hearn, Marcel Robert, Hokuseido Press, Tokyo, 1950

Lafcadio Hearn, Vera McWilliams, Houghton Mifflin Company, Boston, 1946, reprinted Cooper Square Publishers, Inc., New York, 1970

Lafcadio Hearn: A Bibliography, Martha Howard Sisson, The FX Faxon Co, Boston, 1933

Lafcadio Hearn, Writings from Japan, An Anthology edited, with an introduction by Francis King, Penguin, London, 1984

Lafcadio Hearn's American Days, Edward L Tinker, Dodd, Mead and Company, Inc., New York, 1924

Leaves from the Diary of an Impressionist. Early Writings by Lafcadio Hearn. With an Introduction by Ferris Greenslet, Houghton Mifflin Company, Boston and New York, 1911

Letters, (Classica Japonica: Section 6, Lafcadio Hearn, Manuscripts and Letters; 1-2), 2 vols, AMS Press, New York, 1975

Letters from Shimane, Lafcadio Hearn, The Sunward Press, Kyoto, 1934

Letters from the Raven. Letters from Lafcadio Hearn to Henry Watkin, Milton Bronner (ed),

Brentano's, New York, 1907

Letters from Basil Hall Chamberlain to Lafcadio Hearn, compiled by Kazuo Koizumi, Hokuseido Press, Tokyo, 1936

Letters to a Pagan, Lafcadio Hearn, Robert Bruna Powers, (publisher and author of the Introduction), Detroit, 1933 (The letters of Lafcadio Hearn to Countess Annetta Halliday Antona)

Literary Essays, Lafcadio Hearn, Ichiro Nishizaki (ed), Hokuseido Press, Tokyo, 1939

King's Inns Admission Papers, E. Keane, P. Beryl Phair, T. Sadlier (ed), Public Record Office, Dublin, 1982

Manuscripts. (Classica Japonica: Section 6. Lafcadio Hearn, Manuscripts and Letters; 3), AMS Press, New York, 1975

Memoranda for the Lectures at Tokyo Imperial University (Classica Japonica: Section 6. Lafcadio Hearn Manuscripts and Letters; 4), AMS Press, New York, 1975

Miscellanies by Lafcadio Hearn, Albert Mordell (ed), London, Heinmann Ltd., 1924

More Letters from Basil Hall Chamberlain to Lafcadio Hearn, compiled by Kazuo Koizumi, Hokuseido Press, Tokyo, 1937

Mortal Hunger. A Novel Based on the Life of Lafcadio Hearn, Harry Ezekiel Wedeck, Sheridan House, New York, 1947

Occidental Gleanings: Sketches and Essays Now First Collected, 2 vols, Albert Mordell (ed), Dodd, Mead, & Co, Inc, 1925; and Heinmann, London, 1925 (edition used by author)

On Poets, Lafcadio Hearn, R. Tanabe, T. Ochiai, and I. Nishizaki (ed), Hokuseido Press, Tokyo, Third Revised Edition, 1941

On Poetry, Lafcadio Hearn, R. Tanabe, T. Ochiai, and I. Nishizaki (ed), Hokuseido Press, Tokyo, Third Revised Edition, 1941

Percolator Papers, Ellwood Hendrick, Harper and Brothers, New York, 1919

Pettigrew and Oulton's Almanac and Dublin Directory, 1850

Pigot's Directory, Dublin, 1824

Re-Echo, Kazuo Koizumi, Caldwell, Idaho, The Caxton Printers, 1957

Report on the surnames Herron, Hearn, and Hearne, 1728-1940, Genealogical Office, Dublin, MS 803,

Sheridan Le Fanu and Victorian Ireland, W.J. McCormack, Clarendon Press, Oxford, 1980

Sketches and Tales from the French, Translated by Lafcadio Hearn, Edited with a Preface by Albert Mordell, Hokuseido Press, Tokyo, 1935

Slator's Directory, Dublin, 1846

Some New Letters and Writings of Lafcadio Hearn, collected and edited by Sanki Ichikawa, Tokyo, Kenkyusha Publishers, 1925

Stories from Pierre Loti, Translated by Lafcadio Hearn, Julien Viaud, with an introduction by Albert Mordell, Hokuseido Press, Tokyo, 1933

Stories from Emile Zola, Translated by Lafcadio Hearn, Edited with a preface by Albert Mordell, Hokuseido Press, Tokyo, 1935

Stories, Theophile Gautier, Translated by Lafcadio Hearn, TC&EC Jack, London and Edinburgh, 1908

Stray Leaves and Sketches, Edward B. Clarke, Kenkyusha, Tokyo, 1936

The Writings of Lafcadio Hearn, 16 vols, Houghton Mifflin Company, Boston and New York, 1922

The Selected Writings of Lafcadio Hearn, Malcolm Cowley (ed), Citadel Press, New York,

1949; second paperbound edition, 1971

The Dublin University Calendars, University of Dublin, Dublin, various dates

The Dedalus Book of Femmes Fatales, Brian Stableford (ed), Dedalus, Cambs, England, 1992

The Early Writings of Lafcadio Hearn, A Bibliography, O.W. Frost, The Public Library of Cincinnati and Hamilton County, Champaign, Illinois, 1953

The Old Town of Matsue, Shinzo Kukuhara, Japan Photographic Society, Tokyo, 1935

The Idyll: My Personal Reminiscences of Lafcadio Hearn, Leona Queyrouze Barel, Hokuseido Press, Tokyo, 1933

The Parliamentary Gazetteer of Ireland, 1844-5, Dublin, 1845

The Japanese Letters of Lafcadio Hearn, Elizabeth Bisland Wetmore, Houghton Mifflin Company, The Riverside Press Cambridge, Boston and New York, 1910

The Lafcadio Hearn Collection at the Howard-Tilton Memorial Library, Tulane University, Compiled by Ann S. Gwyn, Friends of the Tulane University Library, New Orleans, 1977

The House of Harper, Henry J. Harper, Harper and Brothers, New York, 1912

The Life and Letters of Lafcadio Hearn, Elizabeth Bisland (ed). The editions used are Vols XIII, XIV, and, XV of the Koizumi Edition of the Writings of Lafcadio Hearn, in Sixteen Volumes, Houghton Mifflin Company, The Riverside Press, Cambridge, Boston and New York, 1923.

The New Radiance and Other Scientific Sketches, Ichiro Nishizaki (ed), Hokuseido Press, Tokyo, 1939

The Adventures of Walter Schnaffs and Other Stories, Guy de Maupassant, Translated by Lafcadio Hearn, Edited with an introduction by Albert Mordell, Hokuseido Press, Tokyo, 1931

Things Japanese, Basil Hall Chamberlain, Fifth Revised Edition, London, J Murray; Yokohama, Kelly and Walsh, Ltd, 1905; reprinted in paperback as *Japanese Things*, by Charles E. Tuttle, Co., Rutland, Vermont and Tokyo, 1971

Thom's Directories of Dublin (annual)

Tithe Composition Applotment Books, Public Record Office, Dublin

Toilers in Art, Henry C. Ewart (ed), Isbister & Company, London, 1891 (includes a chapter on Jean Paul Laurens by Richard Hearn)

Under the Bridge, Ferris Greenslet, Houghton Mifflin Company, Boston, 1943

Unfamiliar Lafcadio Hearn, Kenneth Porter Kirkwood, Hokuseido Press, Tokyo, 1935

Walt Whitman, A Life, Justin Kaplan, New York, 1980

Wandering Ghost, The Odyssey of Lafcadio Hearn, Jonathan Cott, Alfred A Knopf, New York, 1991

Watson's Almanac, Dublin, 1826

Ye Giglampz, Crossroad Books, Cincinnati, 1983, Introduction, History, and Notes by Jon C. Hughes, Yeatman Anderson III, and James R. Hunt

Young Hearn, Orcutt William Frost, Hokuseido Press, Tokyo, 1958

INDEX